Awfully Devoted Women

Sexuality Studies Series

This series focuses on original, provocative, scholarly research examining from a range of perspectives the complexity of human sexual practice, identity, community, and desire. Books in the series explore how sexuality interacts with other aspects of society, such as law, education, feminism, racial diversity, the family, policing, sport, government, religion, mass media, medicine, and employment. The series provides a broad public venue for nurturing debate, cultivating talent, and expanding knowledge of human sexual expression, past and present.

Other volumes in the series are:

Awfully Devoted Women

Lesbian Lives in Canada, 1900–65

Cameron Duder

UBCPress · Vancouver · Toronto

20 19 18 17 16 15 14 13 12 11 10   5 4 3 2 1

Printed in Canada on FSC-certified ancient-forest-free paper
(100% post-consumer recycled) that is processed chlorine- and acid-free.

LIBRARY AND ARCHIVES CANADA CATALOGUING IN PUBLICATION

Duder, Cameron, 1962-
Awfully devoted women : lesbian lives in Canada, 1900-65 / Cameron Duder.

(Sexuality studies, ISSN 1706-9940)
Includes bibliographical references and index.
ISBN 978-0-7748-1738-7 (bound)
ISBN 978-0-7748-1739-4 (pbk.)

1. Lesbians – Canada – Social conditions – 20th century. 2. Lesbians – Sexual behavior – Canada – History – 20th century. 3. Lesbianism – Canada – History – 20th century. I. Title. II. Series: Sexuality studies series

HQ75.6.C32D83 2010   306.76'6309710904   C2009-907100-2

---

e-book ISBNs: 978-0-7748-1740-0 (pdf); 978-0-7748-5924-0 (epub)

UBC Press gratefully acknowledges the financial support for our publishing program provided by the Government of Canada
(through the Canada Book Fund) and the British Columbia Arts Council.

This book has been published with the help of a grant from the Canadian Federation for the Humanities and Social Sciences, through the Aid to Scholarly Publications Programme, using funds provided by the Social Sciences and Humanities Research Council of Canada.

UBC Press
The University of British Columbia
2029 West Mall
Vancouver, BC V6T 1Z2
604-822-5959 / Fax: 604-822-6083
www.ubcpress.ca

Contents

Acknowledgments

Awfully Devoted Women began life as an exploration of lesbian and bi-sexual women's subjectivity in English Canada before second-wave feminism. As so often happens, it was prompted by questions arising from a single source. A set of letters and journals of a British Columbia woman, Constance Grey Swartz, led me to wonder about same-sex relationships between women in Canada before the 1970s. I realized that in my reading of lesbian history, I had come across very little on lesbians in Canada and almost nothing on Canadian lesbians before second-wave feminism. It was 1993 and Canadian lesbian and gay history was an emerging but still small field. Now, we have much more scholarship to draw upon, yet we still know relatively little about relationships between women in Canada prior to 1965. My hope is that this book helps to fill that gap.

Many people have shared their expertise and advice during the writing of this book. I would like to thank Lynne Marks, Angus McLaren, Elizabeth Vibert, Aaron Devor and Leila Rupp for their advice during and since the writing of the book and for their enthusiasm generally for the history of sexuality. Each provided crucial feedback and challenged and inspired me to think more carefully and critically, and I am a better scholar for their efforts. The University of Victoria provided fellowship funding for my research, and my time teaching courses there in the history and sociology of gender and sexuality has afforded me the opportunity to do further work in this exciting field. I am grateful to the students in those courses and to colleagues and students at the University of Otago in New Zealand for their engagement with debates in the history of sexuality and for inspiring me during the writing process.

In the late 1980s and early 1990s, the Lesbians Making History (LMH) project of Ontario interviewed a number of women about lesbian community, relationships, and social life in and around Toronto from the 1930s to the 1970s. The LMH interviews are a rich resource of information about lesbian life in postwar Canada. I thank Maureen Fitzgerald, Amy Gottlieb, and all the members of LMH for their work in preserving lesbian histories that otherwise would have been lost and for granting me access to the LMH interviews. Harold Averill is an enthusiastic supporter of research into the lives of the lesbian and gay communities in Canada, especially of research into the lives of those who worked and studied at the University of Toronto. Harold, Ed Jackson, and everyone else involved in the Canadian Lesbian and Gay Archives provide historians of sexuality, and indeed anyone interested in lesbian and gay history in Canada, with access to a wonderful range of resources. I am grateful for the work they do, particularly for the support they have given this project. I also thank the staff of the BC Archives, the University of Toronto Archives, and Library and Archives Canada. Richard Mackie pointed me in the direction of the papers of Constance Grey Swartz. I have told Swartz's story under my former name, Karen Duder, in "Public Acts and Private Languages: Bisexuality and the Multiple Discourses of Constance Grey Swartz," *BC Studies* 136 (Winter 2002-03): 3-24. Pat Gentile was very helpful with the copying of materials from the Charlotte Whitton Papers.

Without the testimonies of the women I interviewed, this study would not have been possible. They provide richness, depth, and humour not usually available in written records, and they allow us a glimpse into a world otherwise unknown. It was a pleasure and a privilege to listen to the narrators' stories. I am tremendously grateful for their willingness to share their memories and for their continued friendship. I am also grateful, as we should all be, for the actions of Dr. Donald Fraser and Mrs. Nancy Fraser Brooks, who could so easily have destroyed the papers of their aunt, Frieda Fraser, upon her death. Instead, they chose to place them in the University of Toronto Archives, and in so doing they have left for the historical record what surely must be the richest collection of papers in Canadian lesbian history. They also gave me personal insights into the character and life of their aunt and into her relationship with Edith Bickerton Williams.

Portions of this book have been published in Karen Duder, "'That repulsive abnormal creature I read of in that book': Lesbians and Families in Ontario, 1920-1965," in *Ontario Since Confederation: A Reader,* ed. Edgar-André Montigny and Lori Chambers, and Cameron Duder, "'Two Middle-Aged and Very Good Looking Females That Spend All Their Week-Ends Together': Female Professors and Same-Sex Relationships in Canada, 1910-1950," in *Historical Identities: The Professoriate in Canada,* ed. Paul J. Stortz and Lisa Panayodotis, and are reproduced here with permission of the University of Toronto Press.

A number of people have supported this project over the years and have sustained me during its evolution into a book. Several have offered incisive and crucial feedback and shared their expertise in the history of sexuality. All have understood the daunting task of writing and have cheered, commiserated, cajoled, and encouraged as needed. I acknowledge particularly Susan Johnston, Carolyn Strange, Sheila McManus, Christie Roome, Becki Ross, Pat Rasmussen, and Janet Sheppard in Canada and Annabel Cooper, Chris Brickell, Rebecca Stringer, Barbara Brookes, Judith Collard, Ros Rice, Trisha Bennett, Su White, and Leslie Turner in New Zealand. Jean Wilson at UBC Press was enthusiastic about the topic from the start and has encouraged and assisted me throughout the book's long journey to completion, particularly when my own interest was waning. Since Jean's retirement, I have been fortunate to work with Darcy Cullen and Ann Macklem, who have guided the final polishing of the manuscript. I thank Jean, Darcy, and Ann for their editorial advice, for their invaluable suggestions, and for their enthusiastic support for the project.

I am very lucky that my partner, Elise Chenier, shares my interest in the history of sexuality and oral history and understands both the joys and the challenges of research. She has prompted me to think in new ways about the work I do, and in the moments of frustration during the writing and editing, she has helped me to remember why I love this work and why it is so very important. *Awfully Devoted Women* could not have been completed without her.

Awfully Devoted Women

Introduction

In 1925 Bud Williams wrote to her partner, Frieda Fraser, "My lamb, it is very hard to be sensible to-night. I'm so awfully thrilled about loving you and vice versa. If you were about, I should probably fall on your neck on the street and kiss you, and disgrace you publicly."[1] In letters written during periods of separation for work and travel in the 1920s and early 1930s, Bud and Frieda wrote often of people's prejudice against women who were "devoted" to each other. They protested the unreasonableness of the fuss being made about such relationships, and they wanted to be left alone to live together in happiness. Both women were aware of the need to be discreet about their relationship for fear of disgracing one another in the presence of others, yet they were also determined in their resistance to family and peer pressure on them to end their relationship. Bud lamented in 1926:

> I haven't the remotest idea of what will be the result of all the fuss about us. It can't be any worse than it has been, can it? Perhaps in time – 20 yrs or so – people will get tired of it and leave us in peace. That is the most we can hope for. I don't suppose they'll be enthusiastic about us even in 100 yrs. However it hasn't made any difference really – we had to exercise tact and discretion, but it hasn't made any difference to our being devoted to each other, really, has it? It is such a delightfully secure feeling to think that various people have been awfully down on it and done their best to spoil it – and they were the ones who could bring more pressure to bear than anyone else – and yet it is still there more than ever. My lamb, aren't you proud of us?[2]

Seventy years later, lesbians spoke to me of their early same-sex relationships from the 1940s to the 1960s and of the same need for secrecy lest
knowledge of their lesbianism have a negative impact on their relationships with family and friends and on their employment. In interviews
about their lives before 1965, they told stories of a fear of being discovered,
of leading a double life, of knowing that they were not supposed to be
"like that" yet wanting to find other women "like that," and of being careful of what they did and said around family, peers, and workmates. A
common theme in their stories was the thought that they were alone and
the knowledge that their desires were regarded as abnormal or immoral,
accompanied therefore by the belief that they could not speak about or
obviously act on those desires in public. Discovery of other lesbians was
both exciting and terrifying. Mary, describing a holiday she took with her
partner, Doris, in 1956, said:

> We thought we were the only two lesbians in the world ... until we went
> with two straight girls to Cape Cod, Provincetown, of all places. When we
> arrived in Provincetown, I remember Doris saying as we looked around,
> "My god, there's more like us around here" ... The clues were that women
> were holding hands and it was so free. The straight girls said, "I think
> they're queer here."[3]

Visibility – its form and its consequences – was a central issue for lesbians between 1900 and 1965, in the years before the bar cultures, lesbian
feminism, and the lesbian and gay rights movement challenged invisibility
and sought to increase public awareness of and to change attitudes toward
lesbians and gay men. There are very few sources that tell us what life was
like before 1965 for a Canadian woman who desired women, particularly
before the 1950s. This book is about such women, their relationships, their
sexual practices, and their communities in that period of greater invisibility. *Awfully Devoted Women: Lesbian Lives in Canada, 1900-65* examines
relationships between upper-middle-class professional women between
1900 and 1950. Correspondence and journals of upper-middle-class
women's relationships reveal that they modified the earlier model of the
romantic friendship. These women did not call themselves "lesbian," yet
their relationships were clearly erotic and outside the bounds of heteronormativity. We know relatively little about upper-middle-class Canadian

lesbian relationships compared to American and British ones, and those scholars who have written of a committed relationship between two women have often been reluctant to discuss it in relation to the possibility of physically sexual involvement. Professional life afforded these women some possibilities of association on the basis of love of women, but requirements of respectability and discretion constrained them in terms of open expression of that love. Canadian women in these kinds of relationships drew upon spiritual and familial metaphors to express their love for one another, and they lived in relationships framed as exemplary of "devotion." They are an important but largely undocumented part of the story of the lesbian past in Canada.

Awfully Devoted Women also discusses lower-middle-class women and their relationships and social worlds from the 1930s to 1965. Interviews with lower-middle-class women who now identify as lesbian address how they explored and attempted to understand their desires for women in the 1940s, 1950s, and 1960s. In most cases, these women were not part of the culture of the public lesbian bar that emerged in the postwar decades. They kept their sexuality hidden from family members and workmates, and either they did not know of other lesbians or they socialized with lesbian friends in ways that would not bring their lesbianism to the attention of others.

Both of these groups of women are an important part of Canadian lesbian history, yet they are little discussed. Lesbian history generally has been less well documented than gay men's history because of ideas about women's limited sexuality, because of the greater legal consequences for male same-sex activity and thus men's greater representation in court and police records, and because of homophobia and a resistance to thinking about the possibility of women's erotic interest in other women. Lesbian invisibility, however, has not resulted only from the homophobia of earlier decades. The ways we have studied lesbian history have also perpetuated the invisibility of some lesbians. Literature on lesbian history between the late nineteenth century and the 1960s is largely about two kinds of female relationship: noble, allegedly nonsexual, and socially sanctioned middle-class "romantic friendships"; and gender-transgressive, sexualized, and pathologized working-class "butch-femme" relationships. These categories have their basis in lived experience, but they are also the main categories by which lesbians and historians have understood, defined, and analyzed lesbian history, to the exclusion of other possibilities.

Both during the period under study and subsequently, the lives of lower-middle-class lesbians have been made culturally unintelligible by lesbians' and historians' desire to restore to the historical narrative the stories of the foremothers of lesbian community and activism, based on preconceived cultural ideals of what constitutes lesbian resistance against homophobia and heterosexist oppression: living openly with another woman, feminist writing or writing extolling the virtues of romantic relationships between women, or living publicly as a lesbian in the sense of clear sexual preference for women, gender transgression, and the formation of social subcultures based on a desire for women. The tendency has been to look for those women who lived openly in relationships with other women and to see these women as the courageous foremothers of lesbian feminists and lesbian communities in the late twentieth century. In focusing on the dedication or the relative openness with which these women lived without men, and in celebrating that as an essential feature of lesbian experience, lesbians have often ignored and made unintelligible the subjectivities of those lesbians who did not live openly as lesbians, were not political matriarchs of the nation,[4] and did not fight for "public" space.[5]

Nan Enstad suggests, writing about young working women at the turn of the twentieth century, that the subjectivities of the women she discusses have been obscured by two things: "contemporary organized politics and historical analyses, both of which searched for political actors who matched preconceived cultural ideals."[6] She further suggests that historians, motivated to restore stories of women's activism to the historical record, actually "narrowed the historical understanding of the diversity of working-class culture and resistance, and foreclosed alternate political subjectivities by the ways they framed their subjects and sources."[7] Like the women Enstad discusses, lower-middle-class lesbians have been obscured by an emphasis on visibility of particular kinds, where to have been visible as a lesbian in the past or to have left behind a record of one's relationship with a woman is celebrated but where living a life now understood as "closeted" is not. As Nan Alamilla Boyd argues, in the post–Stonewall era,

> when political entitlements are linked to public visibility, a language about community based on the relative value of "outness" and "closetedness" has come to structure not only the way historians of gay and lesbian

marker between the "respectable" and "unrespectable" parts of the lesbian community, and for many middle-class lesbians in particular, the bar was an unknown and unexplored site of lesbian socializing.[19]

Scholarship on lesbian and gay history in Canada before 1965 has focused on community, societal pressure and state harassment, and representation, especially in media. Lesbians in Canada grouped together in ways similar to those of their American counterparts, were the target of similar medical, religious, and societal attitudes, were subjected to police harassment and abuse and government discrimination, and had available to them the same limited range of representations of homosexuality in media and medical sources. The twentieth century saw increasing discussion of homosexuality, transforming it from something incomprehensible into something readily viewed and monitored in the public interest.[20] The very public discussions and discovery of sexual deviation, venereal disease, and promiscuity in postwar Canada made the language of sexuality more available to a reading and viewing public than ever before. The twentieth-century expert played a key role in the discovery of all manner of "deviant" sexualities and in the promotion of values and practices thought to combat them. Medical professionals, social workers, educators, and the state all functioned to disseminate categories and theories of sexuality in Canadian society. Although it was the male deviant and predator with whom these professionals were mainly concerned, their categorizations also served to pathologize female same-sex activity.[21]

In postwar Canada the family was the foundation of the nation and "was reified as a primary stabilizing influence on both individuals and the nation as a whole."[22] In this context, non-normative gender or sexual behaviours were seen as resulting in "a spectrum of social problems ... from increasing unwed motherhood, unfulfilled housewives, ineffective and absent fathers, greater incidence of child abuse and family desertion, to the growing threat of the sexual deviant – perceived to be homosexual – stalking young children."[23] That deviant, for most of the period under study, was generally thought of as male, but over the period the amount of comment on female sexual deviancy did increase. It was still the case, however, that many Canadians had little to no knowledge of lesbianism.

One of the challenges in writing lesbian history is that, except for mention in medical sources and in some of the tabloid newspapers, lesbians have received much less attention than gay men. Oral history has been an important methodology for scholars seeking to examine the lives of lesbians who do not appear in written records. Katie Gilmartin interviewed forty women in the Colorado area to determine how their sexual identities intersected with their class, gender, racial, and ethnic identities between 1945 and 1965.[24] She looked particularly at the relationship between lesbianism and class.[25] Gilmartin's analysis is one of only a few that address the relationships and boundaries between working-class and middle-class American lesbians before second-wave feminism. Previous work had largely focused on middle-class *or* working-class lesbians rather than on the relationships between them, the divisions and differences between their communities, and the attitudes of each group toward the other. *Awfully Devoted Women* reveals the differences between the women of the bar culture and those who stayed away from it because of fears of public exposure.

Studying different groups of lesbians has meant deciding how to define "lesbian" and which women to include in the history of lesbian life. Anyone writing about lesbians before the homophile movement and the lesbian and gay rights movement is faced with the question of terminology, for most women who had relationships with women before the 1970s did not use the word "lesbian" to describe themselves, nor did they use other available terms such as "sexual invert." A crucial aspect of debates over who should be included in lesbian history and who should not is whether we can prove that a relationship between two women had a physical, particularly genital, component. This question has been an especially important consideration in studies of elite and upper-middle-class women, whose letters and journals almost never mention physical sexuality.[26] The working-class women of urban bar cultures have been more readily understood as having engaged in physical sexuality, although we should note that this idea about them derives partly from the greater openness with which they expressed physical sexuality and partly from class-based assumptions about greater working-class propensity for sexual behaviours.

Debate over sexuality and definitions of the lesbian continues. Martha Vicinus proposes that the elite women whose lives she examines in *Intimate Friends* were erotically attracted to women, whatever their sexual practices. She reflects on debates of the past twenty years over who gets to be called "lesbian" and who does not and over whether relationships between women prior to the twentieth century can be called lesbian when a terminology of lesbianism and communities of lesbians were not yet part of the social landscape. *Intimate Friends* attempts to avoid the limitations of identity-based history of sexuality and discusses a variety of ways women fashioned personal identity based on "a sexualized, or at least recognizably eroticized, relationship with another woman."[27]

A woman's arrival at some kind of identity based on desire for or relationship with women has been a central aspect of histories of lesbian life. The identity "lesbian" suggests a unity of experience, something shared across broad groups of women in terms of their desire for and relationships with women. A number of activists and scholars have challenged that unity, demonstrating very different experiences for lesbians from different socioeconomic groups and the ways that categories of sexual orientation are themselves social constructs derived from and perpetuating medicalized discourses. Queer theoretical approaches have called into question the enterprise of "uncovering" the lesbian and gay past as though the information located in historical sources – written, oral, or visual – somehow could be seen as a transparent medium through which to know the history of lesbian and gay lives and communities.[28] Many have also criticized the practice of applying modern identity labels such as "lesbian" to people who did not use such labels for themselves. These are useful critiques because they remind us that we cannot "know" how our historical subjects thought about themselves and that we must remember that categories of sexual orientation are neither cross-cultural nor transhistorical. However, as Steven Maynard points out about the privilege involved in calls to give up the search for evidence of homosexual experience in the past, extensive historical reclamation can result in affirmation for those groups whose stories have not yet been made available.[29] There remains a place for historical analysis of lesbian lives in the past, for stories of what it was like to live as a woman who desired women in a period in Canadian history when that experience meant great risk and/or great secrecy. Such analysis does not have to posit that experience as wholly factual, as unmediated by culture, as universal, as unproblematic. *Awfully Devoted Women* does not engage with debates about identity but rather describes the lives of a group of Canadian lesbians who have thus far been neglected in historical studies.

The women whose letters I discuss here never described themselves as lesbians, homosexuals, or sexual inverts. The interview narrators now describe themselves as lesbian, but in the period under study many did not. They simply understood that they were somehow different, that what they desired needed to be kept from their families and work colleagues, and that there were consequences of their relationships becoming known. These two groups of women are divided by period, by class, by identity, and by the means by which we come to know their stories. What connects them, however, is the recognizably erotic, and in many cases recognizably physical, expression of their desire for and of their relationships with women.

Historical evidence of sexuality, particularly of women's sexuality, can sometimes be hard to locate in traditional archival sources. Unless one is examining a form of sexual expression proscribed by law or otherwise dealt with by the state, a record of which might be found in a court document or in the records of a government department, the historian of sexuality must often sift through a significant amount of material before finding evidence of sexual behaviour. In the case of same-sex relations between women, the historian's task is further complicated by an overwhelming gender bias in material regarding homosexuality toward that of gay men.[30] To reveal how Canadian lesbians understood their desires between 1900 and 1965, this book examines love letters and interview testimonies of women who desired women and formed relationships on that basis. Five collections of personal papers provide most of the personal material for the period 1900-50, examined in Part 1, "Awfully Devoted Odd Women." These early-twentieth-century documents reveal same-sex relationships that contained attributes of the romantic friendship but contained a more clearly expressed physicality and awareness of societal attitudes toward homosexuality than was found in earlier relationships between women. They provide a first glimpse into Canadian versions of upper-middle-class lesbian life. The largest is a substantial collection of letters and other personal papers of Frieda Fraser and Edith (Bud) Bickerton Williams. The love letters between Fraser and Williams offer a uniquely intimate picture of a relationship between two Canadian women from the 1920s onward. Also important is the collection of personal papers of Charlotte Whitton, Canadian politician and social reformer, whose sexual orientation has been debated on a number of occasions. A portion of the collection, very personal materials relating to Whitton's relationship with Margaret Grier, was not open to viewing until 1999, and more may now be said about this important figure in Canadian women's history than was possible in earlier studies of her personal life. These two large collections are supplemented by smaller collections in which devoted relationships between women are revealed. Correspondence between Elisabeth Govan and her partner and between Amelia Alexis Alvey and Grace Brodie allow a glimpse into middle-class relationships in the mid-twentieth century, when some norms of sexuality were starting to shift but when pathologization of homosexuality was widespread.

Twenty-two of my own interviews, eight interviews conducted by the Lesbians Making History project, an interview conducted by Elise Chenier, and an interview with one of my narrators conducted by a graduate student provide the majority of the material for 1950 to 1965. Narrators were located in a variety of ways. Some were reached via personal contacts within the local Victoria lesbian community, and those women were able to put me in touch with others. I advertised in newspapers in Victoria, Vancouver, and Toronto, and sent calls for narrators and posters to lesbian and feminist organizations in British Columbia and Ontario. Several Ontario narrators were reached via the Metropolitan Community Church, and several in Victoria were located via the Lesbian Seniors Care Society.[31] In selecting narrators for my own interviews, I chose women who need not have been born in Canada but who had lived in Canada for at least five years between 1910 and 1965. The minimum age for narrators was fifty-five, ensuring that almost all narrators would have reached young adulthood, at the very least, before 1965. I employed a structured yet flexible interview in which narrators responded to a range of set questions but also explored topics of their own choosing and were able to question me and offer contrasting perspectives. Because of the intimate nature of the topic, the interviews began at the most superficial level and worked through to discussion of physical sexuality, many taking several sessions.[32]

From the First World War to the advent of second-wave feminism and gay liberation, these women experienced considerable change throughout their lives. Their dates of birth range from 1913 to 1948, and in their childhood and adult years they witnessed some of the most significant events of the twentieth century. Most important for many of them was the development of their attraction toward women, which, in most cases, eventually resulted in the adoption of a gay or lesbian identity label. The timing of their same-sex attractions varied considerably, twelve of the women having their first same-sex experience while still children and the remainder not exploring same-sex sexuality until adulthood. Despite the differences among them, however, all were raised with heterosexual norms and had to negotiate the tricky terrain of dating, attraction, sex, and relationships. The narrators come from a variety of backgrounds, from very poor working-class families to comfortable middle-class ones. They are overwhelmingly Protestant, with only one narrator, Reva, being Jewish, and one, Chris, being Catholic. Betty is Anglican but was sent to a Catholic school.

All the women interviewed for this study are white. Although many came from working-class or poor backgrounds, most are today comfortably well off. I was unable to locate any Aboriginal lesbians or lesbians of colour who met the criteria for the study in terms of the time of residence in Canada before 1965. The Canadian lesbian community was much less diverse than either its American counterpart in the same period or the community that would form in Canada in the 1970s. Many of the narrators reported that, until the late 1960s at the earliest, the lesbian community contained very few Aboriginal women and women of colour. This opinion is borne out by two of the testimonies from the Canadian film *Forbidden Love*, which examines Canadian lesbians' lives in the 1950s and 1960s, in which the narrators describe the largely monocultural nature of the community.[33] The narrators for this study in some ways form part of a dominant group in society as a whole, yet they are underrepresented in stories of lesbian history. This book provides a perspective from this previously ignored socio-economic group. Also discussed in this study are the testimonies of women involved in Toronto's public bar culture in the 1950s and 1960s. These testimonies, obtained by the Lesbians Making History project in the 1980s and added to by Elise Chenier in the 1990s, show that the Canadian bar culture shared in many ways the characteristics of the American bar cultures described by Lillian Faderman in *Odd Girls and Twilight Lovers* and by Elizabeth Lapovsky Kennedy and Madeline Davis in *Boots of Leather, Slippers of Gold*. Given that Chenier has used these testimonies in her study of the Toronto bar culture, my use of them here is for comparative purposes only.

This book is divided into two parts. The first, "Awfully Devoted Odd Women," examines the early-twentieth-century collections of letters of upper-middle-class Canadian women whose relationships conformed in some ways to the norms of the romantic friendship but in several important ways marked the end of the romantic friendship era and the influence of newer, medicalized discourses of sexuality. In these letters, we see a continuation of some of the language of devotion typical in the romantic friendship era, but we also see that these relationships are markedly different from romantic friendships. The women were profoundly aware of negative societal attitudes toward relationships between women, they used and discussed the new medicalized language to describe such relationships, and they were far more explicitly sexual.

Chapter 1 introduces the reader to the five collections of papers and outlines early-twentieth-century ideas about heterosexuality and about relationships between women, particularly in the North American context. American studies of same-sex sexuality in the nineteenth and twentieth centuries have often relied in part on autobiographical writings, journals, and letters. These sources have been very important for the history of lesbian women because of their relative lack of representation in the records of institutions of punitive control of "deviant" sexuality. There exist medical case records of lesbian and bisexual women, but there are comparatively few instances in which the stories of lesbians and bisexual women come to light in government, police, or court records, sources that have provided at least some means of accessing the lives of gay or bisexual men. The collections used in this part of the book are from middle-class women in professional positions, women who maintained a lengthy relationship with a female partner.

Chapter 2 discusses how women who desired other women were able to locate each other in a period when there did not exist large and visible lesbian communities and political campaigning. How did women discover other women who were similarly "devoted" to women? What linguistic clues and aspects of appearance might have helped them in the formation of social connections? To what degree did they conform to or reject dominant gender? This chapter outlines the importance of school, university, and work in bringing women together in large numbers and in ways that facilitated the exploration of relationships with women. Using particularly the correspondence between Frieda Fraser and Bud Williams, I reveal how women could continue a relationship, and even find other women who were "devoted," without being so outside heteronormative behaviour that they were completely ostracized. In other words, like the women in Vicinus's study, they kept the secret but told it to anyone who was listening. Among their ways of making those connections was a language of devotion and of "odd women," accompanied in some cases by masculine attire.

In Chapter 3 I deal with the question of physical sexuality. Whether or not historians recognize a woman as lesbian has often depended on whether we can show that she engaged in intimate physical activity with another woman. The archival collections on which lesbian historians rely rarely contain specific information about physical sexuality, and whether the historian should make a claim of lesbianism when such evidence is not available has been a contentious issue. Chapter 3 explores the question of physical sexuality in relation to the written sources and suggests that in at least some of them there is sufficient evidence to suggest a physical relationship, even if we cannot prove genital sexuality. More important, however, is the fact that these written records reveal that in the 1920s, 1930s, and 1940s women in same-sex relationships were influenced by the language of sexology, even if they questioned the depiction of same-sex relationships as unnatural and unhealthy, and they were much more aware of the possibility – and indeed the reality – of societal disapproval and familial rejection. These relationships were also much more explicitly sexual. In outlining the ways that early-twentieth-century relationships between women continued some of the language and the appearance of the romantic friendship but clearly were modern and sexually aware, *Awfully Devoted Women* adds a Canadian perspective to the large literature on the transition in women's relationships from the romantic friendship to the modern lesbian.

The letters also reveal that regardless of what we can or cannot conclude with certainty about a physical relationship, these relationships must be included in a history of same-sex relationships, for they were clearly well outside the bounds of heteronormativity, were recognizably erotic, and were understood by the women as lifelong partnerships. Whether we term them "lesbian" when the women themselves did not use the word will remain a matter of debate. We can certainly discuss them as women whose primary emotional and domestic relationships were with women and whose devotion went beyond the usual structures of female friendship.

Part 2, "Lesbian Lives after the Second World War," uses interview material to build a picture of how women who desired other women understood and explored their desires when most of them had not heard of lesbianism and thought that they were unique. Some discovered love with women early, whereas some had relationships with men at first and only later came to a lesbian identity. Chapter 4 looks at the childhood experiences of the narrators and the norms with which they were raised. Although in some parts of Canadian society gender and sexual norms were somewhat modified from the early twentieth century to the 1960s, many of these women lived in families in which traditional roles were emphasized. In Chapter 5 the narrators' testimonies reveal the nature and amount of information they had as children and as young adults about sexuality in general and about homosexuality in particular. Like many women who grew up between the 1930s and the 1950s, they were given very little information about how their bodies worked, about the mechanics of sexual activity, and particularly about homosexuality. Despite living in a period when there was supposed to be considerably more information available than for the previous generation, these women were told relatively little by their parents and the education system. In figuring out their bodies and desires and in beginning to explore sexuality, they had to extrapolate from snippets of information gleaned from family members and friends, from what they saw people do in movies, and from whatever reading materials they could find.

Chapter 6 discusses in specific their sexual practices in same-sex relationships. In some ways, the interwar period and the mid-twentieth century saw great expansion in the discussion of aspects of sexuality, yet in other ways Canadians lacked information about sexual desire and sexual practice. Information about homosexuality was more widespread but was by no means universal, and moreover the information available largely reflected medical constructs of homosexuality as pathological. Some information made its way to the Canadian public in sensationalized tabloid newspaper articles about lurid goings-on in major Canadian cities. Most of the women interviewed for this study were unaware of homosexuality growing up or had some knowledge of gay men but none of lesbians. The interview testimonies complicate the picture we have of women in the mid-twentieth century being much more sexually aware than women of previous generations.

The concluding chapters look at two important aspects of lesbian life in the postwar decades: relationships and community. Chapter 7 offers an examination of lesbian relationships and reveals that most lesbian women hoped for the same things as heterosexual women. Chapter 7 looks at the formation and the nature of lesbian relationships and the difficulties women encountered with their partners. The narrators' testimonies reveal women's longing for relationship, their joy at finding a partner, and their pleasure in coming to an awareness of their desire for another woman, but they also reveal that infidelity, domestic violence, and alcohol abuse were as much a feature of lesbian life as of heterosexual relationships.

Chapter 7 also examines lesbians' relationships with their families of origin. I suggest, tentatively, that in some ways the absolute severing of family ties because of a daughter's lesbianism was more likely to occur from the 1960s onward than before. Prior to the Second World War, a more formal sense of responsibility for one's children and a less medicalized discourse about relationships between women may have worked against parents' desire to completely reject a lesbian daughter. In the later twentieth century, as more Canadians understood relationships between women as pathological, as ideas about familial duty changed, and as it became easier for women to live independently from family and even to find the support of an emerging lesbian community, it may have been more frequently the case that a woman separated completely from her family because of her lesbianism.

Finally, in Chapter 8, this book discusses the lesbian community of the 1950s and the 1960s, specifically how the narrators, who were all in "respectable" jobs in which they were not "out" as lesbians, understood themselves in relation to the working-class bar lesbians of Toronto, Montreal, Vancouver, and the American cities they occasionally visited. The social world of lower-middle-class lesbians was a more private world. Some of the narrators went to the bars at least occasionally and were simultaneously excited and disgusted by the goings-on in the bar culture. Many of them preferred to socialize away from public view and potential police harassment, opting for house parties held in the suburbs. Many others socialized only with heterosexual people and would only later become involved in some form of lesbian community.

The narrators show us that in writing largely about higher-status women in twentieth-century versions of the romantic friendship and about working-class butch and femme women, we have missed a substantial group of Canadian lesbians. They did not leave archival collections preserved because of the author's social status or institutional affiliation, as in the case of the collections discussed in Part 1. Nor did they have a public presence in the form of very visible appearance, marginalized occupations, or contacts with sex work, the drug trade, and the police, as in the case of many of the working-class butch and femme women of urban lesbian bar cultures. They did, however, form social and occupational networks based on same-sex relationships and were part of an expansion of lesbian community in the 1950s and the 1960s. They are part of a broader fabric of lesbian life before 1965, one in which visible relationships between women, claiming of public space by butch and femme women, and establishment of urban communities of lesbians are important but are not the whole story.

Awfully Devoted Women presents a collection of narratives of lesbian life from a period in lesbian history when political organizing among lesbians had not yet started and when the consequences of being identified as a sexual deviant were severe. Lesbian relationships existed in a context of silence and fear and were balanced against the need for familial connection, financial security, maintenance of respectability, and physical safety. Despite these constraints, women who desired women found ways to explore those desires, to form relationships, often long-term ones, and in many cases to establish social networks based on shared attraction to women. Their relationships were hidden from many but were there to be seen by those who knew when and how to see and hear.

Part 1

Awfully Devoted Odd Women

1
Relationships between Women
The "knitting together of mind and spirit"

In *Studies in the Psychology of Sex,* the first parts of which were published in 1897, the sexologist Havelock Ellis wrote that the movement for women's emancipation was "on the whole, a wholesome and inevitable movement. But it carries with it certain disadvantages."[1] The main disadvantage, in his view, was that "having been taught independence of men and disdain for the old theory which placed women in the moated grange of the home to sigh for a man who never comes, a tendency develops for women to carry this independence still farther and to find love where they find work." Ellis, although supportive of some of the aims of the women's movement, reflected a common assumption about its effects: that women's emancipation resulted for some in lesbianism. The women's movement could not, he argued, directly cause sexual inversion, but it could "develop the germs of it."[2]

In one sense, Ellis was right. The coming together of large numbers of women in the workplace, in higher education, in "bohemian" movements, and indeed in feminism *did* give women the opportunity to form intimate relationships with each other. As lesbians, or the various kinds of female "sexual inverts" as they were called in Ellis's day, came together in women-only environments, they were able to realize for the first time that they were not alone in their desires. The workplaces, the universities and colleges, the parties, and the political groups were all sites for the establishment of same-sex relationships between women.[3] Between the turn of the century and the interwar period, such environments became increasingly suspect in the eyes of many; for women attracted to other women, they were worlds of opportunity. The school and the workplace were important sites for the formation of relationships between women, providing numerous opportunities for same-sex social contacts, the like of which disappeared for many heterosexual women upon marriage. Through these contacts, women formed both brief and long-term relationships, sometimes living relatively openly within emerging lesbian communities but more often living very closeted lives.

The few sources attesting to the existence of lesbian relationships in the early twentieth century, before the creation of the bar culture in Canada, come almost exclusively from the upper middle class. Because a public lesbian community, in the form of the bar scene, was established later in Canada than in the United States, we do not have information that would allow the kind of analysis of working-class lesbian life before 1940 found in the two major works on the subject, *Odd Girls and Twilight Lovers* and *Boots of Leather, Slippers of Gold*.[4] Our perspective on lesbian life before the rise of the bar culture in Canada is therefore skewed somewhat in favour of middle-class experiences and perspectives.

Several of the women whose lives are the focus of this study are from this earlier period and from this more privileged economic group. We have only written records of their experiences, in the form of love letters and other correspondence. The earliest of these collections comes from just after the period that Lillian Faderman has described as the "the last breath of innocence" in female-female relationships: from the turn of the century to 1920. Faderman argues that the turn of the twentieth century was "the beginning of a lengthy period of general closing off of most affectional possibilities between women."[5] She traces the emergence of lesbian subcultures and suggests that the twentieth century saw the erosion of the "sexual innocence" of pre-twentieth-century lesbianism, in the form of the romantic friendship, and the creation of lesbian identities and sexual knowledge between and among lesbians. Perhaps not as rapidly colonized by the ideas of the sexologists and Sigmund Freud, Canada was nevertheless party to an increasing obsession with studying, classifying, and controlling sexuality in its many "natural" and "unnatural" forms. Heterosexual as well as lesbian and bisexual women were subject to the trends that Faderman describes. Expressions of romantic love between women, which previously could have been uttered without condemnation, were, by the 1920s, being viewed with suspicion. After 1920 the author of such an expression would have been viewed as psychologically ill or as deserving of whatever negative consequence was meted out to her.[6] Faderman argues that women in twentieth-century America "had to deal with the 'sexual implications' of their attachments. To have disregarded them, as they could in a pre-Freudian era, would have been impossible."[7] No longer was the excessively romantic, self-sacrificing hyperbole of the middle-class romantic friendship enough to disguise any physical content in a relationship between women. Rather, all such relationships could be viewed with the suspicion that they might be pathological and dangerous.

Lesbian women were, to many Canadians, virtually unknown until the postwar period and were invisible in nineteenth- and early-twentieth-century Canadian culture. Because women were assumed to be incapable of the same nature and degree of sexual passion as men, it was inconceivable to many that they could desire each other and could engage in same-sex sexual activity. Most historical scholarship on the subject of relationships between women in the nineteenth century and at the very beginning of the twentieth century concerns British and American women in what have been called "passionate" or "romantic" friendships. These relationships were primarily upper-middle-class and were typified by intense emotional bonds, a very passionate language of devotion that was sometimes almost religious in tone, a sense of duty and fidelity, kissing, fondling, and sleeping together. Whether or not the women had sexual relationships remains a matter of some dispute. Society often perceived romantic friendships as being without a sexual component, and some scholars suggested that this was because women were not perceived as, and did not perceive themselves as, sexual beings. Had physical sexuality been revealed, the women concerned would have been condemned. The traditional argument is that romantic friendships were most likely asexual and were socially acceptable during the eighteenth century and much of the nineteenth but that the rise of sexology spelled the end of the romantic friendship's innocence and, by the early twentieth century, resulted in all relationships between women being regarded with suspicion.

The traditional argument has been challenged in recent years by evidence that the romantic friendship persisted well into the twentieth century, "long after the public recognition of women's sexual desires and passions."[8] *Awfully Devoted Women* adds a Canadian voice to that challenge, demonstrating that the women whose letters I examine conformed in many ways to the language of the romantic friendship, even as they incorporated and disputed the new language of sexology. Also modifying the traditional analysis are studies revealing premarital heterosexual activity, romantic friendships between men, and clear sexual activity in relationships between women in the allegedly asexual romantic friendship. The letters discussed in this book add to that picture too, as they reveal physical relationships.[9]

Although the rapid transformation of the romantic friendship by the new framework of sexology is questioned, it is fair to say that sexology had some influence on people's awareness and interpretation of relationships between women. Ellis's views on the passionate or romantic friendship reflected larger social assumptions about relations between women. Careful to acknowledge that closeness between women was more common than between men and that many passionate friendships were harmless and temporary relationships on the path toward heterosexual matrimony, he nevertheless clearly indicated that he thought many forms of this closeness were abnormal. It was his work, and that of other sexologists of the late nineteenth and early twentieth centuries, that helped to erode the earlier acceptance of passionate friendships between women. By the 1920s even romantic friendships with no sexual element were increasingly classified as abnormal.[10] It became more difficult for women who had grown up with an acceptance of such relationships now to express themselves openly, given the increasingly hostile climate, but the impact was not wholly negative. The sexological discourse was both employed and rejected by women seeking to understand their "nonprocreative" sexuality.

Sexology was a new "science" of sexuality, which arose in the late nineteenth century and became increasingly influential in the early twentieth century. Sexologists attempted "to isolate, and individualise, the specific characteristics of sexuality, to detail its normal paths and morbid variations, to emphasise its power and to speculate on its effects."[11] The sexologists argued that it was possible to isolate and define the nature of what was referred to as the "sexual instinct."[12] Sexuality became something one studied with the lens of science rather than something one pronounced on with the language of religion. Abandoning such moral categories as sin, debauchery, and excess, the new sex pioneers categorized human sexuality as healthy or diseased, normal or abnormal. The construction of the "normal" took place largely by default, as it was primarily the deviations from an a priori ideal about which the sexologists wrote.

The language of the romantic friendship continued well into the twentieth century in middle-class relationships between women, regardless of their assumed pathology. Even though, as discussed earlier, some viewed expressions of devotion between women with suspicion, the linguistic form of the romantic friendship remained popular among certain groups of women into the 1940s. It was a language of the educated middle and upper classes, it was replete with expressions of adoration, loyalty, and devotion, and it often used spiritual or religious imagery in relation to emotion. The hyperbolic nature of romantic friendship language bore considerable relation to literary expressions of heterosexual courtship, especially to very romantic poetry.

In the nineteenth century such a romantic language fitted well both with notions of women's greater emotionality and lesser physical passion and with middle-class assumptions about (respectable) women's greater spirituality, morality, and religious and marital devotion. By the early twentieth century that same language had become entwined with a new, chic, sexualized discourse, partly taken from Freudian and sexological literature and partly the result of changing norms of courtship. It began to include expressions of physical love and words clearly arising from the new sexological and psychological discourses of the twentieth century but retained its characteristic extravagance of imagery and gushing sentiment. Young women could wax lyrical about their devotion for one another, but they combined more general romantic terminology with new sexualized terms, reflecting a new awareness of sexological and psychological ideas and an increasing awareness of sexuality generally, particularly the knowledge that same-sex relationships were viewed negatively and had to be pursued discreetly to avoid loss of reputation.

Of particular interest to the sexologists, and subsequently to historians, were the relationships between first-wave feminism, women's higher education and financial independence from men, and emerging ideas about sexual inversion. Ellis and his contemporaries clearly identified feminism and women's colleges as breeding-grounds for lesbianism. Reacting to female challenges to established gender norms, sexologists and their supporters used same-sex desire as a rubric within which to explain and discredit those women who transgressed the acceptable boundaries of womanhood. In sexological theory, such women represented at the very least an unfortunate lack of femininity, if not a complete sexual inversion. It is certainly true that many early feminists, and many women in women's colleges, had relationships with one another, but this was due to opportunity rather than to the effects of the environment itself. Lillian Faderman shows clearly that "women who live by their brains" sometimes did form romantic relationships.[13]

Despite the pathology, however, the new image of the "lesbian" could be liberating for some, allowing as it did an "authorized" transgression of gender identity. A new stereotype began to emerge in public discourse. As Esther Newton demonstrates,

> From about 1900 on, this cross-gender figure became the public symbol of the new social/sexual category "lesbian" ... From the perspective of Radclyffe Hall's generation ... nineteenth-century models may have seemed more confining than liberating ... Hall and many other feminists like her embraced, sometimes with ambivalence, the image of the mannish lesbian and the discourse of the sexologists about inversion primarily because they desperately wanted to break out of the asexual model of romantic friendship.[14]

The new model of the "sexual invert" at once eroded the earlier respectability of the "romantic friend" and posited a biologically based sexual orientation and gender performance that was argued to be morally right and legal because of its essential nature. A lesbian and gay rights movement based on the biological arguments of the sexologists arose in the late nineteenth century, although it would not bear fruit until the twentieth.

It is difficult to determine precisely the degree to which sexological ideas about sexuality between women permeated Canadian society and over what period.[15] The notoriety of Radclyffe Hall was known to at least some Canadians who were familiar with the controversy surrounding her 1928 novel *The Well of Loneliness,* which was publicized in Canada as well as in Britain by the lengthy obscenity trial that surrounded it. The book's main character, Stephen Gordon, is a self-identified "congenital invert."[16] The book, and Hall herself, became an instant cause célèbre. Hall brought the sexologists' terminology and stereotypes to the public in a manner hitherto unknown and was perhaps the most influential lesbian writer well into the twentieth century. Her presentation of Stephen Gordon was designed to elicit the support of a liberal public who, she thought, ought sensibly to see that homosexuality, as something innate to the individual, ought not to be condemned. She decided to "speak on behalf of a misjudged and misunderstood minority."[17]

Hall presented Gordon as morally upright, despite her biologically flawed nature, yet many were not persuaded by this characterization. After being turned down by several reputable publishers because of the book's theme, Hall was finally successful in negotiating a contract with Cape for the book to be published with packaging that would ensure its being taken seriously. Despite Havelock Ellis's endorsement of the book, and several positive reviews, the British Home Secretary demanded its withdrawal. Subsequently, the publishers of the book and the owners of the premises where copies were held were brought to trial. *The Well of Loneliness* was declared to be obscene and was ordered destroyed, and an appeal was unsuccessful.[18] In the United States, *The Well of Loneliness* was prosecuted in 1929 but was acquitted after a successful defence. In addition to newspaper coverage of the trial, reviews of *The Well of Loneliness* were published in a variety of periodicals, including *The Canadian Forum*.

The liberal Canadian journalist S.H. Hooke reviewed *The Well of Loneliness* and wrote against the censorship of the book. In Hall's defence, Hooke commented that "it is a passionate cry of protest from the side of the abnormal individual against the blind and unreasonable cruelty of society to the unusual type; a protest against the denial to the invert of all emotional outlet." Concerning the ban of Hall's book, he observed that "as a result of the ban ... thousands of people have read the book and become aware of the facts of inversion who would ordinarily never have seen the book, nor become cognizant of the facts which it deals with."[19] Laura Doan regards the trial of *The Well of Loneliness* as a very important moment in lesbian history, "*the* crystallizing moment in the construction of a visible modern lesbian subculture ... a great divide between innocence and deviance, private and public, New Woman and Modern Lesbian."[20]

Lesbians themselves had mixed feelings about *The Well of Loneliness*. Faderman writes that it remained popular well into the 1950s and provided some butch women with a role model in its portrayal of the masculine Stephen Gordon character and her relationship with the feminine Mary.[21] Not all lesbians, however, were happy with its portrayal of lesbian relationships. An American sociological study of lesbians undertaken in the 1920s showed that many lesbians thought that the book portrayed homosexuality in a poor light.[22] Interviews conducted by Vanessa Cosco for her study of lesbians in Vancouver between 1945 and 1969 revealed that some lesbians found the book affirming in that it revealed the existence of others like themselves, whereas others found it depressing and negative toward lesbians and women generally.[23]

Due largely to the extensive publicity surrounding the banning of *The Well of Loneliness,* it became somewhat of a symbol of homosexuality in the eyes of many North Americans in the 1920s and 1930s as well as the standard by which people understood the "sexual invert." *The Well of Loneliness* proved to be a very popular book in the United States, with 100,000 copies sold in the first year of publication, and by the end of December 1928, it was in its fourth printing.[24] We cannot determine with certainty the readership of novels such as *The Well of Loneliness* and thus the range and type of lesbian models in the interwar period in Canada. Knowledge of lesbianism may well have increased dramatically because of expanding coverage in the tabloid press. Steven Maynard argues that "the extensive coverage of the trial, along with follow-up forays into the lesbian world, in a popular tabloid like *Hush,* whose wide circulation surpassed that of elite periodicals, and whose readership reached well beyond medical professionals, suggest that knowledge of lesbianism may have been available to a broader spectrum of the public than we have previously imagined."[25]

Lesbian magazine fiction may have been more available to women than were novels such as Hall's because of the growing popularity of magazine fiction as a genre. In the early twentieth century, before the advent of Freudian theory, much of that fiction was quite frank, for the period, about physical affection between women. Lesbian fiction appeared in such publications as *Ladies Home Journal, Harper's,* and *Strand.* The stories often involved an older and a younger student at a girls' school or women's college. The physical affection portrayed in these stories is without the self-consciousness it would later acquire in the post–Freudian era after the First World War.[26]

Some sexological works were available at least to some Canadians, sometimes through subcultural networks. Elsa Gidlow, who was born in England but grew up in Quebec, confirms that these works were important in her gaining an understanding of her lesbianism. As a teenager during the First World War, she set up a literary group, through which she met Roswell George Mills, who apparently recognized immediately my temperament. He said, "Do you know about Sappho?" I don't remember if I'd heard anything about her, but I went to the library, found writings about her and translations of her fragments, and immediately became interested. Through Roswell – all blessings – I started to hear about some literature that would lead me to some knowledge about myself and other people like me. Other than the literary, I think the first books I read were Edward Carpenter's *The Intermediate Sex,* and Kraft-Ebbing [sic], and Lombroso – and all these were revelatory to me because I could have no doubt, having read them, of where my orientation lay. Though they wrote on a level of morbid psychology, and I couldn't accept the morbidity side of it, it was very interesting to read all this and find out there had been other people like me in the world – and a great many of them, a large number distinguished and outstanding, even if they weren't acceptable in ordinary life.[27]

Together, they read Ellis's *Psychology of Sex* – that is, "such volumes as we were able to get our hands on, as it was mainly available to doctors." Another member of their group, Louis Gross, a graduate medical student at McGill University, helped them to obtain some of the "forbidden" books.[28]

Some of the late-nineteenth- and early-twentieth-century sexological works were available to the public, although they were not widely advertised. In *Between the Acts,* Kevin Porter and Jeffrey Weeks reveal that many of the gay men they interviewed had read the small body of work available to them in the early twentieth century: the works of Edward Carpenter, Havelock Ellis, and J.A. Symonds. They argue that works such as these provided gay men with a vocabulary through which they could give meaning to their feelings and recognize that they were not alone.[29]

The "queer" or "perverse" reading of sexological definitions was widespread. By "queer" or "perverse," I mean the reading of a text, a norm, or an identity in a way not intended by its creator(s). Bonnie Zimmerman defines a perverse reading as one in which the reader is someone who is "highly conscious of her own agency, and who takes an active role in shaping the text she reads in accordance with her perspective of the world."[30] Such an approach was certainly true of many lesbians and gay men in the early twentieth century, who saw in the sexologists' terms a ready-made defence against charges of immorality and vice. If homosexuality was biological, if it was an unchanging condition within a human organism, then moral concerns were irrelevant, and legal punishment and social persecution of homosexuality could not be justified. Rapidly, gay men and lesbians began using the sexological definitions to advance their individual and community rights as best they could.[31]

By the 1920s more authors were writing about homosexuality, and their works were being read by a broader section of the public, although they were not popularized. The extent of the availability of such material to a lay readership is unknown, but there are indications that some sexological works were being read by heterosexual people as well. For example, in 1927 Nettie Bryant wrote to her friend Helene Fraser, mother of Frieda Fraser, advising her on how to handle the lesbian relationship of Frieda and Edith (Bud) Bickerton Williams. Helene had tried without success to discourage the relationship and to tell Frieda the reasons for her opposition. This lengthy letter reveals the conflict between Frieda and her mother over the relationship and the degree to which the relationship was interpreted as unhealthy. Nettie wrote:

> If I can *only* transfer to you, unbroken, my dear old friend, the vision which stands in my own mind with *increasingly persistent clearness and vigour* as a sure, safe, and upright method of meeting this rare problem – and, what is more, though God forbid that it should fail! – it seems to me looking at it in every way possible – it seems to me to be the *one and only* way which will bring everything around in the end!

Nettie wrote a lengthy letter explaining how Helene could change her approach to the problem. She suggested that Helene "say to Frieda that this marked preference for Bud carried on, in opposition to your apprehensive wishes, almost to the line of defiance, is eating your heart out." Helene should remind Frieda that her opposition was not founded on personal dislike but rather that it "lies in a well-founded apprehension, as you believe, that this friendship so-called, is eternally injuring Frieda's life – her development, her career, her health & her future happiness!" She advised her to tell Frieda that

> you have made up your mind to *withdraw* from any further effort in this line – to let Frieda "go to it" just as hard and far and fast as she likes. That you have still one quiet confidence lying in the bottom of your

heart – and that is, that Frieda will never let Bud, or anyone else, crowd you out of that chamber of her affections and her fealty which has always been yours – her own and only mother's. That your only stipulation in making all this over to her is that she will never try to bring you and Bud together, in future: that that *would* be worse than you could carry! But that you give Frieda up to her in every way – she can go just as far as she likes, you give her carte blanche – with this one stipulation that she does not attempt to bring her *to you or to your home.*

In Nettie's opinion, this course of action "would tell forcefully upon Frieda. The generosity of spirit that it would express to Frieda would, of itself, have a favorable re-action ... One cannot barter strong family ties even for a husband to whom one is rightly devoted, without a feeling of great loneliness in the world! How much more so where it is only for the cause of a girl-friend!" Nettie was sure that "this move would do more to loosen Bud's hold on [Frieda] than any amount of opposition would do." Regarding Bud, Nettie remarked:

As to Bud, the reaction that I have felt in realizing that she was not after all of the nature of that repulsive abnormal creature I heard of in that book, has resulted in a more tolerant leniency (perhaps that is expressing it a bit too strongly – as it might seem to you) – even you yourself could not help being conscious if you had read the thing![32]

It is unclear precisely to which book she was referring, but Nettie, in her guidance to Helene, clearly reveals the availability of at least some works attesting to the existence of "abnormal" sexualities and the influence of ideas about same-sex relationships as being detrimental to an individual's personal development and public life.

Also gaining popularity after the First World War were psychological analyses of homosexuality. Henry L. Minton argues that Ellis's "concept of individual and cultural relativism in sex and his tolerance for homo-sexuality had no impact on the medical community."[33] It was Freud who had the larger influence, at least on American paradigms. By 1900 med-ical professionals were beginning to classify sexual deviations more rigor-ously. Sexual inversion, gender inversion, and other forms of sexual "deviancy" became more discrete categories, each with its own set of characteristics. Freud's theories about sexuality began a slow process of separating definitions of homosexuality from those of congenital sexual and gender inversion, yet this change occurred in a very piecemeal fashion. There remained considerable slippage between the two types of theories. As George Chauncey suggests, even Freud's followers in the United States continued to mix his psychological interpretations of homosexuality with earlier, congenital ones.[34] American psychiatrists and psychologists writing in the 1930s associated homosexuality with cross-gender identification, building somewhat on earlier assumptions about inversion. Interwar interpretations, however, did not always have an essentialist basis. Psychiatrist George W. Henry, in his 1937 study of "Psychogenic Factors in Overt Homosexuality," concluded that psychological causes could exacerbate any existing latent tendencies toward homosexuality. In particular, deviation from prescribed gender roles could lead to homosexual tendencies.[35]

Medical, sexological, and psychological works on sexuality increasingly informed the discourses of the medical and psychological professions. It may have been the case that the definitions and terminologies of sexuality used by these professionals with their patients gradually changed in response to these works, but it is impossible to determine without access to medical case files the degree to which this occurred in the period under study. In addition, one must remember that the descriptors developed in these professions may have been used in patients' files but would not necessarily have been mentioned to patients and families themselves, thus keeping the discourse restricted to the medical profession. A few members of the general public, most particularly those deliberately seeking scientific explanations for their own sexuality, gained access to sexological and psychological works, but it is unlikely that their use was widespread. The rapid expansion in published works on sexuality does not necessarily indicate a public well educated on the subject. Such education was most likely class-specific and perhaps even gender-specific. More information on sexuality was available to Canadians, but their degree of access to it varied considerably. The records of the middle-class women whose lives are discussed in this book do indicate a continuation of the earlier language of the romantic friendship and of areas of ignorance about female sexuality, but they also strongly demonstrate that sexological ideas were becoming more influential among middle-class Canadians. These relationships are a transition between the romantic friendship and the modern lesbian relationship.

Women's diaries and letters present the historian of sexuality with many difficulties of interpretation, especially if written before the Second World War. In a period when sexuality was largely not spoken of, and when respectable women were thought to be much less sexual than were men, women naturally tended not to write about their sexual desires and behaviours. It was a rare woman indeed who breached these boundaries of appropriate expression since the consequences for reputation could be severe. Even those literary figures whose works ventured into such areas risked being branded as salacious and improper. Little surprise, then, that the few women's records to be found in public archives and private collections contain little or no material on the authors' sexual activities. Acknowledgment of same-sex desires and activities was even riskier and thus less common. These constraints render the manuscript collections discussed in this chapter particularly significant, for they allow us a rare glimpse into the erotic lives of women whose sexual desires and activities were doubly proscribed.

Frieda Fraser and Edith (Bud) Bickerton Williams

The collection of letters between Frieda Fraser and Edith (Bud) Bickerton Williams is the largest thus far in Canadian lesbian history. It is also a rare and unusual collection in its expressiveness and detail about a passionate relationship between two women. Frieda and Bud wrote to each other in language that was similar to that of romantic friends, but clearly evident in their letters is an awareness of new terms for sexuality, ideas about "unnatural" relationships, knowledge of the possibility of familial and societal disapproval, and awareness of other women in same-sex relationships. Their correspondence also reveals the emotional hardships women had to endure in order to be with one another and clearly illustrates the depth of lesbian passion. It is not known when precisely Frieda and Bud met, but it was during their university years that they formed the intimate relationship that would last until Bud's death in 1979. They date the beginning of their "system of partnership," as they called it, to 1918, and they began the passionate correspondence left to us today during their separation between 1925 and 1927, while Frieda continued her medical training in the United

States and Bud travelled and worked in Europe.[36] Their families, who were largely disapproving of their relationship, also sought to separate them. Bud and Frieda were separated again in the 1930s, when Bud was living in Aurora and Frieda was in Toronto. In 1939 they were finally able to set up house together. They continued to live together until Bud's death.

Frieda Helen Fraser was born in Toronto in 1899, the child of William Fraser, a professor of Spanish and Italian at the University of Toronto, and Helene Zahn. She was educated at home until the age of fifteen and then was sent to Havergal College. She entered University College in the fall of 1917 and graduated with her bachelor's degree in 1922, having specialized in physics and biology. Frieda completed a bachelor of medicine in 1925 and then moved to New York, where she took an internship at the New York Infirmary for Women and Children. She completed her postdoctoral training in chest diseases at the Henry Phipps Institute at the University of Pennsylvania. She then took up the position of demonstrator in the Department of Hygiene and Preventative Medicine in the School of Hygiene in Toronto. She was also a research associate in the Connaught Laboratories. In 1936 Frieda became an assistant professor, and she made full professor in 1949. She retired in 1965 and died in 1992. It was during Frieda's time in New York and Philadelphia that the majority of the letters were written. As a teenager and as an adult, Frieda adopted a boyish and then masculine appearance. She was somewhat reserved, and she enjoyed the outdoors and painting and drawing.

Edith (Bud) Bickerton Williams was also born in Toronto in 1899. Less is known about Bud's background. She too was Presbyterian. That she was of similar social status to Frieda may be indicated by the presence among her remaining possessions of a volume of Henry Wadsworth Longfellow's poetry containing a bookplate with the coat-of-arms of the Williams family, listing the name Sir John Bickerton Williams, Kt., LLD, FSA. Bud's father was "in insurance."[37] Bud spent ten years at "Glen Mawr," a private school for girls. She entered the arts program at University College in 1916 but was an unsuccessful student and failed in her second year. In 1925 she travelled to Britain to work in a bank. Her mother attempted to persuade her to remain in England, but Bud returned to Canada in 1927. In the 1930s she raised poultry in Aurora, Ontario, and then entered the Ontario Veterinary College in Guelph. She graduated in 1941, being only the second female veterinary graduate in Canada and the fifth in North America. She then set up veterinary practice in Toronto, retiring at the age of sixty-five. Bud suffered a stroke in 1976 and another two in 1979, finally succumbing in November of that year. She had a somewhat more feminine appearance than Frieda and was also rather more emotionally expressive.

Frieda and Bud did not encounter family opposition to their undertaking university study and working for a living. Frieda may have been privileged in this regard since she came from a family in which higher education was already valued, her father and one of her brothers also being academics. As noted, her father was in the humanities at the University of Toronto, and Frieda's brother Donald, to whom she was very close, was a scientist. His support may have aided in her being able to pursue the career that she adopted, first as a medical doctor and then as a professor of microbiology. Nor does there seem to have been any opposition to Bud's working in a bank. In fact, Bud's family sent her to England so that she could look after her aunts. Clerical work in the developing banking system was an appropriate employment for a woman of her class. It also had the added "advantage" of keeping her away from Frieda, something Bud's mother desired greatly. It seems from the records available that their upbringing had not included attempts to keep them away from the world of female employment, and thus they had not had to rebel against family wishes in that regard.

Although the ideal and the expected role for all women was marriage and motherhood, it was now rather more customary than it had been just a decade or two earlier for women of Frieda and Bud's class to work before marriage. By the beginning of the interwar period in Canada, many areas of the workforce were opening up for women. Working-class women had long been in paid employment, but a new trend in the 1920s was for a larger number of middle-class women to enter the paid workforce before marriage than had done so in the previous century. No longer was there quite as much stigma attached to the middle-class woman who worked for money, although it should be noted that her employment was to be in respectable and appropriately feminine areas of the workforce, such as teaching, nursing, or good-quality clerical work.[38]

It was the obvious relationship between Frieda and Bud to which their families objected. The Fraser-Williams relationship commenced at the cusp of two important periods in middle-class lesbian history, the era of the romantic friendship and the Freudian era. Their letters are reminiscent in their expressions of love and devotion of some of the letters of nineteenth-century lesbians in romantic friendships, which were assumed to be nonsexual. Similar middle-class values are expressed, and the social milieux they moved in were middle-class in nature. Yet Bud and Frieda clearly had a physical sexuality. Their letters are much less ambiguous than those of other collections. The letters are replete with such terms of endearment as "my lamb," "lambie," and "darling." Writing almost daily when possible, Bud and Frieda discussed not only their jobs, friends, and family events but also the nature of their relationship, societal attitudes toward relationships between women, their future together, and their families' opposition to their relationship. Although they do not analyze their own coming to awareness of their same-sex attraction, their discussions of relationships with friends and family and the continuous expression of the terms of their own relationship reveal a sense of the "rightness" and "naturalness" of their union not unlike that expressed in the more recent oral testimonies used for this study. Their letters also reveal the presence, on both sides, of subjectivity based on same-sex desire in their awareness of their difference from other women, their resistance to societal attitudes toward relationships between women, and their passionate commitment to a long-term relationship.

The two women constantly flatter each other, Bud being the more expressive of the two in this regard. Writing to Frieda for her birthday in 1925, for example, Bud said, "My dear – This carries my best wishes for to-morrow and all my love to you. I am quite used to your getting older as you are doing it so nicely. And it is nice to have you catch up to me again – I am not so lonely. I shall burn two candles for you to-morrow – one as a bribe for the future and one to say thank-you for the past." She continued, flirtatiously, "I hope you're liking the great out-of-doors – please don't pick up a he-man!"[39] She would ask of Frieda, later in 1925, "Do you think we'll get over liking each other in time? It might be simpler in heaps of ways but I couldn't conceive of a worse calamity than to stop loving you, to look at [it] from a purely selfish point of view. O my dear, I've an awful lot to thank you for – especially for showing me what affection is."[40] Bud's feelings for Frieda sometimes affected the way she interacted with other people. "I like it most of the time," she said, because it is not enough to be really painful, but quite often I get took! It is most unexpected and rather inconvenient sometimes. I begin to be so awfully nice to people. Mollie understands so that when I kiss her when we meet in the evening and try to wait on her hand and foot, she doesn't think that I have taken leave of my senses, but is nice and sympathetic back. But with other people, it is not so simple and makes life very much more complicated. But I've told you about it before. I wish I could explain that I'm not being nice and affectionate because of any feelings I have for them but because I like someone else rather hard.[41]

The depth of their feelings for one another is expressed in many letters. In 1926 Bud wrote, "I didn't know that it was possible to miss anyone so much, or that I could love you quite so violently. On having had it happen, I could go on doing it indefinitely without slowing down a bit." Regarding their future together, she said, "The end of our second four years expires this year – what about a new base and for how long? It *will* be amusing to see what we are up to in another eight years – 34, Frieda! And what will we have done?"[42] Frieda also missed Bud, writing the previous year, "It is a most extraordinary arrangement this system of partnership. I suppose it shows the adaptability of the human organism. I didn't realise till lately how much I need you & depend on you & still, or rather because of it I rely much more on myself than without you. Is that clear? It sounds rather cocky but it isn't very."[43]

Frieda and Bud often spoke of their relationship in terms of a "valley," which appears to refer to an imaginary or symbolic and idyllic place where their love was expressed fully. "Frieda dear," wrote Bud,

> I've tried and tried and I can't write about the valley. I've written pages and then torn them up because they don't say at all what I mean. You are a very understanding person, but when I read it over, it doesn't convey what I mean even to me, so I don't think it would to you.[44]

Frieda had similar difficulty describing the valley, but in both cases the descriptions offer images of a tranquil and almost ethereal place where the emotions between the two women surrounded them, communication was almost telepathic, and the criticism of others was absent. The conjuring up of such an imagined place to express their love might suggest to the reader a form of resistance to dominant discourse, in the sense that Frieda and Bud created for themselves an ideal world where their love was not an issue, a world sadly lacking in their real lives.

The valley was a mutually constructed oasis in a homophobic world. This might be thought of as a couple's version of what Nan Enstad, using James C. Scott, calls a "hidden transcript," a "cultural [practice] and knowledge ... not visible to those in power."[45] Enstad is referring to broad cultural practices on the part of subordinate groups who are denied a public voice, but the resistant subjectivities she speaks of can also generate individual practices to produce similar effects. Although created because of social marginalization, and although not a political resistance, the valley served for Frieda and Bud both as a discourse of resistance and as a vision of a different world, where their relationship was allowed to speak its true value.

On several occasions, Bud wrote to Frieda concerning her thoughts on other women's emotional relationships. While in Britain, it seems that she grew to know several lesbian couples, some of whom she compared to herself and Frieda. Once, she wrote to Frieda,

> Helen and I sat up last night until three o'clock discussing liking people, etc. I'm awfully sorry for her, the poor lamb. She likes her family quite well, but I don't think she really knows much about loving and doesn't love anyone at all. I can't think of anything worse, and yet think of the millions of people who do it. She was telling me about Esther and Lucie and how devoted they are, which even Helen couldn't miss. And they seemed to have worked it out rather well. They are awfully happy together and seem to consider it a permanent arrangement – at least, Lucie does, I am sure.[46]

Later in 1925 Bud wrote to Frieda about her friend Mollie, who one night "began to tell me about Edith Clarke, to whom she is devoted. She had never said much about her before, and that little very casually, but I had gathered that she rather liked her. However last night she embarked on the whole tale – their families don't like it and Edith wants to come to London to be with Moll, so there is a devil of a row going on." Bud, in response, told Mollie about her relationship with Frieda. She asked of Frieda,

Do you mind my telling Mollie? I have never wanted to talk about you at all, but when I got started, she was so interested and was rather keen to know because in some ways we are a bit farther on. They have had just the same difficulties with their families, but they really had more time before they got on their ears. Edith and M. lived together here for a bit before there was any opposition, but E. was ill and had to go back to Jamaica, and since then their families have got irate.[47]

The phrase "we are a bit farther on" can be interpreted in two ways. The first, obviously, is simply one of duration of the relationship and suggests that Mollie sought Bud's advice because Bud and Frieda's relationship was the longer of the two. Also in evidence here, however, is a more qualitative suggestion of experience. Bud was able to offer Mollie her advice about family conflicts over same-sex relationships because she and Frieda had gained considerable experience in this area in the preceding years. In her conversation with Mollie, Bud acted as sage or elder stateswoman for relationships between women.

It would appear that in late 1925, Bud and Frieda toyed with the idea of Frieda forming another relationship in Bud's absence. Bud had suggested that Frieda get to know a woman called Gwyn. Bud was initially surprised at the connection that was made between the two, writing to Frieda, "I'm glad you think she is lovely – I do, of course, but I'm always afraid that it is because I like her so much, and discount something. But I was not prepared to find you so impressed."[48] She further commented,

I'm thrilled to death that you could love Gwyn – please do! I can't think of a nicer combination of people and it would be so nice for me ... I couldn't ask for anything more than to have Gwyn my successor, and to be loved by you is the best thing I could wish for her. O my darling, how pleasant it would be! ... My darling lamb, the more I think of you and Gwyn, the nicer it is – do manage it, please![49]

Whatever Bud's statements of encouragement, she was not necessarily very pleased about Frieda meeting someone else. Despite wishing Frieda happiness, and thus expressing a willingness to be "succeeded," Bud became personally rather insecure when it appeared that a close relationship between Frieda and Gwyn might in fact occur. She began to see in Frieda's behaviour changes that might or might not have occurred, the cause of which was the relationship with Gwyn. Her concerns are revealed when she asks,

> Is there anything the matter? The last little bit, you have been different when I have come to see you. Is it that my successor is in sight? You are just as nice as ever, but a little taken up with something that you're not letting me in on. If it is my successor, I am quite prepared to love her too, even if it isn't Gwyn.[50]

In time, Bud and Frieda realized that Gwyn was critical of their relationship. Bud reported to Frieda that "apart from your being a friend of mine, she likes you, but her whole idea of you is somewhat distorted by the peculiar idea she has of our friendship. You are leading me into all sorts of evil, and I am being stupid not to see it. I'm so sorry for her – isn't it a pity she is such an idiot about it?"[51] She further revealed, "it is all based on the fact that it isn't natural for young women to be devoted to each other."[52] Gwyn commented negatively on the relationship on several occasions, and her perspective was similar to that of each woman's family and to dominant attitudes about intimate relationships between women.

Frieda and Bud commented frequently on other people's reactions to their relationship. They were sharply critical of the prevailing views about relationships between women and frequently remarked on the stupidity of the opposition. Frieda said, "Our not being popular is probably due to two things a) people feel left out b) it is against nature." She went on to state, "a) we have done our best [to] rule out & there is no arguing over b) All of which leaves us at the starting point."[53] Even though the two women were not part of a public lesbian culture and did not use the "sexual invert" terminology of the day to express an identity, they resisted the dominant discourse and all attempts to separate them and to deny the validity of their relationship. Bud suggested that having to "exercise tact and discretion" – to monitor their behaviour around others and to be careful how openly they expressed affection – had not affected the quality of their relationship or their commitment to each other. Bud also took pride in their having resisted the forceful pressure of family antagonism.

Bud's complaints about the treatment the two had received and the general absurdity of people's disapproval should not be taken to indicate, however, that she was in favour of all same-sex relationships. In an earlier letter, she wrote, "I think I see exactly what everyone objects to about us, and I'm not sure that I don't agree with them usually, but I am convinced that we are an exception."[54] Unfortunately, Bud does not elaborate on those aspects of the relationship that she might, in others, see as less than desirable. It could be that Bud, who was not in favour of the extremely masculine appearance of some women, might have been commenting on the kind of relationships between women described by such sexologists as Havelock Ellis and increasingly in evidence in England in the 1920s, to which the appellation "sexual inversion" might readily be applied. Many a lesbian in this period sought to distance herself from the pathological terminology of the sexologists, even while others – most notably Radclyffe Hall – were embracing it.[55]

Bud's loquacity on the subject of her relationship with Frieda varied in relation to her assessment of the degree of tolerance of other people. Based on others' reactions to the subject, or their likely reactions, she tailored her information to the particular situation. Bud was aware that their relationship contravened dominant norms, and she sought to preserve and protect the relationship by being circumspect in some situations. For example, in 1925 Bud was talking to her friend Helen about relationships. When Helen remarked that "it must be nice to have someone to whom it mattered whether you were there or not," Bud said that she thought it was. "Then she said something about you and me," Bud wrote to Frieda:

> That we hit it off quite well, and I found that all I could do was agree. I simply couldn't say more or talk about you at all; because she wouldn't understand and it seemed so indecent; although I had said quite a lot about you to the nice Miss Brown coming over on the boat. I thought I had got to the point where I could chat about you now, but I find I can't.[56]

Returning to Canada to visit Frieda in 1926, Bud wrote, "I'm so thrilled at everything I'm nearly in a fit. One old boy that I love on the boat wants to know why I'm so thrilled about getting home and I can't explain that it's because I'm going to telephone you tomorrow night!"[57] If it had been a husband or boyfriend to whom Bud was returning, she might have felt more comfortable expressing her excitement, although still modestly; that she did not do so reveals that she knew what would be the probable reaction to the knowledge that it was another woman she was so excited to see.

Attitudes toward women's relationships sometimes caused the two women considerable mirth. Bud asked Frieda,

> Did I tell you about our maid and your letters? I always get one from you now on Monday morning and she always puts it on top and says with an arch air "Here's your letter, Miss" when she brings them up. And if one comes any other time, she says "Here's an extra one this week," and I have been quite amused by it. But one day she came in for something in the evening when I had been out with Hugh and she gave me a little maternal advice about going out with him so much when there was that man of mine – that doctor – in N.Y. writing to me so regular and me writing to him too! I was so amused that I could hardly restrain my shouts of laughter, but I carefully addressed the next letter that I gave her to post to Dr. Frieda H. Fraser, and nothing has been said since. Aren't you entertained?[58]

That Bud appreciated that their relationship could easily be seen for what it was is indicated by her comment that "I found a nice dedication in a book to-day 'To those who believe that life was made for friendship.' But according to most of our friends we are not in that class, are we? Wouldn't we be counted as too abandoned?"[59] Bud's letters to Frieda suggest a resistance to societal attitudes and a belief that their love would survive social pressures. Discussing their future together, Bud acknowledged in 1926, "I suppose there would be hell raised if we tried to live together."[60]

Frieda commented less often on people's attitudes than did Bud. Her occasional comments reveal that she evaluated societal attitudes at least partly in relation to whether they were intellectually sound. She mentioned to Bud an afternoon tea she had attended: "I went to tea at Gertrude Graden's and found myself suddenly in a rare & intellectual atmosphere. I was immediately introduced to & sat down beside an active middle aged woman with an air whose opening remark was 'Tell me about the contraceptive clinics in Toronto.'" Quite how the conversation turned to the subject of women's relationships is unclear, but Frieda commented, "The problem that seems to be in their minds at the moment was the everlasting odd women. I wonder if there are enough of them to warrant all the fuss & if they are necessarily abnormal or unhappy or mentally deformed."[61] Here, Frieda seems to be commenting that society had blown the magnitude of the "problem" out of all proportion and also that the assumptions about "odd women" were, in her view, incorrect.[62] She continued:

> Gertrude's partner had a pretty idea. She had been reading Lysistrata which seems to be a book deploring the sexlessness of working women in modern times & how it was against NATURE. She wanted to write an essay from the point of view of the amoeba deploring the modern trend & how terrible this new business of sex differentiation was. So utterly against Nature & so forth as the amoeba which was invented before sex differentiation would naturally think it.[63]

A letter of 1926 reveals Frieda being unusually voluble on the subject of societal attitudes toward gender and sexuality. Her letter reveals a mix of scientific knowledge and Freudian ideas interwoven with her own, more personal perspective. The beginning of the letter has been lost, unfortunately, so we do not know what sparked Frieda's unusually long discussion of biologically based ideas of "natural" and appropriate human sexual behaviour. She told Bud,

> there is an outrageously high value put on the passion of men for women & women for men as such – I wonder sometimes whether it isn't a semitic influence – or rather a characteristic of theirs which we have misunderstood & aped while giving it our own racial twist. I'll explain at length if you like – & I'm not rabid about Jews!
>
> When you consider that originally the motive force in question was intrinsically an intermittent mechanism & that now when the need for it is biologically dropping to an extremely low level people keep harping on it as though it were a constantly necessary factor for a normal existence it seems damned silly of them not to say perverse.
>
> No one thinks it indecent of the bees & ants to have developed what is virtually an intersex. In fact they are highly respected. And they do it on the basis of political economy or social hygiene. Imagine what a scandal if some of the workers forgot themselves! And there it seems to be simply a matter of being interested in something else; which a philosopher

might call self sacrifice or self control for the communal good but which a biologist would call a tropism.

Moreover to be truly womanly, take yours truly (generally allowed to be within normal limits even if barely), if one of the ruling instincts of the world is so feeble that in 26 years it has only called attention to itself by my wanting to pat the hair of or kiss the tops of the heads of men engaged in looking down microscopes when I see them from the top, I can't bring myself to take it too seriously.

Of course one could argue a) that I'm setting up a resistance to it a la Freud – allowing that if it is all it is cracked up to be it should surely be strong enough to break down that much.

Or b) that people like me are abnormal. But in that case, though there is no defense, one would have to admit that they manage to rub along in fair numbers.[64]

Frieda's sharp criticism of social norms reveals both awareness of general antipathy toward same-sex relationships and a resistance to that homophobia and also to prevailing gender norms. She clearly regards biological arguments about heterosexuality being for the survival of the species as superfluous in a time when there did not exist the same biological need for reproduction. Her comments on intersex among insects illustrate the influence of early-twentieth-century definitions of a "third sex." It is impossible to determine whether Frieda might have thought of herself in a way we would now classify as "transgender" or simply regarded herself as not traditionally womanly, but she was fully aware and was accepting of her own gender nonconformity. She acknowledged that she was "within normal limits" of womanliness, but her addition of the phrase "even if barely" demonstrates an awareness of her lack of femininity in the traditional sense. That she linked this discussion to her own personal experience at least suggests that Frieda was aware of and comfortable with her own, unfeminine gender performance.[65]

It is clear from this letter that Frieda took philosophical and scientific issue with biological and Freudian notions of the naturalness and rightness of heterosexuality. She found fault with the argument that heterosexuality was the driving human force because in Frieda's case it had little effect beyond the occasional desire to kiss a man affectionately. Countering Freud, Frieda suggested that any force that is natural and strong should easily be able to counter any resistance. Contrary to sexology's tendency to place importance on the sexual instinct as a biological imperative, Freud largely abandoned the association between biology and sexual object choice.[66] He developed a complex theory that portrayed sexuality as a series of conflicting desires and dreams constantly at war with a basic libidinal energy. The nature of sexual expression, and most especially of sexual orientation, indicated to Freud the level of psychological maturity in sexual development. For Freud, matrimonial and reproductive heterosexuality was the most mature and evolved psychological state, whereas homosexuality, masturbation, and other nonprocreative sexual behaviours indicated that a person was "stalled" in the process of sexual development by some unconscious and traumatic crisis, which could be cured only by means of psychoanalysis.[67] Freud's ideas on the subject of sexuality, however, would only gradually inform sexual discourse in the twentieth century. He became increasingly popular with middle-class thinkers during the 1920s, but it was not until the years of the Second World War and the Cold War that Freud's followers became widely influential.

For Frieda and Bud, societal attitudes toward relationships between women were simultaneously amusing, irritating, and oppressive. Their sense of humour about the issue allowed them to defuse some of the stress involved in continuing their relationship in the face of disapproval. Apart from their families and close friends, however, it does not seem that many people knew of the nature of their relationship. It is because of this that Frieda was able to sit quietly at the afternoon tea and listen to the assembled guests discuss "the everlasting odd women," without them being any the wiser that an odd woman was in their presence. And it was not until Bud made it clear by addressing an envelope to "Dr. Frieda H. Fraser" rather than to "Dr. F.H. Fraser" that it occurred to her maid that she might be writing to a woman.[68]

Frieda and Bud found some measure of support among their closest friends, many of whom were similarly "devoted" to women. Others were simply less homophobic than society at large. Their mutual friend B was particularly supportive. In 1926, when Bud was missing Frieda terribly, she expressed to B the desire to quit her job in London and find one in Philadelphia, where Frieda was working. B said to her, "Why don't you? You know you could get a job anywhere." Bud wrote to Frieda, "I was mildly astonished that she thought it would be a good idea but I didn't pursue it further as she went on to say that we got on so well that it was a pity we couldn't live together." B then said to Bud, "Frieda kept thinking all the time we were in Bermuda that it was a pity it wasn't you." Bud later regretted her response, which fortunately did not offend B: "I made the most dreadful remark at which B shouted with laughter and said that I wasn't blest with modesty. Please I said it quite without thinking and I'm sorry I've disgraced you. It was 'Poor dear – I'm sorry it was so bad that she let it show.'"[69]

Elisabeth Govan and B

A further example of changes to middle-class women's relationships in the early twentieth century is the correspondence between B, a Vancouver social worker, and Elisabeth Govan. Elisabeth Steel Livingston Govan was born in Scotland in 1907 and immigrated to Canada with her family. She received her bachelor of arts from the University of Toronto in 1930 and then took a second bachelor of arts at Oxford, graduating in 1932. She followed that degree with a master's in public welfare administration and a diploma in social work from the University of Toronto. In 1938 Govan travelled to Australia to take up a position as a casework tutor in Sydney. The following year, she was appointed to the University of Sydney, and in 1940 Govan became the director of social studies.[70] Govan returned to Toronto in 1945 and took up a junior position as an assistant professor. She completed her studies in 1951 with a doctorate from the University of Chicago and then left the academic world to work on special projects for the Canadian Welfare Council. She returned to the University of Toronto in 1956 to accept a full professorship in social work.

Little is known of Govan's intimate female correspondent B. From the few letters that remain of her correspondence with Govan during the 1940s, it appears that B was studying at the University of British Columbia for a degree in public welfare. Govan, or "Betty," as B called her, had telephoned B some time in 1944 or 1945. That she and Betty had known each other for some time is revealed by her recollection of their reacquaintance. "You were so delightful, Betty-mine," she said. "'Is that Miss M?' 'Yes' 'B' 'Yes' 'Well, this is Betty Govan!!' 'No!!!' 'Yes!' 'It *can't* be.' 'It is.' What would have happened if you had *not* phoned me, I ask you? But you would have, wouldn't you?"[71] The two women may have met each other as early as 1928, when Govan was an undergraduate at the University of Toronto. After Govan had visited B in Vancouver, B remarked to her friend Meg, "'We picked up just where we left off ...' and she immediately sensed my sense of ... revelation, or something. She said ... 'It proved a lot of things for you, didn't it ... because you have changed and grown up almost completely since 1928.'"[72]

The correspondence between Elisabeth Govan and B has been examined by Carol Baines, who quotes the letters at length. Baines seems reluctant to call the relationship a lesbian one, suggesting that, "given the lack of definitive evidence, one can only speculate."[73] Although she does suggest that the early-twentieth-century pathologization of lesbians "may well help us understand some of the ambivalence that Govan experienced" about her personal relationships, Baines seems to be seeking evidence of a physical relationship as proof of Govan's sexual orientation. The letters reveal enough about the depth, passion, and intimacy of the Betty-B relationship to place it firmly outside the boundaries of acceptable heterosexuality, even if Govan and B did not refer to themselves as lesbians or have a genital sexual relationship.

Several letters from B to Betty reveal both the continued use, in the 1940s, of the very hyperbolic language of previous decades and the influence of new ideas about same-sex relationships. B frequently expressed her devotion to Betty. In 1945 she wrote,

> Something has lasted all these years better than we ever dreamed it would ... What is it, darling? ... What do you think? I think – and know – that one of the things is my joy in the way your steady old head works ... Another thing is the spring from which your vitality and enthusiasm and joy in living [springs] forth. Very sweet clear water ... You really aren't any more impervious to feelings than I am ... and we're old and wise enough now to assess things like that quite accurately, aren't we? ... It has moved out of the pathological pitfall it fell into just at first because of my need then ... and now? ... such a very tender affection my Betty ... so very dear and to be cherished, now more than ever.[74]

Precisely what B meant by "pathological pitfall" is unclear. It could be that she simply meant that she had at first been quite obsessed with Govan and perhaps a little too clingy. It could be that they had initially had a physical relationship but had withdrawn from it because of their knowledge that such relationships were regarded as abnormal, and they wished not to be classified or to have to think of themselves in relation to the lesbians who were becoming the subject of increasing public discourse. Whichever is the case, B's use of the word "pathological" illustrates the influence of psychology and of notions of normal and abnormal, healthy and unhealthy relationships. B appears to have felt that her relationship with Betty was very spiritual as well as emotional and that the two had a remarkable connection despite the fact that they spent very little time together in the same city. She wrote,

> Dear Betty-boy ... I only wanted to listen, and look at you, and feel your presence ... and any words of mine were rightly inserted edgewise ... You always go away from me ... that is the pattern for us apparently ... but I still feel you, my dearly beloved child, right to my fingertips. It is a miracle sort of thing that has ... in the words of King James ... been vouchsafed unto us ... It has a religious quality ... perhaps I mean transcendent quality ... and it makes me love the world even more dearly than before ... and feel safer, and freer, and surer. I'm saying all this again because it still overwhelms me ... and yet, had I the faith about which the church preaches, I might have accepted the thing as ordinary. But how blasé ...! Supposing I had had that very reaction ... you would have turned from me in disgust, and I wouldn't have known enough to be disgusted with myself. Thank God for our emotional health, my Betty, and for the mental capacity we both have to recognize a miracle when it happens.[75]

Here again are some elements of the language of the romantic friendship, still present in the 1940s, particularly the linking of a relationship with religion – but with an awareness of the new language of pathology.

B knew well the possible consequences of her relationship, commenting, "I suppose we can't avoid the usual implications of the conservative school ... the biddies who frown upon close attachments between women." Before meeting Betty, B knew that she was not going to fulfil society's expectations of her as a woman. "I faced the prospect of matrimony once," she said, "and decided with a cool sort of half logical knowledge, that I would never be able to face the drudge, nor [be] able to measure up to the usual expectations ... and once that was decided the rest has been easy ... lacking in conflict, I mean."[76] Here, B expresses a belief in the "rightness" and "naturalness" of her desires, present in so many lesbian accounts: once she had decided that marriage, the usual path of womanhood, was not for her, emotional conflict disappeared. She became comfortable with herself and was able to live her life more fully.

Several of B's letters reveal that she missed Betty greatly. In November 1945, she lamented, "I wish you were here. We'd hop up to Pender Harbour and walk in our cedary wood, and paddle on lost lakes and wet a line in the salt sea ... every so often I want you with me rather desperately. Your letter was *good* – and I am completely satisfied, for a little space of time, anyway."[77] Later that month, she told Betty that a friend had said to her, "out of a completely serene sky ... 'You know, it would be a good thing for you to go to the East for a year ...' But you will be in Chicago, so why should I? ... except, if I am ever to have a degree, I'd rather get it in Toronto than here." Money, however, was of concern to her: "I'm an extravagant hussy and would find it awfully hard to endure student poverty," she said. "Would you guarantee me one good meal a week? I could pay it off when you finally get to B.C. [drawing of happy face] – But this sort of chatter is dangerous."[78]

In one of her letters, B described her attraction to Betty:

> You have all the things that would, and did, hoist you almost beyond reach of my earthly eyes ... social poise, academic honours that are staggering in comparison to mine, achievement and prestige in the top drawer of social work ... teaching. Even those dizzy heights couldn't deter me, or send me ricocheting away from you as they might easily have ... Instead we reached out to each other from the ... to be analytical about this ... from the libidinal level ... the warm altogether pleasure of our emotional reaction to each other.[79]

B did not mention the two women sleeping together or being otherwise intimate, but her use of the word "libidinal" to describe their attraction clearly indicates the presence of a sexual desire or at the very least of an awareness of Freudian explanations of their kind of relationship.[80] The sentence follows a passage that can be described as fulfilling many of the requirements of the romantic friendship. B not only expressed loyalty and devotion but also placed the object of her affection clearly on a pedestal, if not in heaven. She described her own eyes as "earthly" and suggested that Betty's attributes placed her beyond earthly terrain.

We see in B's terminology a modern, twentieth-century acknowledgment of physical sexual desire. B regards the word "libidinal" as referring to the women's emotional reaction to each other, but its use in medical discourse generally referred to more physical, and thus more dangerous, passions. It is possible, however, that B was "queering" the notion in the sense that she was able to use the term "libidinal" about feelings between two women without internalizing the pathological interpretation of that desire, which would usually have been directed at lesbians.[81]

Alexis Alvey and Grace Brodie

Amelia Alexis Alvey served with the Women's Royal Canadian Naval Service (WRCNS) from 1942 to 1945. Alvey was born in Seattle, Washington, and later attended McMaster University in Hamilton, Ontario. She was employed as a special technician in charge of photography at the University of Toronto's School of Medicine. Alvey commanded the business-women's company of the Toronto Red Cross Transport Corps and was lecturer to the entire Transport Corps for Military Law, Map Reading, and Military and Naval Insignia. She was chosen as one of the first class of the WRCNS, which began training in August 1942 in Ottawa. Alvey was selected to be acting chief petty officer master-at-arms. She was also deputy unit officer at HMCS Bytown (Ottawa), unit officer with the commanding officer at Pacific Coast HMCS Burrard (Vancouver), unit officer and then lieutenant at HMCS Bytown, and unit officer at HMCS Stadacona (Halifax). After her distinguished career with the WRCNS, Alvey returned to her civilian position at the University of Toronto in 1945. She then joined the University of Washington Libraries, retiring in 1969. She died on 5 June 1996.[82]

Nancy Olson argues that Alvey was lesbian, although she acknowledges that Alvey's identity was unstable and that the Alvey collection contains no explicit statement of that identity or of a physical sexuality. It is in the phrasing of the letters between Alvey and her partner, Grace Brodie, who was also an officer in the WRCNS, and in their joint life that one recognizes her lesbianism.[83] Olson remarks that "Brodie's correspondence to Alvey ... is full of terms of endearment, censored by Alvey as being too personal. There are passages blacked out, though still legible, that demonstrate a physical affection that goes beyond the chaste nature of a romantic friendship."[84] Other material has been removed entirely by the cutting-off of portions of the letters. The letters contain many terms of endearment, the most frequent of which are "Belovedest" and "Own Darling." Brodie wrote effusively, many of her letters revealing her love for Alvey. In October of 1942, during a trip to Vancouver, Brodie wrote to Alvey, "They showed me into a huge room, over looking the harbour and Stanley Park – which would be perfect, if you were here to share it with me."[85]

As Olson indicates, respectability was very important to Alvey, and this importance accounts in part for her censorship of the letters but also for her construction of the collection, in which she emphasized gentility.[86] Her concern about maintaining a respectable reputation can be seen in her desire to live a dutiful and proper life in the military. On 8 December 1942 Brodie advised Alvey, "Had your lovely long letter too, which has raised 1000 questions in my mind! I would certainly go out a bit with Russell, she being the discreet person you know her to be. Certainly she will respect your position and you might get away without anyone knowing about it." Before including this letter in the collection, Alvey wrote a small sidebar identifying the person as a WREN rating. The term "WREN" was the popular name for a member of the British Women's Royal Naval Service and came to be used for women in the WRCNS as well. Ratings were the junior naval ranks, up to the level of chief petty officer, and were inferior in status to commissioned officers. Alvey commented, "Officers were not to consort with ratings."[87] It would appear that this was an ordinary friendship, but Alvey was concerned about it being known that she was friendly with someone of lesser status.

Alvey's concern about keeping up appearances can also be seen in her management of the collection. Not only was she concerned during the war years to behave in an appropriate manner, but she also was later concerned to remove from the letters anything that might reveal the most intimate parts of her relationship with Brodie. Her excisions are interesting, given that the text, in many cases, remains partially visible and given that other parts of the letters, not blacked-out, are equally suggestive to the modern reader.[88] For example, Alvey chose to include a letter in which Brodie wrote, "When I meet you I'm going to be overcome by this efficient, important Third Officer."[89]

Alvey's attempts to maintain a respectable façade during the war years were eventually unsuccessful. The very close relationship between Alvey and Brodie, and Alvey's masculinity, were enough eventually to set off alarm bells in the administration. Canada's military, and indeed society at large, was becoming more adept as the 1940s wore on at identifying "odd women." Alvey began her naval career as a sublieutenant and by May of 1944 was acting lieutenant commander. She was highly regarded by many. By October of 1944, however, her relationship with the naval administration had soured. She was informed by the new director of the women's naval service that she was to be transferred "from her prestigious posting in Halifax, to a clerical position in the photographic division of National Service Headquarters in Ottawa."[90] Later that year, Alvey resigned. Olson argues that the director was pressuring Alvey because her relationship with Brodie had become known within the women's service. She bases this argument on a memo from Alvey to the director in which Alvey stated, "In view of your knowledge of our personal affairs, you will undoubtedly appreciate the importance of my returning to civilian life at the same time as Lt. Brodie. Anything you can do to expedite our release together would be greatly appreciated."[91] It was because of exactly this sort of pressure that many lesbians chose to remain closeted in the war years, fearful as they were of the consequences of lesbian activity.

In Alvey, one sees a more conflicted subjectivity based on sexual orientation than one sees in other relationships discussed here. Respectability was important to all the women, but for Alvey it was important enough to affect her later portrayal of her relationship with Brodie. The requirement for "tact and discretion" affected the behaviour of Bud and Frieda and of Govan and B, insofar as they were unable to publicly express their emotions for one another. In Alvey's case, however, the dedication to respectability compromised her willingness to leave the contents of the letters untouched as late as 1988, when they were donated to Rare Books and Special Collections at the University of British Columbia. By the 1980s she could have surmised that their relationship would not have been viewed as negatively as it would have when the letters were written, yet she still censored them.

Alvey's management of the collection, especially her censorship but inclusion of Brodie's letters, suggests an internal conflict between her sexuality, her notions of class and respectability, and her desire to have her story recorded for posterity. Although she did not resist the dominant discourse to the same degree as Frieda and Bud, and thus did not remain unrepentant about and proud of her relationship with Brodie, she also did not completely remove that part of her life from public consumption. Brodie is present, even if she is muted by Alvey's censorship.

Charlotte Whitton and Margaret Grier

Charlotte Whitton was born in 1896 into a merchant family in Renfrew, Ontario. Intelligent and a keen student, she excelled in her studies at the Renfrew Collegiate Institute and won numerous scholarships. She took her bachelor of arts at Queen's University, followed by a diploma in teaching. In 1918, having left Queen's, she took a position as assistant secretary to the Social Service Council of Canada. She became the assistant editor of the new journal *Social Welfare* and began organizing the Canadian Council on Child Welfare on her own time as a volunteer. In 1926 she was appointed its director. In 1950 Whitton embarked on a career in politics and in 1951 was elected to the Ottawa Board of Control. In 1952 she served as the Canadian delegate to the Commission on Child Welfare at the League of Nations. She was mayor of Ottawa from 1952 to 1956 and again from 1960 to 1964. She retired from civic politics in 1972 and died three years later.

Patricia Rooke and R.L. Schnell suggest that Whitton had a happy childhood, apart from divisions within the family on religious grounds. Whitton was raised to be both a monarchist and a Canadian patriot. She was apparently somewhat of a tomboy and preferred the blacksmith's or the livery stable to traditional girls' play.[92] Whitton began to succeed early at school, "and with such rewards she appears to have begun early to embrace views of innate merit and virtue, where the world fostered the talented and hard-working, and where the self-made man or woman could attain anything desired."[93] Such an attitude was, of course, largely informed by class, and its expression in later life would reveal Whitton to be someone disinclined to recognize the importance of social factors such as poverty in the lives of those less fortunate than she. It was also an attitude, however, that informed her later relationship with her long-term partner, Margaret Grier, as Whitton valued above all else Margaret's worth as a person.

Charlotte Whitton is remembered primarily as "the old lady bitch mayor of Ottawa,"[94] but it was her activism for the cause of child welfare in the early twentieth century that saw her become one of Canada's most influential public figures. Her life's work was the improvement of the condition of children in Canada, and she campaigned tirelessly on the issues of juvenile delinquency and illegitimacy. In keeping with the feminism of her time, Whitton was simultaneously progressive and conservative, deploring society's differential treatment of the mothers and fathers of illegitimate children, while in the next breath arguing against the immigration of groups she regarded as undesirable. She alienated herself from many social workers in 1945 when she published a pamphlet arguing against what she considered the subsidization by the state of the reproduction of "defectives." Throughout her career, Whitton voiced clearly conservative opinions on a variety of social issues. During the Depression, for example, she emphasized the need to differentiate among the deserving and the undeserving poor, and she argued against cash relief on the basis of her suspicion that many who were receiving it were also in receipt of earnings. Mothers fared no better: Whitton argued against giving Mother's Allowance to any but unwed, deserted, or widowed mothers.[95]

From Whitton's later work in the field of social welfare, we can infer the gendered values with which she was raised. Although Whitton herself was never to marry or have children, she nevertheless embodied many of the traditional attitudes of her day. She certainly believed that motherhood was ideally to take place within marriage. Throughout her working life, Charlotte Whitton was often to equate unmarried motherhood with "feeble-mindedness."[96] Although she was one of the few voices in the early twentieth century castigating Canadian society for failing to make responsible the fathers of "illegitimate" children, Whitton was "convinced that unwed mothers were usually of low intelligence and weak morality."[97]

Whitton was inspired by close relationships with women throughout her life. Upon entry to Queen's University, she had become friends with a number of women, especially in a group called the Levana Society, a women-only group whose members shared visions of their futures, wrote poetry to one another, and acted very much as a sorority. Their mentor was Professor Wilhelmina Gordon, who remained important in Whitton's life for some years after she left Queen's. Whitton had found a mentor in Gordon, becoming eventually somewhat her protégée.[98] Gordon was disappointed by Whitton's decision in 1918 not to pursue graduate studies at Bryn Mawr and then Oxford but rather to enter into social work. They nevertheless remained friends.

Whitton maintained "passionate friendships" with several female friends in the Levana Society, particularly Mora, nicknamed "Mo," and

Esther. Letters between these women were written in very passionate and romantic terms. There is also some suggestion of physical contact. In 1917, for example, Mo reminisced about their times together, stating that she missed the "always strong arms about me which used to make me feel so safe and secure."[99]

Rooke and Schnell argue that Whitton was essentially celibate and suggest that her attitudes toward unwed mothers reflect the view that "all women without recourse to licit sexual expression be as strong-willed as she; they must demonstrate the same discipline and self-control."[100] I maintain that Charlotte Whitton was not necessarily as celibate as she has been portrayed, but it is certainly reasonable to suggest that she thought that heterosexual intercourse ought properly to be expressed only in matrimony. It is very likely that this was one of the main values with which she was raised, coming as she did from a family whose early religious practice was Anglican but whose original denominations were Methodist and Roman Catholic.

Rooke and Schnell are at pains to distance their analysis of Whitton's life from any "taint" of homosexuality. On several occasions, they make it clear in *No Bleeding Heart* that, in their opinion, the amorous correspondence between Whitton and other women was simply a playful manifestation of close friendships, belonging "to the literary genre which emerged out of the 'romantic friendships,' which were not uncommon in an era where gender roles were clearly defined and where unsupervised heterosexual interaction and social intercourse were constrained."[101] But whereas Lillian Faderman and others who have discussed romantic friendships place them clearly within lesbian history, Rooke and Schnell seem to agree with those who argue that lesbianism requires proof of a physical sexuality, and in the absence of certain proof of it, they discount the suggestion that Whitton was lesbian.

Around 1918 Whitton met Margaret Grier, who worked for the Juvenile Court and Big Sisters. Grier, who was to become Whitton's *grande passion*, replaced Mo in Whitton's affection. Rooke and Schnell quote Mo's acknowledgment of her defeat:

> I must admit you are a most diplomatic bigamist and an irresistible hubby. It pleases me to think that Marg. has a similar string [referring to a necklace Charlotte had given her] and that I can wear mine in Toronto

without fear of losing eyes or hair ... Give my love to Margaret and tell her I esteem her in spite of her usurpation.[102]

In 1922 Whitton and Grier moved to Ottawa, where Whitton took up positions as secretary to the minister of trade and honorary secretary of the Canadian Council on Child Welfare and where Grier became secretary of the Canadian Tuberculosis Association. They were to live together until Grier's death in 1947. Throughout their relationship, Charlotte Whitton referred to Margaret Grier in terms common to the romantic friendships of the nineteenth century; she wrote in words exalting Margaret's beauty and expressed devotion and commitment to her companion. Grier, as much as one can tell from the few letters she left, was equally expressive. For example, on 27 December 1915 Margaret wrote to "Lottie," saying,

> I must confess I am deeply, head over heels in love with you and it ex-presses itself in an overpowering desire to devour you beginning at your throat of course ... Lottie I am going to keep your letters tied up with ribbon with my lover letters – which I haven't got yet and read them over when I am an old grey haired maid dressed in combinations of lavender and old lace as Myrtle Reid describes – when you are famous I will tell my friends how I used to enjoy kissing the famous authoress on the neck and how I have even slept in her arms.[103]

The main clues that the relationship between Charlotte Whitton and Margaret Grier was something more than a friendship exist in letters writ-ten by Whitton after Grier's death in 1947. As Grier lay dying, Whitton was in Alberta defending her theories at a Royal Commission called by the Alberta government to investigate social welfare in the province in the light of the criticisms Whitton had made in a study she had undertaken at the behest of the Imperial Order Daughters of the Empire.[104] The commission opened its hearings in August 1947 and then adjourned until the fall. Whitton spent the summer at the lake with Margaret and returned to Alberta for the hearings, which resumed on 24 November. Grier had be-come ill in the summer and had had abdominal surgery. A second operation in October weakened her, and she eventually died from cancer on 9 De-cember. Whitton had left Alberta for Ottawa the day before but did not arrive in time to be with Grier when she died. She would later claim that she had been unaware of the severity of Grier's condition and that the doctors had insisted on her return to Alberta, suggesting that, given the importance of the Alberta hearings, Grier would become aware that her condition was critical if Whitton did not go. As Rooke and Schnell argue, it was likely that Grier had also pushed Whitton to return to the commission, knowing that it was an important part of the re-establishment of her waning career.[105] After Grier's death, Whitton began to doubt her own motives and worried that she had allowed her work to take precedence over Margaret. Just a few months after Grier's death, she wrote,

> O do you know where you are, how hourly I realize how much you did all these years for me, how selfish I accepted the service of your love and all the time death tugging at your strength. Did you know all those many recent times when you would say it did not matter, and I thought you were using your blunted weapons to battle me? O darling, did you know and in the shadowing crisis of your life and my obsession with my work did I deny you sympathy, understanding and support? These questions gnaw at me night and day.[106]

Grier's death provoked a crisis in Whitton, and she obsessively pursued a hostile confrontation with the Alberta government.[107] In early 1948 Whitton and two others were charged with conspiracy to commit defamatory libel, after an inflammatory article based on Whitton's information had been published in *New Liberty*. The case against her proved insufficient, however, and a stay of proceedings was declared in April of 1948.[108] Whitton moved on to a new career in civil politics.

Although there is no concrete proof of a physical relationship between Charlotte and Margaret, some information does suggest that the women slept together and shared embraces. That Grier proposed to keep Lottie's letters with her "lover letters," which she had not yet received, need not indicate that she did not think of Lottie as her partner. The word "lover" was associated with male partners, and its heterosexual connotations may have caused Grier (and, as revealed in Chapter 3, Bud Williams) to interpret it as not referring to her love for another woman.[109]

A file of personal letters that Whitton allowed to be opened to researchers only in January 1999 offers more evidence of intimacy in the relationship than was available to Rooke and Schnell. Of particular interest in the collection is a group of ninety-six letters Charlotte wrote "to" her late partner. The two volumes that she named "Molly Mugwamp Makes Believe" represent Whitton's attempt to come to terms with her grief and her guilt, the latter for not having been at Grier's side when she died. In these letters, one can see the depth of this relationship, which lasted thirty years and, in Whitton's mind at least, was to have been a lifelong one.

"Molly Mugwamp Makes Believe" takes the reader on a journey through Whitton's pain as she processed the death of her partner. On the eve of 1948, while Whitton was on a train to Edmonton, she wrote a lengthy letter to Grier in which she said, "This will be the first of the New and Empty Years in which I shall go on alone." She continued,

> Mardie, Mardie, Mardie [Margaret's nickname], I don't yet understand what numbing of my will let them keep me here that Friday night ... I gambled and you died without me. Mardie, they tell me of the light in your eyes when they said you would hear my voice. You and God know the light and peace I denied you by not getting into that room and clasping your poor, beaten body. Oh! Mardie! Mardie, how can I go on? Ours wasn't love: it was a knitting together of mind and spirit: it was something given to few by God: there wasn't anything silly or weak or slavering: it was just that our minds and spirits marched so together that they were the same in two different bodies ... O Mardie, my heart will beat on but all the years, I will walk always with you beside me and this void, this void forever until I too go hence.[110]

In this quotation, we can see the weaving together of the themes of loyalty and devotion and a placing of their love above the earthly. Whitton separates what lay between them from ordinary love when she says not only that God gave it to them but also that it was not "silly or weak or slavering." Given that Whitton was often prone to be rather judgmental about those human instincts that she would have regarded as base, this statement surely suggests that she thought their love to be noble and beyond reproach, and not "basely" sexual. In March of 1948 she wrote,

> Darling: Midnight again and the busy world hushed and just you and I alone together again. O my dearest dear three months gone this early dawn you have been and I left you to die with strangers. Agnes and

Grace are both fine but O Mardie, how terrible it must have been for you, knowing, and how you loved me, that I was letting you down: you see I hoped against hope.[111]

Keenly aware of the date on which her beloved died, Whitton wrote in May, "Darling: Five months ago today! O Mardie I look at your picture, I look at your dear kinky handwriting and I tell myself over and over that you are dead, you, my gracious, gentle radiant Mardie, and I can't believe it."[112] For Whitton, 1948 was a difficult year, and all of the letters from that year in some way express her grief at Grier's death. A month after Margaret's death, Charlotte remembered fondly, "I could almost feel you brush my untidy hair back off my forehead as you would do when you passed me working at my desk at night as you would say goodnight and go down to your room."[113] In 1949 Charlotte wrote, "You will be with me everywhere, always now. Several nights I've dreamed of you, and now you are happy, so happy we both were the other night, lying together in my big bed, joshing as we often did when we had 'breakfast in bed' on Sunday."[114] That Whitton enclosed the phrase "breakfast in bed" in quotation marks may or may not be significant. It is unclear whether this demarcation indicated that the phrase was code for physical intimacy or was simply in some way unusual within her parlance. It is rather the emotional content of the letters that indicates that their relationship was very much akin to a marriage. That Whitton restricted access to the volume of letters may be even more significant. It indicates that they were, perhaps, extremely personal in the sense that they revealed not only her process of coming to terms with her grief but also the depth and the passion of her relationship with Margaret. Even in the alleged absence of a physical relationship, Whitton and Grier were, in all other respects, in a same-sex "marriage."

2

Lesbian Social Worlds, 1900–50

"So there seems to be a fair amount of it about"

Despite the increasing condemnation of same-sex relationships by both medical professionals and laypeople in the twentieth century, women did form both brief and lasting relationships with other women. One of the benefits of wider female movement in the twentieth century was the rise in the number of opportunities lesbian women had to meet others like themselves. It is difficult to determine how women in this period "spotted" other lesbian women, but nevertheless they did find each other and group together socially on the basis of their same-sex relationships. Many were lucky enough to be able to find enough women like themselves to form broad social networks.

Any analysis of lesbian community must take into account the constraints on women's movement and economic independence before the 1960s. Women did have considerably more freedom of movement and economic opportunity than had women of the nineteenth century, but it was still expected that the majority of a woman's life would be spent in economic dependence on a man. And although female friendships were important, they were not to replace the primary relationship with the male breadwinner. The coming together of large groups of women in any setting was therefore not ideal. The majority of women who formed relationships with women did so in isolation or in the context of small social groupings rather than in any kind of mass movement.

Canadian lesbians could not be said to have a formalized community structure based on lesbian identity before perhaps the 1950s. Prior to the 1950s, precursors to lesbian communities were formed in relation to a subjectivity based on shared same-sex desire, although the evidence suggests that identity labels were not used. Women's limited access to public venues, unless they were accompanied by men, and the restrictions of their residential accommodation meant that few were able to form the sort of public networks that men could, with their greater mobility and economic opportunity. It was, however, possible for many women at least to live and socialize together and even to recognize others like themselves. This chapter examines social networks among middle-class women in same-sex relationships. These were not large groups, and they did not have a public profile, but they were networks formed on the basis of a shared and recognized attraction to women.

Middle-class lesbian women were able to recognize each other within middle-class social milieux. Precisely what "signs" they looked for in other women is difficult to determine, but there do exist fragments of evidence suggesting that there were linguistic conventions and visible identifiers aiding in recognition. For example, while travelling with her friend Bess on a cruise ship in Europe, Edith (Bud) Bickerton Williams reported,

> Bess picked up the nicest women from the hospital on board – two nurses, Miss Brown and Miss Scadding. They are head nurses at T.G.H. and quite old – about 45!! – They are very devoted to each other which is enough to make me interested in them even if they weren't such perfect lambs. I was quite thrilled when they said that they had known each other for years and had always planned this trip, and had only managed it this year, and you could tell by the way they looked at each other, just how thrilled they were.[1]

How exactly Bess "spotted" Miss Brown and Miss Scadding is not known since it does not seem from the source material that Bess was herself lesbian or bisexual, but it would seem that they became reasonably friendly toward Bud, in whom they confided,

> Their families had been awfully against their being together so much when they were young but after 20 years they are beginning to get used to it. It is an awfully difficult subject to chat about and it would never be approached if I had to do it, but they suddenly began to talk about it to-day.[2]

Bud commented to her partner, Frieda Fraser, that her new friends "seem to agree with all we think about it, and also that there is no use trying to convince any other people about it – they simply can't see it."[3] Although Bud might simply have connected with most people as fellow travellers, she clearly allied herself with the two women because of their relationship. A temporary social connection, it nevertheless speaks to the importance of recognizing and being recognized as women devoted to other women. Bud and Frieda wrote often about such women, and in quite some detail. That the subject should interest them so greatly shows that finding others like themselves was important to their constructions of self and their confidence in the rightness of their relationship.

Bud's early letters to Frieda spoke often of women's devotion to each other. During her stay in England in 1925, she wrote to Frieda regarding her aunt's cook and housemaid, revealing that her aunt

> told me that her cook and housemaid – who are by way of being ladies – had never had jobs before, but that their families had been rather disagreeable about their being awfully devoted and so they had up and left, and this was the only thing they could do. However, they loved it as it meant living together. So there seems to be a fair amount of it about. And they were certainly the happiest looking creatures. I simply pined to talk to them about it. Aunt F. didn't like it much, but at the time she was ill and couldn't get anyone else who could get on with her nurse and her companion, but she seems to be quite satisfied now. I asked her what her objection was and she said that it wasn't natural! Isn't it funny?[4]

Frieda discovered women who were "devoted" to one another while she was working as a doctor in New York during the late 1920s. She wrote to Bud concerning "two middle-aged & very good looking females that spend all their week-ends together here."[5]

These statements indicate that the language of "devotion," which arose out of the nineteenth-century romantic friendship, operated as a sign of a relationship existing between two women as well as a description of its nature. In other words, the use of such terminology operated in the same way as a red necktie or the word "gay" operated within certain circles in the same period – as a signifier of "queerness."[6] If a shared attraction toward women was suspected in another woman, a middle-class lesbian of the early twentieth century could drop the phrase "awfully devoted" into a conversation, knowing that it most likely would be ignored by those not "in the know" but clearly would be recognized by other lesbian women. It seems reasonable to assume, especially given the frequency with which Bud and Frieda use the phrase and identify others using it, that middle-class lesbians had, in this linguistic code, a lesbian signifier.

Frieda and Bud were quick to notice women who travelled about in pairs. Women with an awareness of their own same-sex desires noticed women whose primary companions were female rather than male and then looked for further signs of a same-sex relationship. To many in mainstream society, even in a period of increasing suspicion of female friendships, two women travelling together were of little interest; to a lesbian woman, they were – unless obviously related to one another or behaving heterosexually – a red flag and were noticed immediately. Frieda and Bud had a finely tuned early-twentieth-century version of "gaydar" and got to know a number of lesbian couples after having spotted them as such.

The emerging professions, such as the medical profession of which Frieda was a part, were frequently (and probably rightly) held to be sites of female-female relationships, especially when women boarded together in large numbers. Any employment or educational institution bringing women into contact with other, unrelated women provided opportunities for same-sex attractions to be realized. Faderman argues that "women who live by their brains" were frequently drawn to each other.[7] Frieda Fraser found such an example in her medical colleague Miss Lawter. In 1927 she wrote to Bud, "Miss Lawter had dinner with me today. I am simply bursting to ask whether her partnership with Miss Cook is disapproved of. If I were you I would know all about it by now."[8]

Bud and Frieda, despite being able to notice and connect socially with other women like them, did not then form a stable network with them in the way that we would understand lesbian community in the present day. There was a feeling of community in the sense that lesbians by this time already shared common behavioural and visible characteristics, such that they were able to recognize one another. They formed friendships with one another and discussed with each other their experience of living in "devoted" relationships when society regarded those relationships as unnatural. Their social networks were fleeting, however, and were not based on a formalized internal structure, consciously realized and rigorously policed, the like of which arose after the Second World War.

Their interactions were also a form of socializing predicated on gender norms of middle-class and educated women of the day. Frieda was quite masculine in appearance compared to Bud, but she did not dress in men's clothes per se. Her style of dress was one adopted by many middle-class women of the 1920s. Both she and Bud would have been horrified by the butch and femme couples they would have seen a decade or two later. The gender norms of the working-class lesbian community signified their sexuality in a way that was largely unacceptable to middle-class women, both in the period when butch and femme roles came to the fore and in the earlier decades when Frieda and Bud were writing. Devotion, as they called it, was not something to be worn publicly and outlandishly; it was something positive but private because social norms required that it be kept hidden.

The correspondence between Frieda and Bud clearly indicates that they were aware of the public disapproval of relationships between women. The women they discussed, while having in many ways the kind of middle-class relationships typical of the romantic friendship era, encountered a public condemnation of their partnerships that would not have occurred a century earlier. A new discourse about the unnaturalness of same-sex relationships is clearly present. One can also see a reticence on the part of both women regarding social inquiries about such relationships. That Bud acknowledges that it is a difficult subject to chat about and one that she would not herself have brought up in conversation, and that Frieda was bursting to ask about Miss Lawter and Miss Cook but did not, clearly indicates that they were both aware that this was a delicate matter and one that should not be discussed openly. The Fraser-Williams letters show, however, that Bud and Frieda actively looked for women like themselves and were critical of the dominant discourse. As Bud commented, "there seems to be a fair amount of it about." The "it," of course, is a shared experience, and this connection should be taken as a form of alliance even when it did not result in the establishment of permanent social networks.

Gender in Lesbian Relationships

The most visible form of lesbian relationship in the period under study was that of the butch-femme couple, a relationship based on the clear demarcation of gender roles, which found expression in both appearance and behaviour. But this form of lesbian relationship did not develop in Canada until the middle of the century, and it was specific to the working-class urban bar culture, although some middle-class lesbians did visit the lifestyle on weekends. There was, especially in the early twentieth century, a distinctly masculine style of dress and manner among some middle-class women. In some cases, this was allied with lesbianism, but in some it was associated merely with feminist politics or even simply the desire to live a life other than that prescribed by dominant gender norms.[9] The "New Woman" of the turn of the century – single, well educated, and economic-ally independent – was often assumed because of her transgression of gender norms also to be lesbian.[10]

Martha Vicinus has argued that we can discover much about late-nineteenth- and early-twentieth-century lesbian mores and also masculine attitudes by examining more carefully than we have previously done the works of the sexologists, who, she suggests, "at the very least made available a sexual discourse to middle-class women."[11] Lesbians, be they middle-class or working-class, have always been defined and had to define themselves in relation to male discourse. That masculinity has been a significant aspect of lesbian life, for some women, and even of nonlesbian gender rebellion, is therefore hardly surprising. In the working-class lesbian communities, masculinity was crucial to butch identity; among middle-class women, masculinity could also be allied to identity but without butch codes of behaviour.

Many middle-class women experimented and played with gender. Flirtation with gender can be found in the few letters that remain to us from B to Elisabeth Govan. In an undated letter written most probably in the 1940s, B wrote to Elisabeth, "Come to me often, Betty boy ... I'm here, and you *can* depend on me entirely, bless you."[12] B called Elisabeth "Betty boy" twice in only a few letters, suggesting that it may well have been a nickname she used frequently. It is unfortunate that Govan's replies have not remained, as it would be interesting to know whether or not she also used masculine terminology about herself.

Bobbed, cropped, and shingled hairstyles became fashionable among some young women in the interwar period. Frieda kept her hair short for much of her adult life. | Frieda Fraser, age 17. University of Toronto Archives, B1995-0044/003P (08) 01

In some cases, gender transgression might be said to be a more fundamental part of a lesbian's subjectivity. Differences in gender performance were present in the relationship of Frieda and Bud, and in Frieda's case it might be argued that masculinity was a more serious and permanent aspect of personality. Several examples serve to illustrate the degree to which Frieda viewed herself as being the masculine partner and Bud the feminine partner. In some ways, this was a relationship between a more "masculine" woman and a "feminine" one. From a relatively young age, Frieda Fraser had sported a very masculine appearance for a woman of her generation.[13] Frieda cut her hair unusually short during her medical internship,

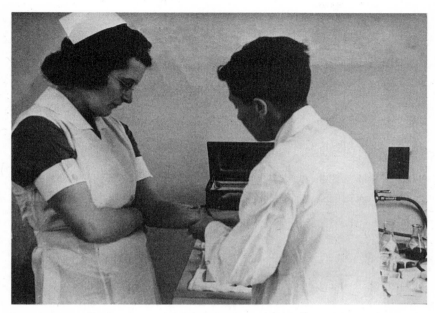

During her medical training, Frieda's hair was cut even shorter than in her adolescent years. Here she wears a version of the shingle cut, one of the more masculine styles of the period. | Frieda Fraser and nurse, n.d. University of Toronto Archives, B1995-0044/003P (07) 01

much to the annoyance of her mother and brother.[14] Nevertheless, her family was forced to tolerate what would be a life-long habit.

Frieda frequently described herself in masculine terms. In a letter of 10 July 1925, she apologized for having forgotten to wish Bud a happy birthday: "Another thing I seem to have over-looked was to wish you many happy returns of the day, now long since past. That's the kind of guy I am – but you must have made up your mind to put up with it long before this."[15] Later that month, she reported to Bud, "My family have induced me to stick back my hair with Kaspar's Anzora. You have no idea what a vast expanse of noble brow it reveals & my hair is so slick a fly would break its neck on it."[16] Bud replied by asking for a picture of Frieda

with slicked hair. I want to decide whether I like it or not, and on that depends whether I'll ever come home or not. If I feel that I can't love you with slicked, I shall stay here, even if I have to resort to the dole.

In the 1920s, some women used hair creams and oils to slick down their short hair in a style called the "Eton Crop." Women wore the Eton Crop under the new cloche hats, fitted close to the head. Frieda does not seem to have favoured hats, however, and simply chose to wear her hair slicked back on occasion. | Frieda Fraser as junior intern (c. 1923), Frieda at top left. University of Toronto Archives, B1997-0027/002P (18)

> But seriously, dear, will you go to a good man in N.Y. and have a decent photograph of yourself done in your best bib and tucker and looking really beautiful? It would give me more pleasure than anything you could do for me at the moment.[17]

Bud liked the picture Frieda sent her, but commented, "You do look masculine, darling. The awful Englishwomen who have that pose have put me off it even more than ever. B looks like a mental case."[18] A stronger indication is a visiting card from 1926, on which the printed text reads, "Miss Frieda Fraser." Frieda crossed out "Miss" and put "Mr."[19] Frieda suggested to Bud in February 1927 that she take

> a job in New York or Montreal or some place after your obligations in England terminate? Have you thought of that? Or is it sound to ignore

it entirely if the Lord is to provide? It would be quite tolerable if a guy could see you every three months provided you were near enough to be reached if anything turned up. You know about that.[20]

Photographs and letters indicate that Bud was the more feminine of the two in this relationship, and both parties acknowledged this. Frieda inquired of Bud in 1927,

> What has possessed you to get a lorgnette (you see I even jib at writing it). I can just imagine how snooty you will [drawing of feminine-looking Bud with bun and dress holding lorgnette to her eyes]. In defence I shall either [picture of small skinny figure crawling away] or more probably the worm will turn and I shall [picture of masculine woman with slicked-back hair and monocle]. You really are asking for it. We will make a pretty pair.[21]

In another letter of 1927, she favoured a masculine identifier, lamenting, "O my lamb if I go on loving you as vigourously [sic] as this it will be very trying. I hope you can stand a lot of letters; that seems to be one of the things that happens. I must stop. It is devilish late but I've been so full of beans lately it is awfully hard to go to bed. And what is the use? You don't give a guy much rest you know."[22]

Individually, these examples of gender play need not suggest more than 1920s "New Woman" fashionableness. Laura Doan suggests that we must be careful in reading "masculine" as synonymous with lesbian, for there was a "pervasive phenomenon of masculine fashion for women."[23] Frieda had a more personal investment in masculinity, however, than someone for whom masculinity was simply a fashion. She consistently and insistently used masculine identifiers. In Canada in the 1920s women do not seem to have adopted the mannish look to the same extent that they did in Europe, England, and the United States, and Frieda was unusual in her degree of masculinity. Gender play and even cross-dressing occurred to an extent among women in the arts, but there is relatively little evidence of professional women who appeared quite as masculine as did Frieda in the 1920s.

In the absence of clear statements about gendered identities or evidence of community based on gender roles, it is impossible to state with any certainty what might have been the meaning of gender in relationships

THE COLLEGE CLUB

PHILADELPHIA BRANCH OF THE
AMERICAN ASSOCIATION OF UNIVERSITY WOMEN

1300 SPRUCE STREET

PHILADELPHIA

In self defence I shall either

or

more probably the worm will turn
& I shall

You really are asking for it.
We will make a pretty pair

Perhaps we had better
find a blind twin
after all

There isn't a blasted thing to write about
I am holding my breath over going home
tomorrow. God knows what will it is.
I am glad you will be holding my hand.

Drawing from letter, Frieda Fraser to Edith Bickerton Williams, 11 March 1927. |
University of Toronto Archives, B1995-0044/036 (11)

between middle-class women. It is clear from these examples that the masculine gender was employed by one partner in a way that suggests an awareness of divergence from femininity. Whether such divergence occurred to the point of a new identity being adopted, either a middle-class version of butch identity or a transgender identity, is impossible to assess. It is certain that, even if Frieda Fraser did feel masculine, this form of masculinity was markedly different from the working-class version in the butch-femme culture after the Second World War.

The records discussed above reveal that in Canada, as elsewhere, there were women who formed relationships with other women and were able to form social networks based on those relationships in a time before lesbian women and gay men campaigned politically for social recognition and acceptance. They did not use identity categories to describe themselves, and they had to be very discreet about their relationships, which flew largely under the radar of heterosexual Canadian society. Middle-class women in same-sex relationships continued to use some of the language of the romantic friendship to express their feelings for one another, but their love letters and journals reveal the strong influence of new psychiatric and psychological terms. Relationships between women were no longer assumed to be nonsexual, and women in same-sex relationships were both more explicit about sexuality and more aware that their relationships might be disapproved of. However, even though historians recognize a wider public discourse on sexuality emerging in the early twentieth century, there has still been the tendency for historians to be very reluctant to discuss relationships between women as having a sexual component unless there is "proof" in the written records of a genital relationship. The extent and nature of physical sexuality between women before the Second World War has remained a topic of debate among lesbian historians. If their letters don't say so explicitly, can we suggest that these women had physical relationships?

3

Physical Sexuality

"How did you get here Miss Brown?"

Although the portrayal of the Victorians as uniformly repressive and prudish is an erroneous one, it is true that the nineteenth century was exemplified by at least the *appearance* of sexual restraint as its defining characteristic. The consequences of women's sexual autonomy were, it was thought, national and catastrophic in nature. The control of sexuality remained a crucial part of all Canadian reform legislation, whether relating to the structure of the urban environment, public health, education, public recreation, or provincial and state welfare assistance. Sex, and by implication the sexuality of women, was a key to the interlocking mechanisms of gender, class, race, and religion. Sex held the future of the race in its grasp. As Mariana Valverde suggests, "The links between sexual excess, mental and moral degeneration, and the decline of the nation were made repeatedly."[1]

Because of the importance placed on sex and on women in the saving of the race from degeneration, the consequences for women of "inappropriate" sexual behaviour were drastic: social approbation was denied, respectability destroyed, financial aid withdrawn, and rights to children negated. Extreme forms of unacceptable sexuality, such as prostitution, were assumed to result in consequences that those in power felt were justified – the wages of sin were public disapproval and even death.[2] The single most important demarcation of acceptable and unacceptable sexuality was whether it was procreative. What was not uniform among the denominations, nor between individuals, was any single belief about the moral correctness of intercourse within marriage for enjoyment rather than expressly for procreation. According to some views, any sexual activity not entered into for the express purpose of conception was inherently sinful. For others, however, and particularly as ideas of the companionate marriage began to merge with acceptance of the mutual physical desires of husband and wife, "normal" sexual intercourse within marriage had pleasure as well as procreation as its focus.

For most Christians, the family was the cornerstone of society: the Christian family provided at once an example of moral living, protection against the sins of the world, and moral education for the young.[3] Of particular relevance to the religious basis of reform efforts and to one of the major agendas of reformers – the education of young Canadians – was the "Self and Sex Series," as it came to be known. The publication in 1897 of *What a Young Boy Ought to Know* marked the debut of a series intended to educate North Americans of all ages in the "proper" relations between the sexes, the healthy expression of sexuality, and the care of the body. Published in Philadelphia and distributed in Canada by the Methodist Church, the Self and Sex Series discussed the body, health, and sex from puberty to old age, promulgating the healthiness and morality of traditional sexual values. Sylvanus Stall, the author of several of the books in the series, urged women to remain pure and to fulfil their roles as good wives and mothers. Premarital sex, masturbation, and infidelity were discouraged for both sexes.[4] Moderation was also urged; not only were the various sexual vices to be avoided, but even within marriage one was to avoid sexual excess.[5]

The Self and Sex Series represented but one of a series of attempts to instil in young minds the behaviours considered appropriate to the living of a moral, Christian life and to the creation of strong and fit Canadian citizens.[6] It is not known how many of these books were distributed in Canada, but given that they were sold to some with the specific intention that they would be passed on from child to child, and from adult to adult, it is reasonable to assume that they had a wide, although by no means universal, readership.

Of considerable concern to moral and social reformers was the impact of urbanization and immigration on the moral fibre of the nation. The nineteenth-century Canadian city, the purported site of much degeneration, was a vibrant and bustling milieu where middle- and working-class Canadians alike found themselves thrust into greater proximity with each other, a proximity that was not altogether comfortable. Increasingly, anglophone Canadians began to feel invaded by immigrants from other cultural groups, immigrants who did not share the values, faith, and family and work relationships held dear by middle-class English Canadians. They began to fear that the Canada they knew was under threat.

The Canada of the early twentieth century was socially and materially different from that of the nineteenth century. By the turn of the century, over one-third of Canadians lived in urban areas.[7] One of the most notable features of twentieth-century Canadian society was its increasing obsession with questions of social decay. In the rapid growth of cities and changing work and recreational patterns, middle-class English Canadians saw a threat to the survival of middle-class morality. Not only were there increasing numbers in the cities of those the middle class saw as unfit, but it was also feared that the very nature of the city itself was conducive to the transgression of appropriate sexual and gender norms. In these new environs, even the respectable might be tempted into morally and physically dangerous activities. It was believed by many that social disorder and moral decay were the inevitable result of rapid changes in the structure of Canadian society and its workforce.

Carolyn Strange's *Toronto's Girl Problem* reveals the tensions between the growing importance of female labour in Toronto's light industries and the concerns of moral reformers that the massive influx of young, single women into Canada's largest city promoted sexual disorder.[8] Assessing the various fears about female employment, which persistently found voice among Toronto's elite, Strange demonstrates that, until the 1910s, single women in urban centres were viewed as women adrift from moral control. Away from the watchful eyes of family and community, young women with leisure time and money to spend were partaking of Toronto's numerous recreations without the benefit of moral guidance. Toronto's urban reformers launched a formal investigation of the state of immorality in their city. The report of the Toronto Social Survey Commission of 1915 portrayed vice as the tawdry underside of the "Queen City." Sexual vice signified a serious breakdown in social organization, one of the alleged sources of vice being the single, working woman.[9]

Strange's analysis bears relevance not only for Toronto but for other Canadian cities as well. Toronto provided numerous opportunities for female independence and recreation, but other urban areas were also likely to provide the environment for unchaperoned female excursions and "terrible scenes of immorality in the parks."[10] Indeed, the opposition to the presence of women in British Columbia's beer parlours demonstrates clearly the assumption, even in the 1920s, that women who socialized publicly were prima facie of loose sexual morals. The banning of women from beer parlours in BC and, subsequently, their segregation from male drinkers were based on the presumption that an unchaperoned woman in a beer parlour either was a prostitute or was of bad character.[11]

The period when Frieda Fraser and Edith (Bud) Bickerton Williams began their correspondence was therefore one of social tensions about gender and sexuality. Women were increasingly visible as paid workers, but their working was not always welcome, and their presence as single women in public was often lamented. Norms of sexuality and marriage had shifted somewhat but still reflected earlier customs and ideas about womanhood. Both Frieda and Bud were aware of the norms regarding marriage and sexuality, and they were obviously privy to some of the new discussion of the moderate sexual freedoms attributed to the "Roaring Twenties."[12] What is not clear, however, is the degree to which that awareness was acquired when they were growing up rather than after they left their respective homes and ventured into university and working life. The tone of their letters often suggests the newness of the knowledge and their surprise at some of the views they encountered among others. There is not, however, any tone of moral outrage that would suggest they were reacting to attitudes that fundamentally challenged their beliefs.

Birth control was a topic of considerable interest in the 1920s and 1930s and one that inspired a great deal of debate among women and men of Frieda and Bud's social class, as well as considerable interest in society generally. Among the most influential campaigners for the new sexual mores were the birth control activists of the early twentieth century. The pioneering English birth control activist Marie Stopes was influential in Canadian society. Her works on fertility, contraception, and marriage proved immensely popular to women and men seeking to enjoy their sexuality within the new "companionate" marriage of the twentieth century while remaining able to limit their family size. Stopes's works, and those of American advocate Margaret Sanger, also influential in Canada, made birth control more acceptable by arguing that it was imperative for the attainment of sexual fulfilment within marriage. Stopes's *Married Love*, which gave advice on how to achieve sexual pleasure in marriage, and her *Wise Parenthood* showed that many in society were keen to break through "the dam of reticence" that had governed discussion of sexuality before their publication in 1918.[13] In Canada the topic of birth control received wide attention, particularly after Sanger's visit to Vancouver in 1923. Stopes and Sanger would prove to be valuable resources to Canadians wishing to improve marital pleasure and limit family size.[14]

Correspondence between Frieda and Bud during the years when the debate was beginning to warm up indicates that they both held values that placed them more on the side of birth control, although they simultaneously displayed considerable ignorance about and even negative opinions of premarital sex. Frieda wrote to Bud in 1924,

> There was a swell discussion at a staff meeting here about birth-control. Did I tell you? I felt awfully ignorant. I don't seem to know the first thing about what every – I was going to say woman in the street but realised that it isn't the homologue of man in the street which is what I wanted. Dr. Baldwin the president of course takes the ancient view that every child is the blessing of god etc. etc. up to 70 x 7 but there are others almost as old who didn't share her views & altogether it was most entertaining. Of course we discussed it afterwards among ourselves. It was then that I felt young & innocent. The young women in this country I think might run your British youth a fairly close race if what you call speed includes that – I have never known exactly what is meant by fast – except from people who mean "my dear she *smokes!*" And I take it that that is an archaic use of the word. One of Ada's friends, a medical man, says that every woman ought to be able to have a baby by the time she's thirty & no damn' questions asked. Isn't that nice? ... I think [the] business of parking babies in homes is poisonous. From what I have seen though I must say that the babies with "no fathers" are much the nicest handsomest & best cared for that I have seen. I don't know what the moral of that is.[15]

Frieda asked Bud about the state of birth control in England. "Are there any contraceptive clinics or have they been shut up?" she inquired. In the United States, during her internship at the New York Infirmary for Women and Children, information was difficult to come by, which Frieda thought was "probably due to the anomalous state of the law and public opinion." Most of Frieda's clients had "only one complaint against fate & that is too many children. It seems dreadfully unfair. Levi [another doctor at the infirmary] remarked one day that all the information about contraception she had ever got was from laymen & she has been practicing about 30 years. I think almost anyone would say the same."[16] So new in public discourse and so scandalous was the subject of contraception that even doctors lacked information.

Bud seemed to place physical sexuality very much within the rubric of heterosexual marriage. In a letter written after her arrival in England, she remembered an occasion when she had had cause to talk to a friend the previous year about sex:

> It was at [a] House party last year on the last night of the second week-end that I found O'Reilly sitting about gloomily outside the sleeping-quarters. I joined her with nips and we sat on the steps going down to the road and were fallen over by the entire house-party for the first hour – but after that we got down to conversation and I gathered that O'R. wanted to be a nun. I said "What nonsense" of course and she said that there didn't seem to be anything else to do. I suggested that she might get married, a great many people did and liked it, etc. and it seemed to be the best thing to do if you were just an ordinary person like most of us. She said flatly that she would never get married and I inquired why. Her reason was that the whole thing was horrible; and then burst out that she hadn't known anything about it, and it had never occurred to her to ask anyone, until the year before at school when she had made some remarks during a discussion about one of the girls being married which had shown her ignorance. The other girls were apparently much amused and had enlightened her. She was simply disgusted and made up her mind then and there that she would become a nun.[17]

O'Reilly's antipathy toward marriage and sexuality was further revealed when she said, "'You know, Bud, I'm not a bit affectionate and I hate touching people – and I would never like being married.'" Bud remembered that, earlier that day, she and O'Reilly had been discussing the showing of affection. She remarked,

> I had been chatting to her about the way we lay about in heaps and were rather affectionate [and] she had been a bit astonished at the way everyone fell on each other's necks ... and she had said that she had always despised

people who did it before and couldn't bear it herself until she came to Bolton, and then she had rather liked it. That it was nice when you or McEvoy or I put our arms around her and said such affectionate things to her, and she supposed that it was because she liked us.[18]

That Bud might have conceptualized her relationship with Frieda as something a little less than or different from marriage is indicated by Bud's response to O'Reilly's opinions. Bud told Frieda,

I reminded her of that and added that you didn't marry anyone unless you liked them a great deal more than that and that then it was all right. She asked me if I didn't think the whole business of sex was simply revolting and I said that I did not, and that if I ever saw anyone I liked sufficiently, I would marry them and be thrilled to death about it, all of [which] seemed to astonish her greatly.[19]

Here, it seems as though Bud considered sex in relation only to people whom she could have married, yet such a perspective does not seem to fit with the rather suggestive letters I discuss below. Many of the letters between Bud and Frieda clearly imply a physically sexual relationship of some description. It may be, however, that Bud had gained the perception, through her childhood and adolescent learning and then in conversations with other young women, that "sex" was really "intercourse" and that physical desire and activity between women were not the same thing as "sex."

It would appear that O'Reilly had had the misfortune, as was common in the early twentieth century, of having been ill informed about sexuality, making its discovery rather shocking. Bud told Frieda, "She also asked me when and how I had found out about it, and I told her. She said that she had never talked to Mrs. O'R. about anything and she had not even told her about the Lord afflicting her [menstruation], and that had been a bit of a shock too."[20] From Bud's tone and wording, one can reasonably assume that her own mother had explained menstruation to her. What is not clear is at what age Bud had found out about sex, although the above quotation does suggest that it was her mother who had told her.

Bud was made aware very shortly after her arrival in England in 1925 that she was rather naive about the sexual goings-on of young women.

"I'm amused at your feeling young and innocent during a discussion on birth-control," she wrote to Frieda in New York,

> but it is nothing to what I feel here. Peg and I had a heart-to-heart talk the other day about our generation here, and I was much enlightened. I have thought they were all rather gay and fast all summer, but put it down to my low mind and the fact that I always like to think the worst of anyone; but after what Peg said, I am feeling very pure and childish. It is most astonishing, Frieda. I thought that all these books about young women who hop off with men for week-ends were exaggerated, or about very isolated cases, but they're not. She says that she is dull and stupid and not a social success because she doesn't, and that it is taken for granted that any girl of more than 22 or so has lovers.[21]

Bud had attended a luncheon in Birmingham "which was composed entirely of unmarried women of between 25 and 30." The women had been discussing birth control, and Bud admitted that she knew nothing at all about Marie Stopes's books on the subject, at which they advised her that perhaps she should read them. When Bud said, "I didn't see why I should as I was not thinking of getting married at the moment and the subject didn't interest me greatly," the women were "awfully amused and said that I should perhaps find such knowledge useful anyway. I was so astonished that my jaw nearly dropped. I had suspected that the girl who said it was living with a man but I didn't expect it to be talked of quite so openly."[22] She asked Frieda whether she thought that she was "feeble-minded" about it. Bud's opinion was that it was acceptable for a woman and a man to have intercourse before marriage if their relationship was a permanent one, but the practice of "going off" with a different person each weekend was "horrible" to her.

Bud's reactions to the opinions she heard expressed in England indicate that she embodied many of the contradictions typical of the early twentieth century. Whether she was raised with the values she came to express or instead developed them in reaction against those of her family is unknown. By the early 1920s, however, by which time she was passing into young adulthood – emerging twentieth-century discourse would have described her as a youth until approximately the age of twenty-five – Bud's attitudes reflected changing sexual mores, yet there remained a clear boundary between acceptable and unacceptable sexual behaviour. Bud, akin to some of the women described in Karen Dubinsky's *Improper Advances,* held that premarital sex was allowable only if marriage was foreseen.[23] Without such an expectation, it was unacceptable.

Did They or Didn't They?

What is it that makes a lesbian a lesbian? The debate over who was and was not a true lesbian was taken up by a number of historians in the 1980s and 1990s because of the difficulty of finding women's records in which sexual activity is mentioned. There remains much disagreement about whether one should include in a history of women's same-sex relationships any woman whose records do not reveal a physically expressed sexuality, particularly a genital sexuality. Sheila Jeffreys's response to the debate was to suggest that the definition of lesbianism as based on genital contact, which had its origins in the sexology of an earlier century, should be questioned so as to challenge its heterosexual foundations. She cautioned, however, that such a questioning would also involve a questioning of lesbian identity, based for so long on the assumption of a genital sexuality.[24] A few historians have argued that nonpenetrative and nongenital forms of sexual expression should also be counted as sex. Karen Hansen, for example, examines the relationship between Addie Brown and Rebecca Primus, two mid-nineteenth-century African American women whose documented physical contact included the fondling of breasts. Hansen has called this "bosom sex." She argues that although it would be inappropriate to call the relationship a lesbian one because the term was not part of the period's cultural consciousness, bosom sex "may have been viewed as natural, pleasurable, and an appropriate means of expressing affection for or attraction to another woman."[25] Hansen regards the Brown-Primus relationship as much more than mere sentiment, calling it rather "a self-consciously sexual relationship."[26] Cases such as the above are a welcome addition to an otherwise dry and narrow lesbian history that rests upon the requirement for genital sexuality or the assumption that it has occurred.

Martha Vicinus has suggested that we think of the "not said" and the "not seen" as conceptual tools. Lesbian and bisexual women's history often involves dealing with the not said (i.e., the lack of source material discussing intimate relationships between women and the lack of identifying labels used by them) and the not seen (i.e., those aspects of same-sex relationships kept out of view for reasons of propriety, fear of exposure, or concern for the sensibilities of one's family). We must be careful not to assume that what is observed and what is visible and stated are all there is to relationships between women. Physical expressions of sexuality take various forms, including, but not restricted to, acts of penetration or genital contact. Moreover, observability should not be taken to refer necessarily to identity: that the historical subject does not use an identifying label about herself need not indicate that she did not have a sexual subjectivity based on same-sex or both-sex desire.

This study treats as potentially indicative of an intimate relationship between two women a diverse range of intimacies, from sleeping together to full vaginal penetration. Relationships between women need not have included a genital component to be included in lesbian history. This is especially the case when available source material indicates other behaviours consonant with the type of relationship found in heterosexual relationships, such as continued sleeping together, expressions of love and extreme devotion, and other forms of intimacy. *Awfully Devoted Women* questions the idea that romantic friendships were not sexual. This study argues, as others have, that the absence of testimony in women's written sources of genital sexuality between women is the result more of linguistic constraints than of an actual absence of genital contact. The evidence provided here adds a Canadian perspective to this still-vibrant debate and suggests that the tendency to equate ignorance about sexuality with a lack of exploration of its physical aspects has led to the erasure of some important elements of lesbian history. If one is to suggest that women before the twentieth century were less likely to have engaged in genital intimacy because women were thought ideally to be passionless and because there was generally less information on sexuality, one is implying that a public discourse of women's sexuality is required for women to act sexually. Such a claim flies in the face of such notable evidence as the diaries of Anne Lister, which show clearly that she engaged in genital sexuality with numerous women during her life in the early decades of the nineteenth century.[27]

This chapter challenges such a viewpoint, arguing instead that even those nineteenth- and early-twentieth-century relationships phrased very much in the noble, moral, and spiritual terms of the romantic friendship could be physical ones. The evidence gained in this study shows that women in the early twentieth century, in contexts of considerable silence regarding sexuality, did engage in physical sexuality with other women. What is required is not an explicit expression of words relating to genital contact between the partners – which, after all, we do not require to regard heterosexual sex as having occurred – but rather the willingness to see beyond the language and norms of the present day in order to think about how women in earlier decades might have obliquely referred to what they were feeling and doing when the risks of doing so were considerable.

Both Bud and Frieda wrote extensively about feeling as though the other were physically present while they were apart, Bud in England and Europe, Frieda in the United States and occasionally back in Canada. Feeling their separation particularly sharply, Bud wrote to Frieda in 1925,

> I don't know what I think about it really – but I do know that it isn't very nice when you aren't about or I'm not feeling that you want me. There haven't been many intervals of that kind fortunately – none at all lately – but I have taken care that there shouldn't be. When I thought you were leaving me, I have screamed and kicked – which is much more effective at this distance than it ever was at close quarters! – or forced myself upon you. I don't know whether it is worth wondering about, but I do quite a lot of thinking without getting anywhere.[28]

A number of the letters between Frieda and Bud indicate clearly that they were in the habit of sleeping together. Several letters suggest at the very least some intimate cuddling, if not genital sexuality. In 1925 Bud wrote to Frieda,

> The funniest thing has happened every night since I have been here. I have wakened up quite suddenly in the middle of the night with the feeling that you were there, and after saying "Everything is all right, dear, and it is so nice to have you," I've rolled over and gone to sleep again almost as if I had a piece of you to hold on to. After the first week, I began to look at the time – it has always been between 4.15 and 5.15 which is, of course, well on towards morning. And it suddenly occurred to me this morning that it would just about [be] the time you were going to bed! Isn't that odd?[29]

That the women may have woken each other regularly is revealed in a letter from Bud to Frieda in 1925, in which she wrote to Frieda, "Yesterday I was awakened by two letters from you – it was nice – almost like having you waken me."[30] A further letter reveals, "Last night you were very close, lamb, almost touchable. And you were there just as much in the morning. It was very pleasant."[31]

It was not unusual for women to sleep together in this period. That what was happening was more than simply two friends sharing a bed is revealed in letters talking about the kinds of risky behaviours that took place when the women were asleep or just waking up. Bud was somewhat upset when she "absolutely disgraced [Frieda] on Sunday – or rather Monday at 3 a.m." She told Frieda, "Moll came back from Paris and wakened me rather gently – I had asked her to – and I embraced her and kissed her much more violently than usual. Oh lambie, it was an awful effort not to weep and to be sufficiently interested in her doings when I woke up properly."[32]

Writing to Bud about a weekend adventure with two of her friends, Frieda wrote, "Tomorrow & the next day are going to be terrible without you because Helen & Anita & I are going to spend Sunday walking in the country taking with us a hunkacheese ... I am going to spend the night there & we will start bright & early on Sunday." She then continued: "as I am going to share Helen's ample bed I hope I don't get absent-minded while asleep. It might be a 'How did you get here Miss Brown?'"[33] During a later trip with another friend, she once again worried about how she might behave while asleep: "we are having a pleasant time in each other's company – at least I am and she is ceasing to be quite so polite. Some time I'm afraid I shall forget in my sleep that it isn't you. I'm amused to notice that B is disproportionately affectionate when half asleep."[34] Clearly, Frieda and Bud were doing much more than simply resting together.

Frieda's letters about their closeness were often phrased in less romantic language than Bud's, she being the more emotionally reserved of the two, and addressed more directly the subject of physical contact. That she and Bud shared a bed is made clear by letters in which Frieda mentioned various aspects of their sleeping arrangements. Writing about consideration between them, she protested in 1926,

This business of your being close is really getting absurd. One night I came down from the delivery room dripping with heat & exertion at about 3 AM & began to apologise quite seriously to you for not bathing before I went back to bed. I didn't realise what nonsense it was till I decided perhaps I had better be a little more considerate of you & get up again.[35]

Frieda spoke frankly of their sleeping together when she teased Bud, "Now I am in bed & yet I don't like to try sleeping because of you. You always were a restless devil weren't you. It is hard to explain how you can keep me awake at this distance."[36] Bud's comments on their sleeping arrangements were less frequent, but she did say in 1926, "You have evidently taught me your trick of not minding which way I face when I'm asleep – I didn't realize it until last night and it was most pleasant."[37]

Other statements are perhaps less suggestive of physical intimacy, yet they do convey the impression of a closeness that went beyond friendship, even of the romantic kind. In a comment to Bud, Frieda seems to suggest, in a flirtatious way, that the women "behaved" on an occasion that presented temptation: "It is nearly as difficult to go to sleep quickly now as any time. I might supplement your observation by reminding you that we were extremely good the last night you were in New York. This tends to prove that if at large we would be quite sensible." A further remark by Frieda seems directly to convey a physical attraction: "The well known law that the attractive force between two bodies varies inversely as the square of the distance & directly as their masses doesn't seem to hold."[38] In turn, Bud commented, "Thank heaven you didn't come to Buffalo, much as I would have liked it. I would have felt so guilty about it. I'm sorry you're having sleepless nights – I wish I could be there to make them more amusing."[39] And more humorous than serious was Frieda's query about "the informa-tion that you don't like being pawed. I shall make a note of it against the future. Do you *mean* anything?"[40] The following month, she reminded Bud: "My dear, I've barely one eye open though it is only nine & I just wanted to remind you as before that I'm there to hold your hand, and indeed all of you."[41]

Commenting on the frequency with which Frieda's letters arrived, Bud joked, "My dear – Cousin Lucy would certainly think that I had a lover – three letters in two days! It is the nicest thing to get them when after the first I had resigned myself to another week! The last one, which reached me this morning only took seven days, isn't that quick?"[42] The following year, she wrote to Frieda, "What a perfectly swell day, darling – 3 letters from you! I'm sure the maid thinks I have a lover."[43] And of course Bud did – just not a male one.

The extent of their passion for each other is revealed in the openness of their affection for one another. They wrote with amusement about public expressions of affection. A bemused Frieda wrote to Bud in 1925, "My dear, I nearly disgraced you about an hour ago. The train had stopped & I was thinking of nothing at all when I suddenly heard myself whisper 'darling!' quite distinctly. Everything else was so quiet that if anyone had been listening they could have heard same at the end of the car. No comments were made anyway."[44]

Some entries suggest a familiarity with and admiration of each other's bodies. A wistful Bud wrote in 1925, "Your letters have your smell quite distinctly when I first open them – hospitaly, I admit, but nice withal! Oh doesn't it sound awful?"[45] It would appear that Frieda was often around when Bud was bathing. Bud remarked, "The only bright spot in my mornings is Enid, who comes in and is rude to me because I won't get out of my bath. The first morning she did it it reminded me so of you that I nearly wept. As a matter of fact, she isn't a bit like you, but you're the only person who makes a practice of being nasty to me in my bath – oh my darling, wasn't it fun?"[46] And describing a theatre production of Peter Pan, she lamented, "The woman who has been doing it was ill and the new one was too much like you for my complete comfort – I've always said that you would make a nice Peter, haven't I? – but her legs weren't as nice as yours."[47] Frieda seemed to appreciate the attention, commenting the following summer, "As you may have gathered from my last letter Don, Alan Shinstone, Elspeth, & I went on a canoe-trip in Algonquin Park. We enjoyed ourselves immensely. I wish you could see me now – very brown very bright eyed & surprisingly well muscled. I hope a little of it stays for you."[48]

The letters between Frieda and Bud were written only a few years after the "innocence" of the romantic friendship had been eroded. As Lillian Faderman suggests, magazine and literary representations of the romantic friendship dwindled once the new discourse of pathological sexuality held sway, and relationships between women were now more readily suspected of having a genital component.[49] But how are we to interpret the actual content of relationships between women in this period of change? It is

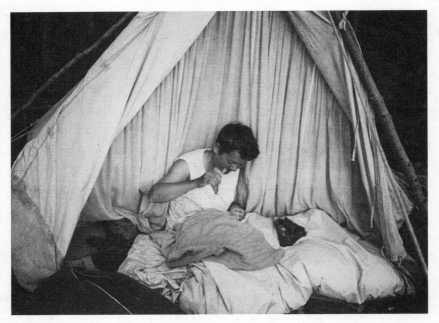

Frieda maintained an interest in outdoor activities and took a number of
camping and canoe trips with friends. | 2nd Bisco trip (summer 1936), Frieda in tent.
University of Toronto Archives, B1995-0044/005P (09), neg. #100

certainly the case that Frieda and Bud were familiar with the new discourse
on sexuality. Frieda in particular, perhaps because of her medical training,
was familiar with views of relationships between women as "unnatural."
But are we to suggest that without that discourse their relationship would
not have had a physical component? If we are to agree that it was the new
discourse that changed everything, then we must also be prepared to accept
that suddenly, when the discourse became more widespread in the 1920s,
their behaviour, and possibly even their entire self-concept, changed in
response to the discourse.[50]

Neither the discourse of female sexual passivity nor that of sexology
was entirely hegemonic, and the period of slippage between the two was
long. Even in the heyday of the discourse of female sexual passivity in the
first half of the nineteenth century, there were those who disputed its
terms. As attitudes changed, and it became increasingly acknowledged
that women had sexual passions, there remained many who saw women's
sexuality as weaker than men's, and even the twentieth-century discourse

of the companionate marriage did not fully erode such views. Sexology, which came into being in the mid-nineteenth century, was not widely influential until the middle of the twentieth century. Even then, one could hardly say that its terms and methods were hegemonic. The patchy nature of public discourse on female sexuality allowed some women to maintain physical same-sex relationships without exposure even as sexology was beginning to focus attention on "sexual inversion."

Those women who contemplated lives without men and lived together as a couple were clearly outside the bounds of heteronormativity. Yet they persevered. In these passages from twentieth-century love letters, one sees the continuation of several themes common to nineteenth-century relationships between women: love, loyalty, and intense devotion. Writing more of the late eighteenth and the early nineteenth centuries, Faderman argues,

> Women who were romantic friends were everything to each other. They lived to be together. They thought of each other constantly. They made each other deliriously happy or horribly miserable by the increase or abatement of their proffered love. They were jealous of other female friends (and certainly of male friends) who impinged on their beloved's time or threatened to carry away a portion of her affections. They vowed that if it were at all possible they would someday live together, or at least die together, and they declared that both eventualities would be their greatest happiness. They embraced and kissed and walked hand in hand, and some even held each other all night in sleep. But unless they were transvestites or considered "unwomanly" in some male's conception, there was little chance that their relationship would be considered lesbian.[51]

The letters between Frieda and Bud and those discussed in Chapter 1 from Charlotte Whitton to Margaret Grier and from B to Elisabeth Govan indicate that their relationships fulfilled several of the above requirements of romantic friendship. Although none of these women suggested that they would die together, there is a similar degree of hyperbole in the language they used to describe their emotions for each other, a similar sense of permanent commitment, and an identical need for constant contact and communication. As I have suggested, this language was not peculiar to lesbian relationships but was a twentieth-century version of middle- and

upper-class courtship language of earlier centuries. In each of these relationships, the love between the women was invested with a religious or
spiritual significance, and the women placed their love above more mun-
dane or earthly loves. This does not necessarily mean that they rejected
physical love, often assumed to be earthly, but rather that they invested
each and every aspect of their relationships, including physical affection,
with a spiritual meaning.

New in twentieth-century love letters between women was an awareness
of societal disapproval of relationships between women, something that
was less a factor in the true era of the romantic friendship. New also was
the physicality of the language; the Fraser-Williams and the Whitton letters
in particular reveal a physical aspect of the relationships that went beyond
the limits described by Faderman in the above passage. Perhaps most
important of all, however, is the moderate infiltration of such words as
"unnatural" and "libidinal," which indicates the influence of sexological
and Freudian ways of conceptualizing relationships. These are medical and
psychological rather than moral terms, ones that were not used about
romantic friends in their heyday before 1850.[52] That some women were
able to blend the language of the romantic friendship with newer ideas
about physical relationships between women should suggest to us that we
are not necessarily discussing two completely different kinds of relationship between women: nonsexual and sexualized. Rather, it was the language
that had changed, not the content of the relationships. It changed from a
language disguising the physical content of relationships to one addressing
it, albeit still obliquely.

Each of the collections discussed in this book was preserved for several decades before being submitted to an archival repository. The letters
of Frieda Fraser and Bud Williams were preserved by Frieda until her death
and then were submitted to the University of Toronto Archives by family
members. Elisabeth Govan kept her private papers until her death, after
which they were archived. And in the case of the Whitton-Grier correspondence and the Alvey-Brodie papers, both discussed in Chapter 1, it was
one of the authors who donated the materials to archives. That these women
kept love letters, journals, and other documents revealing same-sex relationships and did not destroy them suggests that those relationships were
important. All would have known that their papers would be pored over

by family members upon their deaths, yet they chose to retain them. Whitton merely delayed public access to her most private correspondence until 1999, whereas she might easily have submitted only those papers relating to her career and left her private life out of public view. Similarly, Amelia Alexis Alvey could have chosen not to include Grace Brodie's letters in the collection she submitted to the University of British Columbia's Rare Books and Special Collections. Each of these women, in their retention of very revealing documents and, in the case of Whitton and Alvey, in their making those documents publicly available, made a statement about the importance of their same-sex relationships in terms of their sense of self and in terms of the impression they wished to leave behind.

These sources from the first half of the twentieth century were written at a time when, although women were speaking of sex more frequently and were at least acknowledged to have a sexuality of their own, the predominant social attitude was that it was improper to speak frankly of sexual matters, especially in relation to oneself. Even though a few women who were in government positions, were authors of advice literature, or were medical doctors might speak about sexuality, it was almost always about the sexuality of others. It remained inappropriate to speak of one's own sexual activities and desires. That women's letters and journals from the period should be rather enigmatic on the subject is therefore not surprising. If the women discussed had still been alive at the time of writing, it would have been possible to ask the kind of questions of them that would penetrate that veil of secrecy that covered female sexuality before the Second World War.

The opportunity to interview the women about their relationships and also about how their letters and journals are constructed could have verified not only that these were physical relationships but also that it is a combination of social norms about written expression and a lack of modern terminology that makes these sources enigmatic and too easily misread by a modern reader. As it is, we must learn to read sources for the linguistic clues that reveal physical relationships. They are there; it is simply that we have been used to assuming that the "not said" and the "not seen" were therefore also the "did not exist."

Part 2

Lesbian Lives after the Second World War

4

Growing Up under Heteronormativity

After the Second World War, the discursive landscape of Canadian sexuality changed in direct relation to fears arising from the war and to insecurities about Canada's national prowess. The war sparked a number of fears about changing gender norms and their consequences. In particular, crises about women's participation in wartime work and economic factors resulted in a nationwide reinvestment in the traditional, nuclear family.[1] Newspapers and the government mounted lengthy campaigns against those it portrayed as sexual psychopaths or as threats to national security. The campaigns, and the prosecutions and employment terminations that ensued, were focused mainly on gay men, but there were also consequences for women.

The postwar era was one of entrenchment of gender norms, with considerable effort being made to define the "normal" style of Canadian life. Arguments in favour of women's return to the home were not merely about the need for men to be able to return to the jobs they had left; postwar security concerns and changing economic realities underwrote fears about the stability of the nation. The heterosexual, nuclear family was regarded as the building block of the nation and as a bulwark against communism. The nation was the family writ large, and threats to the family were thus threats to Canada as a whole.[2] Psychologists had a crucial role to play in the new postwar obsession with normality. During the war years, psychologists had established a reputation as the arbiters of good health and mental and moral fitness in their role within the military. When the war was over, they sought to build upon that reputation and to extend their role into the whole of Canadian society.

The 1950s was a decade of incipient gender transformations: the gains that women had made in terms of employment opportunities, incomes, and benefits would provide fodder for improvements in the 1960s; the IUD and the contraceptive pill were invented (although they would not come into widespread use until the 1960s); working-class lesbian bar cultures in several large Canadian cities would be among the foundations of later feminist movements based on women's sexual autonomy and freedom of movement; the American sexology and psychology disciplines, with their hostile diagnoses of female sexual deviance, became virtually hegemonic; and Alfred Kinsey's second work, *Sexual Behavior in the Human Female,* caused a ripple across North America with its claim that a substantial proportion of women were enjoying sexual intercourse outside marriage and that some were even engaging in sexual relations with other women.[3]

For the first decades of the twentieth century and earlier, the historian of sexuality must rely on written records. In a study of more recent decades, oral interviews can be conducted to augment the available written records and to provide the historian with the opportunity to question people about very intimate parts of their histories. This chapter and the subsequent chapters on relationships, sex, and community examine the testimonies of the twenty-two women I interviewed. Most of the narrators were in their twenties and thirties in the postwar era. Their testimonies reveal both continuity in older norms of sexuality and changes in roles for women, kinds of sexual knowledge, and opportunities for sexual relationships.

This chapter also discusses interviews conducted by the Lesbians Making History (LMH) project and by Elise Chenier. These interviews, conducted in the 1980s and early 1990s with women who were involved in the lesbian community in Ontario in the 1950s, 1960s, 1970s, and 1980s, focus primarily on community relationships, the bar scene, and politics. Providing rather less material on childhood than do my own interviews, the LMH interviews nevertheless allow glimpses of family relationships based on parents' expectations for their daughters and on reactions to those daughters' wayward desires and actions.

The narrators' testimonies show that their childhood and adolescence were variously happy and unhappy. No consistent theme of alienation from family is revealed, nor does any particular gender performance appear to have predominated in their childhood. Many of the narrators remembered their childhood very positively. The narrators were all raised with the norm that all young women would eventually marry. That message was conveyed to them both overtly and covertly. Many could not remember specifically being told that this was expected of them, but they did remember that they were aware of the expectation as they moved toward adulthood. Such a powerful norm was often expressed in terms such as "that's just the way it was" or "that's just what you did." They were not physically forced in any particular direction but rather were made well aware of the roles they were expected to fill as girls and then as women; alternatives were either not presented to them or were presented negatively.

The narrators may be divided into two broad groups: those who had same-sex experiences as children or teenagers and those who did not. Not all those who did have same-sex experiences before adulthood immediately embraced a lesbian subjectivity. Barb, Pat, Mary, Cheryl, and Pam have always had sexual relationships only with women. Jill, Veronica, Maureen, Bergit, and Jane all left their childhood experiences with girls behind and married, only later to return to lesbian relationships. Of the narrators who did not have same-sex experiences until they were adults, Chris and Lois were the only ones to have been exclusively lesbian. The remaining narrators led heterosexual lives before exploring same-sex attractions.

Many of the women led very average lives as children. Although one or two had unusual parents whose personal lives might have offered more information on sexuality than usual in society, most had very ordinary parents who raised them with the values and norms appropriate for the time. Some were happy children; some were not. There is therefore no common denominator, either among those who did have early same-sex experiences or among those who did not, that would account for their sexualities. From the perspective of the late twentieth and early twenty-first centuries, this is hardly surprising. We now know that sexual orientation crosses all class boundaries and is no respecter of religious affiliation, political persuasion, or family structure. Those who decried homosexuality in the period under study, however, would have found the "cause" of these women's lesbianism or bisexuality in the family; they would have suggested either that it was an inherited characteristic or that it was the product of dysfunctional family life.

Growing up lesbian before second-wave feminism, gay liberation, and the lesbian movement was sometimes akin to living in a vacuum. There existed very little publicly available information about same-sex relationships, and many women remained completely ignorant of their existence. Many were aware of the social condemnation of male homosexuality, but since female homosexuality featured less frequently in media coverage and social discourse, most girls and young women were unaware of the possibility of relationships with other females. They were trained in the norms and expectations of heterosexual matrimony, and bonds with other girls were an important part of their lives but were not supposed to replace the primary bond a girl was eventually to form with a man.

Even in this context of silence, some young women managed to arrive at a lesbian identity. Their experiences may be categorized in several ways. A significant number of young women who formed relationships with other women thought, because they had no access to information about others like themselves, that they were unique and that no one else shared their experience. Many of these women lived for years in a single same-sex relationship before discovering the existence of lesbian community. Others were lucky enough to have found out about the existence of lesbian relationships early in their lives, and they were able to conceive of their sexuality as something shared with others. These women found lesbian communities rather more quickly and labelled their sexuality more readily within the available terminology; they had a framework to explain their desires and experiences. Still other women, even though their desires and actions did not fit neatly into heteronormativity, would develop non-heterosexual subjectivities only later in life. These women married and had children before coming out as lesbians.

In every case, the women interviewed were well aware, as were most women of their generation, that it was expected that they would marry and have children. They weren't necessarily told so explicitly. Often, heterosexual norms were established by inference or by the absence of visible and viable alternatives. Thirteen of the narrators did marry and have children. In several of those cases, a lesbian identity was not explored until the death of or divorce from the husband. The narrators' stories illustrate the strength of normative gender roles in the years before second-wave feminism, but they also show that many women were able to view those norms very selectively or even to reject them outright in favour of a lifestyle abhorrent to society at large.

Gender performance was often associated with sexuality in the late nineteenth and twentieth centuries. Unfeminine behaviour and appearance have long been assumed to be indicators of lesbianism, and lesbians have long been assumed automatically to be gender transgressors. The relevance of nontraditional attire to lesbian culture is predicated on 1970s lesbian-feminist norms and the heterosexist stereotypes that preceded them. Historically, women who dressed androgynously or as men have been assumed to be lesbian. In some instances, such assumptions were and are accurate. Those women who placed themselves at risk of ridicule, assault, and even prosecution because of their attire were often non-heterosexual in their romantic lives as well. However, to assume that all lesbian women dressed in masculine or less than traditionally feminine ways is to obscure the diversity of lesbian experience in that it precludes from observation and recognition those lesbian women who appear traditionally feminine. The sexologists and psychologists whose writings on homosexuality set much of the tone of public discourse on the subject in the nineteenth and twentieth centuries had great difficulty accounting for the feminine lesbian, often regarding her as a less authentic "sexual invert" than her masculine counterpart. Such assumptions were then enshrined within the lesbian community itself with the later lesbian-feminist discourse of androgyny.[4]

Only some of the narrators for this study recalled an early preference for more "masculine" clothes, the stereotypical signifier of lesbianism. Most argued that they had no preference and wore both pants and dresses. Sarah, who was born in Halifax in 1913, remembered that, although she wanted to wear what others were wearing when she was a young adult, she always had a more tailored appearance than her friends. "My mother would have liked me to be a cute little girl," she said, "but I wasn't a cute little girl." She wore "preppy" clothes. The daughter of a naval officer, she was a middle-class child. When her family settled in Victoria, her father bought a large house in a neighbourhood of relatively small houses. Neither of Sarah's parents was strict, but both raised the children with the manners appropriate to their social class. Sarah described the primary values she was raised with as "the good old 'do unto others as you would be done by' and, I think, an open mind more than anything else."[5] Despite their social class, the family did not have a great deal of money, as there was no pension plan for the navy. When Sarah's father died, Sarah's mother was left to raise the children alone. She did not remarry until the children were young adults. Although her family was not wealthy, their social status and expectations clearly placed them in the realm of Euro-Canadian middle-class life.

Sarah left for Toronto when she was eighteen and stayed in a boarding house with a friend. It was not thought at all unusual that she should go out to work, and as her mother knew people in Toronto who could provide an initial contact for Sarah, she was allowed to leave home unaccompanied and join the ranks of young women in clerical work. During the Depression, she lost her job, but she was able to get a succession of secretarial jobs because of her mother's connections in Toronto. She remained in the workforce until just after her marriage at nineteen, giving up when she had a child. In 1943 Sarah joined the air force. Her husband had already joined as an officer. She was a corporal and, like many women in the forces, worked in the accounts section. When Sarah was in the air force, her daughter stayed in Victoria with Sarah's mother. She continued to work after the war in office jobs. She did not begin to explore her lesbian identity until the 1990s, after her husband had died.

Barb was born in Ontario in 1929, the daughter of a Canadian farming couple. Barb was a very tomboyish young woman and was very active around the farm, helping with the manual work: "Always known as a tomboy in the family ... always like to wear my overhauls [overalls], and my plaid shirts, and a straw hat. Oh boy. Spiffy!" Her parents tolerated her gender-bending behaviour. She played most often with the boys and did not care for the traditional pursuits of girls. She preferred the world of Westerns and would sometimes go into town to see a Roy Rogers or Gene Autry film: "After watching those movies I had to go home and play. I would be Gene Autry or I'd be Roy Rogers ... my sisters were a little more, mmm, ladylike around home with Mum, you know ... they liked to sew and knit ... I tried it all, I tried ... never could work out very well, so I gave that up." Barb "hated putting on a dress, or a skirt, or stockings, you know, nylons, and shoes shined up and, oh, boy. I didn't like that at all ... I always had overhauls on ... and always a plaid shirt, and my sisters were always in their skirts or dresses. Had my hair cut, squared off, like cut short. Just showing my ears."[6] As a rural child, Barb was probably lucky in that nontraditional dress was more tolerated than it would have been elsewhere, given that she participated so often in farm work, and she received rather less forced indoctrination in femininity than she might have experienced in an urban family.

The only Catholic interviewed for this study was Chris, who was born in rural Quebec in 1943. Her father, a Scot, was a farmer, and her mother, who was French Canadian, worked as a housewife but also fostered a large number of children. Chris shared the experience of being allowed to dress on most occasions in more boyish clothes. Chris described herself as a strong young woman who was used to doing heavy manual labour around the farm and wearing masculine clothes. She later trained as a nurse.[7]

Mary Louise Adams reveals that advice literature and films of the 1940s rarely explicitly linked "sissy" and "tomboy" behaviour with homosexuality, which would have given credence to biological arguments about homosexuality and would have suggested the futility of the recent regulatory measures and sex education as a prophylaxis against social deviancy. To clearly link behaviour such as Barb's with lesbianism would have suggested that there was a fixed and irrevocable connection between gender performance and sexual orientation. If that were the case, attempts to change the behaviour of "tomboy" girls would be pointless; the aberrant gender performance was simply a manifestation of an innate characteristic. Instead, gender-bending behaviour among children was portrayed as an adolescent condition, often the result of poor parenting, that could be reversed, and it was not necessarily linked explicitly to homosexuality in the 1940s.[8] Sex education was the key to ensuring proper training of girls and boys in gender norms and in appropriate responses to the opposite sex. As sex education became more widespread and was more heavily influenced by ideas of child psychology in the 1950s and 1960s, it began more clearly to reflect the underlying assumption that gender behaviour was linked to psychological pathology. Tomboys, the subject of bemusement before the war, would become signs of femininity gone wrong in the postwar era.

Cheryl was born in 1941 in Newfoundland. She was the youngest of four children. Cheryl's mother died shortly after she was born, and Cheryl's grandmother looked after the children until the family immigrated to Canada (as Newfoundland was not yet part of Canada) when Cheryl was five. Her father remarried and Cheryl acquired another sister and two brothers. Cheryl remembered that her childhood was a happy one, even though her father, a coalminer and steelworker, was poor. Neither of her parents had received much education; Cheryl remembered that her father went "down to the pits" when he was thirteen and that he had a Grade 2 education.

As a child, Cheryl played with both siblings and school friends. She remembered in particular liking to play doctors and nurses, and she remarked that she always wanted to be the doctor. Cheryl was fifteen when she went to work, and she commented that her older siblings were likely even younger. "I was not a teenager," she said, "I did not have a teenage life as most people know a teenage life ... I didn't go to all the things that the other girls did ... And I got a job as soon as I left school. I got a job first dish washing, then pot washing (I graduated) and then I became a waitress, slingin' hash, serving cokes, chips & gravy, cherry cokes." It was at the waitressing job that Cheryl met her first female partner, Robyn, who worked on the soda fountain. In 1959, at the age of eighteen, Cheryl joined the air force.

Like Barb, Cheryl was a tomboy growing up and liked the movie stars Roy Rogers, Dale Evans, and Gene Autry. "I came out of those matinees always, always riding an imaginary horse, and I was never Dale Evans at any time. I was always Roy or Gene or Hopalong ... or the Cisco Kid," she said. Her friend Daphne would play Dale Evans. Cheryl remembered that she wore a great number of hand-me-downs from her sister because they were poor. Her mother made many of their clothes. Girls could not wear pants to school, although in the winter they were allowed to wear overpants on the way to school, but then they had to take them off and wear skirts or dresses. On Saturdays, however, she wore pants. She described herself as "the classic tomboy"[9] and believes that this preference in dress, her admiration of male rather than female movie stars, and a crush she developed on her teacher were the only signs she had as a child that she was in any way different until she formed her first same-sex relationship as a teenager. There is not, however, any necessary and consistent link between gender performance in childhood and sexual subjectivity. Not only do not all tomboys grow up to be lesbians, but also a large number of lesbians either conformed to prevailing norms of feminine dress and behaviour or dressed and played in variously "feminine" or "masculine" ways.

Mildred was born in 1924 in Pittsburgh and remained in the United States throughout the period under study, coming to Canada in 1966. Her experiences, although occurring in America, are important in this study in that they illustrate that higher education and political and social activism were important in the formation of same-sex relationships, just as they were for some of the women whose private papers are discussed in Part 1. Mildred's father was in insurance and her mother was a housewife after marriage but also volunteered extensively.[10] Mildred did her undergraduate and master's degrees at the University of Pennsylvania College for Women in the 1940s, worked in administration for a time, and then did her doctorate. By the early 1960s, just before moving to Canada, she was an assistant professor. Mildred remembered that she had "a very good bringing-up" by her mother. She liked her father, but "insurance, and golf, and cards – that was his life." The youngest and the only girl in a family of three, Mildred was a tomboy who played with her next nearest brother and his friends. Mildred would play touch football and kick-the-can with boys.

Unlike the many narrators who described their childhood recreation as tomboyish, Jane did not play with boys and instead spent most of her time with girls. Her preferred style of dress was "plain and tailored," and she did not like "frills on blouses or anything like that." Jane was born in 1927 in Toronto. Her mother, a housewife and paper-box maker, and her father, a truck driver, were both Canadian and members of the United Church. Jane was the last of four children. Church was important to her when she was growing up, and she enjoyed attending Sunday school and the Sunday evening service. The rest of her childhood, however, was not as enjoyable. She described her family as dysfunctional, and she was treated "with disgust, most of the time" because she was an unplanned child. Her father was a tyrant and was very angry. "He used to sit at the table with the strap beside him," remembered Jane.[11] Jane's upbringing in the 1930s and 1940s was exceptionally strict, and all the children lived in fear of their father. Alcohol was forbidden in the home, mainly because Jane's mother had had an alcoholic brother who eventually committed suicide. She was raised with the traditional values of honesty and hard work, but her father was also prone to indoctrinating the children in anti-Catholic prejudice, something with which Jane said she disagreed even as a child. She spent a great deal of time playing outdoors with a friend from the street.

Bergit was born in Ontario in 1934 to Danish parents. Bergit's family was large compared to that of many of the other narrators: she was the youngest of seven children. Her father was a labourer and her mother was a "chore woman and expert home manager."[12] Bergit described her childhood as very enjoyable, even though she was aware at the time that her family was poor. Her father was of the opinion in the 1930s that "women did not need to be educated, as they would go and get married anyway," and Bergit and all of her older siblings left school at sixteen. Only Bergit's two younger sisters continued their education; their father, by that time, had changed his mind about education for girls. Respectability was important to Bergit's parents, although this did not mean that the children were particularly restricted in their activities. For example, the girls were allowed to wear makeup as long as they "looked respectable."

All the children in Bergit's family were expected to do chores, and it was in this area that Bergit's behaviour differed on gender lines. Bergit most often did outdoor chores, whereas her sisters did many of the indoor ones. Bergit remembered that her brothers went to war while she was growing up. She became the one in the family who shovelled the snow, cut the grass, and piled the firewood. Her sisters cooked, cleaned, and baked. Bergit was also very focused on sporting activities when she was growing up, and she participated competitively in several sports.

It is Barb and Cheryl who best exemplify a common element in lesbian coming-out narratives: unfeminine gender performance as children. Partially because masculinity has underwritten assumptions about lesbianism, and partially because the lesbian-feminist discourse of androgyny, which became virtually hegemonic in lesbian communities in the 1970s and 1980s, reified the tomboy "baby dyke," unfeminine behaviour during childhood has become one of the most enduring symbols of lesbian subjectivity. It is an attribute to which many lesbians refer fondly when telling their life stories, and it forms an early element in many coming-out narratives. Masculine gender performance is portrayed as the first clue to a lesbian identity. This, of course, negates the experiences of the many lesbians who never felt or acted in "unfeminine" ways as children and whose subjectivities do not include masculinity or androgyny. The dominant code of dress among lesbians is based on the experiences of only some lesbians, and it should be acknowledged here that the narrators' testimonies undercut rather than support any suggestion of gender transgression being an integral part of lesbian subjectivity.

It is unfortunate that I could not find femme narrators for this study, as their perspectives on growing up lesbian might have been somewhat different from those presented here. Unlike those women for whom gender transgression was an early element in lesbian subjectivity, femme women experienced same-sex desire without any link to opposite-gender preferences in terms of dress or recreation. None of the narrators identified strongly as femme. Pam, who commented, "I guess I was femme, I suppose," did not hold fast to a femme identity and moved to a more butch role in later relationships.[13]

The Spectre of the Homosexual

One of the most significant events of the twentieth century for lesbians and gay men, both in terms of the formation of communities and in terms of changes in the degree and nature of public knowledge of homosexuality, was the Second World War. Those who "came out" in the 1940s portray the war as a fundamental break with the past. They argue that it was the bringing together of thousands of gay men and, to a lesser extent, lesbians in the military and in war work that propelled them rapidly toward the gay liberation movement of the 1960s and 1970s. Most of the literature on lesbians, gay men, and the war focuses on the United States. Allan Bérubé's *Coming Out under Fire* argues that, because the law in the United States virtually ignored lesbianism, and because the military had built its antihomosexual policies on the basis of the law, lesbians were able to enter the military undetected. Only in late 1942 did the Women's Auxiliary Army Corps (WAAC) respond. In response to a letter impugning the reputations of forty-eight women, including three lesbians, the WAAC required recruiters to examine applicants' local reputations and assess them in relation to nine categories of "undesirable habits and traits of character," one of which was "homosexual tendencies."[14] New psychiatric screening procedures were developed to deal with female as well as male homosexuality.

Bérubé's interviews of six lesbian veterans and six lesbian civilians showed that lesbians, like gay men, found various ways to circumvent the regulations and, once in the military, to socialize with each other. Many lesbians made the service clubs their home, and although they had to be careful not to be too overtly affectionate in public, they managed to form wide social networks based solely on their same-sex attraction. As GIs, lesbian women could also go into the various port cities housing military bases and walk around, alone or in groups, without the same kind of condemnation risked by women before the war.[15]

In Canada's armed services, antihomosexual policies were also employed. The Canadian military placed homosexuality under the heading "psychiatric disorders." Canadian servicemen and servicewomen were discharged under this heading rather than being openly discharged as homosexual.[16] Because of this, we do not have precise figures for the number of women and men discharged from the services during the war because they were lesbian or gay. Ruth Roach Pierson's *"They're Still Women after All"* confirms that the recruitment campaigns for the Canadian Women's Army Corps stopped short in their advertising of any image that might suggest camaraderie to the point of lesbianism because homosexuality could be grounds for a discharge from the military.[17] What her research has not revealed is the degree to which military service was attractive to lesbians regardless of the advertising and the degree to which lesbians were persecuted in the military.

In the United States, the brief period of wartime community building came to an abrupt end for lesbians and gays not because of the end of the war and the disbanding of the women's services but because of the postwar tendency to emphasize conformity to the matrimonial, heterosexual family. The Cold War years were difficult for gay men and lesbians who, despite the antihomosexual policies of the military, had enjoyed a burgeoning social world and sense of freedom in the armed services. Now, in the late 1940s and the 1950s, the nation's attention would be drawn to the rebuilding of the family and to the expansion of the state further into the private lives of Americans. In the case of gay men, campaigns were mounted equating homosexuality with sexual psychopathology and with communism, as both things were regarded as fundamental threats to the sanctity of the American family. Although these campaigns focused mainly on men, lesbians were also the targets of scrutiny and persecution. Those women who chose to remain in the military (which was an option in the United States but not in Canada) were portrayed as a deviant group and were easily stereotyped as lesbian. During the peacetime years from 1947 to 1950, the US military discharged homosexual personnel at triple the rate during the war, and some of the discharges were of women.[18]

The postwar campaigns against gay men and lesbians were also a feature of the Canadian political landscape. For example, Canada took the lead from the United States in instigating the weeding-out of homosexuals from the civil service because of their allegedly greater emotional instability and susceptibility to blackmail. Relying on the scientific opinion of Robert Wake, a Carleton University psychology professor who had investigated the various technological means of identifying homosexuals, Ottawa approved funding in 1963 for the Pupillary Response Test, or "fruit machine," a device intended to detect homosexual response to visual stimuli. Although theoretically capable of testing for homosexuality in both men and women, the Pupillary Response Test was used primarily on men. The results were hardly conclusive, however, and the project was dropped.[19]

The more typical approach to weeding-out homosexuals was a more traditional investigatory technique relying on information gathering and the interrogation of those deemed to be sexually suspect and their associates. The Royal Canadian Mounted Police (RCMP) was primarily responsible for this investigation. The Canadian version of the campaign was more "humane" than its American equivalent. Those investigated did not have to testify at public "loyalty hearings" and were dealt with behind closed doors. Nevertheless, the investigation resulted in the dismissal of over 150 people from government employment, and many more were transferred to other departments or were asked to resign. The investigation was broadened to include people outside the government, and by 1968 the number of suspected homosexuals on file at the RCMP had risen to 9,000, of whom only one-third were federal public servants.[20]

Exactly how many women were persecuted under the government's antihomosexual measures is unclear. Gary Kinsman reveals that, although gay men were known to inform on each other, lesbians resisted the investigators, and lesbian circles were thus not easily penetrated. Nevertheless, the RCMP managed to build files on a large number of lesbians as well as on gay men.[21] Kinsman and Patrizia Gentile indicate that several factors resulted in fewer women being persecuted under the Cold War policies. The texts used by the government and the military to frame the security policies, and the policies themselves, focused primarily on men. Women in the public sector were also largely concentrated in areas where security was not as much a concern. This changed, however, as more security information came to be typed and processed by the growing numbers of female secretarial and clerical staff in the postwar era.[22] Kinsman has argued elsewhere that the campaign against queers was a "major and central part of the Canadian Cold War."[23]

Psychology and psychiatry were vital parts of the postwar re-emphasis of heteronormativity. Before the war, "medical and psychiatric investigations of homosexuality were primarily limited to the pages of professional journals, while the general public's perception of the homosexual – usually male – was shaped by sensational news stories about the sex criminal or religious morality tales about the sex sinner."[24] In the postwar period, medical opinion on homosexuality rapidly infiltrated public thinking via the mainstream media. Much of that opinion rested on assumptions about the intimate link between homosexuality and abnormal or unhealthy family life. The most famous of the American psychologists to promulgate this notion was Frank Caprio, whose works *Female Homosexuality: A Psychodynamic Study of Lesbianism* and *Variations in Sexual Behavior* posited lesbianism as fundamentally pathological.[25] To Caprio, lesbians were subject to a personality disorder and were undisciplined women who had rejected their proper roles as wives and mothers in favour of the masculine role. He argued, "Lesbians suffer from a multiplicity of neurotic health complaints. As a group they do not understand their unconscious. Hence they find it difficult to discipline themselves successfully."[26] In Caprio's view, lesbianism was the inevitable result of the emancipation of women, but it was also allied to dysfunction within the family.

Psychiatrist Edward Strecker, who had served as an advisor to the US army and navy during the Second World War, saw homosexuality as a result of parenting. In *Their Mothers' Sons*, he blamed male homosexuality on frigid, matriarchal, and otherwise problematic mothers. In *Their Mothers' Daughters*, Strecker and co-author Vincent Lathbury derived their claims about female sexualities from ideas about male sexualities and depicted lesbianism as rooted in psychological damage caused by problematic mother-daughter relationships.[27] Although *Their Mothers' Sons* had briefly suggested that immature fathers could implant a tendency in daughters toward lesbianism, for the most part Strecker held mothers to be responsible for the "failure" of a child to develop "normally" toward heterosexuality.

A more positive, although hardly unproblematic, interpretation was held by Alfred Kinsey. Kinsey saw sexuality as more of a continuum than a dichotomy. His interest in the diversity of human sexual practices was expressed in two large studies, *Sexual Behavior in the Human Male*, published in 1948, and *Sexual Behavior in the Human Female*, published in 1953.[28] Kinsey argued that there was no direct link between sexual activity and identity. His data revealed that 37 percent of men and 28 percent of women had had sexual experience to orgasm with someone of the same sex at least once in their lives and that many more had been sexually attracted to others of the same sex.[29] His works served to illustrate that same-sex behaviour was much more common than most North Americans had thought (or wished to believe), and they have since been used to campaign for legal and social recognition of gay men and lesbians. North Americans were not ready for Kinsey's statistics; his research funding was withdrawn, and he came under investigation for seeming to support activities deemed un-American and threatening to the sanctity of both family and nation.

Both lesbianism and bisexuality were linked to broader disruptive trends in postwar American life. The Beat generation in the 1950s allowed and, indeed, argued for sexual freedom and experimentation, which often included same-sex experience. Only just emerging in this period was awareness that young girls and women were among those who were rebelling against normative gender and sexuality.[30] The visible emergence of postwar lesbian communities created the image of a threatening group where previously only individual lesbians had threatened the social order. It was the "many postwar experts and their popularizers [who] sought to give these women a face and a name that the public could recognize for the neurotic, pathological, faulty adjustment that the experts believed it to be."[31]

In an examination of popular psychology in postwar Canada, Mona Gleason demonstrates that psychologists, wishing to sustain the professional prestige established by their employment in the military, broadened their scope in order to take psychology into the innermost recesses of the public mind.[32] Via books, newspapers, magazines, and radio, psychologists gradually increased their hold on the Canadian psyche. A crucial component of the psychologists' work in the postwar period was "educating Canadians in the importance of achieving and sustaining healthy personality development by popularizing their advice and making it accessible."[33] Public knowledge of homosexuality was extended by the inclusion of information on "sex deviations" in dictionaries and medical encyclopaedias, which were available as reference works in libraries and were owned by some Canadian families as well. The entries in these more accessible works were strongly influenced by the psychological and psychiatric discourses of the day and largely presented an image of homosexuality as neurotic and needing psychiatric treatment.[34]

The 1950s and the 1960s also saw the methods developed to detect homosexuals in the military extended to a broader cross-section of Canadian society. Canadian culture, like that of the United States, was increasingly influenced by the new popularity of Freudian-derived theories. Freudian thought enshrined concerns about proper gender behaviour in a number of institutions. At the same time as Canada was attempting to reduce the homosexual "threat" to national security, the government was refining the Criminal Code. In 1949 a federal commission was set up to eliminate inconsistencies in the law in relation to sexual crimes. In 1953-54 sexual offences were moved from "offences against morality" to a new section called "Sexual Offences." In this new definition of sexual crimes, "gross indecency" could be committed by anyone, whereas previously it had been exclusively a male crime. It technically now covered lesbians and heterosexual people. Few women were ever prosecuted under this law for lesbian activity, but police harassment of lesbians did occur, especially in relation to lesbian bars in urban areas.[35]

It would not be until the end of the period under study that the first homophile organizations were founded in Canada, but individuals had campaigned for legal reform for some time.[36] Throughout the 1950s and 1960s, Jim Egan submitted articles on homosexuality to newspapers, and he called on the government to repeal antihomosexual laws. Egan was one of only a few to speak out publicly in Canada in the 1950s, but he was part of an emerging North American movement. Gay and lesbian visibility was increasing in the 1950s and 1960s in the US, and in 1951 the Mattachine Society, North America's first gay rights organization, was formed in Los Angeles. The Mattachine Society aimed to educate the public about homosexuality and to educate homosexuals themselves so that they might become accepted and productive members of mainstream society. One, Inc. was founded in 1952 and began publishing *ONE* magazine a year later. In 1955 the all-female Daughters of Bilitis (DOB) organization was formed in San Francisco. In her recent study of DOB, Marcia Gallo suggests that DOB's goals of lesbian self-knowledge, self-acceptance, public education, involvement in and publicity about research, and lobbying to change laws against homosexuality "reflected the members' beliefs that a conscious, carefully constructed program of discussion, information, and outreach to sympathetic professionals would best advance the nascent movement for gay and lesbian rights."[37] Kristin Esterberg suggests:

> In its early years, the Daughters of Bilitis pursued an integrationist strategy that minimized the boundaries between lesbians and heterosexual women – at a time when the differences between lesbians and heterosexual women may have seemed quite large. In the middle of the 1960s, the DOB began to accentuate the boundaries as it moved toward an alliance with the militant segment of the homophile movement. At the end of the 1960s, as the women's liberation movement flourished, the Daughters of Bilitis and *The Ladder* shifted toward an alliance with the women's movement and pursued a strategy that stressed the commonality of lesbians and heterosexual women.[38]

Both the Mattachine Society and the Daughters of Bilitis were significant in giving gay men and lesbians a voice and a platform, but neither was interested in radically changing society. Rather, homophile organizations argued for education and legal change in the broader society and for the adjustment of gay men and lesbians to society.[39] DOB urged "education of the variant ... to enable her to understand herself and make her adjustment to society."[40] In its paper, *The Ladder,* DOB published reports from psychiatrists and medical professionals on the nature, causes, and impacts of homosexuality. The editors aimed to educate by seeking and distributing the opinions of "experts" of various kinds. Readers condemned many of the reports, however, because they still emphasized the pathological. DOB itself and its lesbian audience were divided on the value of medical and psychiatric perspectives.[41]

The relationship between DOB and the culture of lesbian and gay bars was ambivalent. Although their interests and activities sometimes overlapped, the bars and DOB had fundamentally different agendas:

> bar owners, bartenders, and patrons fought long and difficult battles with the police and state liquor authorities to secure the right to public association. Homophile activism ran in a different direction. Homophile activists worked to integrate themselves into mainstream institutions, seeking acceptance and understanding from outsiders. Underlying this assimilative program was a firm commitment to individual civil rights based on the right to privacy rather than the right to public association.[42]

The relationship between emerging political organizations and gay and lesbian communities was sometimes tense. Marc Stein suggests about Philadelphia that the boundaries between organized politics and communities were never clear. Homophile groups were part of the communities they represented, but they were relatively small and "activists often found themselves at odds with others in their communities, especially when movement strategies of visibility confronted everyday strategies of invisibility and when activists failed to recognize and respect their diverse constituencies."[43]

Canada's first gay community organization was the Association for Social Knowledge (ASK), formed in Vancouver in 1964. ASK was modelled on the Mattachine Society and worked to reform antihomosexual laws and to educate Canadian society about gay men and lesbians. It survived only until 1969. Further groups were founded from 1969 onward.[44] Postwar attitudes toward lesbians were not as hostile as those toward gay men. Lesbian visibility before the 1960s mainly took the form of the public lesbian community of the bar scene in Toronto, Montreal, and Vancouver. The general public were not usually privy to the goings-on of the bar scene and obtained information via newspapers, magazines, the radio, and advice literature. There was little said about lesbianism in these sources until the late 1950s. As Mary Louise Adams points out about advice literature for teens, homosexuals were stereotypically male, and they were adults.[45] Same-sex crushes were approved of for girls, provided they were on people who were worthy of respect and provided they were kept under control and did not involve physical contact.

The rather enigmatic expressions of attitudes toward lesbianism, however, should not be taken as demonstrating a lack of antagonism. What must be remembered is that attitudes can be formed by default, as it were, because of the strength of heteronormative modelling and the lack of positive and viable alternative models. The Canadian public knew full well that heterosexuality was the ideal and that there was a difference between close female friendships and attachments that were "too close" and might be "unnatural." Homoerotic desires had their place in childhood and adolescent development, according to the theories promulgated in the 1950s and 1960s, but they were steps on the path to heterosexual maturity.[46] That their legitimacy was not extended into adult life was a clear message to parents and children alike that homosexuality was not healthy.

By the middle of the twentieth century, images of same-sex relationships and social worlds were increasingly available through mainstream media. Lesbians became the subject of many a magazine or newspaper article. Although some of these were vaguely sympathetic, many were lurid in their hyperbole about the "homosexual lifestyle." With the growth of the "yellow press" in the 1950s, scare mongering about homosexuality became de rigueur. The scandal sheets printed local and international material about lesbians and gay men. In 1955, for example, the *Justice Weekly* printed a story about two London, England, women who had married. Violet Jones, who had desired for some time to change her sex, dressed as a man and married Joan Lee. The judge's comment to the two "lesbians" was that "the fact remains that you made a grave false statement to cover your unnatural passions with a false air of respectability."[47] They were fined £25 each. Such stories, imported from outside Canada, served to titillate the reading public but simultaneously served to foster community awareness among the very people being described.

By 1964 homosexuality had become a more widespread concern. The *Telegram* published a series entitled "Society and the Homosexual," which aimed, after only two months' research on the subject, to present "accurate" information to the public. The first article in the series quoted the Toronto Forensic Clinic as believing that there were 15,000 active homosexual men in the metropolitan Toronto area and a further 150,000 who were latent homosexuals or bisexuals. The article added, "This deviate population is swelled by 6,000 Lesbians and 30,000 other women who live outwardly heterosexual lives but are sporadic or latent homosexuals." The article then went on to chronicle the torrid goings-on in a homosexual club on Yonge Street, where "one pale, ethereal looking Lesbian danced with another who looked and moved like a sack of potatoes rolling down-hill. To the homosexual, particularly, beauty is in the eye of the beholder."[48]

The newspaper reporter then tied the problem of homosexuality to the perceived breakdown in family life. Reporting that Toronto experts dis-agreed with rumours that the proportion of male homosexuals to hetero-sexuals had increased since the war, the paper nevertheless stated that the time was ripe for an increase. As for the cause, the author stated that "the patriarchal society has become the matriarchal society and the lines of familial authority are blurring."[49] Fears about the consequences of women's paid employment and changes in the structure of the heterosexual rela-tionship were manifest in attitudes toward homosexuality, which was thought to be the result of poor parenting. Postwar concerns about dom-ineering mothers and weak or absent fathers were expressed in a variety of media. Most images were of male homosexuality, but lesbians were mentioned more as the 1950s and 1960s progressed.

It would be inaccurate to describe the postwar portrayal of homo-sexuality as uniformly hostile. Clearly, the majority of opinion regarding homosexuality, most particularly gay men, was negative, but there was some degree of tolerance toward homosexuals provided their behaviour was not too extreme in the eyes of the public. Effeminate gay men were seen as somewhat humorous and were ridiculed by the tabloid press, but their gender transgressions were generally tolerated provided they were not extreme.[50] Said tolerance did not necessarily extend very far into the general public or other forms of media. More respectable newspapers and magazines carried stories focused more on the "problem" of homo-sexuality.

By the mid-twentieth century, human sexuality was the subject of in-creasing public debate and journalistic fervour. "Never before," it was argued, "was so much sex information known by so many at so young an age."[51] Canadian newspapers and magazines were replete with sexual scan-dals and speculation, the study of human sexuality became a major pre-occupation of the medical profession and of psychologists, and images of sexuality were widely available in the numerous pulp novels of the period. Sex, the great secret of Victorian society, had acquired a public face. Not only was it now accepted that all Canadians, male and female, were sexual beings, but it was also thought that sexuality was the most important aspect of human psychology – that sex lay at the heart of all relationships, both healthy and unhealthy.

One of the most influential mid-century arbiters of cultural aesthetics was the women's magazine. Canadian magazines, like their American and British counterparts, reflected prevailing gender norms and norms of sexuality while attempting also to appeal to women's changing interests and tastes. The content of magazines changed over the decades in response to changes in the perceived roles and interests of women, but gender prescription was always present. In the 1920s, "magazines could contain a smorgasbord of material, with something for everyone."[52] During the Depression, with advertising revenue and magazine sales decreasing, editors kept only those features that they deemed to have the widest appeal. Mary Ellen Zuckerman argues that editors assumed "that all women resembled the white, middle-class readers they traditionally targeted; and that core subjects existed that were of interest to all women, such as housekeeping and beauty advice." When the Depression was over, magazine fiction rose to a place of prominence in the women's magazines. Most magazine stories focused on love, romance, fantasy, and escape and offered women few nontraditional role models. After the Second World War, magazines published a greater diversity of articles reflecting women's greater participation in the labour force and in business.

It was not until after 1965, however, that women's magazines started to publish many stories about lesbians. *Chatelaine* ran a number of features on lesbians in the late 1960s. *Chatelaine* staff did consider publishing a story on lesbians as early as 1962 but the idea was rejected.[53] The first story was run just after the period this book covers, in 1966, and more regular features on lesbians were not included until the 1970s and 1980s. However, it was possible in earlier years for readers of *Chatelaine* to give the magazine's stories a "queer" reading, and images of lesbianism were particularly important for those Canadian women who lived in rural areas or were not able to partake of the bar culture in Canada's larger cities.[54]

In the period 1920-65, Ontario was the site of considerable gay and lesbian community building and, indeed, of regulatory and discursive reactions to it. Although Montreal also had a significant gay and lesbian population, it was Toronto that became the destination for many a young lesbian seeking others of her kind, especially after the Second World War.

Ontario was also the site of much mainstream and medical publishing on the subject of deviant sexualities in the postwar period. Toronto was the centre of English-language publishing, broadcasting, and cultural production in Canada and was "entwined with the definition of 'national culture.'"[55] It is not surprising that most of the scholarship on lesbian culture in Canada before the gay rights movement focuses on Toronto. Very little has thus far been written about the lesbian and gay communities of Vancouver and other British Columbia towns. Vancouver newspapers did not begin publishing stories and editorials on gay and lesbian issues until the mid-1960s.[56] The availability across Canada of material published in Ontario and the nationwide use of advice literature and films about childhood and adolescent development, however, would have ensured that British Columbians were similarly exposed to theories about homosexuality and its threat to the Canadian nation.

Sexuality was a focus of social anxiety throughout the first half of the twentieth century. Heterosexual sexuality remained the only acceptable form of sexuality, although even the content of heterosexual relations changed. The nineteenth and twentieth centuries witnessed a change from the norm of female sexual passivity to the new ideal of the companionate marriage, in which female sexuality was somewhat permitted, and then to postwar fears about youthful female heterosexuality gone awry. Between 1900 and 1965, female sexuality was increasingly accepted as something that existed – as compared to in the previous century – albeit still at a lesser strength than male sexuality, and its description, theorizing, and policing became the focus of many an advice book, magazine article, and psychological report.

The new century also witnessed the increasing recognition of another kind of female sexuality, one not sanctioned by church or state and one increasingly to be defined in the terms of the new, psychological discourse. Lesbianism began to be discussed by sexologists, doctors, and the judiciary in the nineteenth century. The respectability of the romantic friendship was beginning to erode, and any relationship between women that went beyond close friendship was now deemed pathological. Sexologists and medical doctors began to suspect that relationships between women that were once thought to be healthy and nonsexual were in fact unhealthy.

This new, medicalized discourse was not necessarily hegemonic in North American society, as medical works were not yet widely available.

Most people, until the terms of the discourse began to make their way into mainstream media, regarded homosexuality as unnatural but used non-medical terms to describe it. Further, homosexuality was thought to be a male phenomenon. The limiting of the new discourse to a small, educated elite in society meant that some aspects of the romantic friendship could survive in some circles to the middle of the century. Middle-class women continued to maintain these kinds of relationships even in the face of increasingly negative stereotyping of them. Provided that physical sexuality could be kept secret or was not present, a relationship could still be pursued without arousing hostile reaction. Outsiders might suspect, but they could not prove, that a relationship was of the "pathological" variety.

How, then, *did* people understand the female same-sex relationships in their midst? Many North Americans in the early to mid-twentieth century already had a rubric within which they could simultaneously acknowledge and explain away a relationship between two women who lived together. The spinster, although not meeting dominant standards of heterosexual, matrimonial femininity, was a largely nonthreatening person unless that spinsterhood was accompanied by political activism.[57] Jenéa Tallentire suggests, in fact, that the spinster was not a source of social apprehension because when

> the liminal single woman was creating such alarm, ever-single women professionals in social work and other branches of the justice system held key roles in the surveillance and regulation of the "girl problem" – in short, the tutelage of the "liminal" single woman was in the hands of the mature, "citizen" spinster ... Having passed the transitional stage where most young women pass into marriage, she passes instead into the fully adult independent actor, and her most public roles are those of *securing femininity* – the supervision and training of young women to normative female roles and performances: the *doxa* of gender.[58]

Spinsters were generally conceived of as nonsexual. As Leila Rupp indicates in her discussion of her aunt's relationship with another woman, the outside world could conceive of a spinster as a "maiden aunt."[59] Many North Americans would not have recognized, let alone have had an explanatory model for, a relationship between two women. Several factors account for this. First, despite the new recognition in the twentieth century that women were sexual beings, most North Americans thought in terms of love in relation to women and sex in relation to men. Much of the focus of legal and social policing of same-sex relations was therefore on men rather than women. Further, the tendency to suspect and look for physical sexuality as the crucial aspect of a relationship is a distinctly modern phenomenon.[60] It may be that earlier relationships need to be understood differently, and it may be that the North American public before the 1960s, less inclined to focus on the genital, could more easily distinguish between physical same-sex behaviour, framed as either pathological or immoral, and those relationships that seemed from the outside to be, or actually were, without a physical component.

After the Second World War, particularly in the late 1950s and the 1960s, homosexuality was discussed more frequently in the mainstream media. Although male homosexuality remained the primary focus, the newspaper and magazine articles on homosexuality did discuss lesbianism. Many authors took the approach that the Canadian public needed to be informed of a considerable threat to Canadian society, particularly to the Canadian family. Although some articles attempted to take a balanced and sympathetic approach, many portrayed homosexuality in the most negative ways possible and linked the alleged burgeoning of homosexuality to broader postwar crises and concerns.

The degree to which these new mainstream articles were read by the public is unknown. Information about and stereotypes of homosexuality were increasingly available and would have informed public attitudes to a degree not previously possible. A stronger influence on public attitudes may have been new forms of advice literature for children and adolescents and for the parents raising them. By the postwar era, advice literature was more openly acknowledging homosexuality and was addressing it as a risk factor, and although many of the books and films available to young people and parents may have portrayed same-sex attractions as acceptable during development, they uniformly portrayed physical exploration of those attractions and their continuation into adult life as unhealthy. Heterosexuality was portrayed in this important form of discourse as the ideal and the norm, and positive alternatives were not available.

The following chapters examine how the narrators negotiated dominant discourses of sexuality and developed and explored desires for women.

The women discussed here were in some ways more knowledgeable about sexuality than were women of their mothers' generation, but their knowledge was hardly uniform, and only a few had heard of lesbianism as they were growing up. How, then, did they understand their attraction toward another woman when it arose? At what point did they experience their first same-sex desires, and did they act on them at the time? How did they think of their relationships with women, and did they live in isolation or did they find others like themselves?

Very few of the narrators had heard of homosexuality when they were growing up. The overwhelming majority reported that they did not hear words for same-sex relationships between women until well into their adulthood. Homosexuality was a topic that was rarely discussed in advice manuals or by parents before the Second World War. From the late 1940s on, in an era marked by the growing influence of psychologists, by Cold War fears about communist threats to the nation's stability, and by increasingly strong links between Canadian and American security policy, homosexuality became one of the main forms of deviance against which "normal" heterosexuality was defined, and public discourse on homosexuality increased. As Mary Louise Adams suggests, however, "homosexuality was constructed as so outside the normal teen experience that it was presented in all of the books as an external threat. Homosexuals were other people – not, certainly, teens themselves."[61]

Despite her relatively broad knowledge about sexuality, Sarah had not heard of lesbianism before her early twenties. It was when she was working as a stenographer and receptionist in Toronto in the 1930s that Sarah met her first lesbian, a woman who was a copywriter in the same advertising agency. This woman "and another gal took me up, you might say," and they became friends. Others in the firm used to say of the woman that "she was all things to all people," which Sarah discovered meant that she had relationships with women. That was the first time Sarah encountered the existence of lesbianism.

Sarah grew to know more about homosexuality during her time in Toronto. She was the only narrator to have read the Kinsey reports when they were published in 1948 and 1953. Because she read the newspapers and "moderately serious magazines,"[62] Sarah kept herself informed about current events. She did not read the tabloids, although she did remember looking at the Toronto paper *Hush*. She knew of several gay people through workplace rumour. None of the gay people she knew lost their jobs because of their sexuality.

When Sarah became aware of her attraction toward women in the early 1960s, she began to research the subject of lesbianism. She read *The Well of Loneliness* and other works, and as her husband's health deteriorated she was able to read a range of lesbian books without him suspecting. She had, at some point in her young adult life, heard of the scandal surrounding Radclyffe Hall's book when it was published, but she did not read the book until she became more personally interested in the subject matter.

When Lois was growing up, she had no knowledge of lesbianism. Lois was born in Victoria, British Columbia, in 1919. Her father was a bookie and her mother a music teacher and concert pianist. Lois "was a bit of a problem," so she was sent to St. Margaret's private school.[63] She took her bachelor of arts at Victoria College, graduating in 1938, and then moved to Vancouver to undertake teacher training at the University of British Columbia. She began teaching at the age of twenty. In 1948 Lois moved to Ontario, where she took up a variety of teaching posts. She had married in 1942 and had two sons. Her marriage was rather unusual in that her husband was accepting of her many lesbian relationships and her frequent attendance at lesbian bars such as the one at the Continental Hotel in Toronto. They had an open relationship in the sense that each of them had relationships outside the marriage. They were apart for much of the first twenty-two years of their marriage, as Lois's husband had a teaching job elsewhere. He would return to spend time with her every month or two. Several of her female lovers lived with Lois.[64]

Lois experienced her first attraction toward another girl at the age of ten or eleven. She also previously had crushes on teachers and had been open enough about them for her sister to tell her that there was something wrong with her. Lois's first lesbian relationship occurred in 1940, in her first year of teaching. Lois said she thinks that her parents suspected she was a lesbian when she was in her first relationship, which lasted fifteen years, although she and her partner were apart for much of it. She had thought that there was something wrong with her until she met that partner, also called Lois. Even then, however, she did not know of the words "gay" and "lesbian." It was not until she began socializing at the Continental that she learned words for homosexuality. Lois said that she does not care for the word "lesbian," adding that "'gay' seemed to be something people used, and it was alright." Around that time, she read *The Well of Loneliness* and the pulp novel *The Price of Salt*. As already mentioned, *The Well of Loneliness* became probably the most famous lesbian novel of the twentieth century. Claire Morgan's *The Price of Salt,* published in 1952, was one of the most popular lesbian pulp novels of the postwar era, selling over 1 million copies by 1963.[65]

The Price of Salt was part of a very successful genre that appeared in the 1940s as part of the "paperback revolution" in publishing. In 1939 Pocket Books moved into paperback publishing, greatly expanding its distribution and sales. "Mass market paperbacks" were sold in drugstores, chain stores, bus stations, and airports and featured sensational covers and more accessible content, including more sexually explicit material than in other kinds of books.[66] A great number of paperback novels were published, including some very popular lesbian ones. The most notable of these were *The Price of Salt; Women's Barracks,* by Tereska Torres, published in 1950, which by 1968 had sold over 1 million copies; and the *Beebo Brinker* series, by Ann Bannon, published between 1957 and 1962. *The Well of Loneliness* also became very popular in paperback reprint, selling over 100,000 copies annually.[67]

Lesbians were starved for role models, and although the stories usually ended badly, the lesbian pulp novels provided women with a sense that there were others like themselves. Bannon's *Beebo Brinker* novels "provided a public point of identification for women coming to terms with their own lesbianism" and "often read like a travelogue or tourist guide of Greenwich Village and its homosexual bars."[68] Lesbians gave the books a "queer" reading: "They did the only thing they could – they compromised and turned a blind eye, so to speak, to the homophobic looking relations installed in these texts."[69]

The novels were a topic of much debate among lesbians. The Daughters of Bilitis, the major American lesbian organization of the 1950s and 1960s, held several discussions about the novels of Ann Aldrich (Marijane Meaker), which they regarded as failing to offer depictions of normative lesbians. Del Martin wrote an open letter to Aldrich, published in *The*

Ladder, saying "the cross-section of Lesbian life which you have depicted may be likened to a similar study of heterosexual life in which only the Skid Road characters and the well-to-do are delineated."[70] Martin Meeker suggests that lesbians were caught in a paradox:

> While the paperback original was the main venue in which lesbians could publish stories about their lives and gain a large lesbian readership, it also was a venue that demanded the stories be told in a certain way to appeal to the large base of male readers and to avoid attention from censors. For lesbian writers who sought to reclaim and assert their humanity through literature, the paperback original was the only option – and no option at all.[71]

Marcia Gallo reveals that, perhaps in retaliation to Del Martin's open letter, the next Aldrich book, *Carol in a Thousand Cities,* attacked DOB and the content and style of *The Ladder.* In the end, Gallo suggests, Aldrich's negative comments "fostered knowledge about the organization and its magazine in the very audience DOB was trying to reach: lesbian or questioning women who were buying books about gay people."[72]

Jill, the youngest of the narrators, had heard of homosexuality when she was growing up in the 1950s and early 1960s, although she heard primarily about gay men. She was aware of a lesbian couple who lived close by, and she was familiar with some of the largely pejorative terminology used to describe gay and lesbian people. However, this knowledge, although framed in negative terms, did give Jill a frame of reference for her own emerging desires. Born in England in 1948, Jill did not have a particularly happy childhood. After her family moved to Canada in 1952, when Jill was four years old, they lived in White Rock and then in North Vancouver. Jill commented that she was an unwanted child and thought of her mother as "the iron woman." Her father was quiet until he started drinking, when he became violent toward Jill's brother and mother. Her mother's aggression was taken out on Jill, and Jill's brother was also violent. Jill remembered her childhood as fearful and portrayed herself as being stuck between her two parents. In this climate of fear, Jill withdrew from family life. She commented, "My happiness and safety came because we did live in North Vancouver, and because it was a wooded area, and I would leave the home very early in the morning and I would go out and lie down in the bush, meditate or pray. This was safety for me, and I never came home until it was quite dark at night."[73]

Most of the narrators for this study were more like Lois than like Sarah or Jill – that is, they were not aware of homosexuality when they were growing up, they were not familiar with words for same-sex relationships or even that they existed, and they felt themselves to be unusual or even immoral or abnormal because of their desire for women. As the following chapter reveals, this was part of a general lack of knowledge about sexuality, about their bodies, and about the possibilities of physical pleasure. Although there was much more information about sexuality publicly available, there were limitations on its reach into all groups in Canadian society, and in many ways these women had little more information than women of their parents' generation. Coming to have desire for another girl or young woman, wanting to explore that desire, making the first move, and figuring out exactly what to do when presented with another female body were exciting but stressful journeys into unfamiliar terrain.

5

Sexual Relationships in Postwar Canada

"We found our way to it easily enough"

One of the most difficult things to determine about the lives of women thought to have been lesbian in the early to mid-twentieth century is whether they had physical sexual relationships and, if they did, what sexual practices they engaged in. Given that women generally were somewhat reluctant to record their sexual activities, scant information exists on same-sex female sexuality. What few written sources do exist, such as the collections of letters and journals examined in Part 1, are phrased in somewhat enigmatic terms when it comes to expressions of desire and physical intimacy. Such written sources must therefore be supplemented by the use of oral history, for in interviews the historian can ask probing questions which establish that lesbian women before recent decades did indeed have a physical sexuality.

As suggested in Part 1, this study is situated in relation to two of the major problems that have emerged in recent years in debates over lesbian history: periodization and the importance of genital sexuality. It is often argued that the early twentieth century was a period of gradual (some would say rapid) increase in the availability to the general public of sex education, sexualized romantic fiction, and medical terminology concerning sexuality.[1] A corollary of this argument is that members of the public became increasingly aware of gay and lesbian communities and individuals, especially after the Second World War. Implicit in such a thesis is the idea that those growing up between 1900 and 1965 must necessarily have been more aware of homosexuality and of the negative attitudes toward it than were those of the previous generations. The evidence in this study suggests that this was not necessarily the case.

Most of the women discussed here did come to express their same-sex attractions physically, even though initially many of them were almost as "innocent" of sexual knowledge as were middle-class women of the nineteenth century. What was different was that it was no longer the case that women were thought to be sexually passionless. There was at least an acknowledgment that women could feel sexual passion, but such feelings were still thought appropriate only within heterosexual matrimony. Young women growing up in the twentieth century before lesbian feminism remained, in most cases, as ignorant of lesbianism as were the young women of their mothers' and grandmothers' generations. Despite this vacuum in female sexual knowledge, many of these women discovered and enjoyed physical sexual relationships with other women.

The interviews demonstrate that the naiveté with which young women often approached their first sexual relationship resulted in both uncertainty and curiosity about sexual matters, probably rather more than would occur in the present day. To be sure, the material available to the public in this period acknowledged the sexuality of both men and women, and sought to build an enjoyable sexual relationship between the sexes, yet its primary goal was still to ensure the sexual satisfaction of married couples and the healthy development of the (white) race. And even though more explicit manuals might have been available to adults in Canadian society, the majority of the literature available to young people was enigmatic on some of the crucial aspects of the sexual relationship. The sexual enjoyment of girls, especially in genital terms, was rarely discussed. Moreover, even those who were urging the more comprehensive education of young people in the matter of sex relied on parental willingness to offer such information to their children, a behaviour not customary or comfortable for parents whose own education had been more restricted. Just as today ignorance about sexuality remains surprisingly common in a world lamented as overly sexualized, so too in the early and mid-twentieth century could the youth of Canada – supposedly under the influence of too much sexual information – remain unaware of basic information about sexual relationships. That was especially the case with women's sexuality, particularly with same-sex women's sexuality. Most young women entered into sexual life with little knowledge of what it entailed.

This chapter and the next discuss the sexual lives of the women interviewed for this study. Their testimonies reveal the norms of sexuality they were raised with, the amount of information they were given as they grew up, the kinds of sexual relationships they had, and the sexual practices they engaged in. Lesbian history has, for too long, discussed sexuality very much in the abstract. Lesbian history is about real people with real bodies and real desires. The women discussed in this chapter desired other women, many of them beginning to recognize that desire even as children. When opportunities presented themselves, they acted on those desires, most of them moving very quickly to a genital sexuality. Manual stimulation was the most common form of sexual practice in their early sexual lives with women, but many moved on quite quickly to oral sex as well. Few, however, used or had heard of dildos. Although several of the women described these beginnings as moments of exploration and experimentation, others maintained that they did what came "naturally." Most described their childhood as lacking in information about bodies and sexuality. Only a few had masturbated as children. How, then, were they able to know what came "naturally"?

The majority of the women I interviewed were raised between 1930 and 1965, when the value of sex education was being argued more forcefully than before and when a wider range of medical opinion about sexuality, including homosexuality, was published in sources other than medical journals. Yet the women spoke frequently of ignorance about lesbianism or, indeed, about any form of sexuality. Moreover, they were raised by parents who, although living as adults in this new and "expressive" world, still operated in their parenting under the same feelings of modesty and restraint with which they themselves had been raised. To suggest, therefore, that these women were more knowledgeable than their foremothers may be misleading.

In several cases, the women had a period of bisexual behaviour as they negotiated their coming-out process. Their sexual relationships with men occurred before they were able to live fully as lesbians. Some were married but had desires for or acted sexually with women at the same time. These women argue that they had always been lesbian and had only to find the right person or community to be able to live the life fully. Despite the fact that they did not, in the period before 1965, describe themselves as lesbian, bisexual, or heterosexual, they regard their behaviour as merely a step on the path toward the realization of their lesbian identity, something they did only because it was what society said they should do. Such a linear and progressive portrayal has been crucial to these women's construction of a sense of self in a homophobic environment. Whether or not they possessed, before 1965, a repressed lesbian identity, they did not experience desire for, or physical pleasure with, men. Their experiences with women were more passionate than those with men and felt "right" at the time. In several cases, however, sexual desire for both sexes was present, and neither heterosexuality nor lesbianism can be said to have predominated in the period under study.

Very few of the women in this study used words such as "gay," "lesbian," or "homosexual" about themselves before 1965. Some came to such words only after feminism and gay liberation. Others never used them. They did not use any identity labels with which to explain their attractions to women, yet they clearly had a subjectivity based on those attractions and how they made them different from other women. Most were aware of difference, of attraction to other women, and of the desire to be in relationships and communities with other women who had the same desires.

Sex Education, Morality, and Learning about Bodies
The sex education that these young women received was part of a broader, normalizing education that increasingly regarded youth, especially youthful sexuality, as both the hope and the scourge of the nation. Youth were a force to be manoeuvred, both overtly and covertly, in the direction of appropriate, heterosexual, matrimonial sexuality. As the twentieth century moved on, and it became apparent that premarital sexuality was occurring among the young, sexuality became increasingly the focus of myriad experts, from psychology and other social sciences, whose agenda it was to steer youth toward an appropriate sexuality. Whereas at the beginning of the century most of the sex-advice manuals were aimed at married couples, with a view to their improved sexual enjoyment, in the interwar and especially the postwar era advice literature focused increasingly on dating rituals and how to select the "right" boyfriend or girlfriend. In recognition of the interest young people often had in the opposite sex, these new works attempted to frame heterosexual interest in older, more traditional terms. Teenagers in particular were caught between changing norms. On the one hand, the manuals provided more information about courtship than had previous ones, but on the other, the information was still heteronormative, moral rather than practical, and phrased in obscure

and enigmatic terms, making it difficult for young people to understand fully the desires they were experiencing.

Entirely lacking in advice literature were positive images of lesbianism. There might be moderate acceptance of same-sex adoration as a phase of development in girls, but that same acceptance did not extend to physical relationships between girls or women and to the maintenance of same-sex attractions in adult life.[2] Girls growing up with an awareness of their attraction to other girls or to women were faced either with negative portrayals of their sexuality or with an absence of portrayals. Many internalized the stereotypes available; many more, in the absence of recognizable images, had to extrapolate from or adapt heterosexual norms of behaviour and attractiveness.

By the end of the period under study, considerable anxiety was expressed in many quarters of society about the changing standards of sexuality and morality. Robert K. Kelley, writing originally in the late 1960s, argued that America was "a society in crisis. The old established values and standards are everywhere called into question ... This climate of perplexity certainly affects each one of us."[3] But a climate of perplexity had governed heterosexual courtship from at least the middle of the nineteenth century. What were more pronounced were, perhaps, the more public nature of the discourse and the extent of the anxiety rather than its mere existence. The control of sexual behaviour, most particularly the emerging sexuality of the adolescent, had become of grave concern to postwar North American society.

The main topic of discussion when Sarah was a teenager was boys, but Sarah thought that this was "rather foolish." One of the main opportunities to meet boys was the local dance. Sarah remembered that dances were held by the school when she was a teenager, and she commented that the girls were somewhat prudish about contact with boys. In keeping with the new norms of the twentieth century – Sarah was born in 1913 and was attending school dances in the "Roaring Twenties" – Sarah's mother did not insist that she be chaperoned to dances, requiring only that Sarah have a ride home or that she pick her up. Sarah had a boyfriend as a teenager, but she commented that it was not a passionate love affair: they did not explore physical sexuality to any great degree. "There were not too many people who popped into the back seat with people," Sarah remembered. There was, however, considerable pressure to have a boyfriend; it was "a prestige thing." "You had to have somebody to take you to dances," she said. She recalled that she did discuss the attributes of men with other young women but did not recall precisely what was said. The diary she kept as a teenager did not include entries discussing boys or sexuality.

The links between alcohol and sexuality were a major concern of the early twentieth century, and considerable effort was made by moral reformers to prevent the use of alcohol by the young in particular. In the case of Sarah's social circle, however, class and gendered attitudes toward alcohol consumption operated as a protector. Drinking, although not disallowed in Sarah's circle, was moderate. "Boys were thought not much of if they got drunk," she remarked. Her mother was not opposed to alcohol, and Sarah remembered that there was a great deal of drinking in those days. Each person took a bottle to the dances and hid it under the table, as it was illegal to have it there. It was not illegal to have liquor in private places, so young people would rent rooms and invite friends to their room to drink: "The idea of you going up to somebody's room sounds almost improper, but it was okay, you know, because you weren't alone. There was a whole group of people ... girls and boys."[4] In Toronto, where she frequented beverage rooms in her early twenties, Sarah acquired a reputation for being able to drink five bottles of beer before she had to go to the bathroom. Neither in Victoria nor in Toronto was Sarah concerned about alcohol impugning her respectability, although she does acknowledge that her first sexual experience probably occurred because she had been drinking.

Perhaps the major factor in these women's discovery of sexuality was not alcohol, however, but lack of information. Almost all the narrators revealed that they were given little or no information whatsoever about how the human body worked, about sexual desire, and about physical sexual relationships. Few of them had any sense of how heterosexual intercourse took place. Fewer still had heard of gay or lesbian people, and those who had were certainly not privy to information about the physical aspects of same-sex relationships. Such detailed information, whether about heterosexuality or about homosexuality, was considered dangerous.

It would be easy to assume from the increasing availability of more explicit sex manuals and advice literature and from the increasing interest in sex education that as the century progressed so too did public knowledge about and discussion of sexuality. Oral history allows us to test the validity of arguments that suggest twentieth-century women were more knowledgeable about sexuality than were their predecessors. The postwar era saw an increase in the availability of sex education, but what was regarded as sex education was not necessarily about sex. Sex education was often conflated with gender instruction for girls in particular and might better be described as moral and gender education.

For all young Canadian women, the journey to womanhood was one of heavy indoctrination, confusion, and experimentation with gendered behaviour. For many, it was also a journey through ignorance, for little information was available that might have aided young women in their understanding of the expectations they were supposed to fulfil, the feelings they were having, and the bodily changes they underwent as they moved through adolescence. For those of the narrators who were not Canadian but who were born in other parts of the old empire or the United States and would later immigrate to Canada, growing up was similar. The expectation was that they would marry and bear children, they received little information, if any, about their bodies and about sex, and they received little or no information about alternatives to heterosexual matrimony, or those alternatives were presented very negatively.

The women whose testimonies are discussed here were in their childhood and adolescent years well before more detailed sex education became available in schools in Canada, the United States, and Britain. In the interwar period, more schools began to include sex education in their curriculum. The sex education that was available did outline for pupils the functions of parts of the human body, including those associated with reproduction, but only in a few cases was sexual pleasure addressed. For the most part, lessons and books explained human development without providing any information that might operate as a "how to" and/or incentive to intercourse. In the United States, diverse school programs were developed to inform young people about the physical changes they were experiencing. By the 1940s a substantial shift had occurred from the norms of the early twentieth century, and educators now believed that young people needed knowledge and that "sex education would produce a wholesome regard for sexuality and gender rather than untoward sophistication." As Susan Freeman indicates, "teachers and other professionals wanted young people to gain knowledge and appreciation of sex, but they did not want them, especially girls, to flaunt their bodies or engage in intercourse."[5]

How could one teach about the structure of the body, including genitalia, and reproduction without suggesting exploration of sexual pleasure and producing "untoward sophistication"? The physical facts of development and reproduction were intertwined with material on gender roles, psychology, and society, sexual anatomy was described in functional terms and often associated in the analysis with the urinary system rather than with sexuality, and details of the reproductive organs' specific location on the body and the effects of arousal on those organs were often elided.[6] In particular, although sex education might outline the roles of sperm and egg and talk about the functions of the vagina and the penis, it did not reveal to pupils the exact process of intercourse – how it happened and what it felt like. In Britain there was little specific sex education, and what was available varied enormously because there was until the 1960s no requirement that it be part of the curriculum and no concerted effort to provide it. Apart from some information about menstruation, schoolgirls found out very little about how their bodies worked and what they could expect in relation to sex and reproduction.

Canadian sex education was little better. Concern about a rise in venereal disease rates and juvenile delinquency during the war years had led to arguments being made for school-based sex instruction, or "social hygiene education." In 1944, for example, the Ontario Secondary School Teachers' Federation unanimously endorsed compulsory venereal disease testing for all high school students because of fears about rising venereal disease rates in teens of both sexes. The Department of Education revised its curriculum guidelines to include the study of venereal disease. There were many restrictions on the teaching of the material, however, because of the concern that informing teens about venereal disease would also provide them with information about premarital sexuality. After the war, as fears about venereal disease waned, educators moved toward a "family life education" curriculum that aimed to produce moral and heterosexual teens. The department "produced a Family Life Education curriculum which couched information on menstruation, seminal emissions, sexual intercourse, conception, gestation, and childbirth within a framework promoting the importance of opposite-sex attraction, sexual chastity, marriage, and parenthood."[7] Curriculum materials were controlled so as to eliminate the possibility that they could encourage sexual activity; they were gendered, girls receiving an education aimed more at making oneself attractive and popular as a prelude to marriage and motherhood; and they failed to provide useful information about the human body – for example, introducing information about menstruation at an age when most girls were already past menarche.

An analysis of the amount and kind of information about anatomy, reproduction, and menstruation given to the narrators between the 1920s and the 1950s reveals that assumptions about an increase in public knowledge about sex and sexuality are not necessarily correct. One finds just as much ignorance and shame associated with sexual knowledge in the post-war years as in the 1920s. Because the primary site of sex education was supposed to be the home, the amount of information one received depended entirely on the willingness of parents to provide it, and parents had been raised in decades when the discussion of such things was inappropriate. Many young women reached adulthood with only the most vague understanding of the workings of the body, of sexual orientation, and of sexual pleasure. Despite the new acknowledgment among medical professionals that women did in fact have sexual feelings, few girls and young women were given a framework with which they could understand and experience them.

If a young woman was lucky, her mother or another female relative might tell her about menstruation. Enigmatic pamphlets were sometimes available with sanitary products. Some parents gave their children the rudiments of sex education; midcentury books on conception and birth were made available to some, but such literature did not discuss the sexual activity that was preliminary to fertilization of the egg by the sperm. Reva was born in Montreal in 1931 to an office worker and his wife, both Jewish. Reva's father was Canadian by birth, but her mother had emigrated from Russia. Reva attended public school, and she also attended Hebrew school until she graduated in 1939.[8] Reva reported that, in the 1940s, when she was in grade school, her mother gave her some information:

> She did the routine thing, with the book and the egg and the fallopian tube and the journey, and talked to me about pregnancy. Never explained how the sperm and the egg actually got it together. But, I had a girlfriend who was a year older, and she had a cousin who was even older, and he told us exactly how the sperm and the egg could get together.

When parents or the books they supplied were less than forthcoming, girls such as Reva often relied on peers to provide information.

Families often used fear of premarital pregnancy as a means of policing the sexual behaviour of daughters in the early to mid-twentieth century. Added to the daunting mystery of pregnancy itself was the moral condemnation of those who became pregnant outside marriage. Gossip about young women who did become pregnant before marriage, marginalization of single mothers, and religious and other forms of condemnation and judgment could operate quite effectively as deterrents to early sexual activity. That condemnation did not deter all from engaging in premarital sexual activity served only to intensify stereotypes about it. Those who strayed made very effective examples of young women "gone wrong."

Pam also knew little about the mechanics of sexuality, but she was made well aware of moral precepts. It was made very clear to Pam that there were consequences to be paid for errant sexual behaviour, although morality tales were focused on heterosexual promiscuity. Pam was born in Nova Scotia in 1936 to a coalminer and his wife. They were United Church. The late 1930s and the 1940s were "a time when girls had babies and certainly out of wedlock. A lot of them were shipped off to live with an aunt somewhere. That's all you ever heard, you know. So and so was gone to live with an aunt in Boston or in Halifax." Pam reported that she "was scared to death ... Well, what was constantly told to me [was that] 'good girls make mistakes, once.' But there were a few of them that made that same mistake a number of times. A good girl could get away with one, but after that it was a no-no."[9]

Sarah, who is the oldest of the narrators, received rather more information about the human body than did many others. Her mother talked to her about menstruation, and "she also gave me good old Marie Stopes' book ... *Married Love*." Her mother wanted her "to have all the scientific details," and Sarah remembered being "quite intrigued." It was 1926, and she was thirteen. For a girl of Sarah's age to be given a Stopes book, or indeed any book that explicit, was very unusual in the early twentieth century. Sarah did not talk to her female friends about anatomy or sexuality, but she remembered one friend who "wanted to try some experiments of some kind." Sarah was "a bit surprised by it all ... I didn't do anything very much ... this was when we were quite young ... maybe thirteen, fourteen, twelve." They were having a picnic. Sarah could not remember precisely what her friend wanted to do, but she did remember that she was not necessarily shocked but rather did not want to do it. It was the "you show me yours and I'll show you mine sort of routine ... Well, I'd always seen lots of bodies, so I wasn't a bit surprised." Sarah's father had made the children have a cold bath every morning, so she had seen the male body, and her mother often went around with few clothes on.[10]

A few of the narrators were lucky enough to have lived in households in which aspects of sexuality were discussed reasonably freely. Phyl was born in 1939 in London, England. Phyl experienced her first attractions toward girls at age seven or eight and was never attracted to boys. In 1951, after immigrating to Canada, she worked in a factory and then took clerical work. Phyl knew more about sex than some of the narrators, having heard conversations between her mother and her aunt in the 1930s and 1940s: "Well, my aunt was a nurse, and she was a maternity nurse. She would be telling my mother all of these things that these patients had said and about that's the last time the husband came near them ... I probably first found out that route."[11]

Bergit received almost no information at school and was never given a book on the subject of sex education, but she received some information from her father and sisters. Her parents were flexible when it came to sex, but she remarked, "Mom wasn't one for flaunting herself. She believed that sex was very beautiful and it was for people in love and should be treasured." Bergit was told a little about premarital sex and sexuality generally. "I found out ... that my Mom and Dad had to marry," she said. "But Dad often said that if we got pregnant that we would be responsible for that child, and would have to bring it up as well as we could. It may be noted here that none of my siblings 'had' to get married." Bergit and her sisters were well aware that their parents made love on a frequent basis, knowledge not typical of the narrators in this study. Bergit's family was, in many ways, more open and flexible about sexuality than the families of the other narrators. Bergit was also quite aware of anatomy. For example, she had been menstruating for nine months before her mother found out – not because she was ashamed of it but because "I just knew what to do and that it was natural."[12]

When Jane was a teenager in the 1940s, she became close to an older female cousin who took her to dances. It was this cousin who told Jane about sex, conception, and childbirth. "She helped me grow up, helped me talk about my body and sex and everything. Things that I had never really known the truth about," Jane remembered. Nobody had told Jane about menstruation, for example. Her elder sister had scared her, saying that when she was older, she would get something she would not want, and Jane had no idea what she was talking about. She did find some information in a book entitled *Marjorie's Twelfth Birthday,* which she discovered in her sister's drawer, and it was after reading the book that Jane started talking to her cousin about sex.[13]

Cheryl was told little about anatomy and sexuality and nothing at all about menstruation. Neither she nor her friend Daphne knew what menstruation was, and any mention of it was phrased in euphemistic terms. When Cheryl's older sister Diane or Daphne's sister Elizabeth got their periods, they did not want to go to the store for Modess or Kotex, which they would call "the corn flakes in the blue box." In the late 1940s they would send Cheryl and Daphne to the store for their sanitary supplies:

> So we'd go over into the store, and we'd say, "Could we have some corn flakes in a blue box, please?" and old Mr. Masterson always knew what we wanted. He'd get it, put it in a brown paper bag, and pass it to us like we'd just done a drug deal or something, and we'd go home with this. So Daphne and I, being the smart young girls that we were, figured out why they had to use these. Both Elizabeth and Diane had boyfriends at that point. They were doing it with their boyfriends. We didn't know what they were doing, but somebody told us, "Well, they have to wear those things when they're doing it with their boyfriends" ... Every now and then we had to go and get some corn flakes in the blue box, and we knew it was because they were doing it with their boyfriends.

Cheryl discovered the truth in 1951, when she was ten. Her family went to visit her aunt in Ontario that year, and Cheryl had her first period. "I got to sleep on this sort of chaise longue that they'd borrowed, that my aunt had borrowed from the neighbour," she said. "Well, I woke up in the morning to find a pool of blood and I thought I was dying. I didn't know that that's what Diane was using the stuff for! Oh, I got up, and I felt so awful." Cheryl thought that she had ruined the chaise longue and tried to cover it up. When she felt faint, however, she had to summon her aunt, who explained menstruation to her. "Well, as best she could," Cheryl said, "but she neglected to tell me one very, very important thing – that it can carry on more than one day." She gave Cheryl one of the "corn flake things out of the blue box. She was pregnant, so of course she wasn't using them. Of course, I didn't understand that either." That evening Cheryl's period stopped for a few hours. "So I went to bed and I woke up the next morning in another pool. This time she was not impressed." On her return home, Cheryl availed Daphne of her new knowledge: "Daphne was surprised when I told her it had nothing to do with Diane and Elizabeth 'doing it' and it had everything to do with us getting older, and 'it's part of growing up, you know, and you're going to be like this soon, too.'"[14]

Pam had not been told about menstruation when growing up in the 1940s, and her ignorance about childbirth left her vulnerable to scare-mongering. Some of her girlfriends

> scared the hell out of me, about having a baby, I was going to be split from belly to you-know-what. To the point that I got extremely ill and came home ... My mother wanted to know why I was being so ill, and I told her I just found how babies came. And I was told "oh, that's not true, that wasn't the way it was," but however I was not given too much information.[15]

Betty was born in England in 1928, the daughter of a diplomat and a housewife. She was an only child and was born when her mother was in her late twenties and her father was in his early thirties. Both parents were killed in the air raids on London in 1941. Betty's father was at that time in the army and was on leave. When her parents died, Betty had come under the care of her strict grandmother: "I had a grandmother who ... supposedly raised me the rest of the way after my parents had been killed." The word "supposedly" refers both to the distant and cold nature of her grandmother's care of her and to the difficulty of their relationship. She was educated in a Catholic convent boarding school from age seven to age eighteen. Betty was Protestant. She recalled:

> In those days it was considered a convent education for girls was the thing, and so many Protestants sent their daughters to a convent because they thought the nuns were very strict and they were, some of them (laughter).

And we always had to watch our p's and q's. Ah, so that was what it was, but I was not, along with the others. I was not raised a Catholic. We had religious instruction separately. The Church of England minister ... used to come to the school for the ten of us who were Protestants. We would have our religious instruction right in the school. We would be assigned a space. I can't really recall whether it was on a Saturday or when it was. It possibly was on a weekend, not during school time.[16]

Betty fled as soon as she was able and went to London to find work. At age twenty-one, Betty married a banker who was eleven years older than she. She continued to work after her children were old enough for her to be out of the home. She and her husband immigrated to Canada in 1955, leaving their two sons in England, where her husband thought they would receive a better education. Betty's husband had obtained a posting with a bank in Toronto, and she worked for the government in family and child welfare, where she eventually became involved in personnel and administration.

Because of the death of her parents during the Second World War, Betty was raised with the values of her very strict grandmother and the nuns at her school. The constraints on Betty's behaviour, and on that of the other girls in the convent, were tight. The girls therefore relied on each other to provide information. They took much delight in telling each other scandalous stories at night, gathered around a single bed in the dormitory. Betty recalled one girl, a "very romantic kind of girl, who lived in a fantasy world – knights on white chargers and fairy queens and all that kind of thing," who kept a journal in which she wrote down her romantic stories and poems. A scandal occurred when it was discovered that she had written in her journal about an aunt who had eloped, and the journal was confiscated. Knowledge of this event caused Betty to avoid keeping a journal herself.

Because Betty did not have close family, spending most of the year in the convent and staying with her grandparents only in the summer, she felt left out when others would tell their stories. The stories would often be about romance, relationships, or sexuality. One evening, Betty recalled, one of the girls asked everyone to gather around her bed:

And she said, "When I was at home, something dreadful happened." And we all went, "What? What? What?" And she said, "Well, my brother was home, and he's four years older than me." And we all couldn't see the significance of that, the importance of it. And she said, "I saw his thing." And she said, "And I couldn't say anything, and my eyes were open wide." And we said, something like, "What thing?" This is how innocent an awful lot of us were, you see. We're talking about ... maybe eleven-year-olds, somewhere in that age. And so she would proceed to explain what this thing was, and we all gasped with amazement. And then one or two others got brave, and I can remember one girl saying, "Oh, that's nothing. I saw that years ago."

As the girls grew older, their nighttime conversations changed. They discussed "magazines that we weren't supposed to have, books that we weren't supposed to read, and the more that got smuggled in the better." They were able to get *Vanity Fair* and *Ladies' Home Journal*. These higher-class publications spoke of "beautiful people who never got divorced or had unwanted children," Betty commented. The *Women's Weekly* was

for the little housewife who looked after the husband in those days, who everybody expected should get married. And she got married, and she had kids. The book wouldn't tell you how the kids came, but how to wash the diapers, how to keep the husband happy. Nothing to do with sexually, but how to feed him and wash his shirts, and get the ring around the collar out, and all that sort of thing.

They even read boys' magazines that one of the girls was able to get from her brother. One of Betty's friends later recalled, "Those magazines were the best sex education she ever had."

Betty did not remember her grandmother teaching her anything about relationships or sexuality. She obtained most of her information from informal sources at the school. As it was a Catholic convent school, there was much that was not explained. The girls often asked at catechism how it was possible that the Virgin could have borne a child. The nuns were disinclined to explain. As a Protestant, Betty did not attend catechism with the other girls. She and the other nine Protestant girls were schooled in religious matters by a pastor who would visit. They asked him about the Virgin Mary, but he didn't explain it either. One of the nuns would give them the proverbial "birds and bees" account when they were walking in the woods, but Betty found this to be most unenlightening. Betty remembered one young girl asking, "'Sister, do we have pollen?' and the sister said something to the effect of, 'In a manner of speaking, yes.'"

One of the nuns did believe that the children should be exposed to more explicit literature because, if the girls were sheltered, they would not be prepared for the outside world. However, she had to be careful about the parents. In Betty's opinion, middle-class people sent their girls to the convent to be "shielded from all the nasty things of the common people ... and of course it *was* all the nasty things about the common people that were the most interesting in life ... and so, of course, this was the most sought-after information."

The one saving grace in the convent was another nun "who we today would call a dyke," Betty said, "because she would have her sleeves rolled up. She was a gardener. She would have her habit pulled between her knees and hooked in her rosary belt, and she'd be out there digging up this garden. She had a deep voice." Betty found her one day working with her tomatoes. The sister sat on her milking stool, and with a sable paintbrush she pollinated the tomatoes. When Betty asked why she was pollinating them, the sister replied that she wanted hybrid tomatoes. The nun explained the process of pollination and lamented that the flower garden, which attracted the bees necessary for pollination, was at the other end of the property from the vegetable garden. Betty then asked the sister about humans and pollen. The sister replied:

"No, child, we do not have pollen. We have sperm." So then I learned a new word. So then she said, "You want to know about sperm?" And I said, "Oh yes." And I sat on the ground, in the dirt amongst the tomatoes by Sister's knee, and that's where I got my sex education. And she told me what happened between people, and then when she talked about the male and the female, she said, "Do you know about the male body?" And I said, "One of the girls thought a man, her brother, had a thing," and she said, "That's it. That's the thing we're talking about." So then I've got the thing and the pollen and everything put together. And she told me in a down-to-earth, very easy-to-understand way. So can you imagine what the conversation was about that night in the dorm? I knew something that nobody else knew ... and I told everybody, "I have the biggest story you ever heard."

One or two narrators discovered information about sexuality under their own steam. Cheryl could not remember precisely when she discovered what "it" was, but she knows that she was aware of social disapproval at a young age. When she was approximately ten, her parents went away and left the younger children in the care of her older sister Diane. She awoke in the night and discovered that Diane was not in the bed. "So I thought that she was sleeping in Mom and Dad's bed," she said,

> so I went looking for her, and when I went in to Mom and Dad's room, yes, Diane was there. But so was Russ, her boyfriend, and I knew at that point that there was something wrong with that, because of the way she reacted. Frightened the hell out of her. "Don't tell Mom and Dad," you know. She was just so afraid ... So I knew there was something wrong with what she was doing, but I didn't know what ... So, somewhere along the line ... I guess Daphne and I decided to find out what "it" was. Maybe we found out, you know, whatever it was. But then again, I don't think, I can't remember that it was a big deal one way or the other, you know.

When she was growing up, Cheryl did not see her brothers or parents undressed. Privacy was stressed, and "seeing one another's privates, private parts, was not something that was done." She was "very inhibited" when she was young, yet she knew enough about sexuality to know that there was an "it" that was tantalizing but forbidden (or perhaps tantalizing because forbidden) and that there were consequences for engaging in that kind of behaviour.[17]

Veronica was born in Ontario in 1940 and was raised in Toronto and East York. Veronica did not recall any particular values with which she was raised but commented that her parents were "basically good people."[18] Veronica revealed that her childhood was not as happy as it might have been. Her father was a gambler and often stayed out all night gambling and drinking. She remembered him vomiting in the bathroom afterward and recalled that there was often screaming in the house because of his behaviour.

As a teenager in the 1950s, Veronica dated boys, but she did not feel close to them: "I had so many boyfriends ... who really liked me, but I could never ... and I liked them, but keep your distance kind of thing." Her first sexual encounters were with boys and were "experimentation." Like many of the women in this study, she had been given almost no information about anatomy or sexuality when she was growing up. "There were some books or booklets by my bed or something," she remembered. "I don't think my mother even handed them to me. They were just there, and I think she had a friend come in and talk to me." Veronica did not remember ever being told about negative consequences of sexual activity. "I don't think there was any discussion at all," she remarked.

For several women, friends were the most important source of information about sexuality. Jill described finding out about sexuality from friends in the 1950s, by which time there was theoretically more information available: "I was quite naive. But I had my friend Julia, and we were fascinated, her and I, with things, so we would discuss those kinds of subjects, and I learned a lot from her. I don't know where she got her information, but that was a safe place to learn from, because I didn't have anyone else." Jill's mother had not given her much information, telling her only about menstruation. "She just described menstrual blood, basically," Jill said.

> Sat me in the middle of the kitchen on a chair and paced around me like an army sergeant and ordered me if anything happened to let her know immediately, and did I understand? Yes, I did understand. So when it happened I thought, this isn't happening the way it's supposed to be. There must be something wrong with me, so I didn't go to her ... And in those days they didn't have all the movies and stuff like now. My friend Jenny was given a little book to read by her mother, and so, I thought, "Gee I wish I had one of those books. Why doesn't my mum give me a book?"

Jill was able to look at Jenny's book but not to take it home to read. The book was not particularly specific. "I had no idea what a fellow looked like or anything else," she commented. "In fact, when I was about sixteen, Gail and I were with the manager at the time, and we were sitting down one night discussing things, and we both asked, 'What does a man look like?' and he sat and drew a diagram for us. I thought, 'This is very strange. Is this what it looks like?'"[19]

The narrators were raised with dominant norms as children and adolescents, but like many women of their generation, they were given very little specific information about sexuality, even as late as the 1950s. Many had acquired a basic knowledge of reproduction but did not know the mechanics of lovemaking or of their own bodies. Like most heterosexual women, the early construction of their sexual subjectivities took place in a vacuum; they had somehow to understand their desires without having a framework to describe what they were feeling. The narrators did feel sexual desire when they were growing up, but they lacked a terminology to explain, even to themselves, exactly what it was that they felt and what they should (or should not, according to dominant norms) be doing about it. Only a few of the narrators did know, because of self-exploration, that the female body was a site of considerable pleasure and that there were certain things that could be done to enhance that pleasure.

Masturbation

When the narrators were children and adolescents, there was little discussion of masturbation. Most either knew nothing about it or knew only that it was "bad." Masturbation had been a major concern of medical professionals and advice literature since the nineteenth century. Negative perceptions of masturbation were linked in the nineteenth century to fears about the sexuality of children and about the assumed "race suicide" of the white, middle class in Canada. Michael Bliss has shown that young Canadians at the turn of the century were reading such publications as *What a Young Boy Ought to Know* and *What a Young Girl Ought to Know*. Moralistic publications urged sexual restraint and the proper use of sexuality.[20] What these and other publications had to say about masturbation was either extremely negative or enigmatic and was aimed primarily at boys and men. Perhaps because of notions of propriety and of female sexual passivity, masturbation among girls and women was rarely acknowledged in the early twentieth century.

The interwar and postwar eras, when notions of female sexual passivity had largely been eroded, were little better. Furthermore, as Angus McLaren points out, it is difficult to gauge the impact of injunctions against "self-abuse." Medical professionals dealt mainly with people for whom aspects of sexuality were a problem. Even those progressive advocates of greater knowledge and understanding about sexuality were not advocating the pleasures of masturbation.[21] It is hardly surprising, therefore, that it was little discussed by parents of young girls. Those narrators who knew that it was not approved of did not remember being told anything specific about masturbation. Despite the long history of publications urging the elimination of masturbation, few parents, it seems, were willing to broach the subject directly with their children. It might also be that reprimands early in life, even before they were old enough to read or to understand such phrases as "self-abuse," taught the narrators that they were not to touch themselves. Furthermore, notions of privacy and shame about the genitalia would have instilled in children a reluctance to masturbate.

A few of the narrators did discover masturbation when they were very young. Deborah started masturbating when she was about nine years old: "I couldn't wait for my parents to leave the house," she said. Deborah was born in 1938. She was sent to boarding school, which gave her the opportunity to get away from her parents but also to develop relationships with other girls. She had begun to experience attractions toward girls at a very young age, and as a teenager she began to act on them.[22]

For Maureen, in the 1940s, masturbation was a pleasure and a comfort in a life that involved little warmth and affection:

> I don't think I was much past ten when I learned about masturbation. I would never say the word, and this was my secret ... I was very aware of how my body worked, and I knew how I craved touch – any kind of touch ... I wasn't aware of any attitudes [against it]. I discovered it through playing ... or just such a skin hunger or hunger for touch of any kind.

Maureen's early years were spent in Winnipeg, where she was born in 1938 to a clerk and his wife, a teacher. As her father worked for the rail company, Maureen's family moved frequently when she was growing up, and she does not remember her childhood as an especially happy one.[23]

Jill reported experimenting with masturbation in her teens in the mid-1960s. "I did, when I was about sixteen, seventeen, and I didn't feel anything," she said. When nothing happened, she thought, "'Maybe I'm a dead person or something. Maybe I'm doing this wrong. Maybe I'm not touching the right place, or ...' you know, you can go through all these things. I can't, it didn't do anything for me, so I thought, 'Oh dear,' I felt frigid."[24]

For those who did masturbate and for whom it was a pleasurable experience, touching oneself provided information about the pleasures of physical sexuality less available to others. It provided "hands-on" experience, as it were. That knowledge would later prove useful in the exploration of sexual relationships with other girls. Maureen, for example, knew how to give physical pleasure and what areas of the body to explore precisely because she had done so with herself first. It was not, of course, that girls were ever encouraged to explore the bodies of other girls – or even of boys – but rather that familiarity with one's own body and the pleasures associated with it may have aided some young women when they began finally to explore desires for others of the same sex.

Early Same-Sex Attractions and Experiences

Several factors were important in many of the narrators' journeys toward lesbian subjectivity. Language, events, and relationships with other people are important components in the construction of lesbian narratives, whether one believes, as do many of these women, that sexual orientation is biological and that a lesbian or bisexual identity exists from birth or from a very young age, to be discovered at some point in life, or conversely that sexual orientation is socially constructed and is but one element in an individual's multiple and changing subjectivities. Certain life events bolstered emerging lesbian or bisexual desires: awareness of terminology with which to describe and understand desires at odds with heteronormativity; physical exploration with another person of the same sex; one or more same-sex relationships; and the finding of community based on sexual orientation. Whether early same-sex desires resulted in a rapidly acquired lesbian identity often depended on whether they were understood as something qualitatively different and apart from heterosexuality, whether they were explored with another person, and whether the individual recognized others to be like her. Same-sex desires could too easily be discounted within heterosexist discourse as "a phase" or as curiosity about the female body. With the considerable pressure on women to marry, and the concomitant lack of information about alternatives, many of the women in this study were largely unaware that they wanted something different, even if they experienced same-sex desires.

Mildred experienced attractions toward girls at school, especially during her adolescent years. Three friends in particular were the objects of her crushes. When she was hospitalized with a burst appendix at the age of fourteen, she fell for two of the nurses. "Oh, I was so enamoured of them," she recalled. "After I got out, I'd get them to meet me in town to have a cup of tea or something." It is unclear how Mildred managed to get the nurses to meet socially with her. Mildred was dating boys in her teens and was sexually active with them. She did have a pregnancy scare when she was seventeen and eventually had to confess to her mother that she was no longer a virgin. Mildred's mother took her to the doctor who had performed her appendectomy, and he informed her that she was not pregnant. She had a second pregnancy scare in her early twenties. Mildred did not find out until many years later that peritonitis had destroyed her fallopian tubes and that she could not have become pregnant.

Mildred was attracted to her aunt, who was a lesbian. Her mother knew, apparently. Her aunt "lived with women, one after the other, in Los Angeles," Mildred remembered. She and her mother visited her aunt when Mildred was sixteen, and Mildred fell in love with her aunt. She believes that her aunt was also attracted to her, "but I was way too young, and I was her niece. We didn't have anything to do with each other, except that we had an immense attraction, and my mother saw it. She saw it. She knew. In fact, she was jealous because I liked [her] so much." Mildred identified the attraction to her aunt as a pivotal moment in the formation of her sexuality, but she did not think that she thought of it in relation to such words as "lesbian." "I just knew I was attracted to [her]," she said. It was both a love and a physical attraction. She remembered particularly a night when her aunt came in to kiss her goodnight, "just like an aunt would, you know. But I mean, that was real important to me." Mildred was also attracted to the girls her brother went out with when they were in high school.

Mildred had her first experience of physical sexuality with a woman at college. She regards herself as having been bisexual during her university student years. "After I went to college, of course, I didn't play with the boys any more, except when I dated them." She formed the majority of her relationships, with both women and men, in university settings in the United

States. Her ascription of the word "bisexual" to her activities is a recent one; Mildred did not use any of the common words describing sexual orientation about herself until the late 1960s, when the gay liberation movement made the terminology both more available and more acceptable. In her college days, Mildred simply followed her desires, and she was bisexual in her desire.[25]

Jerry, when interviewed by Elise Chenier in 1992, reported that she had for some time been having feelings of attraction toward girls and women when she began having same-sex relationships in her early teens. The daughter of an air force couple, she was born in England in 1945.[26] Jerry and her parents immigrated to Canada in 1947 and then moved to Toronto when Jerry was fourteen. Her father was an alcoholic who was not involved with the childrearing but had a clear preference for Jerry's younger sister. She recalled the problems with her father beginning at least as early as when she was nine, when she got into "a fist fight" with him because she wanted to live with her aunt. She stayed with friends of the family from age nine to fourteen. Jerry had known since Grade 3 or 4 that she was not attracted to men: "I knew years before because when I was going to public school, I had this uncontrollable urge with a woman." She developed a crush on a girl in her church group, to the point that she was extremely upset when that girl was not the one chosen for Jerry to kiss in a play put on by the group. Jerry later developed crushes on other female friends and was caught holding hands with one of them in a cinema. It was when Jerry made the mistake of confessing her feelings for a female friend of the family who lived next door that her sexuality became known to her family. She reported: "My father said to me, 'You're going to see the padre.' And I said, 'Why?' And he said, 'You're just going to see him.' And then when I got in front of him [the padre], he turned around. He said to me, 'Do you know what a lesbian is?' I said, 'No.'"

Jerry had been aware enough of her emerging sexuality to have pornographic magazines under her mattress when she was growing up. She had obtained two magazines from another girl when she was thirteen or fourteen, and she remembered that they were very explicit for the period. They were not entirely lesbian in content but were "enough to pique my interest. Enough to let me know exactly what I wanted. Enough to let me know exactly what I was because I had no interest in men in any way, shape or form." Jerry's awareness of her lesbianism was enough to propel her toward some of the lesbian hangouts on Yonge Street after she and her family moved to Toronto, and shortly after meeting other lesbians she left home and joined the lesbian community at the age of fifteen.

Betty did not come out as a lesbian until 1994 but can identify attractions she had toward women from a very young age. Many of the girls, including Betty, had crushes on the nuns, "and the nuns responded." Betty thinks that in some cases the affection would be a mother-daughter relationship, but in others it was sexual or romantic. There were also relationships between girls at the school. In one case, there was a duel between two girls over a prefect on whom both had crushes. Both girls were members of the fencing club, and one challenged the other to a fencing duel in the gymnasium. No masks or protective clothing were allowed in the duel. The challenger turned up not with a fencing foil but with a rapier she had taken from the fencing sister's study. The other girl was run through the shoulder and back and bled profusely. The other girls, who did not fully comprehend the seriousness of the event, saw it as "high drama" and were ecstatic. The challenger was expelled from the school. It was very common for the younger girls to have crushes on the seniors. Betty believes that most seniors did not succumb to the adoration, but she remarked that "what happened between the older girls might be another story." She remembered that the sisters cautioned the older teenagers against romantic friendships. Relationships were reported immediately to the mother superior. One senior fell in love with one of the nuns, and in that case the feeling was reciprocated. "The sister left the order," Betty said, "and they left it together."

Betty, although she had several crushes, was unable to recognize the nature of her feelings toward other girls and women. She had a "violent" crush on one of her close friends. Because so many of the girls had crushes, she did not know that her feelings were in any way unusual or that "it wasn't normal." Left alone one day, they kissed, put an arm around each other, and held hands. It went no further, however, and Betty did not explore those feelings again. Betty is sure that she never even knew what a lesbian was until very recently.[27]

Bergit reported that she was not told anything about relationships between people of the same sex, but "most thought it to be unforgiving."[28] Bergit had known that she was different but was not aware of the nature of her difference until she became attracted to a teacher. She had, however, always liked girls more than boys but had played with boys rather than engaging in traditionally female pursuits.

Veronica was not told anything about homosexuality when she was growing up. It was not until she was an adult, and the topic of homosexuality was discussed more openly, that she heard of gay men and lesbians. Despite the lack of information, however, she was able to identify that her English teacher, on whom she had a crush, was in a relationship with another woman:

> All of a sudden, we were very aware that she had a woman friend and we were so intrigued that we used to follow them around. Marilyn [Veronica's partner] lived not too far from where this English teacher lived and we'd drive by. I'd be staying over at her place or something, and in the morning we'd drive. I guess we found that intriguing. Sure enough, there would be Miss W's car outside of the apartment building, you know. I mean, still we didn't know what it was all about.

When asked if she and Marilyn speculated about whether the two women were also making love to each other, as Veronica and Marilyn were, Veronica said, "I guess. Yeah, I guess. But I just loved this woman. She was a very special teacher too."[29]

When she was twelve or thirteen, Cheryl became close to a girl who was very physically affectionate. They used to hold hands going to and from school, and Cheryl "always thought this was the greatest thing since sliced bread." "It just made me feel so great," she remarked, "that this girl was holding my hand." In a gesture that spoke of both heterosexual and butch gender norms, Cheryl played the gentleman when they were out:

> My father used to walk on the outside, 'cause it was the thing to do, you know? My mother never got to walk on the curbside of the road when they were walking. He always walked on the outside because that's what gentlemen were supposed to do. Well ... we'd walk hand-in-hand, but I always placed myself on the outside. And I, I don't think she noticed, but I noticed. I always felt that I needed to be the protector, you know, the one that if anyone was going to get splashed by the traffic, it would be me. Who's the guy, Sir Walter Raleigh? I would have done that too.

Although Cheryl did not realize it until later, this relationship was her first crush. When they held hands, Cheryl would feel "warm inside," and she used to wonder what it would be like to kiss her friend. Her curiosity, however, was not reciprocated. Her friend acquired a boyfriend, and soon the friendship fizzled. Cheryl also remembered having a crush on her teacher in Grade 1.[30]

Sarah did not have same-sex attractions when she was young and regards this as the reason she does not consider being gay "a momentous thing." If she had been aware of it when she was growing up, she thinks, "It would have given me a permanent chip on the shoulder on the subject" because of the "hard time" she might have had in business if her sexuality had been known. When asked whether, in hindsight, she could recognize anything in her childhood or during her marriage that might have indicated that she was a lesbian, Sarah commented that she was "always a take-charge sort of person, and I have a feeling that an awful lot of lesbians are like that." It was not until the early 1960s, when Sarah was fifty, that she realized that she "was in the wrong spot." She became aware that she wanted to be "more than just a friend" to a woman she had grown close to. Sarah had always wanted to have "a close woman friend. I think that was probably telling me something which I didn't catch on to at the time."

In Sarah's opinion, it has always been relatively easy to identify lesbians. She could remember seeing women whom she thought probably were lesbians when she was quite young. "Mostly hairstyle and way of swashbuckling around," she said. She had short hair herself when she was young. Sarah remembered that during the Second World War there were people "who always wore slacks. And I wore them too, but I didn't realize why I did, let's put it that way, 'cause I thought they were comfortable." For Sarah, being lesbian was about preferring the company of women. She accounted for this by stating that her mother was a strong woman. She believes that sexual orientation is genetic, and she suggested that it was upbringing that kept many women from realizing a lesbian identity. "That aura around you, what a woman should do or be, or something like that. I was not very much in favour of doing exactly what everybody thought I should do, and I must admit my mother didn't feel I should." Sarah's mother had, however, inculcated in her the belief that if one promises to do something, then one should do it. When she married, it was her feeling that she had promised to "love, honour and obey her husband," and therefore she stayed with her husband until his death.[31]

The narrators received, for the most part, a standard indoctrination in heterosexual norms as they were growing up. In keeping with the style of the day, however, much of the training they were given took euphemistic and indirect forms. These women were given rather vague information about what to expect from life, particularly from marriage, their expected destiny. Although all were aware, at least on some level, that pregnancy outside marriage was to be avoided, the physical acts themselves that would result in such an occurrence were rarely discussed. Even the nature of the emotional relationship between the ideal heterosexual couple was hardly referred to.

Women were left to discover for themselves what was involved in heterosexual courtship and sexuality. A few had barely any heterosexual contact and certainly did not venture as far as intercourse. Others explored heterosexuality more fully and enjoyed heterosexual sex at the time, either not experiencing same-sex desires or feeling but suppressing them. Some chose sexual relationships with both women and men. A very few had sexual experiences only with girls and women. Yet most were raised with little information about sexuality, very few knew anything whatsoever of homosexuality, and only a handful had explored the pleasures of their own bodies.

What, then, drew these women along different paths, some through marriage and motherhood and only later to a lesbian subjectivity and some more quickly to lesbian and bisexual relationships and then to community socializing on the basis of their sexual orientation? It was largely the congruence of early same-sex desires with other, affirming events in these women's lives that influenced the paths they took. These were moments of affirmation in sexual exploration, in intimate and friendship relationships, and in community. In those moments, when same-sex desire was affirmed as positive, as loving, and as shared, a subjectivity based on same-sex attraction was under construction. The greater and more frequent the affirmation, the more likely these women were to form a lesbian identity early in their lives.

Heteronormative discourse was such a potent force in women's lives that same-sex desires could be explained away, ignored, and buried unless reinforced by intensely physical or deeply emotional relationships with women. Training women for heterosexuality not only involved instilling in them the attributes of femininity, the skills of matrimony, and the desire for motherhood; it also involved, for many women, the suppression or removal of desires that contradicted heteronormativity. Little wonder, then, that many who experienced same-sex desires when young lived heterosexual lives in adulthood until coming to nonheterosexual subjectivities. Same-sex desires would require affirmation in relationships that were not easily explained away if they were to develop into early lesbian subjectivities.

6

Making the Unspoken Plain

Sexual Practice

Information about sexuality was slowly being made available via books and magazines, and greater emphasis was being placed on sex education, but many of the narrators remained rather naive about the functions of the body, most particularly about the physical aspects of intimate relationships. Only a few discovered the pleasures of the body through their experimentation with masturbation, and only some had sexual relationships with boys or men before becoming intimate with girls or women. How, then, did they explore their sexuality as girls and as young women? How did they know "what to do"? Or did they know? And what same-sex desires were experienced by those narrators who did not explore their feelings physically?

This chapter examines the sexual lives of some of the narrators who explored heterosexuality before acting on their same-sex feelings, those who had very early same-sex experiences, and those who had both kinds of experience before 1965. Lois, Barb, Cheryl, and Reva have very vivid memories of the first time they made love with someone of the same sex, and they were able to recount in considerable detail the exact circumstances of the event, which person made the first move, and what the moves were. Many more were able to tell me, in very personal detail, the precise nature of their sexual practices with women before 1965. Assumptions about the prudery of earlier generations will surely be laid to rest by this detailed account of lesbian lovemaking in the years before *The Joy of Lesbian Sex* was published. I remain astonished by and grateful for their willingness to broach private topics such as vaginal penetration, oral sex, and dildos.

Several of the women spoke about the "natural" and "right" feelings they experienced in their attractions toward, and especially in their intimate sexual contact with, girls and women as well as about how ill-at-ease they felt in intimacy with boys and men. The first moments of physical realization of their same-sex desires were, for many, crucial moments in their formation of subjectivity based on same-sex attraction. It was in these moments that they became aware that there was at least one other person in the world who shared their desires. Although they were still aware, on at least some level, that their desires were not regarded as normal, the affirmation of forming an intimate relationship with another girl or woman was a crucial element in their awareness of a shared existence. That these moments are, for many of the women, very well remembered is therefore not surprising, as they form an integral part of their coming-out narratives.

Early Experiences of Heterosexuality

The majority of the women had some dating experience with boys when they were growing up. Most engaged in at least some sexual activity with boys and men, although for many it was merely the obligatory adolescent necking and petting. Thirteen out of twenty-two were married for a portion of the period under study. All the narrators were well aware when they were growing up that women were supposed to marry and have children. Many had not heard of lesbians when they were growing up, but they were aware that their own desires were different. The ideal of heterosexual matrimony was thoroughly enforced, and other options either were not discussed or were shown in a negative light.

Among the narrators who married young and did not explore same-sex desires until they were older was Sarah, who remained married until the death of her husband, feeling that the vow she had made should be kept. She described her physical relationship as indifferent, her husband not being a particularly sexual person himself. They remained "buddies," however, and sex was not a source of conflict in their relationship. Sarah's husband was not her first male lover. She had had her first physical experience in Toronto when she was nineteen. Heterosexual sex never met her expectations, and she was "not particularly impressed by the result, let's put it that way." Because alcohol was a factor in her first encounter, her memories are now hazy. Sarah is sure that if she had been completely sober, it would not have occurred, and she is grateful that she did not become pregnant. No form of contraception was used, although Sarah was aware of the existence of contraceptives because her mother had told her about them. Sarah commented that she was persuaded by her husband to sleep with him and to marry him because she liked him. "I thought, 'This is what you do,' you know." During her marriage, Sarah thought that "there must be something better than this," but she thought that the problem might be her fault. Before the early 1960s, when Sarah first considered that she might be lesbian, she had thought of herself as "not liking to be a heterosexual person, but not really knowing what else to be ... It wasn't that I objected to sex. It was just that I didn't enjoy it. Which I should have done, and I felt I should have done, but I didn't."[1] Being an avid reader, Sarah read many women's magazines – Canadian, American, and British – and was very familiar with the sorts of articles that urged women to please their husbands.

At one of the dances she attended as a young woman, Jane met her future husband. She had dated boys before, but she described them as "kid's stuff." Jane and Jim married when she was nineteen. They were both too young and immature, and the marriage did not last long. Her husband asked for a divorce within a year, and Jane accommodated his request:

> I had to go to this place ... I don't think it was a lawyer. Anyway it was someone who asked me to go to a place and see him in bed with somebody else, like he set it up so that the evidence could be used. So that was okay, and it just took a few minutes and he got the divorce.[2]

Despite Jane's agreement with the divorce, she felt embittered and became "sort of a party girl." She started drinking, attending parties, and having physical but not emotional relationships with men. "I was just, I guess, angry about what families mean and, you know, the marriage break up and that ... Nothing was what it was supposed to be. You know, Cinderella and all that. So I was really acting out of spite and anger for a few years."

Her sexual activities included intercourse without contraception. "This was long before, I didn't even know anything about precautions ... I was lucky." Jane knew that to become pregnant outside marriage was regarded as a grave sin. None of the girls she knew when she was growing up had become pregnant, but Jane knew that "it was not the thing to do." She had so little information about sex, however, that she was ignorant of the need to take precautions. Jane married for the second time in 1951. She regarded it as what she was supposed to do, and all her friends were getting married. It was during this second marriage that Jane began to explore relationships with women.

Jill went out with a number of boys as a teenager. Her friend Jenny would attempt to arrange blind dates for her:

> I would go out on them and say nothing. They never wanted to see me again after that, of course, and I was so relieved. It was my way of handling it. I could make myself extremely boring ... then I had this fellow named Bruce who seemed to be quite pushy, and he came over, and he started to want to fondle me and stuff, and I felt really ... upset over that ... So I felt there was something wrong with me here at this point. I was fourteen then. And all my friends are talking about boys and talking about how good-looking they were and everything.

Jill's friends were determined to get her to date boys. She went out with a few but never became sexual with them. Jill remembered:

> So I just sort of went along with it just to amuse them, but I didn't feel ... and then I had this fellow named Paul when I was fifteen who really cared for me, and he was a really, really good-looking guy, and all the girls were after him, and he was after me. He had a motorbike, mister cool. And so one day I just, I knew by this time, I was fifteen and I knew by this time, and I was really telling people, so I said, "I, I think I'm a lesbian." I never saw him again. I wonder why [laughs].[3]

Jill did later marry, however, and did not explore same-sex attractions while married.

Sarah, Jane, and Jill had heterosexual intercourse more because it was what was expected of them than because they were genuinely attracted to men. As a consequence, sex was not as enjoyable as it might have been if they had felt an attraction. Several of the narrators attempted heterosexual activity but found it not to their liking and did not venture as far as intercourse. Pat, for example, tried dating boys as a teenager but quickly found out that it was not her scene:

Oh yeah ... it felt funny. I had to pretend. I was fifteen, so you had to pretend like you were interested in boys. But what I would do is I had a crush on this gal [Frankie] I used to go to school with, and she had a boyfriend, and he had a friend, so we used to double date. And he used to park the car and I'd be in the back seat, and I'd think, "Oh god, I want, I want out of this." So I used to sit and watch them neck in the front seat and say that I had a stomachache or a headache or something. Anything to get out of necking with this guy. And finally, I must have really discouraged him, because he never proceeded. But no, we used to neck a lot. In those days it was called necking. Nothing serious.

She did not find it pleasant, suggesting instead that "I would much rather have been with Frankie necking." Pat, who would eventually become Mary's partner, was born in Montreal in 1932.[4]

Cheryl's attempts at dating boys were failures. She remembered one night when, "I guess this guy, we went to the movies and so, you know, we sat in the movies, and ah, so he put his arm around me and whatnot and then, by the time we got out of the movie, it was dark ... so we went somewhere and he walked me home, and he kissed me. Well, I guess I could have sang the old Peggy Lee song, 'Is That All There Is?' because, you know ... it didn't do a thing for me."[5]

Chris, who was born and raised in Quebec, did not have sexual experiences with women before 1965 but knew that she was different and knew that her responses to boys were not the same as other girls' responses. She remembered feeling that kissing and cuddling with boys "wasn't right, but I didn't know what I was feeling wasn't right ... That was all I knew ... It was uncomfortable ... I lived with it and carried on."[6]

Some of the narrators, however, experienced heterosexual sexuality as pleasurable and found their male partners attractive at the time. Reva, for example, was allowed to date boys from a young age and enjoyed doing so. Her mother, however, set some parameters on her dating. "My mother gave me dire warnings," Reva said.

She said, "Don't let the boys touch your breasts. It'll make them sag." So this was a little piece of advice ... she would always be awake waiting for me when I came through the door. She'd be right there saying, "I've been waiting for you to come home, now I can go to sleep." She worried about me.

Reva's physical affection with boys would never go far. "I was still a virgin. The person I lost my virginity with was my husband."

Reva's sexual life with her husband was satisfying: "I liked men, yep. It was never the sex that was the problem for me, it was the emotional connection ... It really had nothing to do with sex, although I prefer being sexual with women ... That was okay, it was an okay part of our marriage." Reva commented, "My mother told me that you had to please your husband. I think we all got that message, that it was men that had to be pleased. Who cared if you were pleased as long as they were pleased, you know ... it was always for him, it was never for her. We sort of didn't count all that much." She acknowledged that her husband had attempted to give her pleasure, but she thought that "just generally in the broader culture ... the understanding was that we were there to serve our guys, and that they needed it. We didn't need it, but when they needed it, we'd bloody well better be there, you know, or else."

Reva's husband, apparently, was rather predictable: "I always knew Saturday afternoon we were going to have sex because that's what he did Saturday afternoon. Came home for his break, and, you know ... that was definitely the one day in the week that we were going to." Despite this predictability, however, she regarded him as enlightened and remembered that "we had showers together, and he knew a lot about my anatomy, and he was a good lover." Nevertheless, Reva knew that the broader society held her role to be that of pleasing her man and that, if she did not, there could be consequences: "I knew that I had to please him, or he'd go find another woman. As it was, I found another woman."[7]

Bergit, who began her sexual life with a same-sex relationship discussed later in this chapter, was later to get married and have children. She reported that her sexual relationship with her husband was a satisfying one. "We were companions, we were buddies, we were lovers, we were confidants," she said.

> Many times, we would lie awake all night long and talk about nothing, and um make love, whatever. It was a very satisfying relationship I had with him. But I think that was certainly due to my mental [state] ... the way I did that was to make sure that when I walked down that aisle, because that was a very significant thing in my life, that walk down that aisle. It meant more to me than just getting married. It meant that I would be

sharing that person's feelings and his life, and if I was going to do that, then I would have to devote myself to that, not to that man particularly, but to that situation. And I think that's the reason why everything was so satisfying in my life, or in my marriage.[8]

Never during her marriage was she attracted to another woman: "And I find that extraordinary, I really do, because I am so very much a homosexual. Very much. More now, of course, that I've outed myself ... I often wonder if I were still married to [him] if I wouldn't have been attracted to women. But certainly not in those eleven years was I at all."

Many of the women were fully sexually intimate with men, not objecting to heterosexual activity but not necessarily being fully satisfied either. Even Reva and Bergit, whose sexual relationships with their husbands were perhaps the most satisfying, feel that making love with another woman is a deeper and more satisfying experience than heterosexual sex. For some of the narrators, heterosexual sex has never been something they thought of as appealing.

The norms with which these narrators were raised dictated that they should be attracted to and marry men, and many, thinking that this was what they were supposed to do, at least attempted to live the "normal" Canadian life until their developing desires proved too strong for them to continue or until circumstances had changed in their personal lives, allowing them to explore same-sex attractions. That they stayed in heterosexual marriages for lengthy periods of time should not, however, be regarded necessarily as conformity alone. Many of the narrators, after all, had rewarding relationships with their husbands, even if those relationships were not as fulfilling as later ones with women. Some, such as Jane, for whom marriage was a largely negative experience, do see such periods of heteronormativity as an obstacle they had to overcome in order to fulfil a lesbian identity, but others do not regret their relationships with men.

Early Same-Sex Relationships

The narrators' first encounters with lesbian sexuality reveal a multiplicity of experiences. Some lesbians were influenced in their early exploration of sexuality by the images they saw in films and read in books, but these were largely heterosexual images. The films to which young women went would feature heterosexual romances, and it was up to the young lesbian or bisexual woman to adopt a perverse reading of the images so as to fit them with their own desires. In some cases, the level of identification with characters was based on gender lines rather than on sexuality. Barb and Cheryl both expressed identification with the male characters in Westerns, but only in Barb's case, discussed below, can a link be seen between gender identification with "gentlemanly" behaviour and the first sexual experience.

In most cases, the narrators simply experimented with sexual practices or did "what came naturally." They either extrapolated from their knowledge of heterosexuality or, as Sheila Jeffreys would put it, "discover[ed] the interesting sensations attendant on genital friction and explore[d] the possibility of improving on the sensations."[9] In the early and mid-twentieth century, there were a sufficient number of images of heterosexual couples kissing, hugging closely, and even necking that adolescent curiosity would have led these young women to explore such behaviours, just as it did heterosexual teenagers. Once they discovered sexual pleasure, improving on the sensations took only willingness to experiment and a little time. What these women were doing was not, of course, what the rest of society regarded as "natural," but to the narrators kissing and necking led inexorably, as it often did for heterosexuals, to "petting" and then to genital contact.

The early relationships discussed below suggest that courtship was no more a factor for teenage lesbians than it was for teenage heterosexuals. They did not court in the traditional sense but rather explored physical sexuality fairly quickly. Some of the advice literature available for heterosexual teens addressed the subject of courtship, but it is difficult to determine the degree to which teens were inclined to follow formal courtship rituals rather than following their hormones and burgeoning sexuality. The stereotypical elements of courtship in the 1950s and 1960s – particularly the flowers, especially roses, romantic dinners, and outings to the cinema – were perhaps more common among slightly older people. Most teens had limited financial resources and socialized at parties and dances. Those who had the use of that symbol both of postwar prosperity and of youthful sexuality, the automobile, were able to explore physical sexuality away from the watchful eyes of parents. The cinema did provide many a teen with a place for necking.

What must be remembered is that none of these sites of heterosexual exploration and socializing were suitable for those exploring same-sex desires. There were no teen parties or dances at which the narrators could openly express their sexuality. They could not dance together in the same way that heterosexual couples could. They could not neck in the cinema without fear of being seen, and none of them had use of a car until later in life. They therefore had to make use of the few social opportunities that were available to them, such as sleepovers, babysitting, and school. It was not, therefore, possible either to court or to date in the traditional sense.

Few of the narrators could remember specific courtship rituals they employed or specific instances when someone else courted them. With their very first relationships, one gets the impression that physical desire and uncertainty undermined any tendency to "go slow," and certainly those women who had their first sexual experiences in their teens would not have been familiar enough with the courtship rituals of heterosexuality to employ them with any memorable finesse. Later in life, lesbians employed many of the same courtship rituals as heterosexuals. Some of these practices, however, required discretionary income, and courtship was not necessarily a high priority among those who could ill afford the luxuries associated with it. Nontheless, Reva argued that, in the 1950s, "the courtship was ever more important than the actual final act, and I think the lesbian novels dealt a lot with the courtship, you know, with getting there ... Courtship was a very major part. I think we've lost, actually, some of that, in our quicker paced, let's-get-to-it modern world. I think we've lost that courtship thing a little bit. But I think the courtship was as important as the act." I reminded Reva of the compressed nature of the fictional story in the film *Forbidden Love*,[10] in which a young lesbian from the country arrives in town and goes to the bar, an older woman comes on to her, and later that evening they are in bed together. I asked Reva whether she thought that the story was very fictional or whether she had seen things happening that quickly. She acknowledged that often women "go to the bar and they wait to the end of the evening, and they say 'my place or yours?' and go home and go to bed. I don't know. I've never done that, but I know that I've known women who've done that, and they've told me that's how they do it, that they just want to be sexual, they just wait till the evening and the bar kind of plays itself out and whoever's left."[11]

Barb's first relationship was with a fellow high school student, with whom she used to go babysitting:

> Every night that she went to babysit, she'd often ask me if I'd come and sit with her. So I did, lots of times, and then one night we were there and it happened ... I remember, um, meeting her the next morning and she was just fine about it, and I thought well, now, we're in love, so I have to carry her books to school and do all this stuff. So this went on for quite some time. I thought this was the way I should be doing ... it went on for probably, oh, we went away on weekends or she'd come to my house, or I'd go to her house, you know. That lasted a good year and a bit, I'd say.

It was Barb who initiated this relationship, following a pattern of behaviour that she might well have seen played out on the screen or between other young people. Barb remembered that it was she who made the first move:

> And the music was playing softly, and she was sitting next to ... I think it was a lamp on an end table ... and I reached over behind her and I flicked off the light, and I kept my arm around her and I just grabbed her and kissed her and kissed her and kissed her, on and on. And hugged. And that's the way we were for the whole of the evening ... and she didn't back away or pull away. I thought, oh well, she was just as into it as I was. So, that was the first. And then after that, of course, I got more intimate with her. After the first kiss ... And then we used to, back and forth, to our homes. She would come and stay a Saturday night and we'd be going to a show or something, and I'd go over to her house and stay.

Barb's recollection of their lovemaking suggests that she already knew what it was she wanted to do. Her testimony also reflects the dominant norms of heterosexual courtship:

> And then we got more intimate with touching the rest of our bodies ... It just was a natural feeling. Like, I knew how to do it, you know? I just reached, and that's why I turned off the light. Oh, I don't know why the light off, except that was supposed to be romantic. Romance. You know, the music was playing [and the light] should be dim or off, and

we should be cuddling and kissing and hugging. So that's what we did, for quite some time on the chesterfield. We just kept back and forth kissing each other and hugging and squeezing. I was touching up top and, you know, but that was the way it started. The feelings that it gave me were really, whew! Explosive, you know, inside. Yeah, really, like it was supposed to be.[12]

In 1956, at the age of fifteen, Cheryl had her first lesbian experience with a co-worker who was five years older. Against the wishes of her father, who was very strict, she stayed in town after work one night to attend a party. "Somebody had booze," she remembered. "Rum. The demon rum. And I was still a pretty tender age, and so I hadn't had any rum or anything like that before, so rum and coke." Around three o'clock in the morning, the other girls decided that they needed to get a hamburger from the all-night diner. But one of the girls, Robyn, wanted to remain behind with Cheryl. They were drinking heavily and lying on the double bed:

So, I was kind of laying back there, you know, as the world turned, and she was laying next to me. And then all of a sudden she sort of lifted herself up on one arm, and her face was just right next to mine, and she announced that she was going to kiss me. And being the smart-ass that I was, I said, "So what are you waiting for?" And she kissed me. Oh, my god, this is all right. This never happened when I kissed that boy, or that boy kissed me, you know? Shit. It didn't taste good like this, you know what I mean. Oh my god, all these things started waking up inside of me ... so we had this little sort of necking session.

At this point, Cheryl and Robyn heard the other girls come back. They quickly settled down for the night, as all had work the next morning. The girl with whom Cheryl was supposed to have shared the double bed offered her place instead to Robyn, who was pretending to fall asleep beside Cheryl:

So, there we were. Then Robyn was all over me. She was kissing me, and oh my god, I just, I didn't know what to think. And I mean, I wanted her to do this, but I didn't want three other people in the room with us. So I was sure that they could hear us because my heart was pounding so much that I'm sure they could have heard it across the room, and everywhere else was pounding. You know, throb, throb. I was sure they, oh my god what a position to be in! Oh, jeez, finally, finally, we fell asleep, and the thing is, you know, she started, at one point she started running her hands all over my body like an octopus. Well, we were wearing pyjamas. And she put her hand up underneath my pyjama top and started playing with my breasts and, oh![13]

Eventually, Cheryl and Robyn fell asleep. The next morning, all five girls decided to go out for breakfast. Cheryl said,

And I got up and went to the washroom, and all of a sudden there was a tap, tap. It was one of these single little washrooms, you know, and tap, tap, tap on the door. I mean, it was nothing for two girls to go off to the washroom together, you know, one sort of sitting on the toilet and the other one's sitting on the sink, and yakking to one another, and one's putting her lipstick on or whatever. So tap, tap, tap, so I open the door, and here it was Robyn. She comes in and pulls the door closed and she said, "Do you remember what we did last night?" So all of a sudden, I got all aggressive, well not aggressive, but, "Well of course I remember." So I took her in my arms and kissed her. I said, "This is what we did." So ... we started to see one another, just like we were dating like a boy and a girl were dating.

Despite Cheryl's early attraction toward more masculine role models, she was not the initiator in this first sexual relationship. Robyn's age and greater experience in this instance were more forceful than Cheryl's desire to look after women and take charge of situations, and she was initially passive, although quickly responsive to Robyn's advances. They soon realized that they could not maintain a lesbian relationship in secret in small-town Nova Scotia, so they moved to Ontario when Cheryl was sixteen or seventeen years of age.

Bergit's story is unusual in that she had her first lesbian experience with a somewhat older woman friend when she was sixteen. Bergit already knew that she was "different." When she visited a friend some evenings,

Monica would be there. We would be playing games and things, and Monica was, I guess the term now would be coming on to me, although she did it very discreetly, and very politely. But I became very attracted to her. She was a very, very attractive lady. And this all felt very wonderful, but it, she did it discreetly so nobody really knew. None of my closest friends even knew. Nobody, even to this day nobody ever knew about it.

One night, when Bergit was staying in town with her brother, she and Monica began their relationship:

I walked her home and she said, "Would you like to come in?" And I said, "Okay," so I went in, and by this time I was anxious to be alone with her, but I didn't know why. I mean, I didn't know that this was going to be a sexual thing, I just thought this was going to be a real close, very close, friendship ... Anyway, we got up to the room, and I, she was reading poetry or doing something or other, I don't know what it was, but I was laying on the bed and I fell asleep. And the next thing I knew, I was in bed and she was kissing me and fondling me, and it just felt so wonderful. So the first thing we knew, we were into a full-blown relationship, which lasted, um, I think I was about twenty-one when she suddenly sent me out an invitation to her wedding, [and] I didn't even know she was going to get married.

From the beginning, theirs was a very satisfying sexual relationship. It was "perfect, just perfect. It was like as if it was made for us, and that's why it always felt so good ... we did fit well together. We complemented each other." Because no one suspected the nature of their relationship, Bergit and Monica were able to spend most weekends together.[14]

Pam was also first attracted to a woman when she was in her teens. A family member's son had had to go to the Korean War, and "his mother asked me to sort of entertain [his wife], pay some attention to his wife. She was about seven years older than me. So I paid a great deal of attention to her since she was quite gorgeous, and we had some wonderful moments that I thought, 'Oh, this is not right, and this is not happening' ... I think that's when I knew something was a little strange with me." The relationship involved kissing and some touching but nothing further. The woman left for Toronto but wrote several times to Pam, urging her to follow. Upon arrival in Toronto, however, Pam discovered that the woman was no longer interested in a romantic relationship. Pam was not to have another relationship until 1955, when she was nineteen:

> I went to meet a friend at a bowling alley and, ah, then went out for a beer afterwards. Saw a young woman who was at that time – [they] were almost unheard of – manager of [a utility company], and pretty sharp gal, that obviously wanted to drive me home. Did, asked me if I wanted to go out for dinner another evening. I said, "Yes," and that was the beginning of a thirteen-year relationship.[15]

Lois, whose story is told in the film *Forbidden Love,* said that she has never made the first move with a woman:

> I'm so, I would never make the first move. I told you, I never have. I've always been damn sure that anytime I did anything the woman wanted it. I don't know what that is, the reason for that I can't tell you. But we hugged each other, and I really wanted to kiss her [her first lover] but you know I couldn't, I'm just not the type.[16]

Her first partner was another teacher, also named Lois. "That was after I finished ... college," she said, "and I was, I was going to school. I was teaching high school ... Ah, we just looked at each other and that was that. Love at first sight, I guess." They became attracted to each other, but nothing happened initially. The other Lois left:

> She was going to this other teacher's up the island [Vancouver Island]. So from Cultus Lake when I got there, I wrote a letter and in the letter I said, "Why didn't you kiss me?" you know. A few days later I got a wire: "Arriving in Chilliwack, such and such a time. Meet me." Well, okay, I met her, well you can just imagine. We spent a few days at Cultus Lake. I tell you I can remember just about every detail. But we still didn't make love, I guess is the way you want to put it. Because we didn't know what to do. Oh, am I supposed to tell you all these details? Well, I guess we did and I guess we didn't.

The two women "necked madly" for four days but did not go further. When her partner left, Lois went with her on the train as far as Jasper. They shared a berth.

> So she made love to me. It was marvellous. And then I said, "Want me to do that to you?" So she started to cry. She said, "Oh boy, were you ever inhibited." All of a sudden I felt better. That's what I am. I'm a lesbian!

Deborah's first relationship was with a fellow schoolmate in her boarding school. They shared a dormitory with several other girls and made love at night when supposedly everyone was asleep. I suggested to her that they must have been reasonably quiet. "I don't know," she said, and expanded,

> God help us ... God Almighty, I'm sure everybody was aware of it. I didn't even think it was worthwhile thinking about it. I mean, this is what I wanted to do, right, I'm doing this. I didn't even think if you don't like this ... Egotistical to the extreme, I suppose. Um, it just seemed to me an ordinary thing to do, so I'm doing this.[17]

Deborah believes that the school knew of the relationship and that she paid the consequences when she was not appointed to be the head girl:

> I should have been one of those people, you know, in those girls' school stories that was head girl of the school and all that sort of stuff because I was in ninety thousand sports teams and all that sort of stuff, and I fully expected to be, and ... I got to be vice head of the school, and I'm damned sure that this was because this was a known thing, but they couldn't prove anything.

If the school had been able to prove the relationship, she might have been expelled.

Deborah's next relationship was with a woman who went travelling with her. She remembered that she

> went to England and met up with three women to travel to Europe with, one of which was Canadian, and it was one of those instantaneous, you know, across a crowded room things. It was just fantastic. And the four

of us travelled together for six, eight months in Europe ... but it was still constant pretence. She was seven years older than I was and it was a physical relationship, but it was constantly kept hidden from the other two. She went back to Canada, and some months afterwards I followed.

In 1959 they were in Canada together and the relationship continued, but it was not an equal and honest one. Deborah stated, "We were very, very much in love, but she would continue to go out with men, because that was what, the thing you had to do. I was only, I had turned twenty-one in Europe, she was twenty-seven. I believed she was right, and I attempted to do the same thing." The pressure of heteronormativity caused Deborah to have several relationships with men before she eventually came out as a lesbian.

Reva became attracted toward women in her twenties. Reva's "discovery" of her lesbianism has been made famous by the film *Forbidden Love*.[18] Reva was living with her husband, and her partner lived with her parents. They met at night school in 1958 or thereabout. The story of the two women becoming lovers is well known. Reva reminded me of the events she described in *Forbidden Love*. Her future partner was an avid reader of lesbian pulp novels and had started giving them to Reva to read. She also told her that she thought she was "like that." Reva began to read more and more of the pulp novels. Eventually, Reva began to think that she might be "like that" herself. They quickly formed a relationship after Reva had separated from her husband. Reva was careful not to begin the relationship until after the separation.[19]

Reva and Lois were the only women among the narrators to have read lesbian pulp novels during the period under study, and none of the narrators could remember having read anything specific about lesbians in such publications as *Chatelaine* and *Maclean's*. Although the novels clearly helped Reva to formulate a sense of who she was, the same source material was not available to others in this group. They had, instead, to adopt or adapt heterosexual norms to fit their own experiences. For many, heterosexual experimentation at least provided some experience with dating and necking. There were some narrators, however, who neither had succumbed to heterosexual peer pressure nor were bisexual and who had no experience of opposite-sex relationships before they embarked on same-sex ones.

Phyl remembers that she did not have a boyfriend when she was growing up, nor did she have any interest in boys. She was seven or eight when she first experienced an attraction to another girl. She would get crushes on girls at school and would be disappointed when they would not respond to her invitations. "I can remember [doing] that right up into high school until I was about twelve," she said, "and then I smartened up. I still thought about them, and I still was attracted to them, but I can't [say] any of these people were ever gay. I'm sure they weren't, but [that], however, didn't stop me looking. It still doesn't stop me looking ... And I hung around with girlfriends at school."[20] She was too shy as a child to attempt anything physical with anyone.

Phyl did not have a romantic relationship of any kind before immigrating to Canada in 1959. She settled in Toronto and found a job at a local factory, where she was to meet her future partner. I asked her whether the women in the factory talked about sex. She replied, "They did, but certainly not my side of sex at all." Despite the fact that she had heard her mother and aunt talking about sex, the frank discussion of sex was new to her: "I had never heard, sex was not discussed when I was growing up, in my family anyway. It really wasn't. It probably wouldn't be now, really." Phyl met her future partner on her first day of work at the factory. She was nineteen. "I was kind of scared to work there," she said,

> because I was so shy and I'm not good at meeting new people normally. I looked up and I remember seeing this woman down there, and she had what they called a smock on, like, you know, an overall ... a green one, and most people wore blue. She had a green one on. I remember seeing her there and I don't know what I thought about her, but I wondered what she was doing there. Why would she be here, in this factory? Why would she be here? Doesn't look like she belonged there at all.

There was "just something about her" that made the woman stand out to Phyl:

> She didn't seem to be the type that should be in a factory there, which is kind of strange because she's always worked in a factory, but she didn't seem the type of person that should be there, she should be something

higher. Higher than that. Yes, she attracted me from the instant I saw her. And she was nine years older than me. She wasn't married.

Phyl, in a self-deprecating manner, said that she did not know why the woman was attracted to her, and she put it down to her English background. The woman's stepfather was English, and she liked English people generally.

Phyl knew immediately that they would be more than friends. "Looking back on it now, it was so great that somebody else felt the same way as I did," she remarked, "but at the time I just assumed that that was the way, and yet that had never happened to me before. But I just, it was just, yeah. That was just it. This is going to be." It was only a few weeks before the two women formed a relationship, and within two months it had become physical. It is apparent that, despite not having had prior same-sex experiences, Phyl had enough awareness of her desires and enough of a burgeoning lesbian subjectivity that she was able to recognize the mutual attraction immediately. Her testimony here also illustrates the feeling of affirmation attendant upon a first same-sex relationship.

Maureen began her sexual life with a school friend in Alberta in 1948. "When I was ten," she said,

> [my] friend Katie, I somehow persuaded her that, you know, a bit of experimentation and cuddling – I guess I was so desperate for touch of any kind. So I'm not sure if this would have happened had I not been so desperate for touch. But I remember some cuddling and then, you know, the sleepover at those years. But I guess she did go home and tell her mother something about that, and that's when it was forbidden that I even speak to Katie, let alone ever have her over or even be a friend. So Katie was out of my life.[21]

When Katie's mother was told what had happened, she contacted Maureen directly. "It might have been because it was so hard to reach either one of my parents," Maureen surmised, "or because, I don't think they'd even met my parents. They just knew that this wasn't a usual family. So I had a call from Katie's mother, not with any explanation, just saying, 'For good reason, I don't wish you to speak with Katie again and she most certainly cannot stay at your house, and I'd prefer you ignore her at school also.'" Maureen's family moved two months later because of her father's employment, and she did not see Katie again.

With Maureen's new friend Margaret, who lived across the street in their new town, there was some sexual experimentation, "but always under the guise of – because she's totally heterosexual – 'now what would this feel like?' and 'what do you think it will be like when ...?'" Margaret's family would rent a summer cottage at a nearby lake and would invite Maureen to stay with them. "I know her family felt sorry for me," Maureen said, "and strongly disapproved that there was rarely an adult, let alone a mother, in my home, and that I was there alone nine tenths of the time if I weren't at school, and so they would invite me to come along. Well, the way the summer cottage was set up, I shared a bed and a room with Margaret for a week, and that went on several summers in my teens."

Sexual activity occurred, on and off, throughout her early teen years: "She permitted a bit of it, and once, when we were in our forties, talked about it a bit. She said, 'You know, if you weren't such a strong personality, I never would have let that happen, but at the time it seemed sort of okay.'" By the time Maureen reached her midteens, she was working in the summers and would no longer accompany Margaret to the lake. Margaret also met and began dating her future husband at this time, and her relationship with Maureen became nonsexual.

Mary was raised in Britain and immigrated to Canada in 1951. Mary was born as an illegal immigrant in the United States, but her parents moved to England shortly thereafter. Her father, an ironmonger, and her mother were both English. Mary's mother died when she was young, and her father eventually had to put the children in an orphanage, as he was unable to care for them. After leaving the orphanage, Mary worked in the local mill. She then trained as a nurse. It was during her training that she had her first sexual experience with a woman. "When I think of the things we did then," she said, "I could cringe ... We would sit in the nurses' living room when off duty and have our arms around each other. Never crossed our minds that we were doing anything 'wrong.' Some nurse would be playing the piano, and we'd be singing and looking in each other's eyes, never thinking that we were being indiscreet, it seemed so natural." Their relationship was sufficiently open that the nurses knew that Mary would be in Doris's bedroom when she was off duty. Doris was Canadian and returned to Canada with her family. Mary decided to follow her, against the advice of the matron of the hospital. Mary remembered, "I realize now that she was trying to warn me not to give up my career, and [she] said such things as, 'You know, you see too much of her,'" but Mary told her she was going to Canada.

The relationship with Doris lasted eight years, six of which were happy ones. Things started to unravel after their vacation in Provincetown in 1956, when they discovered other lesbians. Doris went a little wild and had a one-night-stand while in Provincetown, and Mary went home with a butch who taught her "things I couldn't imagine," although she wouldn't let Mary touch her in any way. "I still can't believe I did that, as I was so shy in those days," Mary said.[22]

By the 1950s, Provincetown was well established as a gay resort town, and many Canadian lesbians vacationed there. Karen Krahulik reveals that during the 1940s and 1950s, the arts underwent a renaissance in Provincetown when artists, actors, and entertainers took up residence, and a popular gay world grew and attracted gay men and lesbians from other parts of America and from Canada. In the postwar decades, "white gay men and lesbians, backed by Portuguese and Yankee residents of all sexual orientations, queered Land's End. They did so by creating a thriving gay world there that celebrated rather than demonized gender and sexual alternatives during a time when gay celebrations were prosecutable offenses."[23] Through tourist reports and media stories, Provincetown's reputation for gender-bending behaviour spread quickly.

Mary and Doris, like many lesbians, had no knowledge of lesbianism from family, school, or media, and their trip to Provincetown revealed to them the existence of a large lesbian community. They had not known about Provincetown before the trip, and they were both surprised and delighted. It was after this trip that they sought out lesbian community in Toronto, where they lived. The affirmation of community was an important step in Mary's knowledge of her sexuality because now it was something that she knew she shared with others. They had also met some other Toronto lesbians while in Provincetown and continued to see them socially upon their return.

In 1962 Jill met Laura, her first serious love, in art class at school, when they were both fourteen:

So we became really close friends. We bonded very strongly. Um, at the time she was, she did have another friend and the friendship was wavering a little ... because I came in on the scene – this other friend's name was Diane – um, Diane was holding a pyjama party, and I had heard that Diane was a lesbian, and I got quite excited over that, and then I got quite excited at the thought of a pyjama party ... It turned out to be just the three of us, and there was Diane on one side of me, and me in the middle, and Laura on the other side of me, and during this pyjama party Diane bends over and starts to kiss me. And I was quite enjoying this, when all of a sudden Laura jumps up, quite upset, um, yelling how disgusting this all was etc. etc. But, you know, the funny thing is, about that – I've reflected back on this – um, she never had anything to do with Diane after that again, but she stayed my closest friend. And I think that what she thought was most disgusting was the fact that it was Diane that I was kissing.[24]

School gossip had held that Diane was a lesbian, "and I believed it, too. And now I found out it was true ... For me that was very exciting because I already knew about myself. I just didn't know how to, um, get any contact, so any time I heard that anyone was, I was thinking, hoping, 'Oh. There's got to be a way to make contact here.'" Jill had known about herself since she was twelve: "Yeah, there was a girl, I stayed overnight at her house, and I don't even remember her name, but I remember suggesting that we imitate certain body movements and things, and she lay on top of me and I thought, 'This is wonderful.' And I can remember all these emotions and feelings." Her response to the girl was physical as well as emotional, and she did get aroused. "And that's amazing," she remarked, "when I think, at twelve, twelve going on thirteen. That's just at that age where those things are becoming alive, and yeah, I did feel quite excited. It's incredible."

Her relationship with Laura was a deep one. "This was like, this was a crush," she said. "It was a sudden thing, and it hit me and it was, and then, you know, when summer came, you know, I didn't think of her any more ... But, um, yeah, she called me her 'special.' She was frightened. Her mother was a lesbian. She caught her mother kissing another woman once, and she was pretty upset about that." Laura was in her midteens at the time, and it "wasn't okay for her, it was too shocking." The relationship between Jill and Laura did not become physical. Jill commented,

No, I, I slept with her every weekend and she wanted me to live with her, and my mother stopped that. And that was actually going to be the end result, I'm sure, but my mother didn't like Laura. And I'm sure she must have thought that Laura was my lover. Um, but one day, ah, I was so passionate, and I just, I just asked her, "Could I kiss you?" There was this silence, and then she said, "Oh, go ahead then." And at that I thought, "Oh no. That's not what I wanted to do. Not like that." So I said no, I wouldn't, and we just carried on as normal. And then she gave me this old book, and she wrote in there about being her special friend. And I'm sure that, given time, because she begged me to live with her, um, when I went to England she begged me to come back, um, so we could be together. So had I not have gone, I really truly believe that it would have become something. I needed to give her time. I was ready, but she wasn't.

The desire to kiss Laura was very much a physical one. Jill described her feeling for Laura as one of

pure passion. Yeah. I loved her. I was in love with her. Pure passion. I had to get closer. Just lying beside her was agony. Total agony, I couldn't touch her. Oh, it was horrible. It was the agony and the ecstasy. I could have been in another room and that would have been agony too. But I was right there beside her, and I couldn't touch her, and I just, I don't know what came over me. I just thought, "Oh my god, oh." I don't think I'm usually that bold. Yeah, so, I don't know what would have happened, you know, if I had gone and kissed her. I don't know. Thinking about it now, she might have been extremely responsive to me. She didn't say, "No, that's disgusting." So, I don't know, maybe I lost my chance there. I don't know. I certainly wasn't a threat to her in any way. And she was beautiful, I thought.

These testimonies illustrate the intensity of first same-sex experiences, their consequent importance in the formation of a lesbian identity, and the considerable risk involved in making sexual overtures to someone of the same sex in the period under study. In most cases, either the narrator herself or the girl or woman who would become her partner, at least temporarily, risked not only personal rejection but also exposure as a lesbian when she expressed her attraction physically. Schoolgirl crushes were one thing in the eyes of the public; physical relationships were quite another.

Barb, Mary, Pat, Cheryl, Jill, Deborah, Bergit, and Maureen all moved quickly to sexual activity, many of those relationships including genital sexuality within a matter of days or weeks. It is, of course, difficult to compare them with heterosexual relationships in that we do not have a sense of the average amount of time heterosexual teenagers and young adults spent "necking," then "petting," and then moving to intercourse. Arguably, it took most young heterosexual couples before the late 1960s longer to get to genital contact than a matter of days or weeks. One must consider, however, that the narrators' reporting of early sexual activity in relationships may be an example of reconstruction of the past. We cannot be absolutely sure that the timeframes involved were as compressed as the narrators portray them.

That same-sex relationships between women in this period might have become sexual earlier than most heterosexual ones or that they were explicitly sexual from the beginning may be due to several factors. The most obvious of these is that the threat of pregnancy, which doubtless acted as somewhat of a prophylaxis in heterosexual courtship, did not exist in relationships between women. Women could therefore be sexual with one another without fear of that particular consequence and the social condemnation it always incurred. Also important, however, is that lesbian sexuality was even less discussed in Canadian society than was heterosexual sexuality. Although all of the women discussed here knew on some level that same-sex relationships were disapproved of, it might be said that they lacked the specific social training against sexual activity between women that they had received, to varying degrees, about heterosexual activity before marriage. On a deeper, subconscious level, it might even be the case that some women, already aware that their desires placed them outside the boundaries of sexual normalcy, chose to ignore the rules of acceptable sexual engagement altogether. They already were outside the bounds of respectability – why not in this respect also?

Bisexuality

Many of the narrators for this study had sexual relationships with men before adopting a lesbian identity, and for some it was an enjoyable part of their sexual history. Even those who found heterosexual sex enjoyable, however, do not now define themselves as being bisexual in terms of identity. Rather, most see their opposite-sex relationships as having occurred because heterosexuality was what was expected of women.

During the Second World War, Mildred dated frequently in college. She had sex with several men but did not fully enjoy it. "I don't think I ever had an orgasm," she said. "I didn't enjoy it, no. These few that I chose to, in Los Angeles, but you know, I've often wondered since, did I ever have an orgasm, and I doubt it. I doubt it. I mean, I enjoyed it, in a way, you know, but I didn't have what most people think of as, you know, some great big orgasm."[25] When asked who had been the first woman she slept with, Mildred said, "The one in college who was my roommate, she was the first one. We shared a room, twin beds, at the sorority house. One time she introduced me to lesbian sex ... We were both in our senior years, so I was about twenty-one. So was she." It was the other woman who set the scene for the seduction:

> I came home, I'd been out with this guy I'd been going with a lot, and having not heavy sex but sort of light sex with him. I really liked that guy, Jack, but he, I don't think we ever had intercourse. I don't think so ... But I came home one night and I don't know why, but that night, for some reason, she was set to go and got me into her side, her twin bed, and, ah, initiated me into it. I don't know, I don't know why she all of a sudden decided to do that, but I guess she'd been working up to it for a while or something. But I was quite willing. I was quite willing.

Even though her sexual activity with men was not fully pleasurable, Mildred suggested that she was more bisexual than lesbian in the 1940s. She continued to have relationships with men for some years. Unlike many of the narrators interviewed for this study, Mildred did not feel repulsed by men. In fact, there were several to whom she was very attracted. Moreover, that she did not have orgasms with men should not be taken necessarily as meaning that she was not really attracted to them. Mildred did not have orgasms with all women either. More important, however, Mildred's lack of experience of orgasm with men or women cannot be said to bear any relation to any sexual orientation. After all, if sexual orientation rested on the achievement of orgasm in sexual relationships, many people would hardly be in a position to claim any sexual orientation at all.

It was women to whom Mildred was primarily attracted and with whom she experienced the greater sexual satisfaction. Mildred fell in love,

> really in love, with someone when I was a freshman in college who was a singer ... and I wanted to go to bed with her. In fact, it's one of the sharp memories that I have. And we slept in the same bed together at her family's house, nobody else was there, I don't think. But, I remember ... shaking, I was so, um, intense about this, but she wasn't interested at that time and I didn't have the nerve to even try anything, you know, so we didn't have sex. But I remember the physical, um, emotion that I had over that woman. It was only after I went to Los Angeles and she came out there to Hollywood that we actually had sex together and not very, about twice in all, because she wasn't really as much interested in me as I was in her, you know. But, um, so it wasn't until much later that I actually had sex with her.

Mildred did not form a long-term relationship with a female partner until she met "Ed," with whom she lived for six years, in the 1950s.

Although many of the women interviewed for this study had desires for both sexes before 1965 and had relationships with both, Mildred was the only narrator to suggest that she was bisexual at this point in her life. Several factors may account for this. A major reason, and one that has posed problems for lesbian historians in the past, is the community hostility toward bisexual women, which resulted in many bisexual women either leaving the community or subsuming bisexual desires under a lesbian-identity label. It is always much more difficult to locate bisexual narrators than lesbian ones, as Elizabeth Lapovsky Kennedy and Madeline Davis found in the research that resulted in *Boots of Leather, Slippers of Gold.*[26]

It is also the case that, in the period under study, bisexuality was not a category used in public discourse or medical terminology. The dichotomization of heterosexuality and homosexuality most often resulted in bisexual behaviour being interpreted as incipient homosexuality. Although some might have been prepared to see sexuality as a continuum, few in North America were willing to see same-sex relationships as meaning anything other than that the individual was really homosexual. It is likely, therefore, that many women who experienced bisexual desires and had bisexual sexual experiences ended up having to "choose" between hetero-sexuality and lesbianism, having no bisexual identity category, community, or subcultural norms to hold on to. Many bisexual women probably left the lesbian community to marry, ignoring their same-sex desires, and many may have ignored their opposite-sex desires in order to remain in the lesbian community.

Also important is the structure of the coming-out narrative itself, which necessarily must discount earlier opposite-sex experience as of lesser importance, if not as representative of conformity to heteronormativity. The focus in the coming-out narrative is the end product: the lesbian identity. Behaviour that problematizes a clear identity category must be explained away or excised so as to maintain the integrity of the presently held identity. In such circumstances, few lesbians are prepared to describe themselves as previously having been bisexual or heterosexual, preferring instead to portray heterosexual behaviour as a step they had to go through before they were strong enough to live openly as lesbians.

Sexual Practices in Relationships between Women

In evaluating precisely what sexual practices were known to the narrators, what pleasures they discovered and when, and what behaviours were acceptable and unacceptable to them, one can learn much about the amount of information with which they entered sexual relationships, the degree to which it was possible to experience and explore sexual desires in the absence of knowledge about sexuality, and the similarities and differences between Canadian lesbians' practices and those of their American counterparts. The overwhelming majority of these women had little or no information regarding the mechanics of sexual expression, the nature of their bodies, and the ways different parts of the body could be used sexually, yet they managed, largely through experimentation, to discover a wide range of sexual practices. Most moved very quickly from kissing to fondling to genital activity. Once reached, genital sexuality most often involved clitoral stimulation and vaginal penetration. For many women it also involved oral sex and for a few the use of dildos. And all this in an era of complete silence about the latter two practices especially. Lillian Faderman is right to suggest that many nineteenth-century women must have internalized the passionlessness they were said to represent,[27] but these twentieth-century narrators were not necessarily that much more knowledgeable about sexuality than were their forebears. Although perhaps more aware than nineteenth-century women that they actually *had* desires, they had little idea what to do with them until they tried.

The narrators were able to discover and enjoy a wide range of sexual practices simply by experimentation, even though some of their sexual practices – manual vaginal penetration, oral sex, and the use of dildos – were not discussed in available literature, which suggests that they located sensitive and pleasurable areas of the body and explored various ways of stimulating them to the best of their imaginations and aided by the physical responses of the body. That they did so should caution us to be careful about assuming the absence of any sexual practice simply because it was not spoken of in public discourse. To be sure, greater knowledge did often mean greater expertise and flexibility in sexual practice, which some of the testimonies below illustrate well. But even those who were most ignorant about their bodies were able to find pleasure, including genital pleasure. In recognizing their achievement of pleasure in an era of ignorance, we must also question our previous assumptions about the allegedly nonsexual women of earlier centuries, for surely, however limited their knowledge, they also had responsive bodies on occasion and inquisitive minds, given the opportunity. Opportunities for sexual activity varied by age and class. Very young women lived at home, for the most part, and their behaviour was restricted as a result. They made use of parental absences and ignorance, stole away as often as they could, and used the traditional sleepover in a decidedly nontraditional way. Many of the women in this study had their first sexual experiences with school friends.

Arlene discovered boys at age eight, and at age nine, in 1955, she discovered girls. She spoke to her mother about it: "At one point, about fourteen, I asked my mother if there was something wrong with me, that I didn't like boys. She told me not to worry, it was just a stage, it would go away." The girls were her own age, and most were her classmates. They experimented with the sexuality they saw in films. "There was not really that much to it," she said. "We'd go to the show, and what we saw in the movies, we'd go home and practise. That's what we were doing." They did not discuss what they were doing: "No, either one of us, whichever home we were in – we'd phone our mothers and tell them we were staying overnight, and we'd have supper and we'd go to bed and we'd practise ... We really didn't have any clue."[28] She did not appear to count this early experimentation as sex, however, suggesting that the first time she had sex with a woman was when she ran away from the psychiatric hospital at 999 Queen Street West in Toronto, where she was institutionalized when she was sixteen.

Because of masturbation, Maureen had some idea of physical pleasure from a young age: "I was very aware of how my body worked, and I knew how I craved touch – any kind of touch. But, I know with Katie it was just, 'oh, let's just slip out of our pyjamas ...' You know, just the cuddling, and at that point neither one of us even had any breasts at all ... but there was some touching, and 'what would it be like to kiss a boy?'" Maureen realized even at this early age that she was using words about her body and was taking the lead. There was kissing and fondling, but "with Margaret it became more than that. I think she was interested in how her body worked and, and yet was quite repressed. She's a very mild personality even now, and wouldn't have experimented on her own, and I think was quite pleased to have somebody teach her how her body worked."[29]

Veronica's first lesbian experience was with her school friend Marilyn in the 1950s. During a sleepover at Veronica's house, they became physically intimate. She said that it was initially "just a lot of touching and carrying on and feeling a lot of, you know, very good things." The relationship continued until they both married. They were not dating as such but rather would be drawn to each other whenever they were alone. They continued their sleepovers:

> And there was her poor mother downstairs, you know, I'm sure. You know, we'd be up there ... we're sixteen years old. We were just so enraptured and so carried away, we could have carried on. And I'm sure her mother knew. And I'm sure her mother used to talk to her, Marilyn's aunt, whose daughter is [also a lesbian], she's out there. Maybe this was going on at the same time, you know, in her life, yeah. Yeah, so that was basically it, like in each other's homes. We never went anywhere and expressed anything ... You know, and it was like ... I remember one time Marilyn and I were having a wonderful time and she [Veronica's aunt] arrives, and all of a sudden there we were in the bathroom. I don't know what the hell my aunt was thinking, and you know, I don't know how long we were in there, but it was so good to see her, and it was so, it was wonderful.[30]

Veronica and Marilyn experimented with sex to find out what they liked. "We weren't using vibrators, you know, it was as much as one can do without contraptions," she said.

A high school friend introduced Jane to lesbian sexuality. She had never had desires for other girls. She recalled one night in 1939 or 1940:

> There was one friend ... she'd invite me over to her house and her mother was always out ... we'd be in her room and fooling around, and she was the one that started fooling around sexually ... And we just sort of laughed and it was fun as well as exploration ... I didn't see anything wrong with it, except I was kind of afraid of anybody knowing. But that probably went on for about a year in high school.[31]

Jane was approximately thirteen at the time. It was her friend who made the first move, asking her, "Have you ever tried this?" – to which she replied, "No." Next, "she had me start touching myself, and, ah, she was doing the same. I think there was twin beds in her room. And, ah, she wanted to touch me, and wanted me to touch her and stuff. So it was, um, quite fun, really ... and we would laugh and talk about it ... Wasn't a whole body exploration, it was just the genitals." The encounter, however, did not blossom into a long-term relationship, as Jane discovered aspects of her friend's character that she found disturbing:

> She had some guys come over ... she was all set for it. She was raring to go, she was gonna get these guys and pet and, ah, I don't know, I think it happened for a little while ... I wasn't too impressed with it. Anyway, that was sort of that, and then I guess that part of that time left when I left school, and I really didn't see her again for a long time.

It was not the bisexual nature of the activity that disturbed Jane but rather that her friend was interested in multiple partners at one time. Jane subsequently married twice and had no further same-sex relationships until she came out as a lesbian in the 1970s. "This is what you were supposed to do," she commented. "You were supposed to grow up and get married, and most of the people I knew were doing that."

When I asked Bergit how she and Monica, her first female partner, would make love to each other, Bergit commented,

Well, kissing is kissing, lips onto lips, and certainly she would suck on my ears, and believe it or not, I can't have anybody else do that to this day. I don't know why, it's just a block. I can't do it anymore. And she would, she fondled my breasts, and she caressed my entire body, including my vagina area. And as a result, I had a very satisfying climax. And I did the same to her, and she had one as well. And one of the nicest parts about Monica's and my relationship was that we both wanted to go together, and we most often did. We trained ourselves to do that, because we knew how much fondling each one of us needed to do that. Just wonderful. But yeah, there was nothing that we did to each other that would ever, most of the time I term the whole thing as a missionary attitude toward sex. There was no tools, there was no play tools or anything, it was just done with hands or whatever, lips and hands. Because even to this day I think that I can arouse somebody and they can arouse me without the tools and the play-toys, and to me it's more intense if you can do this, and when I make love, if somebody wants it, I will do it, and vice versa. So nothing is dirty or unapproachable in the lovemaking act to me. So to explain to you what I did is basically physical touching and feeling, um, conversation, words, tenderness, um, exploring. Every part of the body was a sensual area.

They experimented with various sexual practices. Bergit remarked, "Oh, sure. I don't think the experimental stuff ever ends because, you know, the body's such a large area and there's so many sensitive cells on it." Their experimentation, however, did not lead to oral sex. She was not aware of oral sex at this stage of her life. "It's only happened a very few times with me. I think that's a very special thing to do, and unless the [time] is right, unless the temperature of our bodies are right, the emotion is right, I think oral sex should be saved," she said.

Some women were able to gain sexual experience with rather less secrecy than was required if one was still living at home. Some urban, working-class lesbians were able to take advantage of the availability of "no questions asked" cheap accommodation. Joyce reported in her Lesbians Making History (LMH) interview that, in the late 1940s and early 1950s, Toronto lesbians could rent a room on Centre Island if they wanted a private place to have sex: "There were hotels there, yeah. There were two ... And at this particular time we were, I don't know, we didn't even try to hide it. We hold hands, neck in the theatre, we didn't try to hide it."[32] They would also neck in the cinemas in Toronto, where apparently nobody would bother them. Another LMH narrator spoke of renting rooms in Chinatown in Toronto. They would go

> to a room, usually in Chinatown, Cochrane Hotel, eh, and get it for what, six bucks a night, screw your brains out. There was a couple on Jarvis Street too ... they didn't ask questions. You paid your money and that was it. Sometimes three bucks a night, depending on where you went. A lot of us used to go to the Ford Hotel. The Ford Hotel in Chinatown.[33]

Before 1965, during her relationships with her roommate in college, with the singer, and with Ed, Mildred's sexual experience with women "was only lovemaking in bed, not even oral, it was only, you know, hand and so forth. And body contact, but I don't think I ever got into oral sex until much later, um, certainly not in the '40s or '50s. Even in the '60s, I think of that more when I got to Canada [in 1966]." She knew what to do not from any books or other sources but rather from "instinct, I think, just overwhelming attraction to somebody, you know. I didn't read about that kind of thing at that time, at all, so I was just doing what came naturally, I guess." Regarding her partners, she said, "If they had any previous experience, they would have known more than I did, and I think Ed had had at least one previous experience."[34]

I asked Phyl who had made the first move. "I'm not positive," she said. "As far as kissing, it might have been me, I don't know. The rest of it was her." Their first kiss occurred at the house of Phyl's partner, who lived with her mother and stepfather:

> After we finished playing cards, they, by this time it was like eleven, they'd be gone to bed, and we usually, we'd sit and chat for a while. Then we, it was like kids, just like teenagers, we'd be between the front door and the next door in. We would stand in there for ages, you know, talking, and giving little kisses and everything else. And then one time they must have been to bed for a while, and we started kissing, and that's when she started undoing my clothing, but to me it didn't seem anything extraordinary. I didn't even, actually, I quite believe I didn't think anything about it except it was good. But the next day, when I saw her

the next evening, she was quite horrified over this whole thing and she kept apologizing to me, she didn't know what got into her, whatever else, and I looked at her and I said to her, like, "What are you talking about?" She said she'd never done that: "I've never done that before ever in my life. I apologize." And I said to her, "Just don't apologize, and we'll just keep going." And that was it.

That first night comprised mainly kissing and fondling, neither of the women knowing very much about sexuality. Nothing about the evening shocked Phyl:

> See, nothing seemed extraordinary to me. It's like, it's not like one of these great stories where somebody all of a sudden realizes they're a gay and whatever. It's just that my person hadn't come along yet, and now here they were and nothing seemed unusual to me, you know?

Phyl described a close call that occurred only a few months after they had been together. In December 1959,

> at Christmas, we decided to go with a couple of women that we worked with, who certainly weren't gay, to Buffalo for the weekend. Just for a good weekend. And I had never been there, so this was good for me ... Well, this has been the first time I've been away like that with my girlfriend, and so, we were great on the kissing bit. Do you know, your mouth can, my lips completely swelled up. This was in an afternoon when everybody was so tired we each stayed in our rooms. These other two women shared and we two shared. And that worried me sick about that night. We were going out. We were trying to get the swelling down. That, I had forgotten about that. I can remember that and think, "Oh my god." And then my girlfriend's saying to me, "Oh you've got to do something about this," you know. And I was thinking one of these people knew. I guess that worried me. Well, it always worried me what people thought about me, not from the gay sense either ... But nothing was said, and who knows what they thought.

The physical relationship developed from the kissing and fondling. "There was no one particular thing once you got together, and it was everything," Phyl said, "because to me it just seemed all, just the way it was, and there wasn't any one particular thing. No, I just liked anything and everything. Yeah. And also, um, being that close to somebody, just saying whatever you wanted to say, regardless of what it was."[35]

Once Reva's relationship became physical, it developed quite quickly. Although in love with her partner, Reva waited until she had finished with her husband before moving to a physical relationship. After her husband moved out, Reva had the place to herself and her new partner came over regularly, "and it was steamy nights after steamy nights. And I, honest to god, that first time we made love I had never known what real passion was, ever. In spite of all the good times with men, and all the orgasms, and everything else, I had never experienced that passion that I had with her. It was like, 'Wow, where'd this come from?'"[36]

Sexual pleasure with women was different for Reva. She found that the type of connection that occurred between them was different from the connection she had with her husband:

> I think for me pleasurable became the reciprocal side of it. I think with
> men it's more they do it to you, with women we do it for each other, and
> I like that side. I think, I don't know, it's always, it always felt to me that
> there was a little bit of a power thing, like they were the man and I was
> the woman and I had my role and he had his role and we knew what
> those roles were. And with women, I don't find the roles getting in my
> way. It was more reciprocal and more sharing and you could be more
> open in ways, I could be more open in ways that I couldn't be with men,
> even physically more open.

"Right away," she said, "the first time that she and I ventured into a physical side of our relationship, I had already felt this really strong connection in other ways, so the physical thing was just the completion of the circle." She didn't feel the same with her husband: "Like I enjoyed the sex, but it was just sex, it could have been me and my vibrator, I don't know. I mean, what is sex? It's nothing in and of itself, but it was a connecting, it was the way that we touched, the way that we could talk, the way that we could caress afterwards and didn't mean we were going to go another round necessarily. It was just a pleasure all by itself."

Their physical relationship was initially exploratory. Reva commented, "We didn't have a clue. We just kind of tentatively tried this and that. Started off with kissing, we kind of learned our way. It was really slow, it was exploratory." The novels she had read were not very explicit, "so you couldn't really kind of go, 'oh, well, they did that in the book,' you know. They didn't tell you a lot beyond kissing like they did, so we kind of made it up." The novels "talked about, you know, passion, but they didn't talk about how you did this. They didn't say, 'I put my hand into her wet cunt' or, they didn't use that kind of language, it was more genteel, you know?"

Reva may have regarded the novels as genteel, but the broader Canadian society did not. In 1952 the National News Company of Ottawa was charged with eleven counts of having obscene matter in its possession for distribution. The Tereska Torres novel *Women's Barracks* was one of the items of "obscene" literature. It was argued that the novel had the capacity to deprave and corrupt susceptible individuals, particularly children. The lesbian content of the novel, although not its main focus, became the focus of the trial, the Crown attorney arguing that the picture of lesbianism presented in the novel was an inviting one, whereas the defence attorney argued that the book could serve as a cautionary tale against lesbianism.[37] Whether or not lesbians found the pulp novels useful as sex manuals, the judicial system assumed that they would provide exactly the kind of inspiration lesbians were looking for and would even inspire girls and women to become lesbians.

In Reva's opinion, "it was more the story [in the novels] than the explicit sex, and was about you know, lesbian passion and how in the end some man saves [one of the women], and the other one is crushed, or commits suicide. They always had a bad ending, or almost always." She expanded:

> They didn't really go into that much detail. They went into she undressed, her hot hands on her body kind of imagery, you know, the excitement ... but there was nothing, there was not very much to tell you how to proceed really. I don't think, in my recollection, I don't remember that I had any hot tips out of these books. They were just kind of a build-up to the fact that this woman ... allowed this other woman to actually touch her naked body, to kiss her all over, and you never exactly figured out

how they got to the climaxing parts, but you got to use your imagination,
I guess, if you could.

Reva was the only one in their relationship who had had any kind of sexual experience. Even she found it "a little bit [scary]. I thought, 'I know what to do with my husband, I haven't got a clue what to do with her.' And, I don't know, somehow, you know, making love is a natural thing. It really cleared up quickly enough. We found our way to it easily enough."

Pam's innocence about sexual matters was a hindrance to her enjoyment of early relationships. "I wouldn't let anyone even go near me," she said. "I just didn't. I, ah, I was fine, I made love, I wasn't made love to. I just couldn't ... I don't know why, until much later when I did meet with a woman that wouldn't take no for an answer, and I thought, 'Oh my, I've been doing without all this for so long. Poor old me.'"[38] She did engage in oral sex after that point but did not know what a dildo was, although she had heard them mentioned and was always too embarrassed to ask about them. She was lucky to be rescued from her embarrassment by a lover who knew much about the female body and showed her what to do. When she revealed to her lover that she did not know how to masturbate, her lover showed her:

> A girl one time had me on my knees. I was saying, "I don't know." She said, "Well, let me show you." I will never forget it. I didn't, I didn't know, I said, but you see, this was all before this gal that all of a sudden, you know, just threw me over and then said this is it. Well, oh, this feeling, I never had that. All this time, you know, it was like, I don't know, it was like rollin' around doin' nothin'. Now, you know, when I think about it, thanks for the memories, you know. Makin' things come back that I'd rather die of embarrassment.

Pam lamented her ignorance and the lack of information she had had in the early days, commenting: "But it's true, it was stupid, I mean, we didn't know, and nobody talked. There's things today that someone will say to me, 'Did you know such and such?' 'No. Did you?' 'Oh, I just found out.' So, you know, it was things that you never talked about – who did what with who, you know, it was just not said."

Deborah does not think that she and her first partner experimented sexually or that there was a learning curve. She knew what to do. She commented, "No, I don't believe so. It just seemed to me quite an automatic thing." Her early lesbian experiences were not in the least problematic. Rather, it was her later heterosexual activity that was difficult:

> Oh no, it seemed the most natural thing in the world. I had difficulty with heterosexual relationships. That literally was close your eyes and think of England, but I had to find out what this was about, and even with this married man that I had my most long-term heterosexual relationship with, um, I could think of a thousand excuses why we should not be doing this. You know, your wife is on the telephone. It was the idea of being heterosexual that I was trying to achieve. The actual physical, lesbian side of it was the most ordinary thing for me that there was.[39]

"I think I knew right from the beginning what I wanted to do," she said. "I'm sure I grew a little more adept as times went on, but it never was a difficulty." Deborah's testimony on the subject of experimentation is somewhat contradicted, however, by her acknowledgment that the girls did "try things" to see how they would feel: "I think it certainly became, does this feel good? This feels good."

Billie, who was born in Ontario in 1937, joined the air force and later became a police officer. She grew up in a family that was unusual because her mother openly had affairs. Billie was not necessarily talked to about sexuality, but she witnessed her mother with men on several occasions. She does remember that she was caught masturbating and that her mother explained to her that she should not do it, but she did not tell her why.[40] Billie went out with men for a number of years before she became intimate with a woman, but she did not have full heterosexual intercourse. Women in the air force were watched very carefully. In addition, she was afraid of pregnancy and what it would do to her reputation. She does not remember well the first time that she made love with a woman but is sure that she did not make the first move:

> The other woman did. In fact, she would probably do everything. I don't think I did anything at all, and that went on a long time during the affair.

I thought that's the way it was, and I think you do in your first experience because you're not fully aware that you're supposed to participate. This is lovely. I'll do this. I can do this. And I think it was probably years later before I made love to a woman. Got out of the air force, came back, had an affair with her again, and she showed me different things to do, and that's the first time I think I actually participated. I thought you were just supposed to lay here and enjoy this. And she was the one that actually, you know, said to me, "Here's what you do." We spent hours and hours experimenting.

The same woman introduced Billie to oral sex. "The other women had not done that," she said.

And I found that intriguing because I wanted to do that. Like, I, she was a very clean woman, and she smelled like she just stepped out of a bathtub, with baby powder on. That, a woman does that and walks by me, I'm done. You know that smell, that clean? And I found it really, really sexual. It was just a thing. Yes, I did find oral sex exciting, and I wondered why the women before that hadn't done that. You know, it was just something we didn't talk about in those days.

Prior to this experience, Billie's lovemaking was primarily manual stimulation and penetration.

Oral sex, or cunnilingus, has been thought of as the quintessential lesbian sexual practice, but of course it is very commonplace in heterosexual activity as well.[41] However, it was less common among lesbians before the 1970s than afterward, perhaps because the 1970s witnessed strong campaigns to educate women about their sexual pleasure and the health and goodness of their bodies. Oral sex was a surprise that was sprung on Reva by her lover:

I knew that penetration wasn't gonna be part of this picture because we didn't have the equipment, but we had fingers I guess, I don't know. I think that's where it all led, initially. But I think soon enough we figured out what we liked, what we didn't like, what felt good, what didn't feel good, and I remember the first time she said to me, "I want to go down on you." I thought, "What's that?" And I was like, "Wow, this is different."

Question: Now where did she ...?

Reva: Oral sex, I don't know where she got it from. I don't know if she got it out of her head or where or what.

Question: And that was the phrase that she used, "go down on you?" ["I think so," Reva interjected.] I wonder where did she get that information?

Reva: I think that's what she said. I don't remember exactly, but that's what she wanted to do, and it was a new move. I was like, "Oh, okay."

They had been in a relationship for several months before they reached this level of intimacy. "It came out of the blue," Reva said,

> Wasn't anything I read or heard about or knew about, and in fact I thought to myself, "What the hell is she doing? What's happening? What is it?" Well, I liked it, of course, but I was kind of surprised, you know, like it was unlike anything I had done, even with men, up to that point, or had heard of, or that. Okay. So I don't know where she got this, she may have read this in a book because she read many of these books. A book might have talked about it.

Oral sex, however, was not part of their regular lovemaking. They tried it only a few times.

Pat described her own upbringing as cold and inhibited, a point that was brought home to her when she began to date French Canadian women. "A couple of French women that I can think of," she said,

> I could honestly say that they probably taught me an awful lot because they weren't inhibited. I was probably quite inhibited, when I think about it, so when I was with these women, not all together but separately [laughs], they were mostly French Canadian women, now that I think about it, and they were very, very liberal and very open and sex was very important to them, and you learned not to be so uptight about it. So, yeah, I was taught probably by them. You know, I never thought about it like that, but I guess so. Because I must have been uptight, really. But French Canadian women were very open as far as sex is concerned.[42]

Pat did not specify which sexual practices the women taught her but mentioned them during a conversation about oral sex, so it might be reasonable to assume that this was one of them. After Pat returned to Montreal, she met Marg. "Now, Marg was much more experienced than I was," she said, "and I was eighteen, and I didn't know much about women at all. But she taught me. She was bisexual. Yes, she was. I learned a lot ... I guess, maybe it was Marg, maybe that taught me mostly everything I knew. Before it was all like puppy love kind of stuff, you know."

Butches, Femmes, Dildos, and the Border

That some women did know "what to do" has been made clear in several works on the working-class lesbian bar cultures of the early and mid-twentieth century. The most extensive of these, *Boots of Leather, Slippers of Gold,* is a groundbreaking work that challenges lesbian-feminist perceptions of the butch and femme women of the bar culture as uncritically imitative of heterosexuality. In terms of sexuality, it may be said that the butch-femme relationship was a complex dyad in which normative heterosexuality was sometimes copied but often subverted. Kennedy and Davis reveal that the butch-femme relationship created and expressed "a distinctive lesbian eroticism."[43] Although the butch woman was presumed to be the physically active partner, the "doer," and the leader, her role was to please the femme woman rather than to privilege her own satisfaction. Unlike normative heterosexuality in the postwar era, the butch-femme erotic emphasized the feminine partner's pleasure as primary. The butch woman found her pleasure in pleasing the femme woman. The latter was not merely receptive; the femme woman actively sought her own pleasure.

Kennedy and Davis make the point that the butch-femme sexual relationship both imitated and transformed heterosexual patterns.[44] It would be naive to suggest that the butch-femme relationship always operated in this transformative manner and that butches never adopted some of the less desirable aspects of masculinity; there were, in the relationships among women of Buffalo, New York, many instances of abuse. Kennedy and Davis do illustrate, however, that it was in the working-class, butch-femme lesbian community that women's sexual autonomy and pleasure were first promoted, decades before lesbian feminists would write about lesbian sex.

Kennedy and Davis interviewed a wide range of lesbians in Buffalo about their sexual practices in the decades before the 1970s. The most popular sexual practices were dyking, or tribadism,[45] manual stimulation, and oral sex. Only some of the women used dildos; most viewed them as unnecessary to female pleasure. One of the most significant aspects of their research is the revelation that there were a large number of "stone" butches, or "untouchables," in the Buffalo community.[46] The women Kennedy and Davis interviewed varied widely in their degree of knowledge about sex, some knowing what they wanted to do from a very young age and some requiring the assistance of lovers and friends in gaining sexual skills.

In terms of sexuality, Canadian butches and femmes operated with the same roles as did their American counterparts. In her interview for Lesbians Making History, Arlene commented, "Oh, usually, the butches did everything. You know. Femmes got to lay there and enjoy everything."[47] Contrary to the kind of butch mentoring described in *Boots of Leather, Slippers of Gold* and in the novel *Stone Butch Blues*, however, butches in Canada seemed not to be given any instruction in the proper behaviour, sexual and otherwise, of the butch.[48] "Baby butches," as they were called, had to fend for themselves. Arlene said that she knew what to do, even when she had her first sexual experience, which was with a heterosexual woman. Even the butch woman Arlene had met when she was a patient at 999 Queen Street West, her first lesbian friend, did not discuss sex with her: "As far as sex was concerned, it was find out on your own. We talked about – it was more like locker-room talk: 'Oh pick her up, she's good,' this kind of stuff. Nothing ever really, really personal. It just – it was there. It was that simple," she said. "I knew what to do. I don't know how I knew, and I've heard that from a lot of people." Femmes, too, knew what they wanted sexually. Arlene did not know whether femmes talked about sex either: "I don't know. It worked. It was just there. And I've heard this from a lot of people – I've asked the same question of a lot of people, and same thing: it was there. They knew what they wanted, and once they got in bed, they knew what to do. I know that's strange."

Butch and femme roles, however, were not always rigid. Some lesbians moved between categories. Arlene changed from the butch to the femme role when she moved in with a woman who was still living with her common-law husband. At first, the relationship was platonic. The reversal of roles for Arlene occurred when the relationship became sexual: "One thing led to another and we ended up in bed. And she just turned to me very calmly and said, 'You know, I think I can do this better than you.' And it was that simple! No big moral decision, no nothing; it was just: okay. It was just like that: bang. And we lived together like I said. So something worked." Their sexual relationship was a satisfying one, and was often "50-50":

> Not all the time. There were times when she just, "Don't touch me. Let me do it all." But there were other times when there was real, real sexual experimentation going on between the two of us. You'd think: Oh, let's try this, and it would be: Okay, but what you do to me, I do to you! We did – one time my ex-husband was then a friend, he started explaining bondage, and we thought, okay, let's try it. And it was point-blank: What you do to me, I do to you, and when you say stop you stop. Stop came very quickly. And – she started to chicken out: "Oh no, no, no, you're not going to do this." And I said, "Oh yes I am. What you do to me I do to you, in this one." And it was the same thing. You try it; you don't like it; you don't do it again. The biggest thing I found out is that, when you're living with somebody for quite a bit, that people will come up to you and say, "Aren't you getting bored?" And I'd look at them and say, "Are you crazy?" The longer you're with somebody, the more you get to know them, the better things get. And they couldn't understand it.

After she became a femme, Arlene began to be more critical of the sexual aloofness of butches. She remarked, "Well, they seemed not to want to be touched. We'll do to you, but you won't touch us. Which I thought was kind of stupid. I couldn't see how they were getting that much out of it." However, she did not talk to them about it. "That's just the way things were," she said. "There was no sense in sitting down and discussing it. It was the way they felt; that's the way things were. Even now, if you bang into a few of the older ones, they'll say, 'It took me years.' A couple of them, it would be maybe three or four years before they'd let somebody touch them. And then they'd curse themselves: 'My god, now I know what I was missing.'" When asked whether butches had orgasms, she said, "They'd claim they did. Without being touched. They could have orgasms; they just didn't want you touching them. And to me, it never made sense."

When asked whether there was a terminology in Canada to describe "stone" butches, Jan replied, "Yeah. Not *stone* butches. You'd just say, 'She's really dyke, man.' You didn't like the word 'dyke' because if you're a dyke, you used to use a dyke [a dildo], right?"[49] Arlene agreed that there were some butches who preferred to do all the lovemaking. She remarked that being butch "was a sexual thing for a lot of people. There were real sexual barriers."[50] None of the narrators for this study identified as stone butches, and there are fewer reports of stone butches in Canada than there are for the United States. Mary reported having a brief affair with one in the US: "And some butches, you know, like, 'don't touch me.' Isn't that a fact? Going back to that one-night-stand I had in Cape Cod. She would not let me touch her. She was one of those. She was, yeah. And I think about it now. No, she didn't want me touchin' her fanny. That slays me, you know?"[51]

Mildred tended to prefer to make love to women rather than to allow them to make love to her, yet she did not identify as a stone butch. "I did most of it," she reported, "and there were very few, there were some who really were good at making love to me, but a lot of them weren't. I sort of was that type I guess. I didn't like someone else making love to me unless, well, unless they were in some way exceptional, you know." She remembered a notable exception to this general rule:

> I remember, um, with another woman that I had an affair with who was from Chicago, this is one I haven't even mentioned, but she and I had a short, we had one night together in New York when she happened to be in New York and I was in New York. And we went to bed together and she was the kind who absolutely wouldn't let you touch her. She wanted to make love to me, but she said, "No," you know, "you can't do that," you know, "I don't like it." And so I remembered that, because sometimes I've been a little like that, you know, with some people.

Women making love to her did not revolt Mildred. "It was only if I knew that they somehow either felt they didn't want to do it or they weren't very good at it or something that then I'd just, you know, I didn't want 'em to try. In a way, it was more sensitivity to their feelings about it," she said.[52]

Most women interviewed for this study and for the Lesbians Making History project do not seem to have used dildos, a finding that contrasts with research on lesbian communities in the United States for the same period. Most of the narrators had never heard of a dildo until very recently. Billie was one of the few to have been introduced to this particular sexual practice in the 1960s by one of her more experimental partners. "She experimented with everything," Billie said. "I won't go into great detail, but everything. Oral sex, instruments, the whole thing, and I thought, well, maybe that's what kept me going back for another lesson. But I never met, in my span in the '60s and '50s, '60s and '70s even, I don't think I met too many women that would wear a dildo ... One had a vibrator, but that's about all." The woman owned her own dildo, made of rubber, as well. Billie commented, "It was funny, because she was very tasteful about it. She didn't want to offend me, but she wanted to try these things and show me what they could be like, and I thought, 'Okay, I can do this.'"[53]

Neither Reva nor her partner knew anything about dildos, and they did not use them in their sexual relationship. "Never heard of them," Reva said, "was not familiar with that. I think that the old-timey butches were into that. I think they used to wear them all the time sometimes, under their jeans so they'd look, I don't know, well hung or whatever. Ah, no, since I was a soft butch, I never heard about dildos ever, you know."[54] Nor did she remember any of the novels mentioning dildos.

Lois was somewhat scathing about the use of dildos. She and her first lover had developed a satisfying sexual relationship quite quickly. "Well, we used the finger," Lois acknowledged, "and well, um, the other thing – cunnilingus, they call it." Later in their relationship, they experimented further. Lois commented, "Of course, maybe everybody experimented with a dildo, but they didn't work. At least, they didn't work to my satisfaction. I don't know. We tried one or two things like that once or twice, but we never really ... It was enough to satisfy each other, that was all we did."[55]

In neither of Deborah's early lesbian relationships was any form of dildo or other sex toy used. Deborah did not become familiar with dildos until the 1970s, when she was socializing with a larger lesbian community and came to know "a very raunchy couple who would produce the dildos in the late evening." "At parties?" I asked. "Oh yes," she said, "at the drop of a hat, and throw them around and discuss them. I mean, and completely and totally upset older women at the time, so – say I was in my late thirties – maybe [they were] fifty, who would just get up and leave, but, I mean, these were things we just chucked around as toys and thought it was terribly funny. I think these two actually used it, and, but everybody else just screamed with laughter." Deborah's earlier sexual practices did, however, include oral sex.[56]

Phyl "never even knew what a dildo was." She remarked, "Okay, it started in kisses and cuddles and whatever else, oral sex is fine with me, it was great, but I never went into using any things and I still have hang-ups about all this leathery bit." She did not know about oral sex when she was growing up, but she remarked about it, "Nothing's been strange to me. No, that wouldn't have been discussed, for sure, that would not be discussed ... I loved it all, I did ... Nothing shocked me, no. It didn't. In fact, I felt just wonderful that this had all happened."[57]

It was when Pat lived in New York that she was exposed to a broader lesbian community, and she was introduced to new sexual practices. She found New York to be very different from Montreal:

> In New York, I came across the apparatuses and the different, I mean the different, they were much more butch and femme in New York City than it was in Montreal. It was more pronounced in the village [Greenwich Village] in New York when I was there, and there was more sex. More sex, and there was pot, and more drinking, yeah. It was pretty wild in New York. But in Montreal it wasn't as wild as, it wasn't sex, sex, sex all the time, but ... you had a few drinks and, you know, ah, you'd end up in bed together. But there was nothing, no apparatus or anything. I don't remember. My first episode was in New York, and I found, I didn't find that interesting at all. But, um, there was oral sex then. Oh yeah. But you didn't talk about it, you just did it. I mean, you know, you went from a bar or a party to somebody's bed, and that was it. You really didn't make a big deal out of it.[58]

In the absence of much wider research, it is impossible to say with certainty whether Canadian lesbians as a whole were less likely to be stone butches or to use dildos than were American lesbians. Evidence from this small study suggests that this was the case, but a wider range of lesbians would have to be interviewed to be sure. A higher prevalence of butch-femme roles, stone butch identity, and use of dildos in the United States, however, may be accounted for simply by periodization. After all, urban subcultures of lesbians had been in existence in the US since at least the 1920s, whereas in Canada such communities were just beginning to form during the Second World War. Subcultural norms that had become more widespread, if not hegemonic, among certain groups of lesbians in American cities did not have the same amount of time to take hold in Canada before butch and femme identities were critiqued by second-wave feminism.

Historians must be careful when making generalizations about the degree to which women would or would not have maintained physical sexual relationships with one another in particular historical periods. If we suggest that women in the era of the romantic friendship were unlikely to have explored a genital sexuality, we risk ignoring evidence suggesting that behaviour can occur in the absence of a language to describe it. Many of the women in this study were only marginally more knowledgeable about female sexuality than women in the nineteenth century, yet they managed to form sexual relationships and to explore genital sexuality with each other. If this can be shown to be the case in the mid-twentieth century, when relatively little information was available to young women – even though women were now at least assumed to be sexual – then we ought also to be careful about assuming too much ignorance in earlier historical subjects. Offering up the women in this study as necessarily more knowledgeable would do both groups a disservice, for it would undermine the potential for earlier women to have explored their sexuality even though they were not supposed to own one, and it would fail to recognize the significance of the achievement later women made in finding their sexuality in a period still under a veil of silence about lesbianism.

This study suggests that a wide variety of sexual practices featured in the Canadian lesbian landscape before second-wave feminism, yet it also suggests that some practices and roles may have been less prevalent in Canada than in the United States. The most common sexual practices beyond necking were fondling, clitoral stimulation, and vaginal penetration. Oral sex and the use of dildos for penetration were rather less common. All of these practices, when occurring between women, were abhorred by the wider culture, and the narrators were aware that what they were doing was regarded as unnatural. Even so, they eventually followed their desires rather than social norms.

And what of sexual activity and subjectivity? The narrators described their discovery of sexual relationships with women in terms expressing a sense of coming home, of naturalness, and of rightness. Those who had had some heterosexual experience beforehand described it either as unnatural and uncomfortable, or as pleasurable but not as pleasurable or as intense as sexual activity with women. Even those who had no heterosexual experience, and thus no point of comparison, expressed a feeling of naturalness in their same-sex relationships.

For young women growing up with desires they were not supposed to have, the first experience of sexuality could be even more stressful than for young heterosexuals. Everyone must face the fear of rejection, feelings of sexual ineptitude, and concerns about whether sexual activity is appropriate. Young lesbians also had to face the fear of exposure; the potential rejection would be not just an individual rejection of their advances but also a broader social isolation on the basis of sexuality. The risk of losing friends and becoming the target of gossip and harassment was considerable. That they took this first step, even if they did not initiate it, suggests great courage. But there was much at stake, for these women were expressing a developing identity based on their attraction to women. That attraction could be repressed, silenced, or shelved for a time because of heteronormativity, but in the case of all these women it eventually was expressed physically with another woman. When and how that occurred had great import for the development of identity, for it was in that moment of first same-sex intimacy, mutually shared, that most of the narrators received crucial affirmation of their sexuality. When combined with an emotional relationship, physical intimacy was a powerful factor in their awareness of their difference from other girls and women as well as of shared desires for other women.

7

Relationships

Lesbian Couples and Their Families

The postwar years are usually counted as boom years. Canadians were beginning to enjoy greater freedom in geographical movement, urban dwelling, and home ownership, although it must be noted that not all Canadians enjoyed the relative prosperity of the late 1940s and the 1950s. Nevertheless, growing urban areas, changing social relationships, and the greater availability of the automobile fundamentally changed Canadians' recreational lives. The impact was particularly significant for young Canadians. Governments, medical professionals, and church leaders worried about the dangerous possibilities posed by the car and by dances and other social functions at which young girls in particular were not chaperoned by watchful parents or older siblings. Policing the sexuality of youth became paramount.

Because the focus of postwar sexual angst was on heterosexuals and gay men, however, little attention was directed toward lesbian activity. Lesbianism was not completely ignored, but the greater public naiveté about it allowed lesbians a little more latitude in courtship and romance than was given to gay men. Further, an association between two girls or two women was unlikely to cause comment unless it seemed too intimate or unless one or both were masculine in dress or behaviour. Women could be affectionate with one another in public and could live together without it being remarked upon, whereas society viewed men who lived together very suspiciously and unmarried women and men living together as morally reprehensible. These factors meant that women were able to date, fall in love, and even live together without necessarily encountering the hostility of the wider society, once they had gotten over the initial difficulty of finding others like themselves and provided that they kept their sexual relationships out of public view.

In many respects, same-sex relationships were framed in ways similar to heterosexual ones. The rules of courtship and romance were largely the same, as lesbians were indoctrinated with the same norms as heterosexual women. Women in same-sex relationships faced many of the same difficulties faced by heterosexual couples. Most lesbian relationships were positive ones, but abuse, both physical and verbal, was present in the lesbian community and was often linked, at least in the minds of those interviewed, to the use of alcohol and drugs. Infidelity caused grief and the end of relationships. In this regard also, some relationships between women were not necessarily very different from heterosexual relationships. What was different, of course, was the added pressure on relationships of homophobia and the consequent need to remain closeted. Relationships between women could not be lived openly without fear of reprisals, and although a life of secrecy had its own particular thrills, it ultimately placed great pressure on the women concerned and limited both the extent of their social worlds and the depth of their relationships with all but their partners.

This chapter examines the relationships the narrators formed with women in the period under study. How did they establish their romantic relationships? Where did they meet their partners? And what were their relationships like? The narrators reveal that their first same-sex relationships were with fellow school or university students, work colleagues, or girls or women they met socially. In some ways, the formation of lesbian relationships conformed to norms of heterosexual courtship. Because same-sex relationships had to be formed and conducted in secrecy, away from the prying eyes of family, peers, and school and work authorities, there was not the same range of sites for dating and courtship for these women as was the case for their heterosexual peers. Many of those relationships moved quite quickly to sexual intimacy, and in many cases the partners also moved quickly to living together. Most of the narrators had very positive experiences in their relationships with women, but as for heterosexual women, some experienced physical and verbal abuse at the hands of their partners and some lived with partners who were alcoholics. Their experiences reveal that lesbian relationships before 1965 were as varied as were heterosexual ones.

This chapter also analyzes women's relationships with their families of origin.[1] Despite the presence of much more negative perceptions of homosexuality in the period under study than would begin to emerge in the 1970s, lesbians were perhaps somewhat less likely in this period to be fully ostracized by their biological families or to voluntarily sever family relationships because of family antagonism toward their sexuality than were lesbians of the 1970s and 1980s. This was particularly the case before the 1950s. Several factors resulted in families not rejecting lesbian daughters as forcefully as they would during later decades and in lesbians not feeling fully able to break completely with family ties. This is perhaps a little surprising, given that we usually think of these earlier decades as being the more oppressive and as being harder for people who were not heterosexual. We must remember, however, that before the 1960s and 1970s there existed a very strong norm of financial responsibility for one's children, abandonment of one's children was reprehensible, and daughters were less able than they would be in later decades to live a fully independent life. It may have been that although the family of a lesbian daughter thoroughly disapproved of her lifestyle, strong social norms of familial connection and financial responsibility and fewer opportunities for a young woman to be fully independent meant that her family might spend a great deal of effort attempting to change her behaviour but would be less likely to throw her out of the house and ostracize her completely.

It is in their descriptions of their relationships with their families and in their accounts of their first crushes on and relationships with girls or women that one can see the development of the lesbian identities of the women discussed in this study. As young children, many of them began to form attractions toward other girls, and some began to feel that they did not fit prevailing gender norms. They were aware, all of them, that they were eventually supposed to develop relationships with boys and men and that they were supposed to be feminine. Awareness of difference from the norm in these respects led these women to conceal from their families and the broader society those aspects of themselves that they were aware would result in negative reactions.

Relationships are among the most important milestones, or signal events, in many of the narrators' stories. The first awareness of same-sex attraction in the form of a crush on another girl or a teacher, the first exploration of that attraction in a physical sense, the first full sexual experience, the first real lesbian relationship – all of these "firsts" are re-membered in considerable detail compared to other aspects of personal history. They imply the entrance of the individual into a new chapter of life, in which an aspect of self is realized consciously for the first time or is significantly affirmed and thus reinforced.

Establishing and Maintaining Same-Sex Relationships

The testimonies discussed here reveal many similarities between same-sex and heterosexual courtship and relationships, but there were also import-ant differences. Similarities existed because all Canadians were indoctrin-ated with the norms of heterosexual courtship and relationship structure. The differences arose because of the additional pressures of homophobia and consequent secrecy, subterfuge, and social marginalization of same-sex couples. Many of the women attest to the feeling of "naturalness" attendant upon their relationships with women. This naturalness made their rela-tionships with women seem fuller, more emotional, more passionate, and more fulfilling than those with men, but it also meant that their expecta-tions were high and their disappointments consequently profound.

Although the film *Forbidden Love* implies that relationships were often formed in bars,[2] where one woman would pick up another, it was more often the case for the narrators in this study that relationships were formed in other contexts. Bar pick-ups certainly happened, but the women inter-viewed for this study did not frequent the bar scene often enough for it to happen to them – if they had been so inclined. Most of the narrators formed their first sexual relationships at school or with school friends, at work, or through other social networks. As discussed in Chapter 6, many of those relationships became sexual very quickly.

Most relationships, even if they began with a pick-up in a bar, lasted a few years at the very least. Just as it was not acceptable in heterosexual society to have a long string of short-term relationships, it was generally not the case that lesbians were "promiscuous" in their sexuality. Even the majority of the bar women had relatively lengthy relationships. Already present, however, was a feature of lesbian life that would continue to the present: the "get together, move in together," or U-Haul, syndrome, where lesbians more rapidly than heterosexuals moved to the living-together stage of a relationship. As will be revealed in the relationship stories below, many of the women in this study who had relationships with other women after they had left home began living with them very early on in their relationships, often within weeks or months.

In a period when heterosexual courtship tended to be rather long and when living together did not occur until after marriage, such behaviour was unusual. It may have been that if same-sex relationships progressed to the sexual stage much earlier than did most heterosexual ones, these women were already, in their minds, "married." It could also have been that the majority of the women in this study, regardless of their backgrounds, were single, working women on low to midlevel incomes who took advantage of the opportunity to pool their financial resources with someone they loved. Because there was social approval of women living together, they were able to establish homes without fear of heterosexual suspicion.

Same-sex relationships, however marginal they may have been, were heavily influenced by normative rules. Relationships were expected to be long-term, if not permanent. Many women thought that they would be with a partner for the rest of their life. As most women developed their expectations about relationships from their observations of family and friends, from their reading, and from films and other media, lesbian women naturally had expectations similar to those of heterosexual women. They wanted to be with a loving companion who was also a friend in a stable and permanent relationship in which fidelity and honesty were valued and in which resources were pooled. They no more wished to be betrayed by their partners, treated brutally, or lied to than did heterosexual women. The following testimonies reveal that their actual experiences of relationships were as varied as were those of heterosexual women.

There were two pre-eminent sites for meeting future partners, aside from bars and house parties, and those were the school or university and the workplace. This was particularly true of first partners. Subsequent partners could be met in community social activities, but very few women made their first foray into the bar scene or the house parties without first having established a relationship with, or at least a strong attraction toward, another woman. Barb, Bergit, Jill, Maureen, Veronica, and Deborah met their first loves at high school. Reva and Mildred met partners at night school and university respectively. Mary, Phyl, Lois, and Cheryl met partners through work.

Mary followed Doris to Canada in 1951. Doris, having completed her nursing training, was able to work in Canada as a nurse, but Mary was not, as she had six months' training yet to complete. She ended up working in nursing assistant jobs, where the requirements were less stringent. During that time, she and Doris lived together. Mary recalled that their first six years were happy ones, saying "We thought we were the only two in the world." When they first got together, they "wanted to be together all the time."[3] After they came to Canada, they lived with Doris's mother and stepfather for about a year, about as long as many heterosexual couples would have been engaged, and then purchased a house in Richmond Hill. After living there for two years, they moved into an apartment in Toronto to be closer to work.

It was after their move to Toronto that Mary and Doris made the trip to Provincetown discussed in Chapter 6. After having her first taste of the lesbian community, Doris started sleeping with other women, and the relationship began to disintegrate. Around the same time, Mary met Pat, who in 1957 would become her new partner. Mary and Doris met Pat at a lesbian bar at the Continental in Toronto after cooking class one night. They were friends at first: "It wasn't a mad, passionate love thing. We were just very, very good friends. We talked a lot, and it grew into a lot." One night, when Pat was working nights and her roommate, Marion, was at their place, it became obvious to Mary that Doris and Marion were in love. "By this time," she said,

> I knew it was over between Doris and I anyhow. I just knew it. There wasn't the same feeling, and I could sort of see her. And I remember her saying something about that they were in love, and I said, "Well, why don't you live together, then?" And Marion says, "Well, where would you live?" ... I said, "I'll go pick up Pat from work." And it was me that said to her [Pat], "Do you love me?" And she said, "Of course I love you." And I said, "Enough to live with me?" I mean, I was going to live with her ... that's how we got together. And it grew deeper and deeper. It wasn't a fast thing that, it grew after we went to live together.[4]

They began in an apartment and eventually were able to save for a home. Although it was not unusual for couples to have formed sexual relationships out of friendships – many same-sex and heterosexual relationships began in exactly this way – it was unusual for two friends to begin a sexual relationship and move in together simultaneously.

Mildred's primary relationship in the period under study grew out of shared political ideals and intellectualism rather than sexual attraction per se. After some years of very brief relationships of between six months and a year with both women and men, Mildred eventually formed a long-term relationship with "Ed" and lived with her for six years. Both women were university-educated and leftwing. "We were mutually attracted to each other, and mutually got together," said Mildred.[5] Ed was older than Mildred, and she initiated the relationship because Mildred did not have enough nerve. Ed had already had a relationship with a woman. Their relationship was a happy one, although they seemed to spend little time together, as each had her own separate meetings to attend in the evening after work.

As in heterosexual relationships, infidelity was an issue in the lesbian community. The narrators were raised in a society emphasizing fidelity in marriage and in premarital "dating," and the narrators applied that ideal to their same-sex relationships. Several of the narrators reported that they or their partners had had affairs. Lois's first partner, whom she had met while teaching, was "not a faithful lover." "I was. Story of my life, I guess," said Lois. "I could have waited for her 'til kingdom came, but kingdom didn't come and I didn't wait." Several of Lois's partners had affairs.[6]

Mary and Pat each had an affair during their relationship, Pat in 1961. "I was taking, learning how to do leather-craft in those days," said Pat. "Sure you were, dear," Mary responded humorously. Mary was going to night school. Their friend Brenda started dropping over to teach Pat leather-craft. "All of a sudden I felt something," said Mary. "There's something going on here." Mary brought it out in the open and moved out for a few days. "It broke my heart," she remembered. However, their separation did not last very long. Mary returned one day to find the door locked. She finally got in the house and "went nuts" at Brenda. Pat very quickly realized her mistake, and she and Mary came back together. Mary's affair occurred after the period under study.[7]

In the 1950s and the early 1960s, lesbian communities, although growing at a rate most alarming to the broader community, were actually rather small, which meant that one had to find a partner in a small group of people. Very complex social relationships between lovers, ex-lovers, and friends could result. The story Joyce told the Lesbians Making History (LMH) project is emblematic of the nature of lesbian community in these early days, in that it illustrates that the smallness and interconnectedness of lesbian communities could sometimes result in women forming multiple relationships within a small social group over a period of time. When Joyce broke up with her partner, she began to see a woman called Maida, whom she had met at the Rideau Public House at Jarvis and Gerrard Streets in Toronto:

> So she had these friends Val and Ida, whom I met through her, and for some reason I had a fixation on this Val ... So Maida and I parted and I began to live with this Val and then I tried to help Maida. I felt bad because she was a very nice person. So finally, she couldn't stand living alone ... she hadn't formed another relationship, so she phoned us and I said to Val, "We've got an extra room in the house" (we owned a house), and I said, "let's take her in, she's a good friend" etc., so Val said, "All right." So then Val and Ida parted, and Val and I lived together. Ida met someone, so then we had Val and I living together, Maida living with us, Ida was with another woman, and Ida and Maida had originally started out by living together ... and before Val and Ida.[8]

It would seem that serial monogamy was common in the period under study. "It seemed in those days nobody left anybody 'til they had someone else to go to," commented Joyce. The women in this study who were part of any kind of lesbian community after the war rarely were without a partner. The postwar communities, be they based in bars or in house parties, were sufficiently large that women could find other partners if relationships broke up. For those women who were not part of the community, however, a break-up could signal a lengthy spell without another relationship.

The community was often very supportive. Despite their having been in a series of relationships and having broken up with each other and formed new relationships, these women remained friends and were supportive of each other in times of need. That level of support included the willingness to allow an ex-lover of a partner to become a roommate. Even though it cannot be said that the lesbian community was always a happy and egalitarian one, it was one where shared experience of same-sex attraction could potentially blur the differences and antagonisms between people, at least for a time.

An analysis of interview material reveals that the butch-femme relationship, although important, was hardly hegemonic. As other historians have indicated, class differences often determined the degree to which butch and femme were employed as identities. Those women who lived fully in the bar scene also lived fully in butch and femme roles, as it was along these lines that the community was structured until the late 1960s. Those women who were not always in the bar scene, however, or who visited it only occasionally, had a less profound investment in the butch-femme social structure.

Lois, who was involved in the bar scene quite often but who was also a teacher, dressed like a butch "in cowboy boots and shirt and black pants and everything" at the bars, but she argued that she thought that butch and femme roles "were a joke." Lois suggested that she lived the bar life on the weekends because living as a lesbian meant that one was already living a double life, and she maintained that she lived the double life fully, having one life during the week and another on the weekend. It may well be that Lois's perspective on the bar culture has been affected by her involvement in 1970s lesbian feminism, which condemned the butch and femme women for their adoption of masculinity and femininity. Although she may have lived a middle-class lifestyle during the week as a teacher, she was sufficiently involved in the bar scene to have participated in several fights with butches. She also dressed in a very butch manner and wore a knife. That she thought of the roles as a joke at the time is therefore unlikely. It is much more likely that her interpretation of the roles has been altered in the intervening years by political condemnation of butch masculinity and aggressiveness.[9]

Pam commented, "I guess I was femme, I suppose. Debbie was the more aggressive or whatever. It really wasn't all that, to us, but to some of our friends it was very important." It was not until the 1970s, after Pam had broken off her relationship with Debbie and formed a new one, that she switched roles. "I wasn't terribly thrilled with that. I didn't find being butch very great. I mean, in those days, I mean, you paid. Not like maybe today. If you took somebody out for dinner, you bloody well paid for it."[10] Pam seemed to form her gender role in relation to that of her partner, so she was able to switch. Her testimony does not suggest a deeply held subjectivity based on a single gender role but rather a more mutable gender performance formed relationally and dependent on that of a partner. Many lower-middle-class and upper-working-class women were ambivalent about butch and femme roles. They were much more likely to describe themselves as "butchy" or "butchier" and "feminine" than they were to use the identity labels "butch" and "femme." To identify as a butch was to be associated with women who wore men's clothes and whose behaviour and appearance were working-class. Similarly, femme women's femininity was working-class femininity and therefore not the kind the narrators wished to manifest.

The narrators were only occasionally involved in the bar scene, concerned as they were about respectability and the threat to their employment and having, as many of them did, an alternative social world in the form of house parties. Their investment in the structural norms of the bar culture was therefore limited. They did employ gender differentiation in their relationships, but the "butchier" women especially were less likely to invest heavily in the stereotypical butch appearance and behaviour, as it was a very public and therefore dangerous testament of lesbianism. Lois and Pat favoured a tailored and moderately masculine look, especially when visiting the bars or going to house parties, but definitely did not wear men's clothes, as did many of the bar butches.

All the narrators were raised with gender differentiation as a central characteristic of all relationships. That there should be gender differentiation in some same-sex ones is therefore not surprising. Phyl remembered her long-term relationship, formed initially at work and the only one she had with a woman before 1965, as a very egalitarian one. She and her partner had different tasks in the relationship, but they were not based on gendered roles of butch and femme, although Phyl acknowledged that she was the more feminine in terms of tasks around the house than was her partner. Her partner did more of the household maintenance, such as electrical work. Barb and Chris, who grew up on farms and were used to physical labour, were comfortable with more masculine tasks and thus tended to do more of them than their partners. Most of the narrators, however, remembered their relationships differently and recalled sharing tasks in a nongendered way. For the most part, the household tasks they did were traditionally more "feminine" ones, with the exception of yard maintenance. Trades people usually did the more traditionally "masculine" tasks, such as plumbing, carpentry, and electrical work. Because the narrators did not identify as butch or femme, they did not have an investment in gender roles that might have caused them to be more rigid in their adoption of household tasks.

Alcoholism and Abuse in Same-Sex Relationships before 1965

In the postwar era, when ideal gender roles were becoming more rigid – although more people seemed not to be acting in accordance with them[11] – gender became an increasingly crucial aspect of lesbian life, most particularly of working-class lesbian life. Elizabeth Lapovsky Kennedy and Madeline Davis have shown that in the 1950s gender roles became more rigidly defined in the lesbian community of Buffalo, New York. Violence and jealousy increased, and much of it was butch violence directed at femmes. They account for this change not simply in terms of the butch interest in manifesting a masculine persona but also in terms of the new interest in "the tough masculine culture – the violence, jealousy, and solidarity – of the 1950s bar crowd."[12] As the American bar scene became more entrenched in the 1950s and 1960s, and the pressures on lesbians grew as more public attention was focused on them, physical and emotional abuse, alcoholism, and drug addiction became more prevalent.[13]

It has often been assumed in lesbian communities that relationships between women will necessarily be more egalitarian and less abusive than heterosexual relationships. Many women entering relationships with other women for the first time believe that these relationships will automatically be better and closer than their heterosexual relationships, yet the evidence suggests that abuse, both emotional and physical, is present in lesbian communities, as it is elsewhere. Lesbian abuse has only recently begun to be discussed openly, perhaps because lesbians in the past did not want to provide homophobic society with ammunition to level at the community and perhaps because abuse, which is difficult enough to talk about in heterosexual couples, is thought even more traumatic when perpetrated by another woman. But abuse does and did exist in lesbian relationships, and it impacted many of the women interviewed for this study.

Kennedy and Davis suggest that the late 1950s and early 1960s "placed the butch in the vulnerable and stressful position of defender of the community and promoted the fem as the highly desired, but unreliable, refuge or source of security."[14] Living full-time as a butch woman in a decade increasingly hostile to gender nonconformity meant that the butch was increasingly isolated, unemployed, and harassed by police and men in general. In Buffalo, butches increasingly had to live off femmes, they drank more, and they became more insecure emotionally, resulting in the desire to protect the one thing that was important: their relationships. Unfortunately, this sometimes translated into extreme jealousy and even violence.

It is difficult to determine whether the same transition occurred for the Canadian bar cultures. Little information exists for the 1940s with which to compare later decades. Certainly, in the 1950s, violence was a part of the public lesbian community. The fights in bars and at parties, however, were only part of the picture. Abuse within relationships also occurred frequently. Participants in a group interview for Lesbians Making History spoke about one "Big Doris" who "dressed like a man, eh? She used to beat up her little hooker girlfriend, too ... I think she almost killed her."[15]

Abuse was also part of the lives of many women who seldom or never went to the bars. After Cheryl and her partner had moved from Nova Scotia to Ontario, Cheryl began to suffer the effects of abuse. "We moved three or four times," said Cheryl, "and that was getting into the latter part of our relationship, and she became very, very suspicious of who I went to see." If Cheryl arrived home late from work, Robyn would suspect that she was seeing someone. Then Robyn began going out at night

> and then coming home usually with a girl. I had no idea where she went to pick them up. And she didn't bring a lot of them home but she brought several home, and they were all very much alike, she was kind of heavy into the bottle at the time, and they were too ... I'd be sound asleep and all of a sudden I'd get a fist right in the pit of my stomach ... and there were times that she'd accuse me of being with, you know, somebody that I worked with, somebody who was my age who was single ... So it just got from bad to worse ... and there were times that she was really hung over or something like that, there were a couple of times that she took a knife to my throat and threatened that she was going to ram it right through my throat if I didn't tell her the truth.[16]

It was not the physical threats, however, that most frightened Cheryl. "Those were not the things that scared me," she said. Significantly more powerful was the threat of exposure: "You know what scared me? She threatened to tell my parents what we were doing. And I thought, 'Oh my God, this will kill my Dad. If he knows that I'm with Robyn in *that* way.' I mean, I couldn't,

I couldn't have that happen. So under the threat of that, that was the thing that kept me with her as long as I did."

The last straw for Cheryl occurred one night when she finally fought back against the violence. Robyn came home with a woman, and both of them started beating Cheryl up while she was asleep. Cheryl nearly vomited. "So I got up and caught my wind," she said. "I looked at the two of them, and both had been drinking, and I just took one by the side of the head and the other by the side of the head ... and I knocked their heads together. And they just fell to the floor." Cheryl told Robyn that she had had enough and that she did not want to be hit any more. "And all of a sudden, the door kicked open, and Mrs. D – she was our landlady – she was there with her cane, and she pointed the cane, she shook the cane, and she said to the two of them, 'You get out of my house right now this minute, and don't you ever come back.'" It turned out that Mrs. D. had been aware of the abuse for some time. She gave Cheryl a glass of beer and said, "Now, it's about time you took this into your own hands ... it's about time you did something." Cheryl did – she ended the relationship and joined the military the next morning. She still interacted with Robyn, as their families knew each other, and she did not want their break-up to be heard about in Nova Scotia because of family connections. Robyn was to resurface some time later, when Cheryl was stationed with the air force in Nova Scotia. She attempted to persuade Cheryl to return to the relationship, and when Cheryl grew tired of the harassment, she had several of her very butch servicewomen friends advise Robyn politely that she should leave her alone.

Lois also suffered abuse at the hands of a female partner. Lois's second major relationship was with a woman she had met at the Continental,

a lovely woman when she wasn't drinking. Unfortunately, she was an alcoholic. So we lived together for several years, but she tried to kill me a couple of times with hot fat and stuff because she was so drunk she didn't know what she was doing. And I learned you can't live with an alcoholic. But I loved her, tried again, you know. She went to live with her daughter for a while, and I went to meet her at the train when she came back. She looked okay, but all of a sudden I realized that she was drunk – she'd been drinking on the train – so we had to split up because I couldn't take her any more. I couldn't take being attacked.[17]

Lois, like many women in same-sex relationships and also many in hetero-sexual relationships, was disinclined to sever a relationship based on a single or even several instances of abuse. Just as in heterosexual relation-ships a beating was generally viewed as insufficient cause for separation, so too in the lesbian community was there silence about and toleration of abuse. Not only did lesbian women sometimes have to face the disappoint-ment of being abused by another woman, something they did not expect, but there were also no safe houses or institutions to which they could go for safety, save those of friends. A lesbian who went to the police and complained about the abuse she was suffering at the hands of a female partner would hardly have had a sympathetic hearing.

The presence of abuse in a relationship bore no relation to the social class of the individuals concerned. Although many of the women who rarely went to the bars regarded physical violence as an unfortunate aspect of bar life, they themselves were not immune to its effects. Pam's first long-term partner, Debbie, was a violent alcoholic. Alcohol, according to Pam, was a serious problem in the lesbian community of the 1950s and 1960s. Pam acknowledged that drugs were around in that period too, although she said that she "was too dumb to know the difference."[18] As in the case of heterosexual relationships, the presence of alcohol was linked to a higher frequency of domestic violence. Several of the women reported that their partners treated them more violently when they had been drinking. Elise Chenier reveals the prevalence of alcohol and drugs in the working-class bar community.[19] There was also much drinking at the house parties run by lower-middle-class lesbians in the suburbs.

Abuse could potentially affect how a woman felt about her sexuality. Both Cheryl and Pam found it difficult to understand how one woman could abuse another. In Cheryl's case, the abuse received at the hands of her first partner caused her to swear off women. Cheryl joined the air force and decided that she was not going to pursue relationships with women again. She began dating men, and it was two years before she was able to decide that she was fighting her attraction toward women. In the end, her sexual orientation won, but the abuse did permanently change her perspec-tive on same-sex relationships. However, it may be that other women were not as able to recover from abuse from a female partner, and they may have left the lesbian community for heterosexual lives. It is also difficult to determine whether awareness of social isolation and the smallness of lesbian communities kept these women in abusive relationships longer than they would have stayed in abusive heterosexual ones. Both lesbian women and heterosexual women had reasons for staying with abusive partners.

The 1950s and 1960s were hardly times of fully healthy heterosexual relationships either. There remained, in the middle of the twentieth century, considerable domestic violence and alcoholism. Domestic violence would not be addressed in any serious and widespread way until after the period under study. Whereas there existed growing disapproval of spousal abuse in heterosexual society, it was still disapproval based on extent rather than existence, by which I mean that some levels of spousal abuse were tolerated. It was only the more extreme forms that incurred legal penalties. Moreover, women were often assumed to have provoked or otherwise deserved the treatment meted out to them by their husbands.[20] Many narrators for this study had witnessed domestic violence and alcoholism in their own families. Within a context where spousal abuse was tolerated and where the blame for it was placed on the victim, it is hardly surprising that many women remained in abusive relationships.

Relationships were crucial to the formation of lesbian identity in the period under study. In a period when a positive and public recognition of the validity of lesbian identity was absent, when there were no lesbian role models for young women, and when lesbian relationships were seen *inter alia* as inherently unstable, a romantic relationship with another girl or woman was an affirmation of shared sexuality, emotional health, and mutual desire. This is not to suggest that a lesbian identity could not develop in the absence of a relationship but rather that a relationship was an external recognition and validation of that identity. It was in same-sex relationships that women both diverged from the social norm and simultaneously came within it, in the sense of locating themselves within the paradigm of long-term partnership. A same-sex relationship placed them outside the bounds of heteronormativity, but it also gave them what every girl was socialized to want: an intimate and emotional relationship. Provided that one could resist any suggestion that such a relationship was an illness or a sin, a same-sex relationship allowed one to see oneself as participating in the very important world of dating, romance, and even lifelong commitment.

Barb, Pat, Cheryl, Mary, and Deborah in particular experienced very strong same-sex attractions and were able to explore them as children. Unlike some of the other narrators who also experimented sexually with other girls but whose experiences were short-lived, their same-sex experiences involved longer emotional relationships, which may have made them more generative of lesbian subjectivity. After all, physical experimentation could be discounted as mere curiosity or as a phase, something that many children were not supposed to do but did anyway (like masturbation). An emotional and physical relationship was quite another matter. It involved the same kind of activities as "going steady" with a boy.

It was these women, each of whom had established emotional as well as physical relationships with other girls, who continued to have relationships with women, who found lesbian community early in their lives, and who had an early sense of self based on sexual orientation. Other narrators, who had not had lengthy or happy same-sex experiences, may have known about their desires and acted on them occasionally but did not form a subjectivity based on same-sex attraction until later in life. It was the affirmation of the emotional content of early relationships, rather than sex itself, that was the more formative of identity.

In the context of these women's lives, that emotion should have been more consequential than sex is perhaps not surprising. After all, it was with images of emotion, rather than sex, that these women were raised. They, like heterosexual women, were trained to view marriage and emotional commitment as ideals. They were not trained to see sex as separate from emotional commitment, and they most particularly were not trained to see sexual activity as related to any kind of sexual orientation. Although they were desirous of other girls and women, it was emotional connection that they craved and that was the more crucial.

Families and Lesbian Daughters

Although there was, prior to the 1950s and 1960s, disapproval of lesbianism in Canadian society, there was not yet a widespread public discourse about it in the sense of the pejorative and medicalized discourse that would gain hegemony in the 1950s and 1960s. Antipathy toward lesbians in the period before 1950 was therefore based on very vague and often gender-related terms rather than on a specifically pathologizing terminology of illness and dysfunction. Family reactions to lesbian daughters, although certainly based on attitudes about what was "natural" and "moral," were much less often phrased in psychomedical discourse than they would be later in the century, allowing families perhaps to see their daughters as wayward but not as psychologically diseased. From the 1950s onward, lesbianism was described, defined, and policed as a psychological abnormality, and public understandings of it were increasingly informed by the new discourse.

Lesbians' reactions to family attitudes toward their sexuality were themselves mitigated by several factors. Before the 1960s and 1970s, it was more difficult for young women to survive financially without family than it would be later in the century. Many women did not work in paid employment or did so only until marriage, when they were expected to depend financially on husbands, and there were fewer opportunities available for women who wished to live completely independently of family. There was also not yet a lesbian discourse of community and "alternative family" whereby women could visualize living completely separately from their family of origin. Such discourse would not arise until the lesbian-feminist movement of the 1970s and 1980s posited the possibility of lesbian utopias and lives lived in separation both from men and from homophobic families. The evidence for this study suggests, tentatively, that except in the most extreme cases of family antipathy, many lesbians in the first half of the twentieth century may have maintained better – although still difficult – relationships with their families of origin than did lesbians in later decades.

This same period in Canadian history was one without an alternative to the heterosexual, patriarchal family unit. Prior to the formation of large lesbian communities and a broader context of greater opportunities for women's economic independence, there were two choices for lesbians in relation to family: maintained communication with family and absence of family. Family relationships, although problematic for many in this study because of tensions arising from sexuality, were largely not abandoned. There was no structure at this time to replace them, no alternative family where women could feel that they might openly be lesbian and still belong to "family." Duty to family was still a prized value, and a sense of family obligation was strong. Lesbians had therefore to negotiate between sexual orientation and family obligation, between openness and compromise, and between maintenance of family ties and loss of the "rootedness" that family brought.

Mildred's relationship with her mother, although problematic, was without significant conflict on the subject of sexuality. Mildred is sure that her mother knew of her sexuality early on, even though Mildred was engaged for a time in sexual relationships with men. Mildred believes that her being allowed to stay with her lesbian aunt and her aunt's partner in the 1930s and 1940s, when she was a child, indicates that her mother had no fundamental objection to her aunt's sexuality and knew about Mildred's. Although Mildred is sure that her mother was jealous of her closeness with her aunt, Mildred does not think that it was because of antagonism to the aunt's sexual orientation. Nor did her mother ever express any objection to Mildred taking her female partners home to stay in the 1950s and 1960s, and she did not attempt to dissuade her from her sexual orientation.[21]

Lois, who was born in Victoria in 1919, also felt that her family had known of her lesbianism. As revealed in Chapter 4, Lois "was a bit of a problem," and was sent to St. Margaret's private school.[22] Part of her "problem," it seems, was her affection for girls, which was sufficiently obvious that her older sister commented on it when Lois was eleven. Lois had had crushes on girls and teachers from the age of ten or eleven and had talked to her sister about them. Her sister, although not exactly in favour, did not reject Lois out of hand but did suggest to her that same-sex crushes were not normal. Lois thinks that her parents suspected that she was a lesbian when she was in her first relationship, which lasted fifteen years, although she and her partner were apart for much of it.

The tide clearly was turning against lesbian relationships, yet women of the 1930s and 1940s were able to decide not to get married, but rather to follow their passions, with only moderate public condemnation compared to that which would come in the next decade. Increasing female employment allowed young women to leave home and live in same-sex environments. Prevailing gender norms made same-sex living for women socially acceptable, as long as open lesbian sexuality or gender transgression was not present. The Canadian public had to be trained slowly to view female relationships with an eye to lesbian content. Many parents remained ignorant of the possibility or saw it as something that could exist outside their family but not within it. Consequently, many lesbians were able to begin their sexual lives with other girls or women without fear of being caught.

Tolerance may particularly have occurred in the case of girls growing up lesbian in rural areas, which remained somewhat out of the reach of the tabloid newspapers. Parents were perhaps even less likely than their urban counterparts to be able to identify "pathological" behaviours early on. Although they might have been concerned, for example, about their daughters' gender-bending behaviours, the lesser availability of media discussions of links between that and lesbianism might have made them slightly more tolerant and inclined to see it in terms of temporary "tomboy" behaviour. This can only be a tentative suggestion, however, as we lack testimonies from rural parents that would support or refute such a suggestion. Barb's parents tolerated her tomboy behaviour, her cropped hair, and her dressing in "overhauls [overalls] ... plaid shirts, and a straw hat" and saw nothing unusual in it. Although Barb was able to take advantage of her rural surroundings and engage in the sorts of activities and gender performance that a young boy would have been allowed, her appearance would, in the following decades, have been likely to cause suspicion and comment. In the 1930s and 1940s, however, Barb was merely a curiosity, a tomboy who supposedly would grow out of it.[23]

The threat of family reaction to her sexuality was an important consideration for Cheryl and unfortunately was a tool of abuse in her relationship with her first partner. Cheryl had been at pains to keep the nature of her relationship secret, as she feared the reaction of her parents, most particularly of her father. When Cheryl joined the air force, Robyn attempted to stop her leaving by once again raising the spectre of family condemnation. This time, however, Cheryl stood her ground. She realized that her parents would love her no matter what Robyn had to tell them: "I suppose, at eighteen years of age came wisdom. I finally smartened up ... I said, 'My family love me and if you tell them, they will probably be hurt, but they love me and it is not going to make them love me any less. So go ahead and tell them if you want to.'"[24]

Billie is sure that her parents knew of her sexuality, as the subject had been discussed. In the 1940s, when Billie was young, her mother and her aunt had revealed to her that they both had had sexual relationships with women. The implication at the time was that it was a stage that she would pass through, but the fact that the subject was raised at all suggests that her mother and aunt had seen in Billie some signs of lesbian behaviour. Their addressing it so frankly and revealing that they themselves had had same-sex experiences was very unusual for the time. Although Billie's relationship with her parents was made problematic by the household tension resulting from her mother's affairs, it was not made problematic by Billie's sexuality. Moreover, later in life, when Billie began to live fully as a lesbian, her parents did not react negatively.[25]

Postwar discourses of sexuality posited lesbians more forcefully as antagonists to the family, as both the results and the agents of family breakdown. In *The Trouble with Normal,* Mary Louise Adams sets the increasing normalization of matrimonial heterosexuality within a framework of postwar domestic "revival," in which deviance "precluded the homogenization that was seen to be central to Canada's strength as a nation."[26] Homogenization had to involve the protection of the young, who were believed to be particularly vulnerable to persuasion by popular images. The lesbian pulp novels of the 1950s were held in this context to "sway normal girls toward the abnormal, making the latter seem both attractive and possible."[27] Lesbians' relationship to family life began fundamentally to change in this new era of coercive heteronormativity. Whereas in earlier times the concept of family obligation and the lack of female financial independence (or, indeed, a family's need to rely on a daughter's income) might have militated against a family's wish to expel a daughter because of her sexuality, the new discourse allowed families to see their daughters increasingly as enemies, as threats to the health and stability of the family home. Families now had a name to put to their daughters' behaviours and a socially approved framework for their response. For several of the women interviewed by the Lesbians Making History project, this framework often involved psychiatric or psychological treatment. It was often family members who initiated the treatment. Jan reported: "They phoned my family up and they said, 'Did you know that your sister's been seen in Toronto and she's dressing like a man?' My brother came looking for me, my older brother and my older sister. And I met them and they said, 'We're going to put you in the fucking nuthouse: look at you!'"[28]

Tricia came out to her family accidentally. Her mother's tone during a phone conversation had suggested to Tricia that she knew of her daughter's lesbianism, when in fact her mother had assumed that Tricia was going out with a black man. Thinking that her mother had guessed her sexual orientation, Tricia started talking about it. She had been a tomboy and later had been given a copy of *The Well of Loneliness* by her mother, a gift that might have suggested to Tricia that her mother had become suspicious. On revealing her lesbianism, Tricia was told to see a psychiatrist.[29]

Jerry moved to Toronto at the age of fifteen after receiving a hostile reaction to her sexuality. "I was accused of being a lesbian at the age of thirteen by my mother," Jerry said. She continued, "This woman, her name was S. She had a pyjama party one night and there was two other, three other women I think. And S. and I got pretty heavy duty on the chesterfield." Jerry had known fully what lesbianism was, and beneath her mattress at home were two books about lesbian relationships, yet she was careful to deny knowledge when asked by her father and several doctors. After she left home, Jerry's father said to her sister, "'Your sister's a lesbian and I don't want her anywhere near my house. I don't want her anywhere near you.'" Jerry's father was in the air force and might reasonably be expected to have had somewhat greater knowledge of homosexuality than many in the general public, given the high-profile purging of gay men and later of lesbians from the military.[30] He certainly was in command of a wider range of terminology for homosexuality than many would have been, frequently lamenting the fact that his daughter was "queer."[31]

Sometimes a family would do more than simply recommend psychiatric treatment and would actually commit a lesbian daughter. In his study of lesbians and gay men in the American South, James T. Sears was told by a lesbian narrator, Merril,

> Of course, the cops weren't the only ones we had to worry about back then. All it took to be put in a mental hospital was for your husband or parents to bring you in. If you were a woman, of course, you were a possession. You'd show up to the bar one night and ask, "Where's Diane?" A person would reply matter-of-factly: "Oh, she's in a mental hospital. Her mother committed her." Again, this was *not* that unusual. If you were a lesbian then you were infiltrated with "homosexualism." You needed to be purged of this illness through electroshock therapy and lots of medication.[32]

Arlene discovered lesbians in the psychiatric hospital, after her mother had her committed in 1962. She was sixteen. She had been "fooling around" with girls since the age of nine but had not known what a lesbian was until she met several lesbian patients on the ward. At nine, she and her best friend had started acting out the love scenes they saw at the movies. When she was ten, her friend's mother walked in on them making love, asked "What are you doing?" and then started to scream. Arlene fled the house, went home, and overdosed on her mother's sleeping pills. Although it would appear that her friend's mother did not discuss the matter with Arlene's mother, her friend was put in another school, and Arlene ceased most of her lesbian activity until her introduction to lesbians in the hospital.[33]

Arlene revealed that she was committed the same year that she came out to her family as a lesbian, but she said that the reason for the commit-tal was that she was leaving home and her mother did not want her to. Despite the fact that her mother abused her physically, Arlene described her family as a "great one." She was able to tell her whole family, including her grandparents, "This is the way it is: I am a lesbian. I intend to stay one. You can either like me or not see me again." As Elise Chenier comments, however, it is quite likely that her sexual preference was a factor in her mother's decision to have her committed.[34]

Although very difficult, her relationship with her mother was unusual for the time. Her mother eventually insisted on seeing what kind of life Arlene was living and went with her to the Toronto lesbian bars at the Parkside Hotel and at the Continental Hotel. "She just wanted to meet my friends, and see what atmosphere I was in," Arlene said. Her mother became so well known at the Parkside that she was referred to by the other lesbians as "The General" or "Mum." The bar community, according to Arlene, looked to her for assistance when they had problems. It was a different story, however, when it came to Arlene having sexual relationships. "We'd go three to six months with my mother right out of it. She wouldn't talk to me, she wouldn't talk to them." Arlene accounted for this behaviour by suggesting that her mother was jealous of these relationships.

Another Toronto lesbian, Alice, mentioned a friend who was kicked out of a convent when she was sixteen and was discovered in bed with another girl: "And they threw her out because she wasn't Catholic. And her mother sent her to a psychiatrist and she lied to him."[35] The threat of psychiatric treatment was also present for Shirley Limbert:

I was fifteen and proud and not very discreet. I smile to myself as I think of this. I'm still proud to be a lesbian and I'm working on being discreet. Eventually, my mother found out about my lover and me, and she was horrified. At that time, in the late fifties, psychiatric care was recommended as the "cure" for lesbians. I don't think my mother would have gone as far as shock treatments for her only child – they were also considered a part of that "cure" – but the threat was there.[36]

The interviews I conducted also referred to the role of psychiatry. "What psychiatrists do to lesbians is a crime," commented Pat. She remembered that when her father first found out that she was a lesbian when she returned to Montreal from New York, he took her "to a doctor, but unbeknownst to me, didn't tell me it was a psychiatrist. So I walked into this office, and this guy asked me all kinds of silly questions, you know, about my childhood and everything, and it clicked finally that it was a psychiatrist." The psychiatrist called Pat's father in and told him, "Really, she is a lesbian and she married just to hide it from her family, and in her upbringing you certainly didn't help the situation." Pat's father pulled her out of the office saying: "That idiot doesn't know what he's talking about."[37] The psychiatrist had actually been correct, at least about Pat's sexuality and her false marriage, but his linking that sexuality to her upbringing had given Pat's father a means by which to reject the message, for no parent wanted to see themselves as responsible for such a terrible fate.

That Pat lied about her sexuality might, from the perspective of the early twenty-first century, seem to indicate that she was repressing her sexual orientation and was caving in to heteronormativity. One must be careful, however, not to assume that what would be regarded as closetedness today was the same fifty years ago. For Pat to admit her lesbianism at that particular juncture in Canadian history, when sexual "deviance" was increasingly under the purview of psychiatrists and psychologists, could have meant committal or at least parental pressure to undergo therapy. That Pat's father had taken her to the psychiatrist in the first place suggests that he would have deemed treatment appropriate. Lying about one's sexuality in these kinds of circumstance can therefore be seen as conscious self-protection and acknowledgment of one's sexuality rather than as the negation of it. Pat had no intention of changing her behaviour; she wished merely to avoid psychiatric treatment because of it.

Barb and Cheryl, both of whom were required by the air force to see a psychiatrist to determine whether they were lesbian, did not have any ongoing psychiatric treatment. Once they left the air force, they were free to do as they pleased. They did not seek medical treatment, not believing that there was a problem to be treated. Furthermore, because their families did not know the reason for their discharge from the air force, there was no family pressure for them to see a psychiatrist.[38]

Cheryl's previous partner Robyn, however, did end up in the psychiatric ward after Cheryl had joined the air force. Robyn's experience may indicate to us that families could still be somewhat tolerant, even while accepting the psychological discourse regarding lesbianism. Stopping off in Toronto after her basic training, Cheryl found out that Robyn had been admitted to 999 Queen Street West. Robyn's new lover informed Cheryl that it was all her fault, saying, "You left her, and she just couldn't take it." Apparently, Robyn had become suicidal and eventually had to be committed. On Cheryl's first leave from her new base, she went to visit Robyn. Robyn seemed drugged but recognized her. On her second visit, Cheryl found that Robyn had been transferred to the Toronto Psychiatric Hospital at 2 Surrey Place and that she was even more drugged. Robyn's mother had travelled to Toronto as soon as she had heard that her daughter was ill. She and Cheryl got along well, and Robyn's mother informed Cheryl that Robyn had thought that she and Cheryl "would be together like your Mum and Dad are together."[39] Robyn's mother clearly was sympathetic enough to visit her daughter in the psychiatric ward, and she saw her daughter's lesbian relationships as similar in some ways to heterosexual ones, but she did not necessarily approve of her daughter's sexual orientation.

These testimonies reveal that even those lesbians who most clearly transgressed the boundaries of heteronormativity were not necessarily cast out of the family and that attitudes toward lesbians had changed somewhat from the previous decades. Even though many women remained in touch with family members, family concern about their sexuality could be explicit and overt. The new arguments of homosexual pathology clearly were available to parents and were part and parcel of their reactions to their daughters' behaviour. Whereas in earlier decades, opposition could be and was expressed, and some families attempted to keep women apart from one another, from the late 1950s on, families had the added explanations and tools of the psychologists and psychiatrists with which to "understand," describe, and police their daughters' behaviour.

Examining the period 1900 to 1965, one sees a gradual shift in the relationship between lesbians and their families. The familial relationships of Frieda and Bud, discussed in Part 1, and of Mildred and Lois were often difficult because of their sexuality – particularly in the case of Frieda and Bud – but at no time were these women rejected outright by their families, nor was there any suggestion that their behaviour required medical attention. Other women, such as Barb and Cheryl, knew very well that they had to keep their relationships secret because of the potential for family disapproval, but the potential disapproval was not based on psychological discourse. It would not be until they were in the services that this new discourse would become linked with their sexuality.

It is in the testimonies of some of the women whose families came to know of their sexuality in the 1950s and 1960s that one sees the linking of lesbianism with notions of pathology and illness. Family reactions to Jan, Pat, Jerry, and Arlene were clearly based in psychological discourse. Families both understood lesbian sexuality in these terms and sought to police their daughters' sexuality via psychiatric treatment. One sees here a subtle change from previous forms of relationship between lesbians and families: although relationships before 1950 were difficult, they lacked the coercive threat of family rejection and psychiatric treatment that was beginning to emerge in the 1950s and 1960s. Families were exposed to and used the new terms in reaction to lesbian daughters, and their behaviour changed as a result. It is not that reactions prior to 1950 were not negative but rather that the changes in the postwar years resulted in a greater distancing of lesbian daughters from families than had previously been the case.

In the early twentieth century, several factors militated against families of origin rejecting outright their lesbian daughters. There existed perhaps a stronger sense of obligation within some families, although it would be difficult to assess the degree to which this was true across class boundaries, given the paucity of records of working-class women for the years before the Second World War. What is more important, however, is the impact of the postwar discourse about homosexuality. Whereas before the war, families often condemned lesbian relationships with rather vague reasons for their views, the postwar era gave families a new terminology, and an extremely hostile one, with which to reject their daughters' sexuality. In addition, one might suggest that the expanding world of women's work allowed a diminishing of family obligation in the sense that more women could be financially independent. For families, this made the expulsion of the lesbian daughter from the family home less objectionable. The rising standard of living might also have made it easier for some families to give up their daughters' incomes, and the tradition of requiring children who lived at home to give over their wage packet at the end of the week had eroded. Daughters' incomes were usually now their own. For lesbians, this meant the opening-up of the possibility of living one's own life without the scrutiny of family members. Many working-class women in particular moved to Canada's cities for the employment opportunities and also because they could live as lesbians within the emerging lesbian communities.

Certainly, economic independence was a significant factor in forming lesbian relationships and community in the postwar period. Donna Penn argues that "for women, fashioning a lesbian way of life generally required economic independence from men, a situation increasingly possible in the wartime and postwar cities."[40] Chenier suggests,

> Although the military offered women and men alike a unique opportunity to explore and develop same-sex relationships, in Toronto, as in Buffalo, it was the integration of civilian women into blue collar labour industries rather than the homosocial environment of military life that facilitated the formation of public lesbian communities.[41]

Economic independence allowed several of the narrators in this study to live with their partners in the postwar years and even to purchase homes together. Their financial reliance on family was minimal, and consequently they were able to move not only out of the homes they were raised in but also, in many cases, across the country or even from other countries to Canada, allowing them to live lesbian lives completely out of the view of their families.

Ideologues of postwar Canada tried very hard to instil in family life an antagonism toward those who strayed from the path of heterosexual matrimony, yet they were only partially successful. Many lesbians did indeed suffer the consequences of the new, psychological arguments and were marginalized and institutionalized on the basis of their sexuality. Yet, as the sources for this study indicate, family remained important in the lives of many lesbians. The narrators' families did not absorb the new discourse to the extent that they cut ties with their daughters absolutely. It will be the task of further research to examine the degree to which this was true across the nation and across lines of class and race.

With the advent of the social movements of the late 1960s, however, change occurred in lesbians' relationships with their families of origin. Society had come, over the preceding two decades, to see lesbians as antithetical to the family, and lesbians began to see the traditional family as heterosexist. By the 1970s lesbians could be singing "Family of Womon We've Begun."[42] By the 1980s and 1990s one could speak of "lesbian parenting" and "lesbian families" as viable alternatives to the traditional normative family. These ideas are a positive interpretation of lesbian life, in which lesbians are seen once again as capable of family life, albeit with a twist, yet this positive development has its origin in the gradual separation of lesbians from the family unit. Born in antagonism, the alternative lesbian family is the result of a decades-old struggle between lesbian identity and notions of family life.

8

Middle-Class Lesbian Community in the 1950s and 1960s

In the early twenty-first century, we are used to referring to and seeing a lesbian community, whether in the city where we live or represented in media and other arenas. In the 1950s and 1960s in Canada, there were lesbian communities, but they were very small compared to those of today, they existed only in Canada's larger cities, and they were not widely known about. Many lesbians knew nothing of the emerging lesbian communities. Still others knew of the communities based around bars but wanted little to do with them. The formation of community based on sexual orientation has been understood as an essential step in the overcoming of homo- phobia and in the education of society about lesbians and gay men. What we have not as often considered is the shape of that community and whether it was for all lesbians something positive that they wished to participate in. This chapter examines the formation of lesbian community in relation to class differences. In the 1950s and 1960s there existed a sub- stantial middle-class lesbian world outside the universities, government departments, and public welfare organizations, on the one hand, and the downtown bars, on the other. That social world has, until now, remained largely unexplored.

Separation from bar culture was important in many lower-middle-class lesbians' constructions of subjectivity. The bar was a crucial line of demar- cation between "respectable" and "rough" lesbians, and respectability and distance from bar life were key elements in the self-identification of lower- middle-class lesbian women. Much research has examined the 1970s lesbian- feminist disapproval of the butch-femme bar women, yet disapproval had been present within lesbian communities since at least 1940.[1] Prefeminist disapproval was not based on gender analysis but rather was the result of class conflict and concerns about respectability. Lower-middle-class lesbians disapproved of the bar culture, and notions of respectability related to that disapproval were part and parcel of their constructions of self. By organizing their social lives around house parties away from the downtown core or by visiting the bars only occasionally as "tourists," lower-middle-class lesbians created and maintained a class identity distinct from that of the bar women.

Divisions of race were also present within lesbian communities before 1965. In Canada there were very few Aboriginal lesbians or lesbians of colour in the lesbian community before second-wave feminism, and even afterward few felt fully comfortable in the lesbian community. As the film *Forbidden Love* reports, Aboriginal women were more likely to frequent those venues with larger numbers of Aboriginal or black patrons than they were the almost exclusively white lesbian bars. People of colour seldom owned Canada's midcentury gay and lesbian clubs. And although lesbian bars could be found in downtown areas such as Chinatowns, which often housed the greater proportion of cities' nonwhite populations, people of non-European cultures did not necessarily form their clientele. Women of colour might be entertainers, but not many of them were patrons.[2] The predominantly white bars and clubs were often very racist.[3] All the women interviewed for this study were white. Many narrators reported not knowing any lesbians of colour or Aboriginal lesbians during the period under study. Employment, social activities, and location of residence were intimately linked in the pre-1965 period to racial divisions as well as to those of class, and most of the women I interviewed had opportunities that few Aboriginal women and women of colour had access to in the period under study.

In addition to such factors as race and class, the very availability of information about the existence of lesbian communities affected women's ability to meet others like themselves. Many of the women reported that they had no lesbian community in the years before second-wave feminism. In several cases, these women thought that they were alone or, once they had partners, that they and their lover were the only two in the world. Their social worlds were thus largely heterosexual, and they kept their lesbian partnerships separate from family and friends. For these women, the lack of information about the existence of lesbian communities and the prohibitions against same-sex love resulted in a secrecy that was not overcome until the gay liberation movement and lesbian feminism had pushed gay and lesbian communities more forcefully into public view. This chapter does not examine the testimonies of these women but rather focuses on those women who did form community, either in small groups or in large ones, with other lesbians beyond their partners.

A crucial element in the formation of both community and a lesbian identity was the gaining of information about lesbianism. Many lesbians were not part of a community before 1965 simply because they did not know that such a thing existed.[4] Some early-twentieth-century lesbians who were aware of their attraction toward women were lucky enough to be able to read some of the emerging sexological and other literature discussing homosexuality.[5] A case in point is Elsa Gidlow. Gidlow was born in England in 1898 and arrived in Quebec with her family in 1905. When she was a teenager, she founded a literary study group. As mentioned in Chapter 1, it was one of the members of that group, a gay man, who introduced her to the kind of reading that would tell her of other lesbians. In her published memoir *Elsa: I Come with My Songs,* she also remembered:

> Roswell confided his personal crusade to me. He wanted people to understand that it was beautiful, not evil, to love others of one's own sex and make love with them. Roswell had divined my lesbian temperament and was happy to proselytize; the veil of self-ignorance began to lift.[6]

Gidlow's early community was, however, a small and male one. She was not to meet a large number of lesbian friends until the 1960s. Prior to this period, her contact with others like herself was extremely restricted, particularly as her social class would have precluded her involvement in any of the postwar urban bar cultures.

Because of the lack of female participation in same-sex sexual activities in public areas, such as parks and toilets, and the limitations on female use of bars and clubs, there exists very little information about lesbian social activities before the war and postwar work opportunities brought women together in larger numbers than ever before. Those works examining the bar cultures of Montreal and Toronto were the first to discuss the topic of lesbian community. Ross Higgins and Line Chamberland discuss Montreal's "yellow press" in the 1950s and 1960s. Press coverage of the lesbian and gay communities usually portrayed them as perverted and/or humorous. The exposure of "deviants" was one of the main aims of the "yellow press," yet in titillating readers with knowledge of forbidden sexual underworlds, the press was also facilitating the entry into those worlds of women and men who were questioning their sexual orientation.[7] It was these papers to which women and men could turn in order to find out where the bars were and these papers in which they saw others like themselves portrayed, however oddly. Higgins and Ross' study of Montreal scandal sheets shows that lesbians and gay men used the papers to give them access to personal contacts and to the bar scene, even while many papers were adopting a tone of moral outrage to sell more copies to a prurient heterosexual public.[8] Steven Maynard suggests that the Toronto tabloid press, most particularly the paper *Hush,* put into circulation "an evocative, popular language of lesbianism" that might include terminology arising from sexological understandings but was not restricted to an elite readership. Through the tabloids, he argues, people were informed of the existence of lesbianism.[9] Writing about a slightly later period, Becki Ross suggests that the tabloids "contributed to a growing awareness of, and fascination with, 'unorthodox sex exponents,' while playing on heterosexual fears that male and female 'queers' were busily taking over the city."[10]

In her study of lesbian imagery in *Chatelaine* between 1950 and 1969, Valerie Korinek reveals that the magazine published articles – largely negative – about "female homosexuals," their abnormality, and their causes and cures. Korinek also argues, however, that *Chatelaine* published short stories that, using a "perverse" reading, lesbians among its readership could interpret in lesbian terms. Lesbians read stories, illustrations, articles about friendships and other relationships between women, and advertisements and "could easily resist the preferred meanings of the material and opt for alternate interpretations that more aptly reflected their sense of themselves."[11] That women of the period did read such material in a "perverse" manner is confirmed both by the film *Forbidden Love,* for Canada, and by Sherrie Inness, in *The Lesbian Menace,* for the United States.[12]

Few of the women interviewed for this study read the tabloid newspapers. They were not exposed to the lurid accounts of gay and lesbian clubs, scandals, and court cases and had instead to locate their communities in other ways. Nor did they read much about lesbians in the more reputable publications. They therefore remained almost untouched by the trend, described by many historians, of negative media portrayal contributing to the growth of unwanted subcultures, and they relied for the most part on informal networks. Once they had found one individual, either lesbian or gay, who was "in the scene," they were able to meet others. Only some had known, because of novels or casual gossip, that they should look for gay and lesbian bars and clubs. Others stumbled upon lesbian communities accidentally or made their own communities by linking up with a small network of colleagues and friends who shared their sexual orientation. Those narrators whose relationships were formed in the period before urban lesbian communities established themselves and before newspapers publicized their existence, as well as those who lived in rural areas or in towns without a gay and lesbian subculture faced even greater challenges, finding others like themselves. They had to rely exclusively on personal networks and on the limited range of social opportunities available to them.

Single-sex institutions were places where relationships with women could be explored. Women still had to be very discreet about their encounters, but middle-class institutions did at least provide women with social opportunities apart from men.[13] Yet, such institutions, most particularly the American women's colleges, became explicitly linked in this period with lesbian behaviour. Late-nineteenth- and early-twentieth-century antifeminist rhetoric in Europe and the United States often included the charge that higher education masculinized women and could turn them into lesbians. Women's institutions, which coupled higher education with isolation from male company, came under increasing suspicion and had increasingly to police close relationships between women for fear that they might have a lesbian component.[14]

The attitude toward women's colleges changed in response to the new novels about such institutions. Inness demonstrates that, despite the 1920s glamour and mystique of "lesbian chic," the 1920s and 1930s saw the extensive publication of novels about lesbianism in college life that portrayed the women's college as "a nest of perversity." Inness argues that the novels, which marked women's institutions as abnormal and as breeding-grounds for Sapphism, had a considerable influence on how the public regarded single-sex education.[15] Despite the backlash against women's colleges, however, increasing numbers of women sought higher education; some of them were lesbians. The American colleges certainly provided Mildred with opportunities to meet other women. Mildred formed the majority of her relationships, with both women and men, in university settings, where she was first a student and then a faculty member.[16]

Although upper-middle-class women's lives were circumscribed by gender norms and by notions of respectability, their social position afforded them the protection of privilege. They had greater economic backing, in many cases, on which they could rely. It can also be suggested that class bias about sexuality worked in favour of middle-class women, as even in the twentieth century they were assumed to be less sexual than were working-class women. Even though a very sexualized discourse of same-sex relationships was emerging, middle-class women remained somewhat protected from it before the Second World War, partly because of societal assumptions about their degree of physical sexuality. It was less conceivable that middle-class women would be sexually active with each other than it was that working-class women would.[17]

Analyses of gay and lesbian communities have traditionally focused on small geographical areas where gays and lesbians could be found in large numbers. Although most of these studies examine largely working-class communities, there are a few that discuss wealthier enclaves. Esther Newton, for example, has documented the establishment of a prosperous gay and lesbian community in *Cherry Grove, Fire Island: Sixty Years in America's First Gay and Lesbian Town*.[18] Just outside New York City, Cherry Grove became a haven for gays and lesbians in the years before the Second World War. Cherry Grove grew rapidly between 1945 and 1960 and became a weekend resort where wealthy middle-class gay men and lesbians could retreat from their closeted lives in the city and could live openly in a gay environment. Some of the younger women, especially in the 1950s, were more committed to butch and femme identities than were the older women, attesting to the fact that butch and femme roles were not exclusively the province of working-class lesbians and also to the fact that the butch-femme relationship model grew increasingly widespread.[19] Middle-class lesbians were able to be more affectionate and more transgressive in their dress and behaviour in Cherry Grove than they were elsewhere. In the outside world, concern for job security and respectability restricted their expression of lesbianism. The Cherry Grove community provided a safe haven where one's sexuality was validated and affirmed.

The degree to which lesbian community was divided by class can best be seen in the attitudes toward those women who were the most visible lesbians in the middle of the twentieth century: the butch and femme lesbians of urban bar cultures. Openly sexual, transgressing gender norms, and fighting for public space, these women became the symbol of all that was wrong with lesbians – both to heterosexual society and to middle-class lesbians who did not approve of their openness and of their links to crime and drugs.

Bar communities developed in North America between the 1930s and the 1960s. My purpose is not to give a detailed account of the Canadian bar culture, for Elise Chenier has used the Lesbians Making History project and her own interviews to do just that,[20] but rather to offer a context for my narrators' opinions of the bar scene. I shall argue here that antipathy toward many aspects of bar culture formed an important part of the narrators' understanding of who they were as lesbians. Those lesbians involved in the 1950s and 1960s in the homophile campaign for acceptance within the broader heteronormative society were often critical of the visibility of butch and femme lesbians. The rejection of the bar culture and of butch and femme gender roles also took place among lower-middle-class lesbians, women who did not attend university. In the 1950s and 1960s, in particular, it was they who could reasonably have believed that they had more to lose from the public visibility of the bar culture than did university-educated women. As women working in "middling" jobs, they were closer to the bar women in status and social circle, and their personal investment in distancing themselves from the bar culture may therefore have been considerable.

Working-class bar communities began to emerge in the interwar period in the United States. By the 1930s, a large number of words for lesbianism existed, which clearly indicates the existence of a lesbian subculture. Lillian Faderman describes an extensive lesbian argot, which continued the use of a number of terms from the 1920s, including "dyke," "bulldagger," and "gay," and which contained new words as well. The 1930s saw the opening of several women-only bars, such as Mona's in San Francisco, which opened in 1936. These bars were predominantly working-class, although middle-class women did sometimes frequent them.[21]

Elizabeth Lapovsky Kennedy and Madeline Davis chronicle the emergence of a distinct lesbian bar culture in Buffalo, New York, tracing its origins back at least as far as the 1930s.[22] Their study found that the Buffalo bars were hard to find, were sometimes short-lived, and almost always were working-class women's enclaves.[23] Bars were mixed rather than exclusively lesbian, and they were dangerous places. Raids were frequent, particularly in the years immediately before the end of Prohibition.[24] House parties were also an important arena for lesbian socializing, most particularly for black women, who were less inclined to frequent the bars. It was not that they felt that the bars were not welcoming; the black women interviewed preferred parties because it was easier to dance and "let their hair down."[25] White women also frequented house parties. During the 1940s, the bars grew in importance as a social outlet for lesbians, and a distinct subculture began to be associated with them.

In the 1950s and the 1960s, the butch-femme bar culture of the prewar years grew further. The postwar era in both Canada and the United States was one of overt condemnation and repression of homosexuality, yet the subcultures of gay men and lesbians had grown too large to be stifled by the measures employed by the government, the police, and medical experts. Much of the literature available on lesbians in the postwar period is American and focuses on this largely working-class culture. The two most notable studies, Faderman's *Odd Girls and Twilight Lovers* and the Kennedy and Davis book *Boots of Leather, Slippers of Gold,* reveal the growth of a strong and public working-class urban lesbian culture, situated mainly in the bars of the downtown cores of various American cities.

The Canadian Bar Culture

As in the case of the United States, the most visible world of lesbians in postwar Canada was the predominantly working-class butch and femme bar culture. Apart from the film *Forbidden Love,* in which lesbians who lived in Canada during the 1950s and 1960s discuss their lives in the bar scene and in relationships, there is relatively little documentation of this culture in Canadian society. We know that there were many lesbian-friendly bars in Canadian cities in the 1960s, but fewer social outlets of this kind can be found for the previous decades.[26] Canada's lesbians were to come to the bar scene rather later than their American counterparts. As in America, however, bars were frequented on a regular basis only by a segment of the lesbian community – largely working-class women. Middle-class lesbians either avoided the bars altogether or visited only occasionally as "tourists."

Chamberland charts the bar scene of Montreal from 1955 to 1975 and shows that the bar culture was structured along the same butch and femme lines as that of the United States. She also argues that butch and femme roles were strategies for securing and defending public space, in which she is in agreement with the Kennedy and Davis argument that butch-femme couples were the precursors to the lesbian-feminist movement of the 1970s in fighting for women's right to live openly and publicly as lesbians.[27] As Chamberland states, "exposure was needed in order to ensure that lesbian bars became known and accessible. Knowing that such places existed and discovering where they were was a problem. On the other hand, concealment was necessary in order to escape repression."[28]

In Toronto a number of venues became lesbian/gay hangouts from the 1930s onward. During the 1930s and 1940s lesbians and gay men occupied the beach on Hanlan's Point and held parties at the Pearson Hotel on Centre Island. In the 1950s lesbians rented rooms from Heinzmann's piano company and cottages on Toronto Island. By the early 1960s freestanding bars such as Letros and private weekend clubs provided lesbians with social spaces where they could enjoy a dance floor and live music. In the 1960s gay men and women claimed public space in several bars and clubs, such as those at the King Edward Hotel, the Rideau Hotel, and the Continental Hotel.[29]

The most extensive study of a Canadian butch and femme culture is Chenier's examination of Toronto's public lesbian community from 1955 to 1965.[30] Chenier interviewed seven women, in addition to examining the interviews from the Lesbians Making History project, which are also used in this study. Chenier argues that the lesbian bar culture evolved out of lesbians' desire, in a context of social stigmatization, to socialize with other lesbians. The lives of these working- and street-class women were, Chenier suggests, influenced by the links between the bar culture, prostitution, and the drug trade and by the presence of the police. The Continental, like many other lesbian haunts, was in Chinatown, an area already associated in the minds of the police and the public with prostitution, drugs, and other illicit activities. Those who lived the "gay life" full-time were visible:

Butch *and* fem downtowners were identifiable to insiders and outsiders alike: more assertive in staking their claim on physical and social spaces, more willing to challenge conventions concerning sex and gender comportment, and more sexually explicit in their verbal and physical interactions, they comprised a distinct social group of sexual outsiders.[31]

Chenier argues that the character of lesbians in the downtown culture was formed partly by the survival strategies they employed, which included sex work, "rolling" men (pick-pocketing), and dealing in drugs. Lesbians also formed relationships of various kinds with Chinese men. But bar lesbians were not in the bar culture because they desired to create new social spaces for women or because the rough bars were already known to them. They "preferred street bars because the sex trade also provided opportunities to combine remunerative labour with pleasure."[32]

Although the largest lesbian communities in Canada in the 1950s and 1960s were those of Montreal and Toronto, Vancouver also had a lesbian subculture. Less is known, however, about that community. Several of the women interviewed in *Forbidden Love* reveal that the Vanport Hotel was a lesbian hangout in the 1960s. Like the Continental in Toronto, the Vanport was a dangerous and dirty venue where mainly working-class butch and femme lesbians socialized.[33] Several other bars and clubs catered to a gay and lesbian clientele in the early 1960s, among them the Abbotsford Hotel, the Castle Hotel Puss 'n Boots Room, Club 752, the Devonshire Hotel, the Georgia Hotel, the Montreal Hotel, and the Vancouver Hotel.[34] The "heyday" of these bars and clubs occurred in the late 1960s and the 1970s, but in all the above cases the venues had catered to gays and lesbians before 1965. Vanessa Cosco interviewed working-class Vancouver lesbians who were part of the city's butch and femme bar culture and confirmed many of the observations made in *Forbidden Love* about the Vancouver scene.[35] Without further oral histories of women and men who frequented the Vancouver scene in the 1950s, we cannot know precisely how early these and other bars and clubs became gay and lesbian spots.

The mid-twentieth-century bar culture of the larger Canadian cities provided women with a sense of community in that they knew where they could go to be with women like themselves. They had a support group of women who trained them in the roles of the community, who saw them through relationships and struggles with the police and employers, and who fought with them for public lesbian space. However, there was not necessarily a sense of community based on identity shared across class and other lines, and the community that existed was not always supportive. Jerry argued, in fact, that there was no sense of community in the 1950s and 1960s. "You survive, you survive," she commented.[36]

The bar scene was predominantly butch and femme, as Chenier and others have shown, and was often a rough and dangerous world. Barb confirmed that butches dressed like men, with men's clothes, brush-cuts, "the whole works." One butch whom Barb met lived fully as a man, even holding a male job. Even when slacks became more fashionable for women, the butches would wear a more masculine style, favouring slacks with a fly front. She remembered that the couples were easy to spot "because it would be like a guy and a girl together, and the girl would be mostly much more feminine."[37]

Butch-femme roles were an important part of working-class lesbian life in the 1950s and 1960s, and those who were entrenched in the bar scene, especially at the Continental, lived publicly in those roles. Those who were more occasional visitors to the bars flirted with the roles but often did not hold to them very deeply or take them very seriously. Reva's story has been made famous by the film *Forbidden Love* but is worth repeating here. Reva did not feel that she was either butch or femme but rather somewhere in the middle. She and her partner made a trip to New York, and to Greenwich Village in particular, to "look for the lesbians." They went to Greenwich Village because the lesbian pulp novels they had been reading identified the village as a major lesbian area.[38] "You would have laughed if you'd seen us," Reva said:

> She was about five-five, I'm only five feet tall, and she was fairly heavy. I was really skinny in those days. She wore a dress. I wore a red blazer, black pants, and a tie ... the best butch clothes that I could figure out, what a butch wore. And she had her dress, and off we went to look for the dykes. We walked around Greenwich Village, got nowhere, got a cabby, said, "We want to go to a gay bar." He took us to some bar. We went in there and looked around, and couldn't tell "a" from "b." They were very uptight ... People looked at us. I guess we looked really weird ... and that was it. That was our big foray into New York City, and then we never found them.[39]

Even though the two women did not rigidly identify with the butch-femme roles, that was the kind of community they were used to seeing in

Montreal. They were looking for women who were clearly identifiable as lesbians because of their gender performance: "I mean, we didn't know what we were looking for," Reva said. "We were looking for a very obvious butch-femme scene, where all the butches were looking like butches, and all the femmes were looking like femmes, and you could tell them apart, and they'd be in couples, and we'd recognize the thing! But we didn't find that kind of a scene in New York." When they did not find such women, they were confused. However, such a scene was there. Pat married a gay man in 1951 to get away from her family and live in New York. She remembered the New York scene as "wild." Pat was only nineteen when she moved to New York, but she had already attended some gay bars in Montreal, where, as in Toronto, drinking, prostitution, and drugs were a part of bar life. Even so, she was surprised by some of the aspects of the New York scene. Pat recalled that the butch-femme scene in New York was much more rigid than it was in Montreal.[40]

Travelling to other cities was an important part of lesbian life in the 1950s and 1960s if one could afford it. Pam occasionally went to Montreal but made many trips to Buffalo bars. She also went to Detroit, where being butch or femme was a requirement for entry into some of the bars. "If you were a butch, and you didn't have a tie or a jacket, you were actually asked to leave," she remembered, "because that's the way the bar worked." Like Pat, Pam suggested that gender roles were more strongly defined in the United States. Pam remembered one particularly tough Detroit bar called Knit One, Pearl Two, where the female bartender was bald. Pam could hardly tell "if it was male or female."

The butch-femme scene in the United States was more visual to Pam than was the Canadian scene,

> where we were more social. If we did have a party or something, we could go and dance with each other, or somebody else's girlfriend. It wasn't that you were, you know, putting the make on them. You just were, it was dancing. In Detroit, when we'd go to house parties there or to the bars, God forbid if you went over and asked somebody else's girlfriend to dance without asking this butch person's permission to have the dance.

Pam's perspective on this issue is rather different from that of many of the women interviewed for the Lesbians Making History project, who recalled that the Continental was much the same; it was very unwise to ask a woman to dance unless one had the prior permission of her partner. This was particularly the case when asking a femme woman to dance, as the butches were extremely possessive. In England the same rules applied. Rebecca Jennings quotes an interview with Angela Chilton, who explained, "If one of the other butches wanted to dance with someone else's femme, they had to ask the butch, and it was up to the butch whether her femme danced or not."[41] It may be noted that Pam was speaking of the Canadian house parties, many of which she organized, rather than of the bar culture in Canada per se. It may well have been the case that the women who attended Pam's house parties were not as possessive and rigid about gender as were those who attended American house parties and bars or those in the Canadian bar culture.

It is difficult to reconcile the testimonies given on the subject of the Canadian bar scene. All the narrators who visited the bars in Montreal and Toronto attested to the fact that the butch-femme relationship was the predominant mode of relationship among regular bar patrons. Pat, Mary, and Pam argued that the American bar scene was even more rigid in terms of its employment of butch and femme roles. Why, then, was Reva unable to find the sort of community in New York that she was used to seeing in Montreal? It may simply have been an unfortunate coincidence that the bars she and her partner visited in New York were not those of the working-class butch-femme couples. It may also have been that they had dressed in a moderate butch-femme style but in clothes not typical of that bar scene and that the taxi driver may have taken them to a bar frequented by less openly lesbian patrons.

That the differences between Canada and the United States can be attributed to cultural differences is unlikely. Too many of the cultural norms of the butch-femme bar scene were similar, and there was considerable American influence on Canadian lesbians because of the frequent visits Canadian lesbians made to the United States. Rather, it is likely that the greater entrenchment in the American communities of butch-femme norms of behaviour was due to the earlier development of the subculture in the United States. Those works that discuss the bar scene in the US usually identify the 1930s, if not the 1920s, as the starting point for the butch-femme bar scene. In Canada this same culture does not seem to have appeared until the late 1940s. It is therefore reasonable to assume that the additional ten to twenty years of butch-femme culture in America resulted in greater cohesion and definition of subcultural norms. If the butch-femme culture in Canada had developed for a further twenty years, instead of dwindling after the advent of second-wave feminism, it might also have become more rigid and uniform than it was.

The Canadian urban scene was also a little late in developing compared to that in London, England. In the late 1950s Pat and Mary quit their jobs and went to Europe and Britain for several months, spending several weeks working in Chelsea in an area they described as "bohemian." They attended the Gateways Club, which later featured in the lesbian film *The Killing of Sister George*.[42] Through a lesbian couple whom they already knew, they met many British gays and lesbians and went to many house parties. Pat commented, "I found the British people were more kinky than Canadians because they were more open and they used to jump from partner to partner ... and the straight couples would come to the gay bars and sort of be curious about women ... so there was a lot of kinkiness in London." Mary responded, "We loved it. It was so, kind of free."[43] From the perspective of Mary and Pat, Canada lacked the sort of sexual freedom and experimentation typical of some parts of England in the same period.[44]

The Canadian bar culture may have been a little tame compared to the American and British scenes in the same period, but it was "wild" enough to be the subject of much public condemnation, the target of police raids, and the focus of criticism from an emerging homophile movement desperate to persuade North Americans that gay men and lesbians were normal, productive individuals whose lifestyle was not abhorrent. It was also subject to criticism from lower-middle-class lesbians who were sufficiently involved in the urban milieu to know about the bars but largely unwilling to be involved in the bar culture.

"Not the upper crust, but the medium sort of thing": Respectable Lesbians, House Parties, and Bars

For many lesbian women in the years before feminism, community was hard to find and difficult to maintain. Lesbians found community wherever they could, but only some lived openly in the public communities about which lurid articles and novels were written. Lesbian historiography, which focused initially on upper-middle-class educated lesbians, has more recently discussed the highly visible working-class lesbians of the bar culture.

Largely missing from lesbian historiography, however, are those women who arguably were the majority of lesbians before 1965: women who were neither wealthy and highly educated nor poor and involved in the public bar communities of major Canadian cities. They were store clerks, nurses, schoolteachers, and office workers. In suburbs, in isolated couples, and in small groups of friends, they lived behind the walls of respectability. They lived their lesbianism in secrecy, not willing to engage in behaviours that they regarded as "rough" and that they feared would have cost them their jobs. Perhaps because they lived their lives largely unnoticed at the time and were neither highly visible nor politically active, historians have largely neglected them.

Most works on the Canadian bar culture of the 1950s and 1960s focus primarily on those women who lived fully in the bar life. Chenier interviewed a few "uptowners" who visited the bars only infrequently or on weekends, but her emphasis is on the "downtowners," or women who lived "the gay life" full-time in the bar scene. Chenier acknowledges the difficulty for all lesbians of living a lesbian life in a hostile world, but she suggests that social and economic class created a distance between uptowners and downtowners that their shared sexual orientation could not bridge.[45] Chamberland's research on the Montreal bars also suggests that class significantly influenced the mode of lesbian socializing in the 1950s and 1960s and that women's experience of homophobia varied according to class position.[46] Cosco spoke to middle-class lesbians who knew about butch and femme but did not think of themselves in relation to those identities or participate in the bar scene. These were women like the narrators for this study: women in middle-class jobs who kept their lesbianism hidden so as not to jeopardize their employment. One of Cosco's narrators spoke of the life as "like a double closet, triple closet."[47]

One of the few American scholars to explore in depth the social worlds of lower-middle-class lesbians is Katie Gilmartin. Gilmartin argues that "the gay bar was a radically different cultural space for middle-class women ... and for the predominantly working-class clientele that frequented the bars."[48] In her examination of middle-class lesbians' lives in 1950s and 1960s Colorado, Gilmartin found that middle-class lesbians might occasionally have visited the bars but that they did not identify with bar life. In many cases, they distinguished their own lives from those of the bar women, forming their own lesbian identities in relation to other cultural practices and types of community. The public and outspoken world of bar women was anathema to the interests of middle-class women, and class was an integral part of her narrators' struggles over closetedness and the leading of double lives.[49] Secrecy was similarly crucial for lower-middle-class Canadian lesbians. To the narrators in my study, the bar scene was enticing in its openness and its freedom, yet it was filled with traps of other kinds. The women I spoke to have a grudging respect for the toughness of the bar women, particularly the butches, who had to face the most public condemnation and police harassment, but none of the narrators wanted to be as open about their sexuality themselves.

The narrators constructed their narratives of lesbian socializing around antipathy to many aspects of bar culture. They distanced themselves from its more violent and "seedy" aspects, even while often acknowledging an occasional interest in visiting bar life. The narrators formed their initial sense of themselves in an environment hostile to lesbianism and to transgressive gender performance generally, and they also attempted to make careers for themselves in respectable but not necessarily secure and high-status jobs.

To these women, social class and respectability were as important as their lesbianism, which, from their perspective, made interaction with the bar community problematic and dangerous. Class concerns both limited their ability to explore lesbian community in the 1950s and 1960s and informed the ways they developed and responded to community. They were lesbians, certainly, and they socialized on that basis, knew consciously that they were different from the rest of society, and rebelled against heteronormativity to the extent that they were unwilling to live unhappy lives as married women. But they were also women who, whatever their class origins, had achieved middle-class status, respectability, and income, and these attributes informed their self-perceptions and limited their willingness to live openly as lesbians.

One cannot really speak of class conflict among lesbians in Canada before the 1950s. Until the postwar era and the growth of the visible bar culture, lesbians of different classes were so far removed from one another and from public view that even though class differences existed, they were not a source of friction between groups of lesbians. It is with the rise of the bar culture that one sees conflict emerging. The increasing public attention to the subject of homosexuality and the negative portrayals of the bar women as the antithesis of ideal womanhood gave rise to a desire among some lesbians to distance themselves from this new visible culture and to think of themselves, and eventually to publicly portray themselves, as more respectable. Condemnation of the bar culture became common among lesbians from the middle class. The narrators for this study, most of whom were lower-middle-class in the period under study, sought to distinguish their lives and behaviour from those of the bar women. The language they used to describe the bars was often pejorative, particularly when compared with their celebratory tone regarding the house parties that were their primary form of community socializing.

Three negative attributes of the bar scene were repeatedly identified by the narrators: the general seediness of the bars, the frequent fights between women, and the risk of being seen by a work colleague or arrested during a police raid. Many of the women interviewed for this study confirmed that the bars were dirty, violent, and dangerous places to socialize. Barb, Pat, and Mary recalled that many of the bar regulars took and dealt drugs, were prostitutes or pimps, and were very poor. "The [dregs] of society used to hang around there," Pat remarked. "You'd go in there, and you had to wash your hands when you got out."[50]

Fights were frequent in lesbian bars, and several narrators remembered witnessing fights. Barb managed to avoid the fights at the Continental but was aware that they happened.[51] Lois remembered the fights at the Continental. "I used to get in one or two," she said.[52] Reva also remembered hearing about fights, although she was lucky enough not to witness any during her few visits to the bars in Montreal.[53] Personal experience of domestic abuse seemed to temper some women's responses to the fighting. Pam attended various bars and clubs before 1965 and witnessed several fights. When asked whether she ever participated in the fights herself, she replied, "I did enough fighting with the girl I lived with."[54] Cheryl reported that after she and her friends left the air force and moved to Toronto, they started frequenting the Continental and the Music Room. Cheryl found the Continental women

so tough. Oh my God! You know ... I guess we were just so innocent. We just couldn't believe, I mean you'd go in there and you'd sit with your back to the wall ... lots of fights ... always bothered me why people needed to fight. Breaking beer bottles ... and then holding them up to

one another's throats ... And I guess it was because ... I had experienced
the physical abuse at the hands of a woman that, you know, I thought,
"Why does this have to happen?"[55]

The main reason that lower-middle-class women chose to avoid the
bars, however, was the risk of being seen by a colleague from work or being picked up by the police during a raid and losing one's job. Those bars
that allowed an openly lesbian clientele usually reserved a back room for
them, and lesbians could theoretically socialize in privacy. Heterosexual
people did, however, enter the bars to look at them.[56] Many women worried
that these heterosexual "tourists" might include people they knew from
their outside lives. If colleagues from work had seen them in such a venue,
their jobs might well have been in jeopardy.

Pat remembered well the societal attitudes toward gay people. "You
didn't go out of your way to announce that you were gay," she said,
commenting,

> You had to be careful, because the cops ... they'd go out of their way to
> be nasty to you ... so you didn't give them any chance to name-call ...
> so you'd have to be cool in the clubs and walking along the streets. You
> would never think of walking hand-in-hand. I mean, it just wasn't done.
> And you didn't dress as butchy as you would if you were going to a house
> party or something.[57]

At a house party, women were much less likely to be harassed by the police
or by heterosexual people, so they could dress in a more "butchy" way
without fear of it causing them to be the target of abuse. In the bars, the
threat of a police raid was always present.

As a police officer herself, Billie was familiar with the bar scene in
Toronto in the early 1960s. She did not go to house parties until she had
been on the force for a year, and she was closeted in her lesbianism. Her
only experiences of the Continental were of occasions on which she was
part of police raids. She reported that undercover policewomen were used
in the Continental but that she was never required to work undercover.
"I'd have got caught," she said. Her police work meant that socializing at
the Continental was out of the question: "To go to the Continental was
like an excursion into the twilight zone ... some of the women there we

had arrested, so it was impossible." It was not until the early 1970s that Billie would frequent the gay bars socially, and even then it was difficult. The bar women knew by then that she was a police officer and would tell her when the police came in so that she could hide. On one occasion, however, she was seen by a fellow police officer and was warned that she could lose her job.[58]

One should not assume that those lesbians who generally avoided the bar scene were immune to the consequences the regular patrons suffered. Barb remembered leaving the St. Charles one evening with two friends:

> I was walking ahead of them, actually, and the other two were sort of arm-in-arm and they were singing going up the street ... and next thing I know, I was walking just ahead of them and looking in a store window, and I got this on the side of my arm, this squeeze, and "Come on, you're coming with me." I turned around quickly, and there he was – a plain-clothes man [who] said, "You're disturbing the peace. I'm arresting you." I said, "Who are you?" And he said, "I'm police." So I asked to see and he showed me his badge, and in the meantime, there was two of them and they were sitting in a car opposite the bar, St. Charles, and they watched us come out. There's no doubt about it.

One of the women got away through an alley, but Barb and one friend were taken into custody for the night. The next morning, they went to court and pleaded guilty and had to pay a fine. It was much less risky to plead guilty and get the matter resolved than to plead not guilty and spend more time in court, thus risking exposure.[59]

A social life based around bars did not necessarily need to involve the less reputable venues. There were more "upscale" establishments for those who could afford them. In these establishments, a good standard of dress and behaviour was required, and often women were not allowed entrance unless they were in the company of a man. These were not gay or lesbian bars as such but rather establishments that at least tolerated a gay or lesbian presence. Billie did not remember it being illegal for women to enter bars together, but it was the case that some of the bars were restricted to "women and escorts" so that prostitutes could be kept out.[60] Lesbians found their access to the better hotels restricted by this custom, but by and large it was men grouping together who were policed more forcefully than were women.

A gay man often had to have a woman with him to get into places like Toronto's King Edward Hotel. Testimonies in *Forbidden Love* confirm that gay men and lesbians in the 1950s and 1960s often worked together to circumvent such restrictions: they would enter together and then go their separate ways. "What they would do in the men's washroom," one narrator stated, "was none of your business."[61] For those lesbians keen to visit bars but also wishing to maintain a respectable image, such co-operation was vital.

Pam recalled double-dating with gay men on many occasions in the 1950s and 1960s so that she and her partner could gain access to various establishments. The practice was also important for work purposes: "Through to the point that one chap, [he] and I had to stop going to his work especially, because everybody thought we were such a wonderful couple that, you know, why weren't we getting married ... so we had to have a fight and break up because of it." She dated gay men in order to go to dances. "It was a good arrangement," she commented.[62] Lesbians and gay men in middle-class jobs needed to maintain an image of heterosexual respectability. In this respect at least, the two communities were mutually supportive. Barb reported that many of the women went to mixed parties with gay men. "I can remember at one place somebody came to the door for something, and the guys all grabbed a woman so that they'd be standing like this next to each other." If men in particular were found assembled in a same-sex gathering, they could be arrested, so mixed parties were organized.

Class, safety, and respectability were interrelated factors in lesbian socializing in the 1950s and 1960s, and the development of lesbian house parties provided a respectable alternative to the bar scene. The house parties were described by the narrators in much more flattering terminology than were the bars. Not only do their testimonies reveal a feeling of greater safety, but also there is much less condemnation of the activities of the women who frequented the parties. Barb commented: "I think some of the women that I met were women that didn't want to be downtown, you know? A little nervous because they knew about these bars, the people in the city knew about Letros downstairs, and so that was another thing they were nervous about being around, in case of, you know, being picked up." Most of the women whom Barb met at house parties "had the better jobs. We weren't the ritzy people in town, but we all had jobs. There wasn't anyone unemployed at the time, and we all had responsible jobs, you know? ... Not the upper crust, but the medium sort of thing ... Good jobs." Implicit in Barb's comment is a somewhat negative attitude toward the bar women, many of whom were unemployed, were in low-status jobs, or were prostitutes. It is clear that Barb's subjectivity as a lesbian was affected by class considerations. There is no unified lesbian subject here but rather *types* of lesbian, some of them respectable and others not. Barb implied at least three groupings of lesbians: the unemployed, the "medium sort," and the "upper crust." Barb made clear that she and her friends were not of the upper crust but also that none of them belonged to the unemployed category.

Barb revealed that there would be house parties every weekend, and "every weekend there'd be another couple that ... would come in." The parties were large and well organized. The women, however, still had to be careful:

> For the first while, I think, it was, "Drive your car, get a ride, but you better park around the corner," because people across the street, you know, they'll see all these cars and all these women going in and out, with just women, no men. Women going in and out of this house. So try to be a little bit careful ... All the time undercover, hiding, you know? But there was something kind of secret about it, something that really was kind of fun.[63]

Pam held a number of house parties in Toronto in the late 1950s and the 1960s. She and her then partner, Debbie, got to know a number of lesbians through baseball and other contacts. After a ball game, they would take twenty or thirty women back to their two-room apartment. "There was everybody who was anybody," Pam said:

> I never knew that the parties were important. Because people used to say, "Oh, you got an invitation to their party?" I never realized, and I'm sure Debbie went to her grave never knowing these parties were important to some of the gals that we met over the years. And just to be invited to these parties, because there was always somebody going to be there that somebody wanted to meet.

The parties held by Pam and Debbie were significant social events, and they were at a distance from, and out of the reach of, the bar lesbians. Yet these were parties like any other; the women spent their time drinking, dancing, talking, playing games, and otherwise relaxing. Lesbian social-izing was not substantially different from heterosexual socializing in this respect. It was merely that the lesbian house parties, unlike their hetero-sexual equivalents, were held secretly and that the women who attended had to be rather more careful about being seen.

Pam confirmed that the house-party crowd was very different from the bar crowd. "All the girls we knew were in nice positions," she commented,

> and we certainly weren't associated with [the Continental]. Not that we weren't curious, and wanted to go, which I did. It was a very frightening time, but there were a group of us decided one time we'd go down. But we would not go down there, as we were gay. We were going to go down there thinking that we were straight and just happen to fall into this bar by accident. And we went to go in, and some bouncer at the door says, "Well, I suppose you'll want to go into the back, because that's where your crowd is." Our crowd? Excuse me?[64]

However, it wasn't that the less desirable aspects of bar life never intruded on the house parties. There was sometimes excessive drinking, occasional drug use, and even fighting. Barb reported,

> In the group that I was in, I don't think there was ever ... anything that happened. There was once somebody, I think from drinking too much ... somebody wasn't supposed to be there with somebody else at the party, and the other one walked in and grabbed her by the head or the hair. I can remember her grabbing her by the hair and pulling her halfway down the steps at this house ... Nothing serious happened.[65]

Such things were, however, unusual. All of the narrators stated categoric-ally that, unlike the downtown bar women, the women at the house parties were not involved in heavy drugs. They did drink, and there was domestic violence in some relationships, but the fighting common in the bars did not often find its way to the suburbs and rarely took place outside people's homes.

The narrators identified the bar scene as dangerous, violent, and seedy, and although those attributes made the bars risqué and thrilling places to be, the bars did not offer a way of life with which these women chose to remain involved. Their perspective is thus very different from that of the women whose social world centred on the bars. The bar scene was, for working-class lesbians, limiting and liberating, dangerous and simultaneously self-defining. To middle-class lesbians, the bar scene was definitely defining – but in what they regarded as a most unfortunate way.

Historians have argued that the butch-femme culture of the bar scene was the first lesbian community that fought for public space and defended the rights of lesbian women to associate freely with each other and to have sexual lives. It has been shown that 1970s lesbian feminism would have had a much more difficult path to follow without the bar culture that it so soundly condemned. The bar culture had already established lesbian community in urban areas and had provided at least one generation of women with the knowledge that there were many others like themselves in Canada. By giving many lesbian women a social world, lesbian bars of the 1950s and 1960s laid the groundwork for the later community that would demand the right to walk openly on the street and to exist without harassment. The bars were almost as integral to the sense of community and to the subjectivities of those middle- and working-class lesbians who *did not* frequent them as they were to those women who relied on them as their primary or only social outlet. The bar door marked the threshold between two lesbian worlds: the respectable and the unrespectable. It quite literally marked the entry to the first public lesbian community, but it also was a symbolic marker of class difference within the lesbian community as a whole. In a way similar to the narratives of heterosexual sexual danger that placed clear boundaries on women's freedom of movement and expression, and defined the consequences for transgression of those boundaries, the bar represented, to the "respectable" lesbian, the risks involved in very public expressions of lesbian sexuality. The boundary between lower-middle-class lesbians and the butch and femme women of the bars was crucial to their understanding of who they were as lesbians. It was less the case that they defined themselves as being a particular kind of lesbian – other than a "middling" sort – and more that they defined themselves by default – by who it was that they were not. They were *not* like the bar women.

Bisexual Women and the Lesbian Community

The communities discussed above may well have housed, knowingly or unknowingly, a number of bisexual women. There were no bisexual communities as such. It is in the early part of the twentieth century that one begins to see the emergence of publicly acknowledged bisexual activity. It would be inaccurate to portray this as bisexual community, however, given that many of those behaving bisexually seemed to express a general rejection of sexual constraints rather than a bisexual identity per se. Bisexual identity in the modern sense, as a politically and erotically defined sexual orientation alongside, rather than within or between, gay or lesbian identity, is a recent phenomenon. Few before the 1970s argued for bisexuality as an independent sexual orientation, which makes analysis of bisexual history and community extremely difficult.

Scholarship in the history of sexuality has tended to interpret bisexual women's lives in terms of lesbianism – that is, as part of lesbian history rather than as a history unto itself. Lillian Faderman, in a section of *Odd Girls and Twilight Lovers* entitled "The Roots of Bisexual Experimentation," discusses the increasing numbers of women who "were giving themselves permission to explore sex between women." She examines, among other things, the work of the 1920s sociologist Katharine Bement Davis, who surveyed over two thousand married and single women about their erotic experiences and found that 50 percent of the women she interviewed had admitted intense emotional relationships with women, over half of them sexual in nature.[66] There is little evidence revealing to the modern reader the motives for Davis's research. She sought to understand all facets of female sexuality, a fascination arising perhaps from her increasing knowledge of sexual diversity, gleaned from her years of experience as a settlement-house worker in Philadelphia.[67] Whatever her motives for undertaking the study, Davis's research is one of the earliest examples of a large study of female sexual habits and is particularly revealing of the variety of female sexual expression in the early twentieth century.

Faderman suggests that the willingness of the many women Davis studied to engage in sexual relationships with women may have occurred because the mood of the times seemed to permit experimentation. In the 1930s, she argues, the new economic climate and the emphasis on conformity negated the gains of the 1920s, and a "'bisexual' compromise was the best [women] could manage."⁶⁸ In Faderman's view, material circumstances militated against women's opportunities to discover a lesbian identity and to live openly as lesbians. What Faderman has not taken into account, however, is that some of those women might actually have been bisexual, in terms of long-held desires for both women and men or even in terms of a consciously realized identity. It is likely that in the 1920s, when some women were self-consciously "lesbian" and some women were simply experimenting sexually, others were actually bisexual; it is also likely that, in the 1930s, some of the married women Faderman describes as lesbians who adopted a "'bisexual' compromise" were actually bisexual in their desires.

Because there were not early-twentieth-century bisexual communities or a bisexual identity in the modern sense, one must discuss instead those individual women whose desires and/or actions were bisexual and who formed relationships on that basis. Community for bisexuals before 1965 may therefore have to be thought of in terms of links with the lesbian community on the basis of shared sexual attraction to women. Such an analysis, however, risks subsuming bisexual women once again *within* lesbian history and so must be approached with caution.

Several of the narrators for this study reported that they were in relationships with men before they were with women or, in some cases, that they were in relationships with both sexes before beginning to live only as lesbians. As mentioned in Chapters 5 and 6, Mildred had a lengthy period of relationships with both men and women before she finally began seeing only women. She regards herself as having been bisexual, but the term itself was not one that she would have used at the time. She acted on her desires, although she regards her sexual relationships with men as having always been problematic. Yet Mildred was not seeing men because she was internally homophobic or because of heteronormativity. She had the relationships with men for much the same reasons as she did those with women: an intellectual and/or a political rapport.

It is difficult to determine the degree to which Mildred's experience of sexual desire, situated more in relation to shared intellectual and political beliefs than to any particular identity, was common in North American culture. Certainly, many North American female intellectuals, radical in their politics but also in their lifestyles, "challenged the sexual conventions that uphold male dominance, and experimented with radical new ways of thinking and living."[69] In the early twentieth century, when many people in North America were beginning to form the subcultures that would ultimately be the gay and lesbian communities, others incorporated new sexual practices into radical lifestyles based on political belief. As John D'Emilio and Estelle Freedman suggest, "involvement in radical causes, whether as socialists, anarchists, or feminists, imparted a fervor to their erotic experimentation which they defined as an essential, innovative component of revolutionary struggle."[70] In Britain too, in the late nineteenth and early twentieth centuries, there had long been links between radical political thought, especially socialism, and "a fundamental transformation in all relationships, including sexual ones."[71]

Mildred, however, did not articulate her attractions in terms of a conscious revolution in sexual practice as part of a broader political philosophy. She suggested merely that it was on the basis of shared political and intellectual links that she found people of either sex attractive. Nevertheless, it may be said that, in her early sexual life, Mildred's experience fitted within radical political expressions of sexuality in that she chose not to obey dominant conventions of sexual morality and instead explored her desires when and with whom they occurred. Her political beliefs, which ran well against the tide of mainstream opinion, may have aided her in being able to recognize her same-sex attractions as well as her opposite-sex ones and to act sexually with women and also outside the bounds of marriage with men, both of which were unacceptable behaviours in American society at the time.[72]

It is clear from scholarship on lesbian communities and from the tone of remarks made by some narrators that the lesbian community regarded bisexual women with considerable suspicion, as did the heterosexual community. Whereas heterosexuals suspected any woman involved in a relationship with another woman of being a lesbian, lesbians suspected bisexual women of being heterosexuals who were experimenting for a bit of fun. They were therefore not regarded as trustworthy. Such a judgment was based partly on a dichotomous view of sexuality, but it could also be related to gender norms. Kennedy and Davis report that some of the women they interviewed regarded butches as the only "true" lesbians, placing the femmes somewhere in the middle between lesbian and heterosexual and often viewing them as bisexual. Other lesbians regarded any woman who stayed in the scene, butch or femme, as lesbian.

Kennedy and Davis attempt to avoid making judgments about who was and who was not lesbian by describing their narrators instead in terms of persistence and fluidity of membership in lesbian community.[73] Such a strategy still does not adequately acknowledge bisexuality, especially a bisexual community separate from the lesbian community, but it does at least demonstrate that the lesbian community "housed" many different forms of sexuality. Their narrators, however, were not usually as flexible in their view of the community as were Kennedy and Davis. Many narrators made very clear judgments about which women were lesbians and which were not.

Canadian lesbians also made judgments about membership in the lesbian community, and they also differentiated "true" lesbians from those who "moved back and forth" or left the community to get married. Several women used the word "bisexual" in a pejorative sense, usually when they were describing an ex-lover who eventually left the community to get married. Describing the traumatic break-up of a relationship and her ex-partner's departure to the United States, Pat said, "I think she was really bisexual." The phrase was inserted in a set of comments about the woman's being a manipulative, destructive gold-digger. Pat further remembered that many of the exotic dancers in Montreal would "swing both ways."[74]

When asked whether they knew bisexual women, almost all the narrators replied that they did not. It is likely, however, that many of them had met bisexual women in the bar scene or at house parties but had simply been unaware of the fact at that time. Perhaps because of the hostility toward bisexuality in the lesbian community, women going to the bars or the parties may have chosen to express only their desire for women and not their desire for men. Many bisexual women, if they began a relationship with a man, would immediately leave the lesbian community, where that relationship would not have been approved of. It is impossible to know just how many women in Canada before 1965 were bisexual.

The Military and Community

For lesbians in Canada, wartime employment and the return of women to the armed forces in the 1950s were early milestones in community formation. Those of the narrators for this study who served in the military – Sarah, Barb, Cheryl, and Billie – regard it as an important part of their lives. Only one of the women interviewed for this study served in the Canadian armed forces during the first incarnation of the women's divisions during the Second World War. Sarah, who came from a military family, joined the air force in 1942. She had not explored her own sexuality at this point but was aware of other lesbians in the service. Her barrack building housed forty women, and at one corner of the block "there was a gal who had her hair cut [short], which was a real giveaway in those days, and she had a friend ... and we all assumed, but we didn't ever talk about anything like that, that they were a gay pair. This gal definitely was, anyway ... And there may well have been others."[75]

In the 1950s Canadian women were allowed back into the armed forces. The testimonies of several women interviewed for this study confirm that, in the postwar era, the armed services were an important introduction to lesbian community, as they were for American lesbians. It was in the service that many young women who had experienced crushes on, or even had had relationships with, other girls or women discovered that there were many more women like themselves in Canada. The military gave lesbians the opportunity to socialize with large groups of women and to form relationships away from the prying eyes of family. However, the armed forces were not completely safe places for lesbians, given that concern about homosexuality resulted in increasing scrutiny of servicewomen.

Barb and Cheryl were both to bear the brunt of that scrutiny and to leave the military hurriedly before they could be given dishonorable discharges. Their military experiences, at once traumatic and exciting, take centre stage in their life narratives. A considerable amount of detail was remembered, and both women expressed enjoyment of the social aspects of their military years and a sense of pride about having been part of the military's persecution of lesbians. It is not that Cheryl and Barb are glad to have been thus persecuted but rather that in their narratives they portrayed themselves as survivors of that persecution. Their personal triumph was not that they won over the military, for they did not, but rather that the pressure for them to leave did not result in their losing pride in their lesbianism. If anything, it enhanced it.[76] That this particular part of her life story is very important to Cheryl's personal history is further indicated by the fact that it was told in similar detail, and often word-for-word, in the interview I conducted with Cheryl and in an interview conducted by another researcher in 1997.[77]

Barb joined the air force in 1952. She had not had any relationships with other young women since first being with a school friend as a teenager, nor did she have one in the air force until she had passed through her basic training and was on a station. There she met another lesbian woman on the same crew and formed a relationship. On their days off, they would go to nearby towns to spend time together. Their social life also included other lesbian women on the base, with whom Barb and her partner held parties and played ball. She recalled that they would often go out drinking together as a group and did little to hide the fact.

Barb's relationship had been going about a year when one of the five lesbian women she associated with was brought before the authorities and was questioned until she volunteered the names of women she thought were lesbian in the service at the time. The group of young women who socialized together a little too often had been noticed. Barb was brought to the commanding officer. He asked what they had been doing and why they were seen so much together:

> And at that time, I had a car, and I put it down to, you know, well I always have lots of girls in the car, and we were going here and going there because I was transportation for them, you know? So I said, "Well they're just jealous, I have a car."

Barb and her girlfriend were told that they had been seen too much together in her car, playing ball, and going to the recreation centre. She was asked what her feelings were toward the other woman.

Barb and her partner were sent to a psychiatrist in Toronto, escorted by a female air force police officer. They were taken in separately and then together. The psychiatrist asked them what they were doing, and they denied that anything unusual was happening. He asked many questions about their feelings toward each other and whether they had ever slept together or had had any physical contact. Barb did not find him threatening and suspects to this day that the reason he was so gentle with them was that he was himself gay. He sent them back to the station and reported to their commanding officer that they were not lesbians. Barb had known the possible consequences of telling the truth and consequently had chosen to hide the relationship. She did not remember hearing anything specific that would have indicated to her the possible consequences of being "found out," but she did recall that she knew that homosexuality was regarded negatively and that she could be thought of as "queer."

The women received notice that they were to be transferred to different stations. Barb's partner, without her knowledge, went to the medical officer at the station and confessed. She told the officer that she did not want them to be split up and said that the two of them had lied to the psychiatrist. The officer summoned Barb, and the two women were sent to the psychiatrist a second time. When they saw him together, he said to them, "You shouldn't be afraid ... if your feelings are like this." He told them, "You know, there's lots of places in the city that you can go."[78] The two women confessed and received their discharge papers. They received honorable discharges because they had left voluntarily.

Barb speculated that the military may have given her an honorable discharge rather than a dishonorable one because they did not know how far they could take the issue of lesbianism, but such a conclusion does not explain the experiences of those women who *were* thrown out. Clearly, the military was prepared to give women dishonorable discharges if they were unwilling to leave the services voluntarily. It was in late 1954, toward the end of Barb's three years, that she left. She remembered that there had been a major purge of lesbians at all the stations, and she did not think that any of them were ever actually caught in sexual activity. Rather, the purging of lesbians from the forces seemed to occur mainly on the basis of rumour and admission under pressure.

Barb's experience was not uncommon. She was a young woman from the country who had entered the forces after having had only one major relationship with another young woman. In the rural area where she lived, there was no lesbian community. When she entered the military, she found many other lesbian women and began to socialize with them at ball games and parties. The military provided the sort of mass groupings of women that allowed lesbians to discover each other and form alliances based on their sexual orientation. Unfortunately, by the 1950s, officers in the military were alerted to the presence of lesbians and were engaged more forcefully in weeding them out than had been the case during the Second World War. Groups of women who socialized together, were known not to associate with men, and in some cases dressed in a less than feminine way were noticeable on a military base, where behaviour was closely observed. The formation of small communities in the military was liberating for many lesbian women, yet it was dangerous. The behaviour of Barb and her friends was sufficiently open to alert the commanding officer of her base to a lesbian presence.

Cheryl had a similar experience. After moving to Ontario in 1956, Cheryl and Robyn lived very much like a young married couple. "But we didn't know any other women, you know, who were together as a couple. So we didn't know any lesbians or gay men." When their relationship disintegrated in 1959, Cheryl decided to join the forces. It was in the air force that Cheryl finally found the community she had been waiting for. Her first posting was at Clinton, Ontario. During her time at the Clinton base, three women were kicked out of the forces because they were suspected of being lesbians.[79] Cheryl remembered,

> the female officer ... called us all together and vowed to us that if we wanted to be kicked out of the RCAF, then all we had to do was tell them that we were homosexuals. So that sort of put the fear of God into everybody, although, you know, when I joined the air force, I made a vow to myself that if any woman, any woman ever, ever gives me a second look, you know, "in that way," that I would, well, I would probably just give her a piece of my mind!

Her experience with Robyn had soured Cheryl's perceptions of lesbianism, and she resisted her attraction toward women. "So I guess I just wanted to be a normal person," she said, "because I hadn't been normal for the last three years." That the three women were being kicked out because of homosexuality only confirmed her negative view of lesbianism. "I thought, 'See, that's what happens.' Yep. And yet, I had this affinity for, you know, I knew these three people who were being kicked out ... and I knew that they seemed to be like me, you know, like I was."

Despite her reservations about lesbianism, Cheryl found that she formed friendships with "the butchier type of airwoman." She felt that they were all gay, but as long as none of them approached her sexually, she did not mind their company. She was not absolutely positive about the women's sexuality: "I assumed," she said, "and I assumed correctly." She "swore off" women for the first year or so in the air force, but she felt that they had something in common. Cheryl did not call herself gay at that time, nor did she even really know what gay was: "Because of my three years with [Robyn]," she commented, "I thought we were the only ones, and then I found out that there were other people, other women like that."

During her first year in the air force, Cheryl began dating a man. She met Jimmy around six months into her service. Their relationship was not sexual. Cheryl regards herself as having been asexual at this point, and Jimmy was of the opinion that sex should be saved until after marriage, so they did little more than kiss and cuddle. Cheryl's feelings for women, however, began to surface, and eventually it became obvious to her that her relationship with Jimmy would not go further. They were at a restaurant one evening and saw a woman come in and sit down across from them:

> She just kept looking over every now and then, you know. We'd sort of exchange glances. But [Jimmy] exchanged glances with her as well. So I don't know what it was. Maybe she was just looking at us as a nice young couple. Who knows? But when she got up and walked out, and we were sitting by the window, [Jimmy] remarked, "What a beautiful looking woman. What an attractive woman." And I'm sitting there, and I'm thinking the same thing. All of a sudden, the light went on. I thought, "For God's sake, I'm fighting this, I'm fighting it and fighting it." And at that point I've got several friends who are gay and several lesbian friends ... and I didn't discuss it with them, but I knew that they were. So anyway ... it was then that I decided that I needed to do something about it.

After that crucial moment, Cheryl withdrew from her relationship with Jimmy, but she did not immediately begin socializing more frequently with lesbians. It was not until she moved to her new station in Nova Scotia that she began to explore her feelings in greater depth. She began socializing with women on the ball team. She had been on the ball team in Ontario too, but the Nova Scotia one was different: it was "about 90 percent lesbian." Cheryl, a new lesbian friend, her friend's partner, and other members of the ball team would go down to Halifax and visit Africville "because one of these women had a girlfriend down there. And that's where we would go, and we'd sit up and drink all night long."

The ball team had a place they called "the rendezvous" where they met on a regular basis and entertained the navy and army women who would visit. The rendezvous was an open field with a line of trees in front of it. After the ball games were over, they would head for the rendezvous and would drink and "make out." Sometimes there would be as many as fifty or sixty lesbians meeting there. However, such large numbers of women moving about as a group attracted attention, and eventually the air force police followed the women to the rendezvous. Cheryl commented:

> They went and they got the RCMP because they didn't have jurisdiction outside of the base. So they got the RCMP and we were all of a sudden almost surrounded by RCMP, and it was every woman for themselves. They couldn't arrest us because, you know, as soon as somebody screamed that the police are here, any booze or anything, it was gone. So, um, there was nothing that they could do 'cause there was nothing that they could prove.

It was shortly after this incident that Cheryl and six of her friends from the ball team were put under house arrest and were sent to St. Hubert, Quebec, to be interviewed by a psychiatrist who was "trying to help us with our sickness." The air force police had figured out that the women were not meeting in secret to talk about their boyfriends but rather that something else was going on and "that lots of unnatural things were happening." In addition, because of a personal dispute, one of the lesbians had "squealed" on the women. She had been in the air force for a long time but was getting nowhere with promotion. For her to advance to corporal status, Cheryl said, "she just needed some Brownie points, I guess, and unfortunately we were it." The airwoman revealed to the air force police that they were meeting at the rendezvous. She was present that night at the rendezvous and was a known lesbian, yet when the women were put under house arrest, she was not among them. "She was conspicuous by her absence," Cheryl commented. They later learned "on good authority" that she had named the seven of them as lesbians.

The psychiatrist's report was inconclusive, and he could not identify any of them as lesbians. Upon their return to the base, the women were informed that they were going to be split up and would never be on the same base as each other again. Cheryl's new friend and her partner were devastated. They were informed that they would probably never be promoted within the ranks and that they would be sent to the worst stations, "you know, the semi-isolation stations." Cheryl and her friends knew that if they remained in the service, they would be inviting intimidation. She remarked,

> Had we stayed in, we would have been giving them permission to intimidate us, and so we just, five of us decided definitely we were getting out. The other two were younger, they were new in all respects. They were new lesbians, they were new into the air force, new to our station. They thought, "oh no, we don't want to do this," and we, as the older ones ... we in no way encouraged them one way or the other. But they decided they would get out because I think, I think but I don't know, but I think they had a talk with their superiors, and I think their superiors pretty well told them, you know, "You're marked. You're marked women." So they ended up getting out with us. So that was the end of the air force.[80]

Cheryl left the air force in August 1962, just after the point when her three years were up. The week before their arrest, she had signed on for a further four years in the hope that she would get a posting in France. Because she left voluntarily, she received an honorable discharge.

It was in 1956 that Billie joined the air force. Billie was dating a man at the time, but when she announced that she was joining up, he broke it off, telling her "only whores join the armed services." She did not have a same-sex experience until just before she left the air force in 1961. Being in the physical education field, she knew many of the lesbians on the base. They were involved in sports and were quite open about their interest in Billie. Billie now acknowledges that she looked gay, even though she did not identify as such at the time. She had very short hair, almost in a brush-cut, virtually no breasts, and broad shoulders because of her physical education work, and women would approach her because they assumed that she was a lesbian.

Even though Billie was not, at the time, interested in women, she was nevertheless well aware of the lesbian community on the base. In addition to their mutual interest in physical education, the lesbian women would all go off the base as a group every weekend. Everybody in the lower ranks, including Billie's boyfriend at the time, assumed that this was because they were lesbians. Any large group of women socializing together, especially if they did not fit the stereotypical feminine ideal, was assumed to be a lesbian group. Billie recalled that, even though the group of women had a reputation, they nevertheless had to try to keep their sexuality secret. At night, the staff had to take turns on what was called "fire picket duty": "You had to go and check the women who lived in a big dormitory, to see if there was anybody sleeping with them. Other women, presumably. And a lot of my friends, I know, did get what they call a medical release. They were offered that." A medical release enabled a woman to obtain an honorable discharge on unspecified grounds. It saved both the woman herself and the military the embarrassment of a documented dishonorable discharge. Billie reported that she knew of women who were the victims of entrapment: the military authorities, if they suspected that a woman was lesbian, would sometimes get another servicewoman to make a sexual approach to tempt the suspected lesbian into revealing herself.[81]

Given the temporary nature of military life for these women, it might not at first appear that their years in the military were important in terms of community formation. However, for Cheryl, Barb, and Billie, the military was an entrée to a wider lesbian world than they had previously known. Cheryl and Barb had each had but a single same-sex relationship before joining the military, and they knew nothing of the large numbers of women like themselves. Billie entered the military not attracted toward women and soon found a community of women who perhaps suspected she might develop such attractions even before she acknowledged it herself. Moreover, each of these women continued the lesbian friendships they made in the military and remain friends with their fellow servicewomen to this day. Because of their shared experience of romantic liaisons, friendships, sports, and parties while in the military, they formed a long-lasting community.

Sports and Community

Sports were important in the formation of lesbian communities in the military and elsewhere.[82] As Barb reported, many lesbians were involved in sports, especially in ball teams in the 1950s and 1960s. "Most of the women on the ball teams were gay women," she claimed. Barb and her friends also formed a bowling league in the 1950s and called it "Marilyn Monroe." She had always been involved in sports, and in the military she was exposed to the heavy lesbian presence on ball teams.[83] Sports were and are a crucial part of community formation for lesbians. Sporting events were occasions when women could meet each other socially, could be very physical while incurring less comment about their appearance – although femininity was still emphasized in sports – and could gather in large groups without the presence of men.

Among the women I interview, Barb, Cheryl, Pam, Chris, Bergit, and Tricia all identified sports as both a personal interest and a place where they could meet other women. Baseball was by far the most popular lesbian sport. Tricia, interviewed by the Lesbians Making History project, remembered:

> There were baseball teams – they weren't called lesbian baseball teams. Some of them were the industrial league. But you could always be sure, if you went to the baseball games, that some of the team were going to be lesbian. Those baseball teams were going on in the '50s, that's for sure.[84]

When the scouts for the more prominent ball clubs came around, Tricia was chosen to play for a senior team, but her mother would not let her go. "And the only reason she gave me was that the women were too tough. I was devastated and angry." It is unclear from the interview whether Tricia was devastated because her baseball career was over, because she was denied access to the lesbian ball players, or both. That her mother held her back because of the presence of tough women might suggest that she knew that there were many lesbians on ball teams. It could also suggest that she thought that the women were simply unrespectable since women in team sports were often working-class and were thought to be promiscuous.

Lesbians found community wherever they could, but community in the way we usually understand it was not necessarily sought by all lesbians and should not be seen as crucial to lesbian identity and survival. Only some lived openly in the public communities about which articles and novels were written. In suburbs, in isolated couples, and in small groups of friends, other lesbians lived secretly behind the walls of respectability. The interviews done for this study support Elise Chenier's and Line Chamberland's portrayals of lesbian bar culture in the 1950s and 1960s. My own narrators, albeit from outsider perspectives, confirmed the importance of the butch-femme relationship in working-class lesbian life and the links between the bar community and the world of drugs and prostitution. The

Lesbians Making History project interviews acknowledge those aspects of bar culture but also make it apparent that the culture was very important to the women who were "in the life" and that in many ways it was enjoyable. The bar community had its own cultural norms, firmly policed boundaries, and a stake in a very visible lifestyle.

Among lower-middle-class lesbians, one finds ambivalence about the public bar community. The narrators for this study, who, whatever their personal backgrounds, were almost exclusively of upper-working-class and lower-middle-class status as adults before 1965, either did not know of the bar scene, knew of it and avoided it, or visited it only occasionally. All those women who did visit the bars felt uncomfortable there and felt that they did not entirely belong. All portrayed the bar scene in unfavourable terms and had little that was positive to say about the butch-femme scene.

It would be incorrect to portray these women either as closeted middle-class women whose place in lesbian history is therefore marginal or as brave and faultless heroines who countered the odds and formed community in the face of homophobia. They are at once both of these things and neither. Their stories indicate, rather, that class and sexual orientation are always entwined and that they can work with and against each other in the same individual and simultaneously. The narrators' condemnation of the bar women certainly does not do justice to the bar women's courage to fight for public space for lesbians or to the contribution of the bar culture to a vibrant and diverse lesbian history. Their antipathy to the bar culture arose from their middle-class norms. But to portray the narrators as less courageous than the women of the bar culture would be to negate the courage they showed in socializing at all as lesbians.

Conclusion

Most of the "public" discourses regarding sexuality in late-nineteenth- and early-twentieth-century Canada concerned appropriate and inappropriate heterosexuality, as this was the major social concern. Only just emerging in the late nineteenth century, and only gradually spreading beyond the medical profession and the realms of sexology in the twentieth century, was a discourse concerning homosexuality. Few in Canadian society were privy to the new terminologies regarding, and the new methods of policing, those who strayed from the heterosexual path. Most Canadians in the period under study remained ignorant of the new sexual worlds emerging in large cities and were trained to see heterosexual delinquency rather than gay or lesbian behaviours, but they were there.

Exploring same-sex desires, maintaining a lesbian relationship, and forming a social world based on a shared desire for women were all more challenging before 1965, but by no means were they impossible. Learning about lesbians from those earlier decades requires us to look for expressions of desire and social formations that may be unfamiliar to us, accustomed as we are to much greater lesbian visibility than in the past. We need to take account of the factors that caused lesbians of earlier generations to hide their relationships from prying heterosexual eyes and also to look for visual and linguistic clues to their presence, codes that lesbians could use to know and to be known by others like themselves.

It will be helpful to our knowledge of the lesbian past in Canada if we can avoid the tendency to view women who did not fulfil our current requirements of lesbian pride, outness, and visibility as somehow not fully part of a lesbian history we should celebrate. To be sure, the emergence of arguments for lesbian rights, the establishment of lesbian social networks, organizations, support groups, and businesses, the increasing involvement of lesbians in Pride events, legal campaigns, and festivals, and the creation of lesbian zones in cities are all tremendously important parts of Canadian lesbian history. The celebration of some of the precursors of those developments, particularly the public presence of bar lesbians, has been crucial to an understanding of lesbian politics as developing from earlier foundations rather than as rising out of nothing in the post–Stonewall era. In this way, Canadian lesbian historiography supports American and British scholarship in now recognizing the importance of earlier social and political formations. However, if we recognize and celebrate only what is visible and open, we will fail to acknowledge the experiences of those many lesbians who loved women more quietly and were never, or not until after 1965, public in their expression of same-sex desire.

I chose 1965 as the end-date for this study because of the changes that took place in lesbian visibility and community once the movements for lesbian and gay rights and the women's movement put sexuality and gender more firmly in the public eye as issues to be addressed. But the questions I ask here could well be applied to the period after 1965 since it is surely the case for large numbers of Canadian women who were in same-sex relationships in the late 1960s and the 1970s – and even later – that the changes that did occur in societal knowledge of homosexuality and the increase in the range of venues for same-sex social activities had little impact. Revelation of their sexuality at work was still difficult, families did not overnight become welcoming of lesbian daughters, the police were still raiding the bars, and visibility as a lesbian still put one at considerable risk of loss of reputation, employment, and custody of children and even at risk of physical harm. Some Canadian scholarship has revealed how, in the decades of protest and celebration, lesbians and gay men continued to face a great deal of discrimination.[1] Further studies need to be done to flesh out the story of the 1970s and 1980s for those lesbians who were not involved in lesbian or feminist organizing, in bars and clubs, or in parades and protests. They were the majority of lesbians in Canada, but because we have focused on "outness" and on visible community and politics, we know relatively little about their history.

Recognition only of the visible also influences our ideas about sexual practice in the past. Historians of lesbian life continue to deal with the question of sexual activity and whether we need evidence of it to assert lesbian desire or even identity. I have suggested that care needs to be taken not to assume too much sexual ignorance in women prior to the spread of information about sexuality in the twentieth century but also that historians need to be wary of assuming that twentieth-century women were well informed about sexual matters. The evidence discussed in this study demonstrates two things. First, it shows that women who, early in the century, had relationships closely approximating romantic friendships did have physical relationships. *Awfully Devoted Women* contributes Canadian evidence to a growing body of scholarship that complicates earlier claims that romantic friendships were nonsexual. The evidence suggests strongly that when we are looking at historical sources in which sexual activity is not explicitly mentioned, we need to be careful not to assume that the absence of mention means that sexual activity did not occur. Second, this study shows that mid-twentieth-century women, who were assumed to be sexual and allegedly had access to much more information about sexuality than did their forebears, actually knew very little about sexuality and formed sexual relationships largely through experimentation.

Lesbian history traditionally focuses on small groups of middle-class friends who shared a "devotion" to other women and working-class women in the public bar scene. Until recently, little attention has been devoted to lower-middle-class and upper-working-class women whose social worlds existed largely away from the bar scene. I have sought to bring to light the histories of this largely neglected group of Canadian lesbians and to show how, in different decades and at varying ages, they began to explore same-sex desires. All of these women formed friendships and social networks based on their same-sex desires. The nature of those networks, and the degree to which lesbian relationships were visible, varied according to the period and the class of the women involved. They were all, however, women whose primary relationships were with women, and those relationships were erotic in nature and, in most cases, physically sexual. Only some, however, were lived in public view. Most lesbians from Canada's elite or from the larger ranks of teachers, nurses, clerical workers, and factory workers experienced their desire for women as only one of many aspects of life, one that held considerable risk for their relationships with family and for their employment. They did not feel that they could be fully open about their lives. Yet they were there, and they are visible if we look in the right places.

Notes

Introduction

1 University of Toronto Archives, Fraser Family Personal Records, B95-0044 (hereafter Fraser Records), sous-fonds II, box 010, file 03, Edith Bickerton Williams to Frieda Fraser, 1 December 1925.

2 Fraser Records, sous-fonds II, box 010, file 04, Williams to Fraser, 19 June 1926.

3 Mary, personal interview, 24 September 1998, and personal communication, 20 May 2009.

4 Unlike the lesbians discussed in Lillian Faderman's latest work, *To Believe in Women: What Lesbians Have Done for America – A History* (Boston and New York: Houghton Mifflin, 1999).

5 Unlike those discussed in Elizabeth L. Kennedy and Madeline D. Davis, *Boots of Leather, Slippers of Gold: The History of a Lesbian Community* (New York and London: Routledge, 1993), and in Elise Chenier, "Tough Ladies and Troublemakers: Toronto's Public Lesbian Community, 1955-1965" (MA thesis, Queen's University, 1995).

6 Nan Enstad, *Ladies of Labor, Girls of Adventure: Working Women, Popular Culture, and Labor Politics at the Turn of the Twentieth Century* (New York: Columbia University Press, 1999), 51.

7 Ibid., 117-18.

8 Nan Alamilla Boyd, "Who Is the Subject? Queer Theory Meets Oral History," *Journal of the History of Sexuality* 17, 2 (May 2008): 186.

9 Elizabeth L. Kennedy, "'But we would never talk about it': The Structures of Lesbian Discretion in South Dakota, 1928-1933," in *Inventing Lesbian Cultures in America,* ed. Ellen Lewin (Boston: Beacon Press, 1996), 16-17.

10 Ibid., 34.

11 Martha Vicinus, *Intimate Friends: Women Who Loved Women, 1778-1928* (Chicago: University of Chicago Press, 2004), 230.

12 Ibid., emphasis in original.

13 Kennedy and Davis, *Boots of Leather.*

14 See, for example, Lillian Faderman, *Odd Girls and Twilight Lovers: A History of Lesbian Life in Twentieth-Century America* (New York: Penguin, 1992); Esther Newton, *Cherry Grove, Fire Island: Sixty Years in America's First Gay and Lesbian Town* (Boston: Beacon Press, 1993); Marc Stein, *City of Sisterly and Brotherly Loves: Lesbian and Gay Philadelphia, 1945-1972*, 2nd ed. (Philadelphia: Temple University Press, 2004); Nan Alamilla Boyd, *Wide-Open Town: A History of Queer San Francisco to 1965* (Berkeley: University of California Press, 2003); the community histories in Brett Beemyn, ed., *Creating a Place for Ourselves: Lesbian, Gay, and Bisexual Community Histories* (New York: Routledge, 1997); Katie Gilmartin, "'We Weren't Bar People': Middle-Class Lesbian Identities and Cultural Spaces," *Gay and Lesbian Quarterly* 3 (1996): 1-51; and Rebecca Jennings, *Tomboys and Bachelor Girls: A Lesbian History of Post-War Britain, 1945-71* (Manchester, UK, and New York: Manchester University Press, 2007).

15 Chenier, "Tough Ladies"; Elise Chenier, "Rethinking Class in Lesbian Bar Culture: Living 'The Gay Life' in Toronto, 1955-1965," *Left History* 9, 2 (Spring/Summer 2004): 85-118. Chenier's work is discussed in greater depth in Chapter 8.

16 Line Chamberland, "Remembering Lesbian Bars: Montreal, 1955-1975," in *Gay Studies from the French Cultures: Voices from France, Belgium, Brazil, Canada, and The Netherlands*, ed. Rommel Mendès-Leite and Pierre-Olivier de Busscher (New York: Harrington Park Press, 1993), 231-69.

17 See Chenier, "Tough Ladies"; Chenier, "Rethinking Class"; Chamberland, "Remembering Lesbian Bars"; and Vanessa Cosco, "'Obviously then I'm not a homosexual': Lesbian Identities, Discretion and Communities in Vancouver, 1945-1969" (MA thesis, University of British Columbia, 1997).

18 Rochella Thorpe, "'A house where queers go': African-American Lesbian Nightlife in Detroit, 1940-1975," in *Inventing Lesbian Cultures in America*, ed. Ellen Lewin (Boston: Beacon Press, 1996), 41.

19 Histories of romantic friendships, Boston marriages, and other relationships among middle-class women largely examine the lives of women whose class privilege allowed them not to work in paid employment and women who were in salaried positions in educational institutions or in the government and civil service. The histories of working-class communities of butch-femme couples largely address the lives of women in lower-waged positions. Chenier also shows that many of the women in Toronto's butch-femme culture survived through prostitution. The majority of women in this study were in midlevel clerical positions or such middle-class employment as nursing or teaching. It is this group that Chenier describes as "uptowners," who visited the bars only occasionally.

20 Steven Maynard, "Through a Hole in the Lavatory Wall: Homosexual Subcultures, Police Surveillance, and the Dialectics of Discovery, Toronto, 1890-1930," *Journal of the History of Sexuality* 5, 2 (October 1994): 207-42.

21 For an analysis of sexual deviance in postwar Canada, see Elise Chenier, *Strangers in Our Midst: Sexual Deviancy in Postwar Ontario* (Toronto: University of Toronto Press, 2008).

22 Mary Louise Adams, *The Trouble with Normal: Postwar Youth and the Making of Heterosexuality* (Toronto: University of Toronto Press, 1997), 38.

23 Mona Gleason, *Normalizing the Ideal: Psychology, Schooling, and the Family in Postwar Canada* (Toronto: University of Toronto Press, 1999), 82.

24 Katie Gilmartin, "'The very house of difference': Intersections of Identities in the Life Histories of Colorado Lesbians, 1940-1965" (PhD diss., Yale University, 1995).

25 Gilmartin, "'We Weren't Bar People.'"

26 The diaries of Anne Lister are a notable exception. Lister wrote explicitly, albeit in code, about her desires, her sexual practices, and her many relationships with women. See Helena Whitbread, *I Know My Own Heart: The Diaries of Anne Lister, 1791-1840* (New York and London: New York University Press, 1992).

27 Vicinus, *Intimate Friends*, xix.

28 There is an extensive literature on the construction of sexuality, on the problems of identity-based approaches to the history of sexuality, on definitions of sexual orientation, and on the idea of "evidence" generally. See, for example, Boyd, "Who Is the Subject?"; Steven Maynard, "'Respect Your Elders, Know Your Past': History and the Queer Theorists," *Radical History Review* 75 (1999): 56-78; Donna Penn, "Queer: Theorizing Politics and History," *Radical History Review* 62 (Spring 1995): 24-42; Leila J. Rupp, "'Imagine My Surprise': Women's Relationships in Historical Perspective," *Journal of Lesbian Studies* 1, 2 (1997): 155-76; Joan W. Scott, "The Evidence of Experience," *Critical Inquiry* 17 (Summer 1991): 773-97; Martha Vicinus, "Lesbian History: All Theory and No Facts or All Facts and No Theory?" *Radical History Review* 60 (1994): 57-75; Jennifer Terry, "Theorizing Deviant Historiography," *differences* 3 (Summer 1991): 55-74; Donald Morton, ed., *The Material Queer: A LesBiGay Cultural Studies Reader* (Boulder, CO: Westview Press, 1996); and David M. Halperin, *How to Do the History of Homosexuality* (Chicago: University of Chicago Press, 2002).

29 Maynard, "'Respect Your Elders,'" 64.

30 For a discussion of some of the problems involved in researching gay and lesbian history, see Steven Maynard, "'The Burning, Wilful Evidence': Lesbian/Gay History and Archival Research," *Archivaria* 33 (Winter 1991-92): 195-201.

31 Four women came forward in response to newspaper advertisements. A further seven were found via contacts with women's organizations, the Lesbian Seniors Care Society of Victoria being particularly helpful. The remaining narrators were contacted via personal community contacts in Victoria and Toronto and via the Metropolitan Community Church and a related women's gathering. The Metropolitan Community Church, or MCC as it is affectionately known, is a Christian church founded in 1962 with the specific aim of welcoming gay men and lesbians unable to worship in

mainstream churches. It has since expanded to include bisexual, transgender, transsexual, and intersex people.

32 Two exceptions to these restrictions were made. Mildred, an American, did not immigrate to Canada until the final year under study. However, her background as a student and then faculty member in women's colleges in the United States links her to an important part of the historiography on women's relationships, and she was included in the study because of that experience. The youngest of the narrators, Jill, was only fifty when interviewed but provides a British Columbia perspective. She also possessed sufficient awareness of her sexuality as a teenager in the early 1960s to render her perspective on sexuality an important one. Pseudonyms are used for all narrators except Lois and Reva, whose stories are already in the public domain via the film *Forbidden Love* and who requested that their real names be used.

33 Lynn Fernie and Aerlyn Weissman, dirs., *Forbidden Love: The Unashamed Stories of Lesbian Lives* (National Film Board of Canada, 1992). The film blends oral testimonies, photographs, and written sources with a fictional story in the style of the lesbian pulp novels of the 1950s and 1960s.

Chapter 1: Relationships between Women

1 Havelock Ellis, *Studies in the Psychology of Sex*, vol. 1 (New York: Random House, 1937), 262.

2 Ibid.

3 For a discussion of sexologists' views about same-sex environments and their dangers, see Martha Vicinus, *Intimate Friends: Women Who Loved Women, 1778-1928* (Chicago: University of Chicago Press, 2004), 206-8.

4 Lillian Faderman, *Odd Girls and Twilight Lovers: A History of Lesbian Life in Twentieth-Century America* (New York: Penguin, 1991); Elizabeth L. Kennedy and Madeline D. Davis, *Boots of Leather, Slippers of Gold: The History of a Lesbian Community* (New York and London: Routledge, 1993).

5 Faderman, *Odd Girls and Twilight Lovers*, 4.

6 Lillian Faderman, *Surpassing the Love of Men: Romantic Friendship and Love between Women from the Renaissance to the Present* (New York: William Morrow, 1981), 297.

7 Ibid., 142.

8 Leila J. Rupp, "Romantic Friendship," in *Modern American Queer History*, ed. Allida Mae Black (Philadelphia: Temple University Press, 2001), 17.

9 For discussion of romantic friendships and their decline, see, for example, Faderman, *Surpassing the Love of Men*; Faderman, *Odd Girls and Twilight Lovers*; Rupp, "Romantic Friendship"; and Karen Lystra, *Searching the Heart: Women, Men, and Romantic Love in Nineteenth-Century America* (New York and Oxford, UK: Oxford University Press, 1989), 7.

10 Faderman, *Odd Girls and Twilight Lovers*, 49.

11 Jeffrey Weeks, *Sexuality and Its Discontents: Meanings, Myths and Modern Sexualities* (London and New York: Routledge, 1985), 65-66.

12 Ibid., 143.

13 Faderman, *Surpassing the Love of Men*, 226-27.

14 Esther Newton, "The Mythic Mannish Lesbian: Radclyffe Hall and the New Woman," in *The Lesbian Issue: Essays from SIGNS*, ed. Estelle B. Freedman, Barbara C. Gelpi, Susan L. Johnson, and Kathleen M. Weston (Chicago: University of Chicago Press, 1985), 10.

15 For a discussion of the diversity of sexological texts available in the late nineteenth and early twentieth centuries, and the responses to them, see Vern L. Bullough, "The Development of Sexology in the USA in the Early Twentieth Century," in *Sexual Knowledge, Sexual Science: The History of Attitudes to Sexuality*, ed. Roy Porter and Mikulas Teich, 303-22 (Cambridge, UK: Cambridge University Press, 1994); Lesley Hall, "'The English Have Hot-Water Bottles': The Morganatic Marriage between Sexology and Medicine in Britain since William Acton," in *Sexual Knowledge, Sexual Science: The History of Attitudes to Sexuality*, ed. Roy Porter and Mikulas Teich, 350-66 (Cambridge, UK: Cambridge University Press, 1994); and Vicinus, *Intimate Friends*, 202-8.

16 Radclyffe Hall, *The Well of Loneliness* (London: Cape, 1928).

17 Una Troubridge, "The Life and Death of Radclyffe Hall," in Richard Ormrod, *Una Troubridge: The Friend of Radclyffe Hall* (New York: Carroll and Graf, 1985), 163.

18 Richard Ormrod, *Una Troubridge: The Friend of Radclyffe Hall* (New York: Carroll and Graf, 1985), 176-84; Leslie A. Taylor, "'I Made Up My Mind to Get It': The American Trial of *The Well of Loneliness*, New York City, 1928-1929," *Journal of the History of Sexuality* 10, 2 (2001): 253.

19 S.H. Hooke, "A Biological Sin," *Canadian Forum* 9, 103 (April 1929): 243-44. See also Steven Maynard, "Radclyffe Hall in Canada," *Centre/Fold* 6 (Spring 1994): 9.

20 Laura Doan, *Fashioning Sapphism: The Origins of a Modern English Lesbian Culture* (New York: Columbia University Press, 2001), xii, emphasis in original.

21 Faderman, *Odd Girls and Twilight Lovers*, 173.

22 Faderman, *Surpassing the Love of Men*, 322.

23 Vanessa Cosco, "'Obviously then I'm not a homosexual': Lesbian Identities, Discretion and Communities in Vancouver, 1945-1969" (MA thesis, University of British Columbia, 1997), 27.

24 Taylor, "'I Made Up My Mind to Get It,'" 261.

25 Steven Maynard, "'Hell Witches in Toronto': Notes on Lesbian Visibility in Early-Twentieth-Century Canada," *Left History* 9, 2 (Spring/Summer 2004): 201.

26 Lillian Faderman, "Lesbian Magazine Fiction in the Early Twentieth Century," *Journal of Popular Culture* (1978): 805, 809.

27 Quoted in Nancy Adair and Casey Adair, *Word Is Out: Stories of Some of Our Lives* (New York: New Glide/Delta, 1978), 17.

28 Ibid., 17; Elsa Gidlow, *Elsa: I Come with My Songs – The Autobiography of Elsa Gidlow* (San Francisco: Booklegger Press, 1986), 72.

29 Jeffrey Weeks and Kevin Porter, eds., *Between the Acts: Lives of Homosexual Men, 1885-1967* (London and New York: Routledge, 1991), 3.

30 Bonnie Zimmerman, "Perverse Reading: The Lesbian Appropriation of Literature," in *Sexual Practice/Textual Theory: Lesbian Cultural Criticism*, ed. Susan J. Wolfe and Julia Penelope (Cambridge, UK: Blackwell, 1993), 139.

31 Faderman, *Odd Girls and Twilight Lovers*, 58-59.

32 University of Toronto Archives, Fraser Family Personal Records, B95-0044 (hereafter Fraser Records), sous-fonds II, box 001, file 17, Nettie M. Bryant to Helene Fraser, 23 April 1927, emphasis in original.

33 Henry L. Minton, "Femininity in Men and Masculinity in Women: American Psychiatry and Psychology Portray Homosexuality in the 1930s," *Journal of Homosexuality* 13, 1 (Fall 1986): 8.

34 George Chauncey, "From Sexual Inversion to Homosexuality: The Changing Conceptualization of Female 'Deviance,'" in *Passion and Power: Sexuality in History*, ed. Kathy Peiss and Christina Simmons, with Robert A. Padgug (Philadelphia: Temple University Press, 1989), 102.

35 Minton, "Femininity in Men," 2.

36 The letters between them, and other papers relating to their relationship and to their personal and working lives, were donated to the University of Toronto Archives by Donald Fraser and Nancy Fraser Brooks, nephew and niece of Frieda, after Frieda's death in 1992.

37 Nancy Fraser Brooks, "A few answers," personal e-mail, 23 November 1999.

38 Veronica Strong-Boag, *The New Day Recalled: Lives of Girls and Women in English Canada, 1919-1939* (Markham, ON: Penguin, 1988), 41-42.

39 Fraser Records, sous-fonds II, box 010, file 03, Edith Bickerton Williams to Frieda Fraser, 29 August 1925.

40 Fraser Records, sous-fonds II, box 010, file 03, Williams to Fraser, 2 November 1925.

41 Fraser Records, sous-fonds II, box 010, file 03, Williams to Fraser, 29 December 1925.

42 Fraser Records, sous-fonds II, box 010, file 04, Williams to Fraser, 6 February 1926, emphasis in original.

43 Fraser Records, sous-fonds III, box 036, file 06, Fraser to Williams, 10 July 1925.

44 Fraser Records, sous-fonds II, box 010, file 03, Williams to Fraser, 28 November 1925.

45 Nan Enstad, *Ladies of Labor, Girls of Adventure: Working Women, Popular Culture, and Labor Politics at the Turn of the Twentieth Century* (New York: Columbia University Press, 1999), 121.

46 Fraser Records, sous-fonds II, box 010, file 03, Williams to Fraser, 5 November 1925.

47 Fraser Records, sous-fonds II, box 010, file 03, Williams to Fraser, 14 December 1925.

48 Fraser Records, sous-fonds II, box 010, file 03, Williams to Fraser, 18 November 1925.

49 Fraser Records, sous-fonds II, box 010, file 03, Williams to Fraser, 25 November 1925.

50 Fraser Records, sous-fonds II, box 010, file 03, Williams to Fraser, 28 November 1925.

51 Fraser Records, sous-fonds II, box 010, file 05, Williams to Fraser, 13 July 1926.

52 Fraser Records, sous-fonds II, box 010, file 05, Williams to Fraser, 20 July 1926.

53 Fraser Records, sous-fonds III, box 036, file 08, Fraser to Williams, 27 March 1926.

54 Fraser Records, sous-fonds II, box 010, file 04, Williams to Fraser, 28 May 1926.

55 Faderman, *Surpassing the Love of Men*, 322.

56 Fraser Records, sous-fonds II, box 010, file 03, Williams to Fraser, 2 November 1925.

57 Fraser Records, sous-fonds II, box 010, file 04, Williams to Fraser, 27 June 1926.

58 Fraser Records, sous-fonds II, box 010, file 04, Williams to Fraser, 9 January 1926.

59 Fraser Records, sous-fonds II, box 010, file 04, Williams to Fraser, n.d.

60 Fraser Records, sous-fonds II, box 010, file 04, Williams to Fraser, 27 March 1926.

61 Fraser Records, sous-fonds III, box 036, file 07, Fraser to Williams, 7 February 1926.

62 "Odd women" could be lesbians, spinsters, or "New Women." The term describes those women who did not conform to prevailing gender norms and norms of sexuality and who were noticed by and were of concern to heterosexual and gender-normative society. Such terms were often used to define and pathologize those women whose gender and sexual nonconformity made them unusual to broader society and whose politics often made them a threat as well.

63 Fraser Records, sous-fonds III, box 036, file 07, Fraser to Williams, 7 February 1926.

64 Fraser Records, sous-fonds III, box 036, file 9, Fraser to Williams, n.d. 1926. Frieda's comment in this letter about a "semitic influence" is not the only remark she made about Jews. Frieda did not often comment on ethnicity, but she did on several occasions express opinions that were reflective of widespread anti-Semitism in medicine at the time. Another of these instances, in which Frieda's comments were even more clearly anti-Semitic, is discussed by Katherine Perdue in her article "Passion and Profession, Doctors in Skirts: The Letters of Doctors Frieda Fraser and Edith Bickerton Williams," *Canadian Bulletin of Medical History/Bulletin canadien d'histoire de la médecine* 22, 2 (2005), 276-77.

65 Frieda's gender performance is discussed further in the next chapter.

66 His views clearly maintained predominant gender norms, which were predicated on essentialist ideas about the "natural" and "appropriate" roles of the sexes.

67 Weeks, *Sexuality and Its Discontents*, 127-56.

68 It should be noted that the custom of the day was that a male doctor would use initials, whereas a woman would put her first name. It was perhaps Bud's use of Frieda's initials when addressing letters that was the more unusual rather than the maid's "ignorance."

69 Fraser Records, sous-fonds II, box 010, file 05, Williams to Fraser, 11 August 1926.

70 Carol Baines, "Professor Elizabeth Govan: An Outsider in Her Own Community," in *Challenging Professions: Historical and Contemporary Perspectives on Women's Professional Work,* ed. Elizabeth Smyth et al. (Toronto: University of Toronto Press, 1999), 47-48.

71 University of Toronto Archives, Elisabeth Steel Livingston Govan Records, B79-0027 (hereafter Govan Records), box 3, file 4, B to Elisabeth Govan, 19 November 1945, emphasis in original.

72 Govan Records, box 3, file 4, B to Elisabeth Govan, n.d., ellipses in original.

73 Baines, "Professor Elizabeth Govan," 60.

74 Govan Records, box 3, file 4, B to Elisabeth Govan, n.d. 1945(?), emphasis in original.

75 Govan Records, box 3, file 4, B to Elisabeth Govan, n.d., emphasis in original.

76 Govan Records, box 3, file 4, B to Elisabeth Govan, n.d.

77 Govan Records, box 3, file 4, B to Elisabeth Govan, 8 November 1945, emphasis in original.

78 Govan Records, box 3, file 4, B to Elisabeth Govan, 19 November 1945.

79 Govan Records, box 3, file 4, B to Elizabeth Govan, n.d. (1940s).

80 All uses of the word "libidinal" listed in the second edition of the *Oxford English Dictionary* are examples of psychological discourse, most listed as occurring for the first time in 1922. Strictly speaking, the libido was thought to be any psychic energy emanating from the id, but most commonly it is regarded as a sexual force. Certainly, by the 1940s, when B was writing to Govan, the word "libidinal" was specifically sexual in meaning.

81 It should be noted here that Freud was not as condemnatory of homosexuality as were his followers. As Jeffrey Weeks comments, "What for Freud was an abnormality of sexual object choice, that in the first place needed explanation, has since taken on the characteristics of an illness which demands curing." See Weeks, *Sexuality and Its Discontents*, 150-51. Freud did not believe that homosexuality per se could be cured. It was his more conservative followers who used his ideas to devastatingly pathologize homosexuality and turn it into a social problem requiring therapeutic intervention.

82 University of British Columbia, Rare Books and Special Collections, A. Alexis Alvey Fonds, AII B2 (hereafter Alvey Fonds).

83 Nancy Olson, "Assembling a Life: The (Auto)biography of Alexis Amelia Alvey, 1942-1945" (MA Thesis, Simon Fraser University, 1998), 64-65.

84 Ibid., 66n49. Brodie did not keep Alvey's letters, and thus the correspondence is one-sided. It is nevertheless apparent that this was a very passionate relationship on both sides.

85 Alvey Fonds, Grace Brodie to Alexis Alvey, 5 October 1942.

86 Olson, "Assembling a Life," 49, 71.

87 Alvey Fonds, Grace Brodie to Alexis Alvey, 8 December 1942.

88 The blacked-out portions are not given here for reasons of confidentiality. The collection was donated to the University of British Columbia's Rare Books and Special Collections in 1988.

89 Alvey Fonds, Grace Brodie to Alexis Alvey, 18 December 1942.

90 Olson, "Assembling a Life," 40-50.

91 Alexis Alvey to Adelaide Sinclair, 13 September 1944, cited in ibid., 53.

92 Patricia T. Rooke and R.L. Schnell, *No Bleeding Heart: Charlotte Whitton, a Feminist on the Right* (Vancouver: UBC Press, 1987), 7-8.

93 Ibid., 8.

94 Patricia T. Rooke, "Public Figure, Private Woman: Same-Sex Support Structures in the Life of Charlotte Whitton," *International Journal of Women's Studies* 6, 5 (1983): 414.

95 Rooke and Schnell, *No Bleeding Heart,* 87-88.

96 Ibid., 22-23.

97 Ibid., 25.

98 Rooke, "Public Figure, Private Woman," 414.

99 Cited in ibid., 416.

100 Rooke and Schnell, *No Bleeding Heart,* 25-26.

101 Ibid., 32.

102 Mo to CW, 10 October 1921, cited in ibid., 37.

103 Library and Archives Canada, Charlotte Whitton Papers, MG30, E256, vol. 133 (hereafter Whitton Papers), Margaret Grier to Charlotte Whitton, 27 December 1915. This letter is contained in the R.M. Grier File of the collection. However, according to Rooke and Schnell, *No Bleeding Heart,* 28, Charlotte did not meet Margaret until after she moved to Toronto in 1918.

104 Rooke and Schnell, *No Bleeding Heart,* 129-30.

105 Ibid., 132-33.

106 Whitton Papers, "Molly Mugwamp Makes Believe," vol. 1, Whitton to Grier, 31 March 1948.

107 Rooke, "Public Figure, Private Woman," 422-23.

108 Rooke and Schnell, *No Bleeding Heart,* 136-41.

109 Indeed, the description of lesbian partners as "lovers" was not common until the late 1970s and the 1980s, when it became, in many lesbian circles, the preferred word.

110 Whitton Papers, "Molly Mugwamp Makes Believe," vol. 1, Whitton to Grier, New Year's Eve, 1947-48.

111 Whitton Papers, "Molly Mugwamp Makes Believe," vol. 1, Whitton to Grier, 9 March 1948.

112 Whitton Papers, "Molly Mugwamp Makes Believe," vol. 1, Whitton to Grier, 9 May 1948.

113 Whitton Papers, "Molly Mugwamp Makes Believe," vol. 1, Whitton to Grier, 10 January 1948. The letters in these volumes are stained with Whitton's tears.

114 Whitton Papers, "Molly Mugwamp Makes Believe," vol. 2, Whitton to Grier, 27 March 1949.

Chapter 2: Lesbian Social Worlds, 1900–50

1 University of Toronto Archives, Fraser Family Personal Records, B95-0044 (hereafter Fraser Records), sous-fonds II, box 010, file 03, Edith Bickerton Williams to Frieda Fraser, 30 June 1925, emphasis in original.

2 Fraser Records, sous-fonds II, box 010, file 03, Williams to Fraser, 2 July 1925.

3 Fraser Records, sous-fonds II, box 010, file 03, Williams to Fraser, 2 July 1925.

4 Fraser Records, sous-fonds II, box 010, file 03, Williams to Fraser, 22 August 1925.

5 Fraser Records, sous-fonds III, box 36, file 11, Fraser to Williams, 5 March 1927.

6 George Chauncey, *Gay New York: Gender, Urban Culture, and the Making of the Gay Male World, 1890-1940* (New York: Basic Books, 1994), 52.

7 Lillian Faderman, *Surpassing the Love of Men: Romantic Friendship and Love between Women from the Renaissance to the Present* (New York: William Morrow, 1981), 226-27.

8 Fraser Records, sous-fonds III, box 36, file 11, Fraser to Williams, 14 March 1927.

9 For discussion of motivations for and reactions to women's cross-dressing, see Laura Doan, *Fashioning Sapphism: The Origins of a Modern English Lesbian Culture* (New York: Columbia University Press, 2001); Laura Doan, "Passing Fashions: Reading Female Masculinities in the 1920s," *Feminist Studies* 24, 3 (Autumn 1998): 663-700; Alison Oram, *Her Husband Was a Woman! Women's Gender-Crossing in Modern British Popular Culture* (London and New York: Routledge, 2007); Esther Newton, "The Mythic Mannish Lesbian," in *Hidden from History: Reclaiming the Gay and Lesbian Past*, ed. Martin Duberman, Martha Vicinus, and George Chauncey, 281-93 (New York: Meridian, 1990); and Julie Wheelwright, *Amazons and Military Maids: Women Who Dressed as Men in the Pursuit of Life, Liberty and Happiness* (London and Scranton, PA: Pandora, 1989).

10 Martha Vicinus, *Intimate Friends: Women Who Loved Women, 1778-1928* (Chicago: University of Chicago Press, 2004), 205; Carroll Smith-Rosenberg, *Disorderly Conduct: Visions of Gender in Victorian America* (New York: Alfred A. Knopf, 1985), 265.

11 Martha Vicinus, "'They Wonder to Which Sex I Belong': The Historical Roots of the Modern Lesbian Identity," *Feminist Studies* 18, 3 (1992): 485.

12 University of Toronto Archives, Elisabeth Steel Livingston Govan Records, B79-0027 (hereafter Govan Records), box 3, file 4, B to Elisabeth Govan, n.d., emphasis in original.

13 Frieda had adopted the outdoor boyish look in her adolescent years.

14 Interview with Donald Fraser and Nancy Brooks, nephew and niece of Frieda Fraser, 15 December 1997.

15 Fraser Records, sous-fonds III, box 036, file 06, Fraser to Williams, 10 July 1925.

16 Fraser Records, sous-fonds III, box 036, file 06, Fraser to Williams, 27 July 1925. See Figure 3.

17 Fraser Records, sous-fonds II, box 010, file 03, Williams to Fraser, 16 August 1925.

18 Fraser Records, sous-fonds II, box 010, file 04, Williams to Fraser, 2 June 1926.

19 Fraser Records, sous-fonds III, box 036, file 09, Fraser to Williams, n.d. 1926.

20 Fraser Records, sous-fonds III, box 036, file 11, Fraser to Williams, 24 February 1927.

21 Fraser Records, sous-fonds III, box 036, file 11, Fraser to Williams, 11 March 1927. See page 72 for the drawings themselves.

22 Fraser Records, sous-fonds III, box 036, file 11, Fraser to Williams, 6 February 1927.

23 Doan, *Fashioning Sapphism*, 99.

Chapter 3: Physical Sexuality

1 Mariana Valverde, *The Age of Light, Soap and Water: Moral Reform in English Canada, 1885-1925* (Toronto: McClelland and Stewart, 1991), 106.

2 See, for example, Karen Dubinsky, *Improper Advances: Rape and Heterosexual Conflict in Ontario, 1880-1929* (Chicago: University of Chicago Press, 1993); Susan Johnston, "Twice Slain: Female Sex-Trade Workers and Suicide in British Columbia, 1870-1920," *Journal of the Canadian Historical Association* 5 (1994): 147-66; and Carolyn Strange, *Toronto's Girl Problem: The Perils and Pleasures of the City, 1880-1930* (Toronto: University of Toronto Press, 1995). An analysis of the consequences thought likely to befall the wayward, especially wayward women, can be found in Judith Walkowitz, *City of Dreadful Delight: Narratives of Sexual Danger in Late-Victorian London* (Chicago: University of Chicago Press, 1992). Sander Gilman's *Difference and Pathology: Stereotypes of Sexuality, Race, and Madness* (Ithaca, NY: Cornell University Press, 1985), shows clearly that the linking of images of pathology and immorality has a long history in European culture.

3 Neil Semple, *The Lord's Dominion: The History of Canadian Methodism* (Montreal and Kingston: McGill-Queen's University Press, 1996), 342-43, 363-64; Valverde, *Age of Light*, 58-60; Brian Clarke, "English-Speaking Canada from 1854," in *A Concise History of Christianity in Canada*, ed. Terrence Murphy and Roberto Perin (Toronto: Oxford University Press, 1996), 289.

4 For a discussion of the Self and Sex Series, see Michael Bliss, "'Pure Books on Avoided Subjects': Pre-Freudian Sexual Ideas in Canada," Canadian Historical Association, *Historical Papers* (1970): 89-108; Valverde, *Age of Light*, 31, 69, 70; and Lana Castleman, "Self, Sex, and Moral Reform in English Canada, 1890-1920," *Blurred Genres* 2 (Winter/Spring 1994): 35-49.

5 Michael Bliss, "How We Used to Learn about Sex," *Maclean's*, March 1974, 61.

6 Canada's "pioneer sex educator," Arthur Beall, was a nationalist who told boys and girls that "if they really loved Canada they would become builders of the nation by thinking only clean and noble thoughts and producing clean and noble children." See ibid., 66.

7 The population of Canada in 1901 was 5,371,315, of whom 2,182,947 lived in Ontario. Of the total population, some 1,867,260 lived in urban areas of 1,000 persons or more. See M.C. Urquhart and K.A.H. Buckley, eds., *Historical Statistics of Canada* (Toronto: University of Toronto Press, 1965), 14-15.

8 Strange, *Toronto's Girl Problem*.

9 Carolyn Strange, "From Modern Babylon to a City upon a Hill: The Toronto Social Survey Commission of 1915 and the Search for Sexual Order in the City," in *Patterns of the Past: Interpreting Ontario's History,* ed. Roger Hall, William Westfall, and Laurel Sefton MacDowell (Toronto and Oxford, UK: Dundurn Press, 1988), 256.

10 Strange, *Toronto's Girl Problem*, 59.

11 Robert A. Campbell, "Ladies and Escorts: Gender Segregation and Public Policy in British Columbia Beer Parlours, 1925-1945," *BC Studies* 105-6 (Spring/Summer 1995): 119-38.

12 Historians have questioned the degree to which the 1920s really constituted a period of new sexual freedoms, given the strength of existing norms and the class specificity of sexual experimentation. Nevertheless, it may be said that for the social class of which Bud and Frieda were a part, there was a new mood of sexual adventure and a new acknowledgment of women's sexual pleasure.

13 Roy Porter and Lesley Hall, *The Facts of Life: The Creation of Sexual Knowledge in Britain, 1650-1950* (New Haven, CT, and London: Yale University Press, 1995), 208-9. *Married Love* sold 17,000 copies in its first year alone and went through five editions. *Wise Parenthood* was also extremely popular.

14 Angus McLaren and Arlene Tigar McLaren, *The Bedroom and the State: The Changing Practices and Politics of Contraception and Abortion in Canada, 1880-1980* (Toronto: McClelland and Stewart, 1986), 55-59.

15 University of Toronto Archives, Fraser Family Personal Records, B95-0044 (hereafter Fraser Records), sous-fonds III, box 036, file 05, Frieda Fraser to Edith Bickerton Williams, 5 December 1924, emphasis in original. Available information suggests that this would have taken place during Frieda's training at the University of Toronto.

16 Fraser Records, sous-fonds III, box 036, file 07, Fraser to Williams, 19 February 1926.

17 Fraser Records, sous-fonds II, box 010, file 03, Williams to Fraser, 19 August 1925.

18 Fraser Records, sous-fonds II, box 010, file 03, Williams to Fraser, 19 August 1925.

19 Fraser Records, sous-fonds II, box 010, file 03, Williams to Fraser, 19 August 1925.

20 Fraser Records, sous-fonds II, box 010, file 03, Williams to Fraser, 19 August 1925.

21 Fraser Records, sous-fonds II, box 010, file 03, Williams to Fraser, 17 December 1925.

22 Fraser Records, sous-fonds II, box 010, file 03, Williams to Fraser, 17 December 1925.

23 Dubinsky, *Improper Advances.*

24 Sheila Jeffreys, "Does It Matter If They Did It?" in *Not a Passing Phase: Reclaiming Lesbians in History, 1840-1985,* ed. The Lesbian History Group (London: Women's Press, 1989), 22-24, 28.

25 Karen V. Hansen, "'No Kisses Is Like Youres': An Erotic Friendship between Two African-American Women during the Mid-Nineteenth Century," *Gender and History* 7, 2 (August 1995): 200.

26 Ibid., 183.

27 Helena Whitbread, ed., *I Know My Own Heart: The Diaries of Anne Lister, 1791-1840* (New York and London: New York University Press, 1992).

28 Fraser Records, sous-fonds II, box 010, file 03, Williams to Fraser, 4 November 1925.

29 Fraser Records, sous-fonds II, box 010, file 03, Williams to Fraser, 23 July 1925.

30 Fraser Records, sous-fonds II, box 010, file 03, Williams to Fraser, 29 December 1925.

31 Fraser Records, sous-fonds II, box 010, file 04, Williams to Fraser, 27 June 1926.

32 Fraser Records, sous-fonds II, box 010, file 04, Williams to Fraser, 14 February 1926.

33 Fraser Records, sous-fonds III, box 036, file 06, Fraser to Williams, 12? December 1925 (question mark in original).

34 Fraser Records, sous-fonds III, box 036, file 08, Fraser to Williams, 29 April 1926.

35 Fraser Records, sous-fonds III, box 036, file 09, Fraser to Williams, n.d. June 1926.

36 Fraser Records, sous-fonds III, box 036, file 11, Fraser to Williams, 5 March 1927.

37 Fraser Records, sous-fonds II, box 010, file 05, Williams to Fraser, 24 September 1926.

38 Fraser Records, sous-fonds III, box 036, file 11, Fraser to Williams, n.d. March 1927.

39 Fraser Records, sous-fonds II, box 010, file 05, Williams to Fraser, 20 July 1926.

40 Fraser Records, sous-fonds III, box 036, file 11, Fraser to Williams, 11 April 1927, emphasis in original.

41 Fraser Records, sous-fonds III, box 036, file 12, Fraser to Williams, 17 May 1927.

42 Fraser Records, sous-fonds II, box 010, file 03, Williams to Fraser, 1 August 1925.

43 Fraser Records, sous-fonds II, box 010, file 04, Williams to Fraser, 6 February 1926.

44 Fraser Records, sous-fonds III, box 036, file 11, Fraser to Williams, 13 January 1927.

45 Fraser Records, sous-fonds II, box 010, file 03, Williams to Fraser, 2 December 1925.

46 Fraser Records, sous-fonds II, box 010, file 04, Williams to Fraser, 6 January 1926.

47 Fraser Records, sous-fonds II, box 010, file 04, Williams to Fraser, 19 January 1926.

48 Fraser Records, sous-fonds III, box 036, file 12, Fraser to Williams, 3 August 1927.

49 Lillian Faderman charts this period of change in *Surpassing the Love of Men: Romantic Friendship and Love between Women from the Renaissance to the Present* (New York: William Morrow, 1981), 297-313.

50 As I have earlier acknowledged, however, the Fraser-Williams correspondence is highly unusual. Further research would have to be done to support the argument I make here, as this one collection cannot be generalized to all women of the period.

51 Lillian Faderman, *Surpassing the Love of Men: Romantic Friendship and Love between Women from the Renaissance to the Present* (New York: William Morrow, 1981), 84.

52 As previously mentioned, the word "libidinal" was not used before the early twentieth century, when psychological discourse began to be influential. References to same-sex relationships as "unnatural" or as "against nature" were much older but began to be deployed much more widely from the middle of the nineteenth century, when sexual behaviour was linked more clearly to biological paradigms than previously.

Chapter 4: Growing Up under Heteronormativity

1 Ruth Roach Pierson, *"They're Still Women after All": The Second World War and Canadian Womanhood* (Toronto: McClelland and Stewart, 1986), 216-17.

2 Mary Louise Adams, *The Trouble with Normal: Postwar Youth and the Making of Heterosexuality* (Toronto: University of Toronto Press, 1997), 21-23; Mona Gleason, *Normalizing the Ideal: Psychology, Schooling, and the Family in Postwar Canada* (Toronto: University of Toronto Press, 1999), 81-82.

3 Alfred Kinsey, *Sexual Behavior in the Human Female* (Philadelphia and London: W.B. Saunders, 1953).

4 In the 1970s and 1980s, lesbian political theory argued against gender and posited both femininity and masculinity as patriarchal in origin. Feminine behaviour and attire were especially the target of lesbian antagonism, symbolizing as it did to lesbian feminists the oppression of women and particularly the making of women into sexual objects. In their attempts to remove gender from appearance and to adopt a genderless, or "androgynous," self-representation, lesbians tended to wear pants rather than dresses, often cut their hair short, particularly in the 1980s, and refused to wear makeup or otherwise conform to feminine norms. The result was, of course, an appearance that was rather more masculine than truly androgynous.

5 Sarah, personal interview, 5 August 1998.

6 Barb, personal interview, 15 May 1998.

7 Chris, personal interview, 22 September 1998.

8 Adams, *Trouble with Normal,* 95-98.

9 Cheryl, personal interview, 4 November 1998.

10 Mildred, personal interview, 1 May 1998.

11 Jane, personal interview, 1 October 1998.

12 Bergit, e-mail interview, 10 June 1998.

13 Pam, personal interview, 30 September 1998.

14 Allan Bérubé, *Coming Out under Fire: The History of Gay Men and Women in World War Two* (New York: Plume, 1990), 28.

15 Ibid., 102-3, 106-8.

16 Gary Kinsman, *The Regulation of Desire: Homo and Hetero Sexualities,* 2nd ed. (Montreal: Black Rose Books, 1996), 150.

17 Pierson, *"They're Still Women after All,"* 158.

18 Bérubé, *Coming Out under Fire,* 258-63.

19 Daniel J. Robinson and David Kimmel, "The Queer Career of Homosexual Security Vetting in Cold War Canada," *Canadian Historical Review* 75, 3 (September 1994): 340-41; Kinsman, *Regulation of Desire,* 177-81. It proved very difficult for the researchers to find gay men willing to undergo the test, and lesbians were even less forthcoming.

20 Robinson and Kimmel, "Queer Career," 323-24, 343; Kinsman, *Regulation of Desire,* 174.

21 Kinsman, *Regulation of Desire,* 175.

22 Gary Kinsman and Patrizia Gentile, *"In the Interests of the State": The Anti-Gay, Anti-Lesbian National Security Campaign in Canada: A Preliminary Research Report* (Sudbury, ON: Laurentian University, 1998). See also Gary Kinsman and Patrizia

Gentile, *The Canadian War on Queers: National Security as Sexual Regulation* (Vancouver: UBC Press, 2010).

23 Gary Kinsman, "The Canadian Cold War on Queers: Sexual Regulation and Resistance," in *Love, Hate, and Fear in Canada's Cold War*, ed. Richard Cavell (Toronto: University of Toronto Press, 2004), 124.

24 Kate Adams, "Making the World Safe for the Missionary Position: Images of the Lesbian in Post-World War II America," in *Lesbian Texts and Contexts: Radical Revisions*, ed. Karla Jay and Joanne Glasgow (New York and London: New York University Press, 1990), 264.

25 Frank Caprio, *Female Homosexuality: A Psychodynamic Study of Lesbianism* (New York: Citadel, 1954); and Frank Caprio, *Variations in Sexual Behavior* (New York: Citadel, 1955).

26 Caprio, *Female Homosexuality*, 305.

27 Marc Stein, *City of Sisterly and Brotherly Loves: Lesbian and Gay Philadelphia, 1945-1972*, 2nd ed. (Philadelphia: Temple University Press, 2004), 134-35.

28 Alfred Kinsey, *Sexual Behavior in the Human Male* (Philadelphia and London: W.B. Saunders, 1948); and Kinsey, *Sexual Behavior in the Human Female*.

29 Jeffrey Weeks, *Sex, Politics and Society: The Regulation of Sexuality since 1800*, 2nd ed. (London and New York: Longman, 1989), 242; Lillian Faderman, *Odd Girls and Twilight Lovers: A History of Lesbian Life in Twentieth-Century America* (New York: Penguin, 1992), 140. Kinsey was not particularly interested in rigid definitions of sexual preference, claiming as he did that there existed a range of human sexuality, from fully heterosexual in activity (the Kinsey 0) to fully homosexual (the Kinsey 6). Nevertheless, many used his data to support a dichotomous view of sexuality, leaving bisexual people somewhere in a blurry and vague middle ground. American society and, indeed, many scholars writing about sexuality seem not to have heeded his warning that "one must learn to recognize every combination of heterosexuality and homosexuality in the histories of various individuals." See Kinsey, *Sexual Behavior in the Human Male*, 617.

30 Wini Breines, "The 'Other' Fifties: Beats and Bad Girls," in *Not June Cleaver: Women and Gender in Postwar America, 1945-1960*, ed. Joanne Meyerowitz (Philadelphia: Temple University Press, 1994), 383-84, 392.

31 Donna Penn, "The Sexualized Woman," in *Not June Cleaver: Women and Gender in Postwar America, 1945-1960*, ed. Joanne Meyerowitz (Philadelphia: Temple University Press, 1994), 368.

32 Mona Gleason, "Psychology and the Construction of the 'Normal' Family in Postwar Canada, 1945-60," *Canadian Historical Review* 78, 3 (September 1997): 447. Donna Penn has argued that the same process occurred in the United States, where "after the war, the psychiatric world was in a position to consolidate its power as an agent of cultural authority." See Penn, "Sexualized Woman," 363.

33 Gleason, *Normalizing the Ideal*, 83.

34   Vanessa Cosco, "'Obviously then I'm not a homosexual': Lesbian Identities, Discretion and Communities in Vancouver, 1945-1969" (MA thesis, University of British Columbia, 1997), 16-17.

35   Kinsman, *Regulation of Desire*, 160-61, 169; Tom Warner, *Never Going Back: A History of Queer Activism in Canada* (Toronto: University of Toronto Press, 2002), 19; Elise Chenier, *Strangers in Our Midst: Sexual Deviancy in Postwar Ontario* (Toronto: University of Toronto Press, 2008), 91.

36   Kinsman, *Regulation of Desire*, 230-35.

37   Marcia M. Gallo, *Different Daughters: A History of the Daughters of Bilitis and the Rise of the Lesbian Rights Movement* (New York: Carroll and Graf, 2006), 13.

38   Kristin G. Esterberg, "From Accommodation to Liberation: A Social Movement Analysis of Lesbians in the Homophile Movement," *Gender and Society* 8, 3 (September 1994): 426.

39   Elizabeth L. Kennedy and Madeline D. Davis, *Boots of Leather, Slippers of Gold: The History of a Lesbian Community* (New York and London: Routledge, 1993), 67-68. See also Warner, *Never Going Back,* 57-59.

40   Esterberg, "From Accommodation to Liberation," 430. For further information about DOB activism, see, for example, Stein, *City of Sisterly and Brotherly Loves.*

41   For an analysis of *The Ladder* and its publication of conflicting opinions about homosexuality, see Kristin G. Esterberg, "From Illness to Action: Conceptions of Homosexuality in *The Ladder,* 1956-1965," *The Journal of Sex Research* 27, 1 (February 1990): 65-80.

42   Nan Alamilla Boyd, *Wide-Open Town: A History of Queer San Francisco to 1965* (Berkeley: University of California Press, 2003), 160.

43   Stein, *City of Sisterly and Brotherly Loves,* 185.

44   Warner, *Never Going Back,* 59.

45   Adams, *Trouble with Normal,* 92.

46   Ibid., 92-93.

47   *Justice Weekly,* 15 January 1955, 14.

48   *Telegram,* 11 April 1964, 7.

49   Ibid.

50   Eric Sutliff, "Sex Fiends or Swish Kids? Gay Men in *Hush Free Press,* 1946-1956," in *Gendered Pasts: Historical Essays in Femininity and Masculinity in Canada,* ed. Kathryn McPherson, Cecilia Morgan, and Nancy Forestell (Toronto: Oxford University Press, 1999), 159.

51   Library and Archives Canada, Canadian Penal Association, June 1948, Kenneth H. Rogers, "Interim Report of the Committee on the Sex Offender," RG 33/131, Acc. 84/253, vol. 2, 23.

52   Mary Ellen Zuckerman, *A History of Popular Women's Magazines in the United States, 1792-1995* (Westport, CT: Greenwood Press, 1998), 102.

53 Barbara Freeman, "From No Go to No Logo: Lesbian Lives and Rights in *Chatelaine*," *Canadian Journal of Communication* 31 (2006): 818.

54 Valerie Korinek, "'Don't Let Your Girlfriends Ruin Your Marriage': Lesbian Imagery in *Chatelaine* Magazine, 1950-1969," *Journal of Canadian Studies* 33, 3 (Fall 1998): 83-109.

55 Adams, *Trouble with Normal*, 5.

56 Kinsman, *Regulation of Desire*, 252.

57 For information on attitudes toward spinsters and on the links made between spinsterhood and politics, see Sheila Jeffreys, *The Spinster and Her Enemies: Feminism and Sexuality, 1880-1930* (London and Boston: Pandora Press, 1985).

58 Jenéa Tallentire, "Everyday Athenas: Strategies of Survival and Identity for Ever-Single Women in British Columbia, 1880-1930" (PhD diss., University of British Columbia, 2006), 118, emphasis in original.

59 Leila J. Rupp, *A Desired Past: A Short History of Same-Sex Love in America* (Chicago and London: University of Chicago Press, 1999), 5.

60 See ibid., 7-10; and Faderman, *Surpassing the Love of Men*, 17-18.

61 Adams, *Trouble with Normal*, 92.

62 Sarah, personal interview, 5 August 1998.

63 Lois, personal interview, 3 October 1998.

64 Lois's social life has been made public in Lynn Fernie and Aerlyn Weissman, dirs., *Forbidden Love: The Unashamed Stories of Lesbian Lives* (National Film Board of Canada, 1992). The community in which she socialized and her relationships with women are discussed in later chapters.

65 Yvonne Keller, "Pulp Politics: Strategies of Vision in Lesbian Pulp Novels, 1955-1965," in *The Queer Sixties*, ed. Patricia Juliana Smith (New York and London: Routledge, 1999), 2-3.

66 Martin Meeker, "A Queer and Contested Medium: The Emergence of Representational Politics in the 'Golden Age' of Lesbian Paperbacks, 1955-1963," *Journal of Women's History* 17, 1 (2005): 167.

67 Keller, "Pulp Politics," 2-3.

68 Diane Hamer, "'I Am a Woman': Ann Bannon and the Writing of Lesbian Identity in the 1950s," in *Lesbian and Gay Writing: An Anthology of Critical Essays*, ed. Mark Lilly (London: Macmillan, 1990), 51. See also Becki Ross, "Dance to 'Tie a Yellow Ribbon,' Get Churched, and Buy the Little Lady a Drink: Gay Women's Bar Culture in Toronto, 1965-1975," in *Weaving Alliances: Selected Papers Presented for the Canadian Women's Studies Association at the 1991 and 1992 Learned Societies Conferences*, ed. Debra Martens (Ottawa: Canadian Women's Studies Association, 1993), 269.

69 Keller, "Pulp Politics," 3. The construction of lesbian stereotypes in fiction is discussed in Sherrie A. Innes, *The Lesbian Menace: Ideology, Identity, and the Representation of Lesbian Life* (Amherst: University of Massachusetts Press, 1997).

70 Del Martin, "An Open Letter to Ann Aldrich," *The Ladder,* April 1958, 4-6, quoted in Meeker, "Queer and Contested Medium," 172.
71 Meeker, "Queer and Contested Medium," 181.
72 Gallo, *Different Daughters,* 68-69.
73 Jill, personal interview, 30 May 1998.

Chapter 5: Sexual Relationships in Postwar Canada

1 See, for example, Mary Louise Adams, *The Trouble with Normal: Postwar Youth and the Making of Heterosexuality* (Toronto: University of Toronto Press, 1997), 158-65; Sherrie A. Inness, *The Lesbian Menace: Ideology, Identity, and the Representation of Lesbian Life* (Amherst: University of Massachusetts Press, 1997); Jeffrey Weeks, *Sex, Politics and Society: The Regulation of Sexuality since 1800,* 2nd ed. (London and New York: Longman, 1989); Angus McLaren, *Twentieth-Century Sexuality: A History* (Oxford, UK: Blackwell, 1999); and Lillian Faderman, *Odd Girls and Twilight Lovers: A History of Lesbian Life in Twentieth-Century America* (New York: Penguin, 1992).
2 Sherrie Inness indicates that, in the interwar period, "schoolgirl crushes, complete with ardent love letters, kissing, hand holding, and bed sharing, were considered normal relationships for high school and college women"; see Inness, *Lesbian Menace,* 34. Even in the 1950s, suggests Mary Louise Adams, advice books such as *On Becoming a Woman* "constructed a continuum of affectional and sexual ties" beginning with same-sex ones and later developing into opposite-sex relationships; see Adams, *Trouble with Normal,* 93.
3 Robert K. Kelley, *Courtship, Marriage, and the Family,* 2nd ed. (New York: Harcourt Brace Jovanovich, 1974), 25.
4 Sarah, personal interview, 5 August 1998.
5 Susan K. Freeman, *Sex Goes to School: Girls and Sex Education before the 1960s* (Urbana and Chicago: University of Illinois Press, 2008), 70-71.
6 Ibid., 72-79.
7 Christabelle Sethna, "The Cold War and the Sexual Chill: Freezing Girls Out of Sex Education," *Canadian Woman Studies/Les cahiers de la femme* 17, 4 (Winter 1998): 58.
8 Reva, personal interview, 5 August 1997.
9 Pam, personal interview, 30 September 1998. For information on attitudes toward unmarried motherhood, see Andrée Lévesque, "Deviants Anonymous: Single Mothers at the Hôpital de la Miséricorde in Montréal, 1929-1939," Canadian Historical Association, *Historical Papers/Communications Historiques* (1984): 168-83; Margaret Little, *"No Car, No Radio, No Liquor Permit": The Moral Regulation of Single Mothers in Ontario, 1920-1997* (Toronto: Oxford University Press, 1998); and Adams, *Trouble with Normal,* 68.
10 Sarah, personal interview, 5 August 1998.
11 Phyl, personal interview, 28 September 1998.
12 Bergit, personal interview, 29 September 1998.

13 Jane, personal interview, 1 October 1998.
14 Cheryl, personal interview, 4 November 1998.
15 Pam, personal interview, 30 September 1998.
16 Betty, personal interview, 28 September 1996.
17 Cheryl, personal interview, 4 November 1998.
18 Veronica, personal interview, 27 September 1998.
19 Jill, personal interview, 30 May 1998.
20 See Michael Bliss, "'Pure Books on Avoided Subjects': Pre-Freudian Sexual Ideas in Canada," Canadian Historical Association, *Historical Papers* (1970): 89-108.
21 McLaren, *Twentieth-Century Sexuality,* 28-29.
22 Deborah, personal interview, 28 September 1998.
23 Maureen, personal interview, 25 September 1998.
24 Jill, personal interview, 30 May 1998.
25 Mildred, personal interview, 1 May 1998.
26 Jerry, interviewed by Elise Chenier, 23 November 1992. Both of Jerry's parents were in the air force. The pseudonym "Jerry" is that chosen by Chenier in her use of this interview in Elise Chenier, "Tough Ladies and Troublemakers: Toronto's Public Lesbian Community, 1955-1965" (MA thesis, Queen's University, 1995).
27 Betty, personal interview, 28 September 1996.
28 Bergit, personal interview, 29 September 1998.
29 Veronica, personal interview, 27 September 1998.
30 Cheryl, personal interview, 4 November 1998.
31 Sarah, personal interview, 5 August 1998.

Chapter 6: Making the Unspoken Plain

1 Sarah, personal interview, 5 August 1998.
2 Jane, personal interview, 1 October 1998.
3 Jill, personal interview, 30 May 1998.
4 Pat, personal interview, 24 September 1998.
5 Cheryl, personal interview, 4 November 1998, and personal communication, 9 May 2009.
6 Chris, personal interview, 22 September 1998, and personal communication, 9 May 2009.
7 Reva, personal interview, 5 August 1997.
8 Bergit, personal interview, 29 September 1998.
9 Sheila Jeffreys, "Does It Matter If They Did It?" in *Not a Passing Phase: Reclaiming Lesbians in History, 1840-1985,* ed. The Lesbian History Group (London: Women's Press, 1989), 27.
10 Lynn Fernie and Aerlyn Weissman, dirs., *Forbidden Love: The Unashamed Stories of Lesbian Lives* (National Film Board of Canada, 1992).
11 Reva, personal interview, 5 August 1997.

12   Barb, personal interview, 15 May 1998.

13   Cheryl, personal interview, 4 November 1998, and personal communication, 9 May 2009.

14   Bergit, personal interview, 29 September 1998.

15   Pam, personal interview, 30 September 1998.

16   Lois, personal interview, 3 October 1998.

17   Deborah, personal interview, 28 September 1998.

18   Fernie and Weissman, dirs., *Forbidden Love.*

19   Reva, personal interview, 5 August 1997.

20   Phyl, personal interview, 28 September 1998.

21   Maureen, personal interview, 29 May 1998.

22   Mary, personal interview, 24 September 1998 and personal communication, 20 May 2009.

23   Karen Christel Krahulik, *Provincetown: From Pilgrim Landing to Gay Resort* (New York and London: New York University Press, 2005), 152.

24   Jill, personal interview, 30 May 1998.

25   Mildred, personal interview, 1 May 1998.

26   Elizabeth L. Kennedy and Madeline D. Davis, *Boots of Leather, Slippers of Gold: The History of a Lesbian Community* (New York and London: Routledge, 1993).

27   Lillian Faderman, *Surpassing the Love of Men: Romantic Friendship and Love between Women from the Renaissance to the Present* (New York: William Morrow, 1981), 16.

28   Arlene, LMH interview, 6 May 1987.

29   Maureen, personal interview, 29 May 1998.

30   Veronica, personal interview, 27 September 1998.

31   Jane, personal interview, 1 October 1998.

32   Joyce, LMH interview, 16 November 1985.

33   Jerry, interviewed by Elise Chenier, 23 November 1992.

34   Mildred, personal interview, 1 May 1998.

35   Phyl, personal interview, 28 September 1998.

36   Reva, personal interview, 5 August 1997.

37   Mary Louise Adams, *The Trouble with Normal: Postwar Youth and the Making of Heterosexuality* (Toronto: University of Toronto Press, 1997), 158-65. See also Adams's chapter "Margin Notes: Reading Lesbianism as Obscenity in a Cold War Courtroom," in *Love, Hate, and Fear in Canada's Cold War,* ed. Richard Cavell, 135-58 (Toronto: University of Toronto Press, 2004).

38   Pam, personal interview, 30 September 1998.

39   Deborah, personal interview, 28 September 1998.

40   Billie, personal interview, 23 September 1998.

41   Alfred Kinsey, *Sexual Behavior in the Human Female* (Philadelphia and London: W.B. Saunders, 1953), 257-58, 467. Kinsey's data suggested that, compared to 20 percent of females with some coital experience and 46 percent with extensive coital experience

who had accepted male stimulation of their genitalia, and 16 percent and 43 percent respectively who had performed oral stimulation of male partners, 78 percent of those women who had had extensive same-sex relationships listed oral stimulation of the genitalia as a common sexual technique.

42 Pat, personal interview, 24 September 1998.

43 Kennedy and Davis, *Boots of Leather,* 191.

44 Ibid., 192.

45 The term "tribadism" refers to the practice of rubbing together, or what the women Kennedy and Davis interviewed referred to as "friction." One of their narrators spoke of it as "when a butch and a fem, the fem plays the woman part and the butch plays the male part, and the male lays on the female just like a man would do to a woman, except for there's no intercourse." See ibid., 227.

46 A stone butch was a lesbian who did not like to be touched sexually and who obtained the entirety of her sexual pleasure in the act of sexually pleasing a femme. Many stone butches reported being able to achieve orgasm without being touched. See ibid., 208-9.

47 Arlene, LMH interview, 6 May 1987.

48 Leslie Feinberg, *Stone Butch Blues: A Novel* (New York: Firebrand, 1993).

49 Group LMH interview, 19 October 1985.

50 Arlene, LMH interview, 6 May 1987.

51 Mary, personal interview, 24 September 1998.

52 Mildred, personal interview, 1 May 1998.

53 Billie, personal interview, 23 September 1998.

54 Reva, personal interview, 5 August 1997. A soft butch was a lesbian whose gender performance was on the masculine side but not to the same degree as those who held to firm butch identities. A soft butch did not necessarily have to be in a relationship with a femme, and gendered behaviours were not as rigidly defined for soft butches as they were for those in butch-femme relationships.

55 Lois, personal interview, 3 October 1998.

56 Deborah, personal interview, 28 September 1998.

57 Phyl, personal interview, 28 September 1998.

58 Pat, personal interview, 24 September 1998.

Chapter 7: Relationships

1 Parts of this chapter have been published in Karen Duder, "'That repulsive abnormal creature I read of in that book': Lesbians and Families in Ontario, 1920-1965," in *Ontario Since Confederation: A Reader,* ed. Edgar-André Montigny and Lori Chambers (Toronto: University of Toronto Press, 2000), 260-83. Some pseudonyms have been changed in this new version.

2 Lynn Fernie and Aerlyn Weissman, dirs., *Forbidden Love: The Unashamed Stories of Lesbian Lives* (National Film Board of Canada, 1992).

3 Mary and Pat, joint personal interview, 26 September 1998.

4 Mary, personal interview, 24 September 1998, and personal communication, 20 May 2009.

5 Mildred, personal interview, 1 May 1998.

6 Lois, personal interview, 3 October 1998.

7 Mary and Pat, joint personal interview, 26 September 1998.

8 Joyce, LMH interview, 16 November 1985.

9 Lois, personal interview, 3 October 1998.

10 Pam, personal interview, 30 September 1998.

11 Crises about gender occasioned by the dramatic shifts of the Second World War resulted in an increased emphasis on the return to an ideal of heterosexual matrimony, in which the woman remained at home with children and the man was employed in a well-paid job with a sufficient income that his wife would not have to work. Many women continued to work, however, especially before marriage and then again when children were older. Some "experts" in Canadian society argued that the new postwar suburbs resulted in the masculinization of women and in absentee fatherhood, both considerable threats to the family. See, for example, Veronica Strong-Boag, "Home Dreams: Women and the Suburban Experiment in Canada, 1945-1960," *Canadian Historical Review* 72, 4 (December 1991): 471-504; Veronica Strong-Boag, "'Their Side of the Story': Women's Voices from Ontario Suburbs, 1945-1960," in *A Diversity of Women: Ontario, 1945-1980*, ed. Joy Parr, 46-74 (Toronto: University of Toronto Press, 1995); and Mary Louise Adams, *The Trouble with Normal: Postwar Youth and the Making of Heterosexuality* (Toronto: University of Toronto Press, 1997).

12 Elizabeth L. Kennedy and Madeline D. Davis, *Boots of Leather, Slippers of Gold: The History of a Lesbian Community* (New York and London: Routledge, 1993), 316-17, 320.

13 Elise Chenier has dealt with the topic of drug use and drug pushing and with the links between the drug scene and prostitution in her work, so I shall not deal with those subjects here. See Elise Chenier, "Tough Ladies and Troublemakers: Toronto's Public Lesbian Community, 1955-1965" (MA thesis, Queen's University, 1995); and Elise Chenier, "Rethinking Class in Lesbian Bar Culture: Living 'The Gay Life' in Toronto, 1955-1965," *Left History* 9, 2 (Spring/Summer 2004): 85-118.

14 Kennedy and Davis, *Boots of Leather*, 320-21.

15 Group LMH interview, 19 October 1985.

16 Cheryl, personal interview, 4 November 1998, and personal communication, 9 May 2009.

17 Lois, personal interview, 3 October 1998.

18 Pam, personal interview, 30 September 1998.

19 Chenier, "Tough Ladies."

20 For further information on domestic violence, see Annalee Golz, "'If a Man's Wife Does Not Obey Him, What Can He Do?' Marital Breakdown and Wife Abuse in Late

Nineteenth-Century and Early Twentieth-Century Ontario," in *Law, Society and the State: Essays in Modern Legal History,* ed. Louis A. Knafla and Susan W.S. Binnie, 323-50 (Toronto: University of Toronto Press, 1995); and Cynthia R. Comacchio, *The Infinite Bonds of Family: Domesticity in Canada, 1850-1940* (Toronto: University of Toronto Press, 1999).

21 Mildred, personal interview, 1 May 1998.

22 Lois, personal interview, 3 October 1998.

23 Barb, personal interview, 15 May 1998.

24 Cheryl, personal interview, 24 November 1998, and personal communication, 9 May 2009.

25 Billie, personal interview, 23 September 1998.

26 Adams, *Trouble with Normal,* 23.

27 Mary Louise Adams, "Youth, Corruptibility, and English-Canadian Postwar Campaigns against Indecency, 1948-1955," *Journal of the History of Sexuality* 6, 1 (1995): 113.

28 Jan, LMH interview, 19 October 1985.

29 Tricia, LMH interview, 21 September 1986.

30 See Gary Kinsman, *The Regulation of Desire: Homo and Hetero Sexualities,* 2nd ed. (Montreal: Black Rose Books, 1996), 148-212; and Daniel J. Robinson and David Kimmel, "The Queer Career of Homosexual Security Vetting in Cold War Canada," *Canadian Historical Review* 75, 3 (September 1994): 319-45.

31 Jerry, interviewed by Elise Chenier, 23 November 1992.

32 Quoted in James T. Sears, *Lonely Hunters: An Oral History of Lesbian and Gay Southern Life, 1948-1968* (Boulder, CO: Westview Press, 1997), 43, emphasis in original.

33 Arlene, LHM interview, 6 May 1987.

34 Chenier, "Tough Ladies," 84.

35 Alice, LHM interview, 16 November 1985.

36 Shirley Limbert, "Coming Out x Three," in *Lesbian Parenting: Living with Pride and Prejudice,* ed. Katherine Arnup (Charlottetown, PEI: Gynergy Books, 1995), 269.

37 Pat and Mary, joint personal interview, 26 September 1998.

38 Their stories about their lesbianism being discovered by the military authorities are told in Chapter 8.

39 Cheryl, personal interview, 4 November 1998, and personal communication, 9 May 2009.

40 Donna Penn, "The Sexualized Woman," in *Not June Cleaver: Women and Gender in Postwar America, 1945-1960,* ed. Joanne Meyerowitz (Philadelphia: Temple University Press, 1994), 364.

41 Chenier, "Tough Ladies," 37.

42 Title of a Linda Shear song, cited in Becki Ross, *The House That Jill Built: A Lesbian Nation in Formation* (Toronto: University of Toronto Press, 1995), 57.

Chapter 8: Middle-Class Lesbian Community in the 1950s and 1960s

1 Many scholars have discussed lesbian-feminist criticisms of the bar culture, particularly of the butch-femme relationship that formed its basis. See, for example, Lillian Faderman, *Odd Girls and Twilight Lovers: A History of Lesbian Life in Twentieth-Century America* (New York: Penguin, 1992); Elizabeth L. Kennedy and Madeline D. Davis, *Boots of Leather, Slippers of Gold: The History of a Lesbian Community* (New York and London: Routledge, 1993); Sheila Jeffreys, *The Lesbian Heresy: A Feminist Perspective on the Lesbian Sexual Revolution* (Melbourne: Spinifex, 1993); Elise Chenier, "Tough Ladies and Troublemakers: Toronto's Public Lesbian Community, 1955-1965" (MA thesis, Queen's University, 1995); Joan Nestle, ed., *The Persistent Desire: A Fem-Butch Reader* (Boston: Alyson, 1992); and Becki Ross, *The House That Jill Built: A Lesbian Nation in Formation* (Toronto: University of Toronto Press, 1995).

2 Lynn Fernie and Aerlyn Weissman, dirs., *Forbidden Love: The Unashamed Story of Lesbian Lives* (National Film Board of Canada, 1992). The racialized nature of the nightclub entertainment industry in postwar Vancouver is discussed in Becki Ross and Kim Greenwell, "Spectacular Striptease: Performing the Sexual and Racial Other in Vancouver, B.C., 1945-1975," *Journal of Women's History* 17, 1 (2005): 137-64.

3 Vanessa Cosco, "'Obviously then I'm not a homosexual': Lesbian Identities, Discretion and Communities in Vancouver, 1945-1969" (MA thesis, University of British Columbia, 1997), 43.

4 Bergit, for example, knew nothing of lesbians and never sought contact outside of her first relationship. Phyl and her partner thought that they were the only two in the world and socialized only with heterosexual women. Despite increases in the amount of literature available about sexuality, and in the press coverage of gay activity, Bergit and Phyl did not realize that there would be others like themselves, with whom they could form social networks. Bergit, personal interview, 29 September 1998; Phyl, personal interview, 28 September 1998.

5 Sexological literature had, of course, been in publication since the middle of the nineteenth century, but it was in the early to mid-twentieth century that its circulation began to expand from an almost exclusively medical readership to a larger readership among the general public.

6 Elsa Gidlow, *Elsa: I Come with My Songs – The Autobiography of Elsa Gidlow* (San Francisco: Booklegger Press, 1986), 72-73.

7 Ross Higgins and Line Chamberland, "Mixed Messages: Gays and Lesbians in Montreal Yellow Papers in the 1950s," in *The Challenge of Modernity: A Reader on Post-Confederation Canada*, ed. Ian McKay, 422-31 (Toronto: McGraw-Hill Ryerson, 1992).

8 Ibid., 428-30.

9 Steven Maynard, "'Hell Witches in Toronto': Notes on Lesbian Visibility in Early-Twentieth-Century Canada," *Left History* 9, 2 (Spring/Summer 2004): 194.

10   Becki Ross, "Dance to 'Tie a Yellow Ribbon,' Get Churched, and Buy the Little Lady a Drink: Gay Women's Bar Culture in Toronto, 1965-1975," in *Weaving Alliances: Selected Papers Presented for the Canadian Women's Studies Association at the 1991 and 1992 Learned Societies Conferences,* ed. Debra Martens (Ottawa: Canadian Women's Studies Association, 1993), 269.

11   Valerie Korinek, "'Don't Let Your Girlfriends Ruin Your Marriage': Lesbian Imagery in *Chatelaine* Magazine, 1950-1969," *Journal of Canadian Studies* 33, 3 (Fall 1998): 105.

12   Fernie and Weissman, dirs., *Forbidden Love;* Sherrie A. Inness, *The Lesbian Menace: Ideology, Identity, and the Representation of Lesbian Life* (Amherst: University of Massachusetts Press, 1997), 79-100. *Forbidden Love* uses interviews with lesbians who were involved in lesbian communities in the 1950s and 1960s, supplemented with film footage and a fictional romance, to describe lesbian life in postwar Canada.

13   Faderman, *Odd Girls and Twilight Lovers,* 107-8.

14   Lillian Faderman, *Surpassing the Love of Men: Romantic Friendship and Love between Women from the Renaissance to the Present* (New York: William Morrow, 1981), 229, 235; Inness, *Lesbian Menace,* 35.

15   Inness, *Lesbian Menace,* 38-39.

16   Mildred, personal interview, 1 May 1998.

17   One of the many holdovers from nineteenth-century discourse was the assumption that working-class women were by nature more likely to be promiscuous and that they did not know how to behave demurely. Their families hid the fact that middle-class girls and women also engaged in "bad" behaviour.

18   Esther Newton, *Cherry Grove, Fire Island: Sixty Years in America's First Gay and Lesbian Town* (Boston: Beacon Press, 1993).

19   Esther Newton, "The 'Fun Gay Ladies': Lesbians in Cherry Grove, 1936-1960," in *Creating a Place for Ourselves: Lesbian, Gay, and Bisexual Community Histories,* ed. Brett Beemyn, 145-64 (New York: Routledge, 1997).

20   Elise Chenier, "Tough Ladies and Troublemakers: Toronto's Public Lesbian Community, 1955-1965" (MA thesis, Queen's University, 1995); Elise Chenier, "Rethinking Class in Lesbian Bar Culture: Living 'The Gay Life' in Toronto, 1955-1965," *Left History* 9, 2 (Spring/Summer 2004): 85-118.

21   Faderman, *Odd Girls and Twilight Lovers,* 107-8.

22   Kennedy and Davis, *Boots of Leather,* 31.

23   Ibid., 33-36.

24   Elizabeth L. Kennedy and Madeline D. Davis, "'I Could Hardly Wait to Get Back to That Bar': Lesbian Bar Culture in Buffalo in the 1930s and 1940s," in *Creating a Place for Ourselves: Lesbian, Gay, and Bisexual Community Histories,* ed. Brett Beemyn (New York: Routledge, 1997), 33.

25   Ibid., 35.

26   Donald W. McLeod, *Lesbian and Gay Liberation in Canada: A Selected Annotated Chronology, 1964-1975* (Toronto: ECW Press/Homewood Books, 1996), 277-86.

27   Kennedy and Davis, *Boots of Leather*, 378-80.

28   Line Chamberland, "Remembering Lesbian Bars: Montreal, 1955-1975," in *Gay Studies from the French Cultures: Voices from France, Belgium, Brazil, Canada, and The Netherlands,* ed. Rommel Mendès-Leite and Pierre-Olivier de Busscher (New York: Harrington Park Press, 1993), 263.

29   Ross, "Dance to 'Tie a Yellow Ribbon,'" 271-72.

30   Chenier, "Tough Ladies"; Elise Chenier, "Rethinking Class in Lesbian Bar Culture: Living 'The Gay Life' in Toronto, 1955-1965," *Left History* 9, 2 (Spring/Summer 2004): 85-118.

31   Chenier, "Rethinking Class," 86, emphasis in original.

32   Ibid., 107.

33   Fernie and Weissman, dirs., *Forbidden Love.*

34   McLeod, *Lesbian and Gay Liberation in Canada,* 278.

35   Cosco, "'Obviously then I'm not a homosexual.'"

36   Jerry, interviewed by Elise Chenier, 23 November 1992.

37   Barb, personal interview, 15 May 1998.

38   In her study of Vancouver lesbians, Vanessa Cosco spoke to one lesbian woman who had read the novels and discovered that lesbian bars existed. See Cosco, "'Obviously then I'm not a homosexual,'" 26.

39   Reva, personal interview, 5 August 1997. See also Fernie and Weissman, dirs., *Forbidden Love.*

40   Pat, personal interview, 24 September 1998.

41   Rebecca Jennings, *Tomboys and Bachelor Girls: A Lesbian History of Post-War Britain, 1945-71* (Manchester, UK, and New York: Manchester University Press, 2007), 122.

42   Robert Aldrich, dir., *The Killing of Sister George* (American Broadcasting Company, 1968).

43   Mary and Pat, joint personal interview, 26 September 1998.

44   Paris and Berlin were also important cultural centres for lesbians and gay men.

45   Chenier, "Tough Ladies," 212-13.

46   Chamberland, "Remembering Lesbian Bars."

47   Cosco, "'Obviously then I'm not a homosexual,'" 50.

48   Katie Gilmartin, "'We Weren't Bar People': Middle-Class Lesbian Identities and Cultural Spaces," *Gay and Lesbian Quarterly* 3 (1996): 1.

49   Gilmartin's article is based on some of the research done for her "'The very house of difference': Intersections of Identities in the Life Histories of Colorado Lesbians, 1940-1965" (PhD diss., Yale University, 1995).

50   Pat, personal interview, 24 September 1998.

51   Barb, personal interview, 15 May 1998.

52   Lois, personal interview, 2 October 1998.

53 Reva, personal interview, 5 August 1997.

54 Pat, personal interview, 24 September 1998.

55 Cheryl, personal interview, 4 November 1998, and personal communication, 9 May 2009.

56 In Fernie and Weissman, dirs., *Forbidden Love,* Stephanie Ozard describes an occasion on which the women at her table, who were being stared at by a group of heterosexual "tourists," made a sign that said "Please Do Not Feed the Animals" and put it on the edge of their table.

57 Pat, personal interview, 24 September 1998.

58 Billie, personal interview, 23 September 1998.

59 Barb, personal interview, 15 May 1998.

60 Billie, personal interview, 23 September 1998.

61 Carole Ritchie-Mackintosh, interviewed in Fernie and Weissman, dirs., *Forbidden Love.*

62 Pam, personal interview, 30 September 1998.

63 Barb, personal interview, 15 May 1998.

64 Pam, personal interview, 30 September 1998.

65 Barb, personal interview, 15 May 1998.

66 Faderman, *Odd Girls and Twilight Lovers,* 63.

67 John D'Emilio and Estelle B. Freedman, *Intimate Matters: A History of Sexuality in America* (New York: Harper and Row, 1988), 171-72.

68 Faderman, *Odd Girls and Twilight Lovers,* 99.

69 Judith Schwarz, Kathy Peiss, and Christina Simmons, "'We Were a Little Band of Willful Women': The Heterodoxy Club of Greenwich Village," in *Passion and Power: Sexuality in History,* ed. Kathy Peiss and Christina Simmons, with Robert A. Padgug (Philadelphia: Temple University Press, 1989), 120.

70 D'Emilio and Freedman, *Intimate Matters,* 229. Sexual experimentation was more often heterosexual exploration before and outside of marriage than it was bisexual, lesbian, or gay exploration, and the degree of sexual freedom in the early twentieth century varied by gender as well as by class. For an examination of the effects for women of "modern love," see Ellen Kay Trimberger, "Feminism, Men, and Modern Love: Greenwich Village, 1900-1925," in *Powers of Desire: The Politics of Sexuality,* ed. Ann Snitow, Christine Stansell, and Sharon Thompson, 131-52 (New York: Monthly Review Press, 1983).

71 Jeffrey Weeks, *Sex, Politics and Society: The Regulation of Sexuality since 1800,* 2nd ed. (London and New York: Longman, 1989), 175.

72 Mildred, personal interview, 1 May 1998.

73 Kennedy and Davis, *Boots of Leather,* 386.

74 Pat, personal interview, 24 September 1998.

75 Sarah, personal interview, 5 August 1998.

76 Cheryl, personal interview, 4 November 1998; Barb, personal interview, 15 May 1998.

77   Cheryl, interviewed by C.S., 20 January 1997, personal collection of Cheryl.
78   Barb, personal interview, 15 May 1998.
79   One of these women subsequently became a friend to Cheryl.
80   Cheryl, personal interview, 4 November 1998.
81   Billie, personal interview, 23 September 1998.
82   As Susan Cahn indicates, the mannish lesbian athlete was a particularly powerful stereotype in postwar America. See Susan Cahn, "From the 'Muscle Moll' to the 'Butch' Ballplayer: Mannishness, Lesbianism, and Homophobia in U.S. Women's Sport," in *Lesbian Subjects: A Feminist Studies Reader,* ed. Martha Vicinus (Bloomington and Indianapolis: Indiana University Press, 1996), 42. Although the image was a negative stereotype used against all female athletes, there was an element of truth in it. Sport, particularly baseball, was one of the few opportunities for long-term single-sex female bonding and thus was a crucial part of community for many a lesbian, as indeed it is today.
83   Barb, personal interview, 15 May 1998.
84   Tricia, LMH interview, 21 September 1986.

Conclusion

1   See, for example, Gary Kinsman, *The Regulation of Desire: Homo and Hetero Sexualities,* 2nd ed. (Montreal: Black Rose Books, 1996); Becki Ross, *The House That Jill Built: A Lesbian Nation in Formation* (Toronto: University of Toronto Press, 1995); and some of the testimonies in Katherine Arnup, ed., *Lesbian Parenting: Living with Pride and Prejudice* (Charlottetown, PEI: Gynergy Books, 1995).

Selected Bibliography

Archival Sources

Library and Archives Canada
Canadian Penal Association, June 1948, Kenneth H. Rogers, "Interim Report of the Committee on the Sex Offender," RG 33/131, Acc. 84/253, vol. 2
Charlotte Whitton Papers, MG30, E256, vol. 133

University of Toronto Archives
Fraser Family Personal Records, B95-0044
Elisabeth Steel Livingston Govan Records, B79-0027

University of British Columbia, Rare Books and Special Collections
A. Alexis Alvey Fonds, AII B2

Newspapers and Magazines
Canadian Forum (Toronto), April 1929
Georgia Straight (Vancouver), 13-19 September 1968
Globe and Mail (Toronto), 13 November 1963 to 22 June 1965
Justice Weekly (Toronto), 1946-64
Maclean's (Toronto), 22 February to 7 March 1964
Saturday Night (Toronto), 26 November 1955
Telegram (Toronto), 11 and 14 April 1964
Toronto Daily Star (Toronto), 1960-65
Vancouver Province (Vancouver), 14 August 1964
Vancouver Sun (Vancouver), 1960-65

Other Sources
Adair, Nancy, and Casey Adair. *Word Is Out: Stories of Some of Our Lives*. New York: New Glide/Delta, 1978.

Adams, Kate. "Making the World Safe for the Missionary Position: Images of the Lesbian in Post-World War II America." In *Lesbian Texts and Contexts: Radical Revisions*, ed. Karla Jay and Joanne Glasgow, 255-74. New York and London: New York University Press, 1990.

Adams, Mary Louise. "Almost Anything Can Happen: A Search for Sexual Discourse in the Urban Spaces of 1940s Toronto." *Canadian Journal of Sociology* 19, 2 (1994): 217-32.

–. "Margin Notes: Reading Lesbianism as Obscenity in a Cold War Courtroom." In *Love, Hate, and Fear in Canada's Cold War*, ed. Richard Cavell, 135-58. Toronto: University of Toronto Press, 2004.

–. *The Trouble with Normal: Postwar Youth and the Making of Heterosexuality.* Toronto: University of Toronto Press, 1997.

–. "Youth, Corruptibility, and English-Canadian Postwar Campaigns against Indecency, 1948-1955." *Journal of the History of Sexuality* 6, 1 (1995): 89-117.

Aldrich, Robert, dir. *The Killing of Sister George.* American Broadcasting Company, 1968.

Andreadis, Harriette. "Theorizing Early Modern Lesbianisms: Invisible Bodies, Ambiguous Demarcations." In *Virtual Gender: Fantasies of Subjectivity and Embodiment*, ed. Mary Ann O'Farrell and Lynne Vallone, 125-46. Ann Arbor: University of Michigan Press, 1999.

Arnup, Katherine, ed. *Lesbian Parenting: Living with Pride and Prejudice.* Charlottetown, PEI: Gynergy Books, 1995.

Baines, Carol. "Professor Elizabeth Govan: An Outsider in Her Own Community." In *Challenging Professions: Historical and Contemporary Perspectives on Women's Professional Work*, ed. Elizabeth Smyth, Sandra Acker, Paula Bourne, and Alison Prentice, 44-64. Toronto: University of Toronto Press, 1999.

Beemyn, Brett, ed. *Creating a Place for Ourselves: Lesbian, Gay, and Bisexual Community Histories.* New York: Routledge, 1997.

Beemyn, Brett, and Mickey Eliason, eds. *Queer Studies: A Lesbian, Gay, Bisexual, and Transgender Anthology.* New York and London: New York University Press, 1996.

Bennett, Judith M. "'Lesbian-Like' and the Social History of Lesbianisms." *Journal of the History of Sexuality* 9, 1-2 (January-April 2000): 1-25.

Bérubé, Allan. *Coming Out under Fire: The History of Gay Men and Women in World War Two.* New York: Plume, 1990.

Black, Allida Mae, ed. *Modern American Queer History.* Philadelphia: Temple University Press, 2001.

Bliss, Michael. "How We Used to Learn about Sex." *Maclean's*, March 1974, 38, 61-66.

–. "'Pure Books on Avoided Subjects': Pre-Freudian Sexual Ideas in Canada." *Canadian Historical Association, Historical Papers/Communications Historiques* (1970): 89-108.

Boyd, Nan Alamilla. "Same-Sex Sexuality in Western Women's History." *Frontiers* 12, 3 (2001): 13-21.

–. "Who Is the Subject? Queer Theory Meets Oral History." *Journal of the History of Sexuality* 17, 2 (May 2008): 177-89.

–. *Wide-Open Town: A History of Queer San Francisco to 1965*. Berkeley: University of California Press, 2003.

Breines, Wini. "The 'Other' Fifties: Beats and Bad Girls." In *Not June Cleaver: Women and Gender in Postwar America, 1945-1960*, ed. Joanne Meyerowitz, 382-408. Philadelphia: Temple University Press, 1994.

Bullough, Vern L. "The Development of Sexology in the USA in the Early Twentieth Century." In *Sexual Knowledge, Sexual Science: The History of Attitudes to Sexuality*, ed. Roy Porter and Mikulas Teich, 303-22. Cambridge, UK: Cambridge University Press, 1994.

Cahn, Susan. "From the 'Muscle Moll' to the 'Butch' Ballplayer: Mannishness, Lesbianism, and Homophobia in U.S. Women's Sport." In *Lesbian Subjects: A Feminist Studies Reader*, ed. Martha Vicinus, 41-65. Bloomington and Indianapolis: Indiana University Press, 1996.

Campbell, Robert A. "Ladies and Escorts: Gender Segregation and Public Policy in British Columbia Beer Parlours, 1925-1945." *BC Studies* 105-6 (Spring/Summer 1995): 119-38.

Caprio, Frank. *Female Homosexuality: A Psychodynamic Study of Lesbianism*. New York: Citadel, 1954.

–. *Variations in Sexual Behavior*. New York: Citadel, 1955.

Castleman, Lana. "Self, Sex, and Moral Reform in English Canada, 1980-1920." *Blurred Genres* 2 (Winter/Spring 1994): 35-49.

Cavell, Richard, ed. *Love, Hate, and Fear in Canada's Cold War*. Toronto: University of Toronto Press, 2004.

Cavell, Richard, and Peter Dickinson, eds. *Sexing the Maple: A Canadian Sourcebook*. Peterborough, ON: Broadview Press, 2006.

Chamberland, Line. "Remembering Lesbian Bars: Montreal, 1955-1975." In *Gay Studies from the French Cultures: Voices from France, Belgium, Brazil, Canada, and The Netherlands*, ed. Rommel Mendès-Leite and Pierre-Olivier de Busscher, 231-69. New York: Harrington Park Press, 1993.

Chauncey, George. "From Sexual Inversion to Homosexuality: The Changing Conceptualization of Female 'Deviance.'" In *Passion and Power: Sexuality in History*, ed. Kathy Peiss and Christina Simmons, with Robert Padgug, 87-117. Philadelphia: Temple University Press, 1989.

–. *Gay New York: Gender, Urban Culture, and the Making of the Gay Male World, 1890-1940*. New York: Basic Books, 1994.

Chenier, Elise. "The Criminal Sexual Psychopath in Canada: Sex, Psychiatry and the Law at Mid-Century." *Canadian Bulletin of Medical History/Bulletin canadien d'histoire de la médecine* 20, 1 (2003): 75-101.

–. "Rethinking Class in Lesbian Bar Culture: Living 'The Gay Life' in Toronto, 1955-1965." *Left History* 9, 2 (Spring/Summer 2004): 85-118.

–. *Strangers in Our Midst: Sexual Deviancy in Postwar Ontario*. Toronto: University of Toronto Press, 2008.

–. "Tough Ladies and Troublemakers: Toronto's Public Lesbian Community, 1955-1965." MA thesis, Queen's University, 1995.

Clark, Anna. "Anne Lister's Construction of Lesbian Identity." *Journal of the History of Sexuality* 7, 1 (1996): 23-50.

Clarke, Brian. "English-Speaking Canada from 1854." In *A Concise History of Christianity in Canada,* ed. Terrence Murphy and Roberto Perin, 261-360. Toronto: Oxford University Press, 1996.

Comacchio, Cynthia R. *The Infinite Bonds of Family: Domesticity in Canada, 1850-1940*. Toronto: University of Toronto Press, 1999.

Cosco, Vanessa. "'Obviously then I'm not a homosexual': Lesbian Identities, Discretion and Communities in Vancouver, 1945-1969." MA thesis, University of British Columbia, 1997.

Davis, Madeline D., and Elizabeth L. Kennedy. "Oral History and the Study of Sexuality in the Lesbian Community: Buffalo, New York, 1940-1960." *Feminist Studies* 12, 1 (Spring 1986): 7-26.

D'Emilio, John. *Sexual Politics, Sexual Communities: The Making of a Homosexual Minority in the United States, 1940-1970*. Chicago and London: University of Chicago Press, 1983.

D'Emilio, John, and Estelle B. Freedman. *Intimate Matters: A History of Sexuality in America*. New York: Harper and Row, 1988.

Doan, Laura. *Fashioning Sapphism: The Origins of a Modern English Lesbian Culture*. New York: Columbia University Press, 2001.

–, ed. *The Lesbian Postmodern*. New York: Columbia University Press, 1994.

–, ed. *Old Maids to Radical Spinsters: Unmarried Women in the Twentieth-Century Novel*. Urbana and Chicago: University of Illinois Press, 1991.

–. "Passing Fashions: Reading Female Masculinities in the 1920s." *Feminist Studies* 24, 3 (Autumn 1998): 663-700.

Doan, Laura, and Jay Prosser, eds. *Palatable Poison: Critical Perspectives on* The Well of Loneliness. New York and London: Columbia University Press, 2002.

Duberman, Martin, Martha Vicinus, and George Chauncey, eds. *Hidden from History: Reclaiming the Gay and Lesbian Past*. New York: Meridian, 1990.

Dubinsky, Karen. *Improper Advances: Rape and Heterosexual Conflict in Ontario, 1880-1929*. Chicago: University of Chicago Press, 1993.

Duder, Cameron. "'Two Middle-Aged and Very Good Looking Females That Spend All Their Week-Ends Together': Female Professors and Same-Sex Relationships in Canada, 1910-1950." In *Historical Identities: The Professoriate in Canada*, ed. Paul J. Stortz and Lisa Panayodotis, 332-50. Toronto: University of Toronto Press, 2006.

Duder, Karen. "'That repulsive abnormal creature I read of in that book': Lesbians and Families in Ontario, 1920-1965." In *Ontario Since Confederation: A Reader*, ed. Edgar-André Montigny and Lori Chambers, 260-83. Toronto: University of Toronto Press, 2000.

Duggan, Lisa. "The Social Enforcement of Heterosexuality and Lesbian Resistance in the 1920s." In *Class, Race, and Sex: The Dynamics of Control*, ed. Amy Swerdlow and Hannah Lessinger, 75-92. Boston: G.K. Hall, 1983.

–. "The Trials of Alice Mitchell: Sensationalism, Sexology, and the Lesbian Subject in Turn-of-the-Century America." *Signs* 18, 4 (Summer 1993): 791-814.

Duggan, Lisa, and Nan D. Hunter. *Sex Wars: Sexual Dissent and Political Culture*. New York and London: Routledge, 1995.

Ellis, Havelock. *Studies in the Psychology of Sex*. New York: Random House, 1937.

–. *The Task of Social Hygiene*. London: Constable, 1912.

Enstad, Nan. *Ladies of Labor, Girls of Adventure: Working Women, Popular Culture, and Labor Politics at the Turn of the Twentieth Century*. New York: Columbia University Press, 1999.

Esterberg, Kristin G. "From Accommodation to Liberation: A Social Movement Analysis of Lesbians in the Homophile Movement." *Gender and Society* 8, 3 (September 1994): 424-43.

–. "From Illness to Action: Conceptions of Homosexuality in *The Ladder*, 1956-1965." *The Journal of Sex Research* 27, 1 (February 1990): 65-80.

–. *Lesbian and Bisexual Identities: Constructing Communities, Constructing Selves*. Philadelphia: Temple University Press, 1997.

Faderman, Lillian. "Lesbian Magazine Fiction in the Early Twentieth Century." *Journal of Popular Culture* (1978): 800-17.

–. "The Morbidification of Love between Women by 19th-Century Sexologists." *Journal of Homosexuality* 4, 1 (Fall 1978): 73-90.

–. *Odd Girls and Twilight Lovers: A History of Lesbian Life in Twentieth-Century America*. New York: Penguin, 1992.

–. *Surpassing the Love of Men: Romantic Friendship and Love between Women from the Renaissance to the Present*. New York: William Morrow, 1981.

–. *To Believe in Women: What Lesbians Have Done for America – A History*. Boston and New York: Houghton Mifflin, 1999.

Feinberg, Leslie. *Stone Butch Blues: A Novel*. New York: Firebrand, 1993.

Fernie, Lynn, and Aerlyn Weissman, dirs. *Forbidden Love: The Unashamed Story of Lesbian Lives*. National Film Board of Canada, 1992.

Ford, Ruth. "Speculating on Scrapbooks, Sex and Desire: Issues in Lesbian History." *Australian Historical Studies* 106 (April 1996): 111-26.

Forel, August. *The Sexual Question: A Scientific, Psychological, Hygienic and Sociological Study*. 2nd ed. New York: Medical Art Agency, n.d.

Forsythe, Carolyn J. "'Whatever My Sex, I'm No Lady': Charlotte Whitton, Politician; Welfare Pioneer." *Makara* 2, 4 (1977): 27-31.

Foster, Marion, and Kent Murray. *A Not So Gay World: Homosexuality in Canada*. Toronto: McClelland and Stewart, 1972.

Freedman, Estelle B. "'The Burning of Letters Continues': Elusive Identities and the Historical Construction of Sexuality." *Journal of Women's History* 9, 4 (Winter 1998): 181-200.

–. *Maternal Justice: Miriam Van Waters and the Female Reform Tradition*. Chicago and London: University of Chicago Press, 1996.

Freedman, Estelle B., and John D'Emilio. "Problems Encountered in Writing the History of Sexuality: Sources, Theory and Interpretation." *Journal of Sex Research* 27, 4 (November 1990): 481-95.

Freedman, Estelle B., Barbara C. Gelpi, Susan L. Johnson, and Kathleen M. Weston, eds. *The Lesbian Issue: Essays from SIGNS*. Chicago: University of Chicago Press, 1985.

Freeman, Barbara. "From No Go to No Logo: Lesbian Lives and Rights in *Chatelaine*." *Canadian Journal of Communication* 31 (2006): 815-41.

Freeman, Susan K. *Sex Goes to School: Girls and Sex Education before the 1960s*. Urbana and Chicago: University of Illinois Press, 2008.

Freud, Sigmund. *Three Essays on the Theory of Sexuality*. New York: Avon, 1962.

Gallo, Marcia M. *Different Daughters: A History of the Daughters of Bilitis and the Rise of the Lesbian Rights Movement*. New York: Carroll and Graf, 2006.

Gentile, Patrizia. "Searching for 'Miss Civil Service' and 'Mr. Civil Service': Gender Anxiety, Beauty Contests and Fruit Machines in the Canadian Civil Service, 1950-1973." MA thesis, Carleton University, 1996.

Gibson, Margaret. "The Masculine Degenerate: American Doctors' Portrayals of the Lesbian Intellect, 1880-1949." *Journal of Women's History* 9, 4 (Winter 1998): 78-103.

Gidlow, Elsa. "Casting a Net: Excerpts from an Autobiography." *The Body Politic* 83 (May 1982): 27-30.

–. *Elsa: I Come with My Songs – The Autobiography of Elsa Gidlow*. San Francisco: Booklegger Press, 1986.

Gilman, Sander. *Difference and Pathology: Stereotypes of Sexuality, Race, and Madness*. Ithaca, NY: Cornell University Press, 1985.

Gilmartin, Katie. "'The very house of difference': Intersections of Identities in the Life Histories of Colorado Lesbians, 1940-1965." PhD diss., Yale University, 1995.

–. "'We Weren't Bar People': Middle-Class Lesbian Identities and Cultural Spaces." *Gay and Lesbian Quarterly* 3 (1996): 1-51.

Gleason, Mona. *Normalizing the Ideal: Psychology, Schooling, and the Family in Postwar Canada*. Toronto: University of Toronto Press, 1999.

–. "Psychology and the Construction of the 'Normal' Family in Postwar Canada, 1945-1960." *Canadian Historical Review* 78, 3 (September 1997): 442-77.

Goldie, Terry, ed. *In a Queer Country: Gay and Lesbian Studies in the Canadian Context*. Vancouver: Arsenal Pulp Press, 2001.

Golz, Annalee. "'If a Man's Wife Does Not Obey Him, What Can He Do?': Marital Breakdown and Wife Abuse in Late Nineteenth-Century and Early Twentieth-Century Ontario." In *Law, Society and the State: Essays in Modern Legal History*, ed. Louis A. Knafla and Susan W.S. Binnie, 323-50. Toronto: University of Toronto Press, 1995.

Hall, Lesley. "'The English Have Hot-Water Bottles': The Morganatic Marriage between Sexology and Medicine in Britain since William Acton." In *Sexual Knowledge, Sexual Science: The History of Attitudes to Sexuality*, ed. Roy Porter and Mikulas Teich, 350-66. Cambridge, UK: Cambridge University Press, 1994.

–. *Hidden Anxieties: Male Sexuality, 1900-1950*. Cambridge, UK: Polity Press, 1991.

Hall, Radclyffe. *The Well of Loneliness*. London: Cape, 1928.

Halperin, David M. *How to Do the History of Homosexuality*. Chicago: University of Chicago Press, 2002.

Hamer, Diane. "'I Am a Woman': Ann Bannon and the Writing of Lesbian Identity in the 1950s." In *Lesbian and Gay Writing: An Anthology of Critical Essays*, ed. Mark Lilly, 47-75. London: Macmillan, 1990.

Hansen, Bert. "American Physicians' 'Discovery' of Homosexuals, 1880-1900: A New Diagnosis in a Changing Society." In *Framing Disease: Studies in Cultural History*, ed. Charles Rosenberg and Janet Golden, 104-33. New Brunswick, NJ: Rutgers University Press, 1992.

Hansen, Karen V. "'No Kisses Is Like Youres': An Erotic Friendship between Two African-American Women during the Mid-Nineteenth Century." *Gender and History* 7, 2 (August 1995): 178-208.

Harvey, Brett. *The Fifties: A Women's Oral History*. New York: Harper Perennial, 1993.

Higgins, Ross, and Line Chamberland. "Mixed Messages: Gays and Lesbians in Montreal Yellow Papers in the 1950s." In *The Challenge of Modernity: A Reader on Post-Confederation Canada*, ed. Ian McKay, 422-31. Toronto: McGraw-Hill Ryerson, 1992.

Hooke, S.H. "A Biological Sin." *Canadian Forum* 9, 103 (April 1929): 243-44.

Horn, Mildred A. *Mother and Daughter: A Digest for Women and Growing Girls, Which Completely Covers the Field of Sex Hygiene*. Toronto: Hygienic Productions of Canada, 1946.

Inness, Sherrie A., ed. *Delinquents and Debutantes: Twentieth-Century American Girls' Cultures*. New York and London: New York University Press, 1998.

–. *The Lesbian Menace: Ideology, Identity, and the Representation of Lesbian Life*. Amherst: University of Massachusetts Press, 1997.

–. *Tough Girls: Women Warriors and Wonder Women in Popular Culture*. Philadelphia: University of Pennsylvania Press, 1999.

Jay, Karla, and Joanne Glasgow, eds. *Lesbian Texts and Contexts: Radical Revisions*. New York: New York University Press, 1990.

Jeffreys, Sheila. "Does It Matter If They Did It?" In *Not a Passing Phase: Reclaiming Lesbians in History, 1840-1985*, ed. The Lesbian History Group, 19-28. London: Women's Press, 1989.

–. *The Lesbian Heresy: A Feminist Perspective on the Lesbian Sexual Revolution*. Melbourne: Spinifex, 1993.

–. *The Spinster and Her Enemies: Feminism and Sexuality, 1880-1930*. London and Boston: Pandora Press, 1985.

Jennings, Rebecca. "From 'Woman-Loving Woman' to 'Queer': Historiographical Perspectives on Twentieth-Century British Lesbian History." *History Compass* 5-6 (2007): 1901-20.

–. "The Gateways Club and the Emergence of a Post-Second World War Lesbian Subculture." *Social History* 31, 2 (May 2006): 206-25.

–. *Tomboys and Bachelor Girls: A Lesbian History of Post-War Britain, 1945-71*. Manchester, UK, and New York: Manchester University Press, 2007.

Johnston, Susan. "Twice Slain: Female Sex-Trade Workers and Suicide in British Columbia, 1870-1920." *Journal of the Canadian Historical Association* 5 (1994): 147-66.

Keller, Yvonne. "Pulp Politics: Strategies of Vision in Lesbian Pulp Novels, 1955-1965." In *The Queer Sixties*, ed. Patricia Juliana Smith, 1-25. New York and London: Routledge, 1999.

Kelley, Robert K. *Courtship, Marriage, and the Family*. 2nd ed. New York: Harcourt Brace Jovanovich, 1974.

Kennedy, Elizabeth L. "'But we would never talk about it': The Structures of Lesbian Discretion in South Dakota, 1928-1933." In *Inventing Lesbian Cultures in America*, ed. Ellen Lewin, 15-39. Boston: Beacon Press, 1996.

–. "Telling Tales: Oral History and the Construction of Pre-Stonewall Lesbian History." *Radical History Review* 62 (Spring 1995): 59-79.

Kennedy, Elizabeth L., and Madeline D. Davis. *Boots of Leather, Slippers of Gold: The History of a Lesbian Community*. New York and London: Routledge, 1993.

–. "'I Could Hardly Wait to Get Back to That Bar': Lesbian Bar Culture in Buffalo in the 1930s and 1940s." In *Creating a Place for Ourselves: Lesbian, Gay, and Bisexual Community Histories*, ed. Brett Beemyn, 27-72. New York: Routledge, 1997.

Key, Ellen. *Love and Marriage*. New York and London: G.P. Putnam's Sons, 1912.

Kinsey, Alfred. *Sexual Behavior in the Human Female*. Philadelphia and London: W.B. Saunders, 1953.

–. *Sexual Behavior in the Human Male*. Philadelphia and London: W.B. Saunders, 1948.

Kinsman, Gary. "The Canadian Cold War on Queers: Sexual Regulation and Resistance." In *Love, Hate, and Fear in Canada's Cold War,* ed. Richard Cavell, 108-32. Toronto: University of Toronto Press, 2004.

–. "Character Weaknesses and Fruit Machines: Towards an Analysis of the Anti-Homosexual Security Campaign in the Canadian Civil Service." *Labour/Le travail* 35 (1995): 133-61.

–. *The Regulation of Desire: Homo and Hetero Sexualities.* 2nd ed. Montreal: Black Rose Books, 1996.

Kinsman, Gary, Dieter K. Buse, and Mercedes Steedman, eds. *Whose National Security? Canadian State Surveillance and the Creation of Enemies.* Toronto: Between the Lines, 2000.

Kinsman, Gary, and Patrizia Gentile. *The Canadian War on Queers: National Security as Sexual Regulation.* Vancouver: UBC Press, 2010.

–. *"In the Interests of the State": The Anti-Gay, Anti-Lesbian National Security Campaign in Canada: A Preliminary Research Report.* Sudbury, ON: Laurentian University, 1998.

Korinek, Valerie. "'Don't Let Your Girlfriends Ruin Your Marriage': Lesbian Imagery in *Chatelaine* Magazine, 1950-1969." *Journal of Canadian Studies* 33, 3 (Fall 1998): 83-109.

–. *Roughing It in the Suburbs: Reading* Chatelaine *Magazine in the Fifties and Sixties.* Toronto: University of Toronto Press, 2000.

Krafft-Ebing, Richard von. *Psychopathia Sexualis.* 1882. Reprint, New York: Surgeons Book Co., 1925.

Krahulik, Karen Christel. *Provincetown: From Pilgrim Landing to Gay Resort.* New York and London: New York University Press, 2005.

Laycock, S.R. "Homosexuality – A Mental Hygiene Problem." *Canadian Medical Association Journal* 63 (September 1950): 245-50.

Lesbians Making History Collective, "People Think This Didn't Happen in Canada – But It Did." *Fireweed* 28 (Spring 1989): 81-86, 142.

Lévesque, Andrée. "Deviants Anonymous: Single Mothers at the Hôpital de la Miséricorde in Montreal, 1929-1939." Canadian Historical Association, *Historical Papers/Communications Historiques* (1984): 168-83.

Lewin, Ellen, ed. *Inventing Lesbian Cultures in America.* Boston: Beacon Press, 1996.

Lilly, Mark, ed. *Lesbian and Gay Writing: An Anthology of Critical Essays.* London: Macmillan, 1990.

Limbert, Shirley. "Coming Out x Three." In *Lesbian Parenting: Living with Pride and Prejudice,* ed. Katherine Arnup, 265-70. Charlottetown, PEI: Gynergy Books, 1995.

Little, Margaret. *"No Car, No Radio, No Liquor Permit": The Moral Regulation of Single Mothers in Ontario, 1920-1997.* Toronto: Oxford University Press, 1998.

Lystra, Karen. *Searching the Heart: Women, Men, and Romantic Love in Nineteenth-Century America.* New York and Oxford, UK: Oxford University Press, 1989.

Marcus, Sharon. *Between Women: Friendship, Desire, and Marriage in Victorian England*. Princeton, NJ: Princeton University Press, 2007.

Martens, Debra, ed. *Weaving Alliances: Selected Papers Presented for the Canadian Women's Studies Association at the 1991 and 1992 Learned Societies Conferences*. Ottawa: Canadian Women's Studies Association, 1993.

Maynard, Steven. "'The Burning, Wilful Evidence': Lesbian/Gay History and Archival Research." *Archivaria* 33 (Winter 1991-92): 195-201.

–. "'Hell Witches in Toronto': Notes on Lesbian Visibility in Early-Twentieth-Century Canada." *Left History* 9, 2 (Spring/Summer 2004): 191-205.

–. "In Search of 'Sodom North': The Writing of Lesbian and Gay History in English Canada, 1970-1990." *Canadian Review of Comparative Literature/Revue Canadienne de Littérature Comparée* (March-June 1994): 117-32.

–. "The Maple Leaf (Gardens) Forever: Sex, Canadian Historians and National History." *Journal of Canadian Studies* 36 (Summer 2001): 70-105.

–. "Radclyffe Hall in Canada." *Centre/Fold* 6 (Spring 1994): 9.

–. "'Respect Your Elders, Know Your Past': History and the Queer Theorists." *Radical History Review* 75 (1999): 56-78.

–. "Through a Hole in the Lavatory Wall: Homosexual Subcultures, Police Surveillance, and the Dialectics of Discovery, Toronto, 1890-1930." *Journal of the History of Sexuality* 5, 2 (October 1994): 207-42.

McCreary, John K. "Psychopathia Homosexualis." *Canadian Journal of Psychiatry* 4, 2 (1950): 63-74.

McLaren, Angus. *Our Own Master Race: Eugenics in Canada, 1885-1945*. Toronto: McClelland and Stewart, 1990.

–. *Twentieth-Century Sexuality: A History*. Oxford, UK: Blackwell, 1999.

McLaren, Angus, and Arlene Tigar McLaren. *The Bedroom and the State: The Changing Practices and Politics of Contraception and Abortion in Canada, 1880-1980*. Toronto: McClelland and Stewart, 1986.

McLeod, Donald W. *Lesbian and Gay Liberation in Canada: A Selected Annotated Chronology, 1964-1975*. Toronto: ECW Press/Homewood Books, 1996.

McPherson, Kathryn, Cecilia Morgan, and Nancy M. Forestell, eds. *Gendered Pasts: Historical Essays in Femininity and Masculinity in Canada*. Toronto: Oxford University Press, 1999.

Meeker, Martin. "A Queer and Contested Medium: The Emergence of Representational Politics in the 'Golden Age' of Lesbian Paperbacks, 1955-1963." *Journal of Women's History* 17, 1 (2005): 165-88.

Meyer, Leisa D. *Creating G.I. Jane: Sexuality and Power in the Women's Army Corps during World War II*. New York: Columbia University Press, 1996.

Meyerowitz, Joanne, ed. *Not June Cleaver: Women and Gender in Postwar America, 1945-1960*. Philadelphia: Temple University Press, 1994.

Minton, Henry L. "Femininity in Men and Masculinity in Women: American Psychiatry and Psychology Portray Homosexuality in the 1930s." *Journal of Homosexuality* 13, 1 (Fall 1986): 1-22.

Mitchinson, Wendy. *The Nature of Their Bodies: Women and Their Doctors in Victorian Canada*. Toronto: University of Toronto Press, 1991.

Morton, Donald, ed. *The Material Queer: A LesBiGay Cultural Studies Reader*. Boulder, CO: Westview Press, 1996.

Murphy, Terrence, and Roberto Perin, eds. *A Concise History of Christianity in Canada*. Toronto: Oxford University Press, 1996.

Nestle, Joan, ed. *The Persistent Desire: A Fem-Butch Reader*. Boston: Alyson, 1992.

–. *A Restricted Country*. New York: Firebrand Books, 1987.

Newton, Esther. *Cherry Grove, Fire Island: Sixty Years in America's First Gay and Lesbian Town*. Boston: Beacon Press, 1993.

–. "The 'Fun Gay Ladies': Lesbians in Cherry Grove, 1936-1960." In *Creating a Place for Ourselves: Lesbian, Gay, and Bisexual Community Histories*, ed. Brett Beemyn, 145-64. New York: Routledge, 1997.

–. "The Mythic Mannish Lesbian." In *Hidden from History: Reclaiming the Gay and Lesbian Past*, ed. Martin Duberman, Martha Vicinus, and George Chauncey, 281-93. New York: Meridian, 1990.

–. "The Mythic Mannish Lesbian: Radclyffe Hall and the New Woman." In *The Lesbian Issue: Essays from SIGNS*, ed. Estelle B. Freedman, Barbara C. Gelpi, Susan L. Johnson, and Kathleen M. Weston, 7-25. Chicago: University of Chicago Press, 1985.

Olson, Nancy. "Assembling a Life: The (Auto)biography of Alexis Amelia Alvey." MA thesis, Simon Fraser University, 1998.

Oram, Alison. *Her Husband Was a Woman! Women's Gender-Crossing in Modern British Popular Culture*. London and New York: Routledge, 2007.

Ormrod, Richard. *Una Troubridge: The Friend of Radclyffe Hall*. New York: Carroll and Graf, 1985.

Palmer, Alice Freeman, and George Herbert Palmer. *An Academic Courtship: Letters of Alice Freeman and George Herbert Palmer, 1886-1887*. Cambridge, MA: Harvard University Press, 1940.

Peiss, Kathy. *Cheap Amusements: Working Women and Leisure in Turn-of-the-Century New York*. Philadelphia: Temple University Press, 1986.

Peiss, Kathy, and Christina Simmons, eds., with Robert Padgug. *Passion and Power: Sexuality in History*. Philadelphia: Temple University Press, 1989.

Penn, Donna. "The Meanings of Lesbianism in Post-War America." *Gender and History* 3, 2 (Summer 1991): 190-203.

–. "Queer: Theorizing Politics and History." *Radical History Review* 62 (Spring 1995): 24-42.

–. "The Sexualized Woman." In *Not June Cleaver: Women and Gender in Postwar America, 1945-1960,* ed. Joanne Meyerowitz, 358-81. Philadelphia: Temple University Press, 1994.

Perdue, Katherine. "Passion and Profession, Doctors in Skirts: The Letters of Doctors Frieda Fraser and Edith Bickerton Williams." *Canadian Bulletin of Medical History/ Bulletin canadien d'histoire de la médecine* 22, 2 (2005): 271-80.

Pierson, Ruth Roach. *"They're Still Women after All": The Second World War and Canadian Womanhood.* Toronto: McClelland and Stewart, 1986.

Porter, Roy, and Lesley Hall. *The Facts of Life: The Creation of Sexual Knowledge in Britain, 1650-1950.* New Haven, CT, and London: Yale University Press, 1995.

Porter, Roy, and Mikulas Teich, eds. *Sexual Knowledge, Sexual Science: The History of Attitudes to Sexuality.* Cambridge, UK: Cambridge University Press, 1994.

Richardson, Mattie Udora. "No More Secrets, No More Lies: African American History and Compulsory Heterosexuality." *Journal of Women's History* 15, 3 (Autumn 2003): 63-76.

Riordan, Michael. *Out Our Way: Gay and Lesbian Life in the Country.* Toronto: Between the Lines, 1996.

Robinson, Daniel J., and David Kimmel. "The Queer Career of Homosexual Security Vetting in Cold War Canada." *Canadian Historical Review* 75, 3 (September 1994): 319-45.

Rooke, Patricia T. "Public Figure, Private Woman: Same Sex Support Structures in the Life of Charlotte Whitton." *International Journal of Women's Studies* 6, 5 (1983): 412-28.

Rooke, Patricia T., and R.L. Schnell. *No Bleeding Heart: Charlotte Whitton, a Feminist on the Right.* Vancouver: UBC Press, 1987.

Ross, Becki L. "Bumping and Grinding on the Line: Making Nudity Pay." *Labour/Le travail* 46 (Fall 2000): 221-50.

–. "Dance to 'Tie a Yellow Ribbon,' Get Churched, and Buy the Little Lady a Drink: Gay Women's Bar Culture in Toronto, 1965-1975." In *Weaving Alliances: Selected Papers Presented for the Canadian Women's Studies Association at the 1991 and 1992 Learned Societies Conferences,* ed. Debra Martens, 267-87. Ottawa: Canadian Women's Studies Association, 1993.

–. *The House That Jill Built: A Lesbian Nation in Formation.* Toronto: University of Toronto Press, 1995.

Ross, Becki L., and Kim Greenwell. "Spectacular Striptease: Performing the Sexual and Racial Other in Vancouver, B.C., 1945-1975." *Journal of Women's History* 17, 1 (2005): 137-64.

Rothblum, Esther D., ed. *Classics in Lesbian Studies.* New York and London: Harrington Park Press, 1997.

Rothblum, Esther D., and Kathleen A. Brehony, eds. *Boston Marriages: Romantic but Asexual Relationships among Contemporary Lesbians.* Amherst: University of Massachusetts Press, 1993.

Rupp, Leila J. *A Desired Past: A Short History of Same-Sex Love in America.* Chicago and London: University of Chicago Press, 1999.

–. "'Imagine My Surprise': Women's Relationships in Historical Perspective." *Journal of Lesbian Studies* 1, 2 (1997): 155-76.

–. "Romantic Friendship." In *Modern American Queer History,* ed. Allida Mae Black, 13-23. Philadelphia: Temple University Press, 2001.

–. "Toward a Global History of Same-Sex Sexuality." *Journal of the History of Sexuality* 10, 2 (2001): 287-302.

Sahli, Nancy. "Sexuality in 19th and 20th Century America: The Sources and Their Problems." *Radical History Review* (Spring/Summer 1979): 89-96.

–. "'Smashing': Women's Relationships before the Fall." *Chrysalis* 8 (1979): 17-27.

Schwarz, Judith, Kathy Peiss, and Christina Simmons. "'We Were a Little Band of Willful Women': The Heterodoxy Club of Greenwich Village." In *Passion and Power: Sexuality in History,* ed. Kathy Peiss and Christina Simmons, with Robert A. Padgug, 118-37. Philadelphia: Temple University Press, 1989.

Scott, Joan W. "The Evidence of Experience." *Critical Inquiry* 17 (Summer 1991): 773-97.

–. *Gender and the Politics of History.* New York: Columbia University Press, 1988.

Sears, James T. *Lonely Hunters: An Oral History of Lesbian and Gay Southern Life, 1948-1968.* Boulder, CO: Westview Press, 1997.

Seidman, Steven. *Romantic Longings: Love in America, 1830-1980.* New York: Routledge, 1991.

–, ed. *Queer Theory/Sociology.* Cambridge, MA, and Oxford: Blackwell, 1996.

Semple, Neil. *The Lord's Dominion: The History of Canadian Methodism.* Montreal and Kingston: McGill-Queen's University Press, 1996.

Sethna, Christabelle. "The Cold War and the Sexual Chill: Freezing Girls Out of Sex Education." *Canadian Woman Studies/Les cahiers de la femme* 17, 4 (Winter 1998): 57-61.

–. "Wait Till Your Father Gets Home: Absent Fathers, Working Mothers and Delinquent Daughters in Ontario during World War II." In *Family Matters: Papers in Post-Confederation Canadian Family History,* ed. Lori Chambers and Edgar-André Montigny, 19-37. Toronto: Canadian Scholars' Press, 1998.

Smith, Patricia J. "'And I Wondered If She Might Kiss Me': Lesbian Panic as Narrative Strategy in British Women's Fictions." *Modern Fiction Studies* 41, 3-4 (1995): 567-607.

Smith-Rosenberg, Carroll. *Disorderly Conduct: Visions of Gender in Victorian America.* New York: Alfred A. Knopf, 1985.

Smyth, Elizabeth, et al., eds. *Challenging Professions: Historical and Contemporary Perspectives on Women's Professional Work*. Toronto: University of Toronto Press, 1999.

Snitow, Ann, Christine Stansell, and Sharon Thompson, eds. *Powers of Desire: The Politics of Sexuality*. New York: Monthly Review Press, 1983.

Stein, Marc. *City of Sisterly and Brotherly Loves: Lesbian and Gay Philadelphia, 1945-1972*. 2nd ed. Philadelphia: Temple University Press, 2004.

Stekel, Wilhelm. *Bi-Sexual Love*. New York: Emerson Books, 1946.

Stopes, Marie. *Enduring Passion: Further New Contributions to the Solution of Sex Difficulties – Being the Continuation of* Married Love. 4th ed. London: G.P. Putnam's Sons, 1932.

–. *Married Love: A New Contribution to the Solution of Sex Difficulties*. 12th ed. London: G.P. Putnam's Sons, 1923.

–. *Wise Parenthood: The Treatise on Birth Control for Married People*. 12th ed. London: G.P. Putnam's Sons, 1925.

Strange, Carolyn. "Bad Girls and Masked Men: Recent Works on Sexuality in US History." *Labour/Le travail* 39 (Spring 1997): 261-75.

–. "From Modern Babylon to a City upon a Hill: The Toronto Social Survey Commission of 1915 and the Search for Sexual Order in the City." In *Patterns of the Past: Interpreting Ontario's History*, ed. Roger Hall, William Westfall, and Laurel Sefton MacDowell, 255-78. Toronto and Oxford: Dundurn Press, 1988.

–. *Toronto's Girl Problem: The Perils and Pleasures of the City, 1880-1930*. Toronto: University of Toronto Press, 1995.

Strong-Boag, Veronica. "Home Dreams: Women and the Suburban Experiment in Canada, 1945-1960." *Canadian Historical Review* 72, 4 (December 1991): 471-504.

–. *The New Day Recalled: Lives of Girls and Women in English Canada, 1919-1939*. Markham, ON: Penguin, 1988.

–. "'Their Side of the Story': Women's Voices from Ontario Suburbs, 1945-1960." In *A Diversity of Women: Ontario, 1945-1980*, ed. Joy Parr, 46-74. Toronto: University of Toronto Press, 1995.

Strong-Boag, Veronica, and Anita Clair Fellman. *Rethinking Canada: The Promise of Women's History*. 2nd ed. Toronto: Copp Clark Pitman, 1991.

Sutliff, Eric. "Sex Fiends or Swish Kids? Gay Men in *Hush Free Press*, 1946-1956." In *Gendered Pasts: Historical Essays in Femininity and Masculinity in Canada*, ed. Kathryn McPherson, Cecilia Morgan, and Nancy Forestell, 158-78. Toronto: Oxford University Press, 1999.

Tallentire, Jenéa. "Everyday Athenas: Strategies of Survival and Identity for Ever-Single Women in British Columbia, 1880-1930." PhD diss., University of British Columbia, 2006.

Taylor, Leslie A. "'I Made Up My Mind to Get It': The American Trial of *The Well of Loneliness*, New York City, 1928-1929." *Journal of the History of Sexuality* 10, 2 (2001): 250-86.

Tennenbaum, Joseph. *The Riddle of Women: A Study of the Social Psychology of Sex.* New York: Lee Furman, 1936.

Terry, Jennifer. "Theorizing Deviant Historiography." *differences* 3 (Summer 1991): 55-74.

Thompson, P.G. "Sexual Deviation." *Canadian Medical Association Journal* 80 (March 1959): 381-89.

Thorpe, Rochella. "'A house where queers go': African-American Lesbian Nightlife in Detroit, 1940-1975." In *Inventing Lesbian Cultures in America*, ed. Ellen Lewin, 40-61. Boston: Beacon Press, 1996.

Tinkler, Penny. *Constructing Girlhood: Popular Magazines for Girls Growing Up in England, 1920-1950.* London: Taylor and Francis, 1995.

Torrie, Rachel. "Making Space for Rural Lesbians: Homosexuality and Rurality in British Columbia, 1950-1970s." MA thesis, Simon Fraser University, 2007.

Traub, Valerie. "The Rewards of Lesbian History." *Feminist Studies* 25, 2 (Summer 1999): 363-94.

Trimberger, Ellen Kay. "Feminism, Men, and Modern Love: Greenwich Village, 1900-1925." In *Powers of Desire: The Politics of Sexuality*, ed. Ann Snitow, Christine Stansell, and Sharon Thompson, 131-52. New York: Monthly Review Press, 1983.

Urquhart, M.C., and K.A.H. Buckley, eds. *Historical Statistics of Canada.* Toronto: University of Toronto Press, 1965.

Valverde, Mariana. *The Age of Light, Soap and Water: Moral Reform in English Canada, 1885-1925.* Toronto: McClelland and Stewart, 1991.

Van de Velde, Theodoor Hendrik. *Ideal Marriage: Its Physiology and Technique.* 4th ed. Trans. Stella Browne. New York: Random House, 1965.

Vicinus, Martha. *Intimate Friends: Women Who Loved Women, 1778-1928.* Chicago: University of Chicago Press, 2004.

–. "Lesbian History: All Theory and No Facts or All Facts and No Theory?" *Radical History Review* 60 (1994): 57-75.

–. *Lesbian Subjects: A Feminist Studies Reader.* Bloomington and Indianapolis: Indiana University Press, 1996.

–. "'They Wonder to Which Sex I Belong': The Historical Roots of the Modern Lesbian Identity." *Feminist Studies* 18, 3 (1992): 467-97.

Walkowitz, Judith. *City of Dreadful Delight: Narratives of Sexual Danger in Late-Victorian London.* Chicago: University of Chicago Press, 1992.

–. *Prostitution and Victorian Society: Women, Class, and the State.* Cambridge, UK: Cambridge University Press, 1980.

Warner, Tom. *Never Going Back: A History of Queer Activism in Canada.* Toronto: University of Toronto Press, 2002.

Weeks, Jeffrey. *Sex, Politics and Society: The Regulation of Sexuality since 1800.* 2nd ed. London and New York: Longman, 1989.

–. *Sexuality and Its Discontents: Meanings, Myths and Modern Sexualities.* London: Routledge and Kegan Paul, 1985.

Weeks, Jeffrey, and Kevin Porter, eds. *Between the Acts: Lives of Homosexual Men, 1885-1967*. London and New York: Routledge, 1991.

Weininger, Otto. *Sex and Character*. 6th ed. London and New York: William Heinemann and G.P. Putnam's Sons, 1906.

Wheelwright, Julie. *Amazons and Military Maids: Women Who Dressed as Men in the Pursuit of Life, Liberty and Happiness*. London and Scranton, PA: Pandora, 1989.

Whitbread, Helena. *I Know My Own Heart: The Diaries of Anne Lister, 1791-1840*. New York and London: New York University Press, 1992.

Zimmerman, Bonnie. "Perverse Reading: The Lesbian Appropriation of Literature." In *Sexual Practice/Textual Theory: Lesbian Cultural Criticism*, ed. Susan J. Wolfe and Julia Penelope, 135-49. Cambridge, UK: Blackwell, 1993.

Zuckerman, Mary Ellen. *A History of Popular Women's Magazines in the United States, 1792-1995*. Westport, CT: Greenwood Press, 1998.

Index

Printed and bound in Canada by Friesens

Set in Rotis and Minion by Artegraphica Design Co. Ltd.

Copy editor: Robert Lewis

Proofreader: Dianne Tiefensee